ANTHEM

Anthem

*Social Movements and the Sound of Solidarity
in the African Diaspora*

Shana L. Redmond

NEW YORK UNIVERSITY PRESS
New York and London

NEW YORK UNIVERSITY PRESS
New York and London
www.nyupress.org

Parts of the Introduction and chapters 1 and 2 were previously published as "Citizens of Sound: Negotiations of Race and Diaspora in the Anthems of the UNIA and NAACP," *Black and African Diaspora: An International Journal* 4, no. 1 (2011): 19–39.

References to Internet websites (URLs) were accurate at the time of writing.
Neither the author nor New York University Press is responsible for URLs that
may have expired or changed since the manuscript was prepared.

LIBRARY OF CONGRESS CATALOGING-IN-PUBLICATION DATA
Redmond, Shana L.
Anthem : social movements and the sound of solidarity in the African diaspora / Shana L. Redmond.
pages cm
Includes bibliographical references and index.
ISBN 978-0-8147-8932-2 (hardback) — ISBN 978-0-8147-7041-2 (pb)
1. African Americans—Music—Political aspects. 2. Anthems—Political aspects. 3. Civil rights movements—History—20th century. 4. Music—United States—Political aspects. I. Title.
ML3917.U6R43 2013
782.42089'96—dc23

                            2013023733

New York University Press books are printed on acid-free paper,
and their binding materials are chosen for strength and durability.
We strive to use environmentally responsible suppliers and materials
to the greatest extent possible in publishing our books.

Manufactured in the United States of America

10 9 8 7 6 5 4 3 2 1

Also available as an ebook

CONTENTS

ACKNOWLEDGMENTS

Anthem is the product of labor; it is some of the evidence of years of reading, listening, interpreting, writing, conversing, and soul searching. It is also a *labor of love*, however, due to the many people whom it brought me into contact with, formally and informally. It is a nearly overwhelming honor to thank the many people who have oriented me on my life's course. To imagine the many hours spent on my behalf by the individuals and communities acknowledged here is humbling. The names on the printed page do not do justice to most of the relationships that I signal, but I nonetheless take this opportunity to try to make your efforts legible.

In a very real sense, my intellectual genealogy begins with those who taught me as a child in Wisconsin. Their support helped me to develop the determination that has made all of what I've done possible. Thank you Mona Lewis, Patricia Dickert, Greg Nyboe, Rick Weigel, Mary Jo Perry, Wm. Mark Murphy, and especially Everett McKinney. My time at Macalester College introduced me to the "life of the mind" with a three-dimensionality that I continue to note and cherish. The friends with and from whom I learned so much are still with me: Sarah Fuentes, Cyndy Harrison, Chad Jones, Grant Loehnig, Sele Nadel-Hayes, Auyana Orr, Kwame Phillips, and Kara Von Blasingame. Professors Mahmoud El-Kati, Robert Morris, and Leola Johnson fomented my passions for the study of Black life and culture and trusted my process, even as they challenged me on it. Peter Rachleff has, for more than a decade, been my biggest cheerleader. He modeled for me the political necessity of this work as well as its limits, encouraging me to be the intellectual that I desired to be while also being the activist that I needed to be. For being my mentor and so much more, I thank him.

The journey begun in the Midwest led me east to a community of thinkers who continue to influence my every action. While at Yale University I had the pleasure of being part of numerous contiguous communities who made me again, helping me to get closer to the promise of this work and this life. A shout-out to my peoples who sustained me: Mike Amezcua, Kimberly Juanita Brown, Martina Forgwe-Fongyen, Stephanie Greenlea, Brandi Hughes, Nicole Ivy, and Melissa Mason. Aaron Carico, Amanda Ciafone, Alejandro Delgado, Dan Gilbert, Chris Johnson, Uri McMillan, Bethany Moreton, Theresa Runstedtler, Melissa Stuckey, Brandon Terry, and Sam Vong helped me to process and fight as well as smile and laugh. My colleagues in GESO and the broader UNITE HERE community in New Haven challenged me in ways that I couldn't have predicted and sharpened my analysis of the academy and other industries. Thank you Jeffrey Boyd, Brenda Carter, Mandi Isaacs-Jackson, Mary Reynolds, and David Sanders, the members of Locals 34 and 35, and organizers Lisa Bergmann and Andrea van den Heever. I so appreciate the university staff who labored in order to make my path a smooth one: Janet Giarratano and Geneva Melvin held me down during my time in African American studies, Liza Cariaga-Lo and Pat Cabral in the Office for Diversity and Opportunity counseled and supported me, and Yvette Bernard was a generous aide as I sought employment. During my studies Glenda Gilmore and Paul Gilroy sat and thought with me, Alondra Nelson facilitated my growth as a teacher, and Gerald Jaynes and his partner Pat graciously opened their home to me on a research trip. I had the good fortune to train under three amazing scholars while at Yale—mentors who believed in me and my project and continue to provide guidance: my profound gratitude is offered to my chair, Hazel Carby, for attuning me to the stakes of this work, her wise counsel, and good humor; Michael Denning for his critical eye and contagious enthusiasm; and Matthew Frye Jacobson for his big-picture narrative and constant encouragement. In addition to those on my committee, I had the opportunity while in New Haven to learn from two individuals who continually show me how to be a better scholar and person: David and Martel Montgomery embody the courage and integrity that I aspire toward every day. I am so proud to call them family. Though David has departed, he is with me now and always.

Beyond my institutional affiliations, I have been mentored and cared for by scholars who model for me how theory meets praxis. First among them is Robin D. G. Kelley, an incomparable thinker, mentor, and comrade. Vijay Prashad and Ruth Wilson Gilmore ground and inspire me. George Lipsitz has been a constant reservoir of knowledge and zeal. This book was made possible through the brilliance and friendship of two men with whom I shared limited time but unlimited benefits; I often smile at thoughts of Rudolph P. Byrd and Clyde Woods, two fierce and observant men who made every community that they touched better and who have forever marked my thinking, my work, my life.

I have benefitted from a number of intellectual communities along this path. The Mellon Mays Undergraduate Fellowship and Social Science Research Council continue to be a resource for me all these years later; the Institute for the Recruitment of Teachers grew my confidence and my opportunities; the Erskine Peters Dissertation Fellowship at the University of Notre Dame assisted me in finishing and brought me into communion with Richard Pierce; a year in the James Weldon Johnson Institute for the Study of Race and Difference at Emory University connected me to Dr. Byrd, Calinda Lee, Lawrence Jackson, and Vincent Lloyd, and allowed me time to write; as did the Woodrow Wilson Career Enhancement Fellowship for Junior Faculty, which additionally made possible the important counsel that I received from Brent Hayes Edwards. Funding through the Advancing Scholarship in the Humanities and Social Sciences fellowship from the University of Southern California facilitated my passage to South African archives. Archival workers across the country and world made this project viable; thank you to those librarians and archivists at the Beinecke Rare Book and Manuscript Library at Yale University where the project began, the Wisconsin Historical Society (Madison), and the Library of Congress. I especially thank Steven Fullwood and his colleagues at the Schomburg Center for Research in Black Culture in New York City and Randall Burkett at the Manuscript and Rare Book Library (MARBL) at Emory University. In South Africa, the staff of the National Heritage and Cultural Studies Centre at the University of Fort Hare (UFH) provided the space and resources necessary to excavate crucial materials. Bernhard Bleibinger of the Music Department at UFH was a gracious host and guide, and Graeme Gilfillan of the ZM Makeba Trust offered important documents and information while I was in Johannesburg.

Robin D. G. Kelley, Vincent Lloyd, and Fred Moten read the entire manuscript. They understood the passions of this project and complicated and refined them, in the process helping me to reveal the reasons why we sing. Friends and colleagues, including Barry Shank, Ivy Wilson, the "New Americanists" group (composed of Aaron Carico, Brian Chung, Amanda Ciafone, Daniel Gilbert, Sarah Haley, A. Naomi Paik, and Jason Ruiz), the School of Unlimited Learning (SOUL) collective at the University of California, Santa Barbara, and the SoCal women of color LOUDies, encouraged me and read portions of the book. For their LOUD mentorship I acknowledge Grace Hong and Jodi Kim especially. Thanks are due to Tisha Hooks and Derek Gottlieb who provided their fine editorial and indexing skills. For their attentiveness to and comments on the book, I also thank the anonymous readers for Duke University Press and New York University Press. I've experienced a meeting of the minds in working with my editor Eric Zinner; thanks and gratitude are due to him as well as Ciara McLaughlin, Alicia Nadkarni, Dorothea Halliday, and the rest of the staff at NYU Press for their diligence and for making my first foray into book publishing a joy.

Colleagues from the University of Southern California, both near and far, have taught me a lot about community and achievement in this industry; thank you all. Macarena Gomez-Barris, J. Jack Halberstam, Sherman Jackson, Kara Keeling, Josh Kun, Richard Meyer, Viet Nguyen, Manuel Pastor, Sally Pratt, Laura Pulido, John Rowe, George Sanchez, Nayan Shah, Francille Rusan Wilson, and Carol Wise have offered friendship and advice along the way. Sarah Banet-Weiser, Todd Boyd, R. Taj Frazier, Michelle Gordon, Nitin Govil, Sarah Gualtieri, Edwin Hill, Lanita Jacobs, Neetu Khanna, Dorinne Kondo, David Lloyd, Maria-Elena Martínez, Michael Preston, Ricardo Ramírez, David Román, Karen Tongson, and Diana Williams gave above and beyond any expectation. The staff of American Studies and Ethnicity (ASE) is fantastic and made my professional work much more manageable; thank you Kitty Lai, Jujuana Preston, and Sonia Rodríguez. For their research assistance with the book, I thank ASE graduate students Yushi Yamazaki, who found and translated documents for chapter 2, and Tasneem Siddiqui, who accompanied me to the South African archives. From my time at Yale on to USC, my students have challenged me in innumerable ways and I appreciate it all. Angel Hernandez, Victor Kwansa, Tasneem Siddiqui, David Stein, Alessandra Williams, and the graduate students in my Spring 2013 Research Methods in African American Studies course remind me why I do what I do. Thank you.

It's been proven to me again and again that it's less important where I'm from than where I'm at. Atlanta was home thanks to Charles Greenlea III, Vincent Lloyd, and Reggie and Gigi Wilborn. Kirstie Dorr, Aisha Finch, Kai Green, Sara Clarke Kaplan, Uri McMillan, Yusef Omowale, Anthony Ratcliff, Dylan Rodríguez, Denise Sandoval, Damien Sojoyner, and Deborah Vargas make my SoCal community real. Erica Edwards is a brilliant and unique sister-friend-mentor at whom I regularly marvel. Although not in SoCal, Jason Ruiz resides here with me in spirit and has brightened many a day with his wit. My cousins Shereta Redmond and Tywone Redmond have housed and moved me on multiple occasions—from Racilla to New York City—made me laugh, and cheered me on.

These final words are for those who will never be too far away. Grandaddy (Booker T.) and Granmama (Roberta) are gone now, but their dedication to making a way for my father gave me my chance. The aspirations of Grandpa (Harry) and Grandma (Marilyn) showed me how to make my own. Sarah Haley has done more to shape me as a person than any other; for all that she is and all that she brings to my life she remains "the star of a story I'll always tell." LaDonna, my sister, tries a little harder every day and gave me my two loves—Alani and Akari, the sweetest, most promising niece and nephew I could hope for. My best friend and brother Jessie Jr. has taken hits but gains strength from the fall and expects nothing less from me. His humor and honesty revitalize me. My mother Sheryl continues to be kind, even in a world that isn't, and reminds me to only control that which is mine to manage. Lastly, a note to and for my father, Jessie Sr., who has taught me that life is for living. He made a way from nothing and never allowed anyone else to define his humanity, making him the most accomplished person I know. His love and example prove to me that I can do anything.

Introduction

Anthem: Toward a Sound Franchise

Get them to sing your songs and they'll want to know who
you are.
—Paul Robeson

Music is a method. Beyond its many pleasures, music allows us to
do and imagine things that may otherwise be unimaginable or seem
impossible. It is more than sound; it is a complex system of mean(ing)s
and ends that mediate our relationships to one another, to space, to our
histories and historical moment. The *movement* of music—not simply
in response to its rhythms but toward collective action and new political modalities—is the central exposition of *Anthem*. Within the African diaspora, music functions as a method of rebellion, revolution,
and future visions that disrupt and challenge the manufactured differences used to dismiss, detain, and destroy communities. The anthems
developed and deployed by these communities served as articulations
of defense and were so powerful that they took flight and were adopted
by others. Marginalized groups around the world have taken advantage
of the special alchemy that musical production demands, including the
language, organized noise, and performance practices that represent,
define, and instruct the performers and receivers of these musics. The
statement by Paul Robeson used here as epigraph acknowledges these
processes by situating music as a meaning-making endeavor, one that
is strategically employed to develop identification between people
who otherwise may be culturally, ideologically, or spatially separate or

distinct from one another. Through "get[ting] them to sing [his] songs" Robeson compelled sounded and embodied action, thereby constructing an audible global public with the potential to radically adjust their political circumstances.

The songs of tragedy and triumph that Robeson offered to arouse beleaguered workers offer evidence of the transformative elements of music and performance. They are not the only such evidence. *Anthem* is an interdisciplinary cultural history that charts multiple acts in diasporic music making that have transformed Black political cultures. From the Black South's demand to "Lift Ev'ry Voice and Sing" to the Black women workers who declared "We Shall Overcome," certain songs have helped to sustain world-altering collective visions. While they are compelling, it is more than the artistry or charisma of the music or performer that draws people together.[1] In the ways that they symbolize and call into being a system of sociopolitical ideas or positions, the songs that I analyze as anthems are devices that make the listening audience and political public merge. Listening to Black anthems is a political act in performance because it mobilizes communal engagements that speak to misrecognition, false histories, violence, and radical exclusion. The songs carried alternative theorizations and practices of blackness, becoming representations that were sought out, not stumbled upon. Unlike standard national anthems, Black anthems were not ubiquitous but instead were performed selectively, and even when their usage was not formalized there was always some clarity of *ends* engendered by the performance. Collectively singing and listening within these choice circumstances, then, was a method of participation within the freedom dreams and liberation projects of an emergent diaspora.

Through anthems, the delineation between art and politics as well as listener and actor is blurred. Anthems demand something of their listeners. In performance they often occasion hands placed over hearts or standing at attention. Yet more than a physical gesture, anthems require subscription to a system of beliefs that stir and organize the receivers of the music. At its best this system inspires its listeners to believe that the circumstances or world around them can change for the better—that the vision of freedom represented in the song's lyrics and/or history are worth fighting for in the contemporary moment. Black communities boast remarkable histories of struggle for freedom through collective mobilizations that often expand beyond the level of the nation, and their anthems are the sound texts that most poignantly record the political issues and contests that arise therein.

Anthem investigates the music that organized the Black world in the twentieth century. As performative political acts, this music is able to mobilize Black populations in service of a particular set of goals through careful attention to and debate over intragroup conceptions of community, racial formation, and political affiliation. These anthems are transnational texts composed of *a set of musical forms* and *a set of organizing strategies* within Black movement cultures and are bound together by African derived performance techniques, Western art traditions, attachments to social justice organizations, iconic performers and performances, relationships to exile, and collective visions of freedom. In their performances around the world they take with them myriad histories and struggles that both ground and invent the audience's relationship to their sociopolitical present.

There is a politico-theological basis for the composition and performance of anthems that disrupts any easy categorization of Black-produced texts as such. Within the ancient Western traditions of the antiphon from which the word "anthem" derives, the call-and-response that lies at the center of Black musics was used as a response to a sovereign body, initially the godhead. The word of God was recited to the congregation, who in turn answered with their anthem, a song style that by the nineteenth century was delivered by a nation in response to their government. This type of response, whether it be to a God figure or state formation, relies upon performances of acquiescence and obedience, two techniques of survival under domination employed only selectively by the African descended. Black cultural practice was the release, the counternarrative that did not identify response as its sole, or even primary, imperative. There were other communicative and methodological strategies at play. Black anthems were not intended as responses to the state/nation, nor to local authorities, although their practice and performance by an organized group of Black women and men initiated an exchange between the surveilling and listening state (local, national, international) and the movement actor and/or organization.[2] An inability to recognize the politico-sonic decentering of a governing subject of response (the Godhead/nation) by the African descended has led recent critics of Black anthems to erroneously identify their projects as nonracial and, by extension, apolitical.[3] As a movement strategy, anthemic musical exchange was a social relay practiced, first and foremost, among the organization, its members, and those whom they sought to mobilize.[4] Motivated by the need to instill the ethics of self-determination and pride in their members, these movement organizations first negotiated relationships to their families, friends, and neighbors.[5] Because there were elements of intraracial difference that conditioned these engagements, these actors did not capitulate to the political as a static realm of engagement controlled from the top down; the political was wherever three or four gathered in the name of justice and labored to speak to one another. This intensive effort at political struggle through racial formation is the process and project, for example, that allowed "We Shall Overcome" to grow from a locally situated protest song to an anthem that transgresses the ideo-temporal frames used to simplify and contain Black movement activity.

When placed alongside Western definitions and practices, the anthemic formation described above approximates a counteranthem, in that there is a critical engagement with the form already embedded within Black anthems. The anthems of the African descended represented here engaged in parallel political projects with those of the liturgical or national variation; they were similarly imagined as effective and powerful performances of cohesion, yet they were situated as internal communiqués and acts of political performance that resisted the containments and fixity of nations and rights—both of which were barriers to the imaginations that through Black music condoned improvisation and exploration, demand and accountability beyond rhetoric.[6] I am interested in pursuing the anthem as it moves in excess of these limits not as a way of setting Black anthems up as an antidote per se but as a way of foregrounding the ways in which Black musics have remixed the modalities of the state in order to foster alternative exercises and experiences of freedom and justice. Beyond a rights paradigm that privileges only those principles and persons established and enlisted, Black anthems negotiated and announced the ambitions and claims of those whose very bodies threw into crisis the normativity of rules and liberties. Black anthems construct a "sound franchise," which I argue is an organized melodic challenge utilized by the African descended to announce their collectivity and to what political ends they would be mobilized. These conversations did not exist outside of the political geographies in which the performers gathered, yet neither were they defined by them. This "franchise" works inside of tension by signaling the presence of a state even as the Black anthems work against or in defiance of its privileges. Composed of a series of alternative performance practices developed and executed to counteract the violent exclusions and techniques of silencing contained within the governing structures of white supremacy, the sound franchise is also proactive and in advance of these codified structures because it works toward an ideal that exceeds the rights bestowed by any particular nation, thereby ushering its performers into formative international solidarities.[7] The terminology of the franchise signals the duplication of these texts across community, time, and space, and like the corporate models, these anthems are situated in differently located, yet aligned, political conditions, thereby becoming representatives or approximations of the original in performance rather than an exact replica.

Anthem begins from the premise that an analysis of the composition, performance, and uses of Black anthems allows for a more complex reading of racial and political formations within the twentieth century and expands our understanding of how and why diaspora was a formative conceptual and political framework of modern Black identity. Scholastic emplotments of the African diaspora grew through anticolonial histories during the Cold War and carry with them an attachment to political struggle, an attachment that I preserve in *Anthem*. The African diaspora is a "dynamic, ongoing and complex phenomenon stretching across time and geography" that has in the past decade been challenged to also consider not only (in)voluntary movement but also what Hazel Carby and Tina Campt discuss as the "settling" of those populations.[8] The art/work of these communities demonstrates the "production" of identity described by Stuart Hall that, like diaspora, "is never complete, always in process."[9] My use of the signifier "Black" throughout *Anthem* is a way to call attention to the overlapping projects of diaspora and racial formation that actively seek recognition in mutual struggle. "Black" signals a transnational culture composed of but always negotiated by a group of individuals who share a common ancestry in Africa. Because it too often is used to dismiss or obscure difference, "Black" in

Anthem is duly troubled through those who make sounds in its name. So too is Africa, which is represented not only as a site of struggle and imagination but also as the progenitor of a flexible set of transferable knowledges of technique and performance that, as Olly Wilson argues, organize "Black music" as "the common sharing of a core of conceptual approaches to the process of music making [that] is not basically quantitative but qualitative."[10]

The sound productions of political actors are undervalued within Black movement literatures, even those histories of well-known and appreciated groups and figures such as the Universal Negro Improvement Association under Marcus Garvey. While scholastic adjustment is part and parcel of any academic project, I am less interested in revising previous accounts of these figures and movements than I am in demanding that we listen to them. Through an intense engagement with their sounds, I argue that new perspectives and consequences are realized. I will again situate these organizations and movement organizers within Black freedom struggles, but I do so in order to document the ways in which the musical performance of anthems both guides and throws into crisis their political aims and objectives. Like any effort at representation, these anthems are flawed and embody contradiction; there are exclusions embedded within their composition—whether textual or musical—that limit their effectiveness and reach. They are not universally held or appreciated—at best, they speak to and for *most* of the people *most* of the time (more likely, they managed speech for *some*). In this respect, they are not unlike any other national anthem in that their communities are selectively imagined and exclusive. Black anthems also are similarly powerful, however, because they exhibit efforts by the African descended to compose an alternative politics and repertoire of belonging, sometimes defined and/or practiced as nationalism, other times as camaraderie or affiliation. Whatever the terminology, these pieces demonstrate the vivid imaginations and performances of solidarity employed by the African descended.

The impulse behind each anthem's composition and performance was unique, but each creatively combined racial and political insights and proscriptions. This tandem imperative, in which one was necessarily conjoined to the other in theory and praxis, produced dense texts that changed the contemporary realities and futures of the composers, performers, and their audiences. Their sonic experiments grew and conjured new projects and structures of identification that challenged, at various moments, white supremacist modernity, Western empire, two-party politics in the United States, settler colonialism, patriarchy, and capitalism. In the absence of free speech, the vote, and other methods of state-sanctioned political participation, Black men and women constructed their own methods and spheres of subjection, influence, and communication. Music has been centrally configured within this project, both pre- and post-Emancipation, and has, according to theorist Fred Moten, evidenced the impossible commodity speech rued by Karl Marx that has pushed against, undermined, and reconfigured value. Black music remains that horizon of "both the performance of the object and the performance of humanity"[11] but is recalibrated through Black anthems, which, as collectively imagined and practiced speech acts, attempt to mobilize sonic rebellions outside of financial exchange. Although multiplied in performance, differences in language and location meant that these anthems, most often, were not experienced as ritualized tomes; performance condones, and oftentimes demands, innovation and change, and these pieces, even if regulated, remained dynamic. They did, however, carry resonances of both technique and position. These anthems are projects of political accumulation; from performance to performance the text grew to incorporate other histories, voices, and political circumstances. In this way, Black anthems cannot be isolated within one incident or performance—they must be understood comparatively. With this expressive vehicle at their disposal, the African descended used their spheres of influence to define new culturo-political communities in direct defiance of the regimes erected to contain them. The most powerful of these articulations were the anthems, which constituted Black political thought in performance.

Black anthems are dense texts that expose the negotiations at work between the West and its Others, the marketplace and the commons, and the individual and the collective. The Western hymn tradition that influenced many of the arrangements for European anthems was not the sonic landscape into which Black anthems were launched. The development of Black anthems occurred at a moment of increased capital gains for Black popular music. Mamie Smith's 1920 hit for Okeh

Records, "Crazy Blues," set into motion an industry-wide investment in Black music through "race records." Blues and jazz took center stage as the popular representations of Black America and became mediating tools in race relations.[12] Black anthems, more than Black popular music, insightfully document these articulations because their use and practice are not primarily motivated by financial imperatives; they instead may be described as motivated by what historian Robin Kelley terms "freedom dreams," ideas and artistic practices attached to movements of conscience. While Black musics have traditionally been a hybrid of sentience and principle, emotion and movement, Black anthems are particularly capable of creating "a world of pleasure, not just to escape the everyday brutalities of capitalism, patriarchy, and white supremacy, but to build community, establish fellowship, play and laugh, and plant seeds for a different way of living, a different way of hearing."[13] The circulation of 1920s Black movement anthems offered a potent political counterpoint to the mass-produced "race records" of the time in that they publicly grappled with how the "race" of "race records" was (and should be) constituted. Through that, they liberated the collapsed Black identity of the marketplace by articulating associations and communities of both race ("a different way of living") and sound ("a different way of hearing").

The six songs discussed and analyzed within *Anthem* are the political acts of performance that defined and called attention to Black cohesion and, through this sound franchise, mobilized hundreds of thousands, if not millions, of the African descended and their allies in the twentieth century. The music in these scenes of political struggle was more than a "soundtrack" for the events surrounding it. These sonic productions were not ancillary, background noise—they were absolutely central to the unfolding politics because they held within them the doctrines and beliefs of the people who participated in their performance, either as singers or listening audience. Those involved in the performance were actively engaging in a quest for alternatives to their political present and were assisted in imagining and enacting that change by the songs on their lips and in their ears: the anthems. These texts were not envisioned or managed by culture brokers in order to accompany the movement actors; the anthems were, instead, the music made by those actors who proactively arranged their own sonic treatises. The reach of the anthem was proportional to the reach of the movement, although it often exceeded it. As the organizations and political communities grew, so too did their anthems, yet it was not unidirectional. Anthems allowed these groups to connect with populations beyond their immediate reach (through staff, organizers, literature) and therefore were both a result of movement momentum and a propelling force behind it.

While certain universals are apparent, the complicated interplay of performer and audience is specific to each of these songs. Some of the anthems were written with four-part harmonies that organically lace together a rich communal performance, while others are solo-voiced anthems whose performers embodied the political struggles of an aggrieved global majority and, through their complicated relationships to the nation, became troubadours for various movements. The attachment of these songs, performers, and performances to political struggle differently configured the acts and actors through a process of meaning making that centered the stakes involved in musical production and performance. This act of "musicking," to borrow from musicologist Christopher Small, was agentive and future-sighted in its forecast of the music's effects.[14] It was an organized and *organizing* effort in which the individual singers were no longer soloists: they were, within movement struggle, the embodied amplifier for a collective who refused the limitations of the term "audience" and instead became a "public."[15] Drawing upon philosopher John Dewey,[16] I contend that Black diasporic publics grew in response to their radical exclusion from an imagined Great Society and communicated with one another through music in order to form and mobilize its alternative: the locally driven "Black counterpublics" described by political scientist Michael Dawson, which are antibourgeois and harbor critiques of liberalism. Although far from perfect, these counterpublics have the potential to "provide the institutional and political base to facilitate communication and criticism across . . . diverse elements."[17] Twentieth-century musico-political counterpublics were composed of members of Black and interracial social justice organizations, radical of-color intellectuals and cultural workers, and allied actors from myriad class and national backgrounds. This diverse constellation of movement participants grounded the various camps engaged in organized struggle, yet, far from being uncritically unified, these organizations and their extended publics worked under tension. In addition to external political and social pressures, there were internal struggles for recognition and acceptance that were often (and perhaps unknowingly) played out in the performance of their anthem.[18] The multivocal antiphony characteristic of Black music is, through these anthems, identifiable as both the straightforward layering of sound (call-and-response) and the intracommunity contests embedded within and emboldened by that exchange. Gender, nation, and class are all negotiated affiliations within these organizations, and their anthems demonstrate, through composition and text, the ways in which members and performers were instructed and constructed within their political community and imaginary.

The genealogy of Black music details the ways in which it has served as a laboratory for the interplay of racial solidarity and struggle. An Afro-Anglophone tradition of resistance among the enslaved is heard in the spirituals and field hollers, which carried messages of rebellion and techniques of survival. These messages have continued unabated throughout the twentieth century, taking shape through rags, art music, the behemoth of jazz, folk, soul, and, most recently, the lyrical urban symphonies of the disinherited through hip-hop. Leverage is constituted through this musical method in myriad ways: as communication and strategy to listening comrades or enemies, flight through performance or technologies of sound, and finance through recording industries. In *Anthem*, I investigate the first and second of these effects. Black anthems are particular incubators for intraracial dynamics and relationships because they are attached to on-the-ground mobilizations. As ethnomusicologist Kyra Gaunt argues, "Musical play is a vital environment within which black folks . . . learn to improvise with what it means to be dominant and subordinate in musical and nonmusical relationships."[19] This "play," as a three-dimensional practice, is pronounced within anthems and accounts for the sound and innovation of musical acts, the uneven participation within them, as well as the politics that are mobilized through their performances. Power is, therefore, present throughout and working on multiple, and sometimes competing, registers.[20] Guided by a desire to further materialize the powerful "blues epistemology" theorized by Clyde Woods,[21] *Anthem* builds on literatures of Black music and social movements—an especially present consideration in jazz and hip-hop studies[22]—by situating the anthems discussed here as productions that organize sound and community in dense and fantastic ways.[23]

Music is a participatory enterprise that requires certain performative knowledges in order for its political and movement aims to be realized. Racial communities have long participated in the protective subterfuge of coded language and performance practice, commonly referred to as "insider" and "outsider" knowledges. The "dissemblance" employed by Black women and theorized by historian Darlene Clark Hine models the strategies that accompany minority life under majority rule.[24] The musical literacy of the performers and audiences for Black anthems covered the spectrum, from the formally trained to the illiterate, yet technical precision was less important than the experiences of living a life of difference. Anthropologist James Scott uses the idea of public and hidden transcripts to discuss the ways in which oppressed peoples communicate with power and one another. Public transcripts are the "open interaction between subordinates and those who dominate," while hidden transcripts are those that "[take] place 'offstage,' beyond direct observation by powerholders." These texts and spaces are not uniform or absolute. As he notes, "Power relations are not, alas, so straightforward that we can call what is said in power-laden contexts false and what is said offstage true. Nor can we simplistically describe the former as a realm of necessity and the latter as a realm of freedom." What is true, according to him, "is that the hidden transcript is produced for a different audience and under different constraints of power than the public transcript."[25] Black anthems are neither condoned as public texts nor completely absented from the public sphere as hidden text, yet they similarly rely on codes produced through the intimacy of difference that demand observance of cultural practices in relation to a majority society, even as they double back to challenge that culture and society. Black arts have their own tradition of "speaking truth to power." This speech, as theater scholar David Krasner argues, includes "[c]ountercodes, innuendoes, and subtle shifts in emphasis [that] suggest that the significance underlying [Black] performances was open to broader interpretations," while also signaling an acknowledgment by performers, composers, and audiences of their access to a "multifaceted cultural (ethnic) capital," which, drawing on sociologist Pierre Bourdieu, makes meaning for those with the cultural expertise to understand the code.[26]

The anthems investigated here combined both understated and explicit overtures within their compositions and performances, situating their impact as both affirmations of the unique knowledges of the African descended and rebellion against the diffuse violences of white rule on a global scale.

The state and nation as contiguous, though distinctly employed, geopolitical configurations are disarticulated within the worlds of the anthems described in this book. Black anthems are transnational by design and reach publics beyond the scope of their place of origin. While a number of the songs are situated within certain national contexts and grow from specific conditions of bondage, violence, and exclusion, their narratives resist the fixity of place and follow the indictments of anthems by encouraging identification from and by a number of communities. Within Black anthemic production, this mass of individuals is bound not by geography but instead by their intersectional conditions as raced and (post)colonial subjects and their shared freedom drive/impulse. There is, however, engagement with the state/nation and/or its representation through these texts, not only in their molding/ modeling of the genre but also through sonic and textual employments that play off of the entrenched knowledge of existing national anthems. Black cultural production has historically functioned as a rebuttal to the state's power to control and manipulate national consensus, yet the African descended have creatively employed the state's rubric of cohesion through productions of musical iconography. For example, the national anthem of the United States, "The Star-Spangled Banner," haunts chapter 1's "Ethiopia (Thou Land of Our Fathers)," the anthem of the Universal Negro Improvement Association (UNIA) and is replayed in an augmented form within the composition. The anthem of the African National Congress (ANC) under investigation in chapter 6, "Nkosi Sikelel' iAfrika," was wed to the anthem of the apartheid regime, "Die Stem van Suid-Afrika," in the postdemocracy moment, with both texts now hailed as co–national anthems. Both of these examples demonstrate the insidiousness of the state in sonic histories and the ways in which the violences of the state are (re)entrenched through music even in the pursuit and wake of racial justice victories.

The Black and interracial organizations that these anthems represent serve to rebut, reorient, or reimagine the state's role in the lives of Black citizens, not replace it as the sole object of allegiance. These anthems are intended to conjure alternative affiliations that meet people where they are, in their communities, churches, schools, and organizations while also allowing them to grow through the mobilizations within those "translocal" spaces.[27] They are not meta-texts in the same way as national anthems; they derive their power not from a rigid and controlled nationalism—although as the UNIA demonstrates, nationalism was part and parcel of the organizing framework for some of these songs—but from identification with communities excluded from the promises of the nation. These anthems are connected to one another through histories of struggle and political techniques more so than through sonic methods or composition; they are sounded and performed differently but all fall along a continuum of Black political practice theorized by Cedric Robinson as the Black Radical Tradition.[28] Their tie to a history of dissent makes their articulations all the more dangerous within the hostile societies of their birth and employment. The surveillance techniques of the state condone the patrolling of all methods of speech, and music is a conspicuous avenue of political thought that is carried on air, through throats and fingers, and into the ears of the listening "counterintelligence" agencies.[29] This sound, while detectable and traceable, cannot be contained or wholly stopped, making its dissemination more fluid and its impact that much more powerful than the written word. While the written compositions and organizations and, later, their performers and performances often were banned and outlawed, the sounds and utterances produced in their name would not be silenced. As Harry Belafonte famously argued, "You can cage the singer but not the song."

Music is at the center of this project for this flight but first and foremost because it creates collective engagement in performance and contributes to a dense Black performance history that continually configures Black citizenship through shared ambitions and intersectional identities. Without dismissing the urgent reminder offered by literary scholar Brent Edwards that "space is privileged and richly varied" in diaspora, it is important to consider the "reciprocal relationship[s]" of social theorist Paul Gilroy's description that within diaspora "can serve as an ideal communicative situation even when the original makers of the music and its eventual consumers are separated in time and space."[30]

Black anthems exercise their power across and between national borders, languages, and cultures precisely because they are dialogic without requiring a literate tradition; while absolutely crucial, the compositions as material evidence are not the primary texts within my analysis here—they are instead their performances, those interpretations that tell us who the performers and audiences were and why they were on stage, in the room, auditorium, or field at that moment on that day. Nina Simone's performances of "To Be Young, Gifted and Black" drew people together and into conversation with each other; without exceptionalizing her as a singular figure, it is necessary to note that often it literally was her voice that put them in the same place at the same time. The power of these acts, then, is not simply as sonic art—as important as that is; it is also pedagogical and organizational in that these performances compelled reactive and proactive engagements and debate, all of which contributed to political alternatives in the present.

These anthems constitute differently configured diasporic formations that link people to one another through and beyond race into communities organized by imaginations of freedom from and an end to hierarchies of difference. Black anthems are both the rationale and vision for these imaginations. As manifestos based in political practice and mobilization, Black anthems are able to model a three-dimensional platform for communities in struggle on a global scale. Within and between their multiple iterations, they are composed of prominent artist-activists, social justice organizations, and large ground-level mobilizations by Black and allied communities who are brought into communion with one another not simply through the assumed knowledge of their racial kinship but instead through their daily choice to actively engage in resistance efforts. The diasporas for these anthems then are not assumed but chosen and speak to the lived experiences of communities under siege. While the conditions for each community and individual are particular, these songs reflect universal cadences of struggle that are dynamic and adaptable to different communities, locations, and issues. The myriad requests to reprint and translate "Lift Ev'ry Voice and Sing" are but one example of these anthems' reach and impact beyond their communities of origin. In this respect, the diasporas of political thought and performance that I discuss here are, to follow Gilroy, announced more by their "routes" than their "roots," yet precisely their foundations in Black traditions allow their passage domestically and abroad.[31] Neither they nor the political scenarios that they inspired can be removed from the originary knowledges and experiences envoiced through these anthems.

These diasporas are held together not only by alternative and studied political visions and performance but also by alternative sensory engagements. The song in concert with its history and present mobilization develops the "anthemic event," which privileges hearing over seeing, another grand departure from diasporas based in race and sight. To hear the struggles of others—versus the *hearing of* or seeing of them— requires a different level of engagement with the communities represented therein. The mechanics of listening are technological as well as biological and allow for these texts to be adopted in other national contexts where language and culture otherwise limit international communications. To hear Black anthems, whether live or on wax, is to be a part of the event itself; singing and listening, therefore, involve pronounced political stakes within the anthemic event. In those scenes, the performing body exhibits an acknowledgment of the project taking place and the relations that made it possible. The community of performance and its environment is therefore dynamic and begins to challenge narratives of the state as an equally incorporative, undifferentiated unifying entity and the exclusive infrastructure of global power. Black anthems construct an alternative constellation of citizenship—new imagined communities that challenge the "we" of the "melting pot" or democratic state, yet install new definitions of "we" in its place.[32] Exposed here is a fundamental tension within their construction and use: Black anthems replicate certain functions of state propaganda, albeit toward different ends and with different actors—actors who, historically, are structurally powerless. Black anthems are the evidence of a cumulative project of identity formation and political agency mobilized through culture, which, when taken together, construct parallel movements of solidarity and influence.

Far from working in isolation, these anthems built off of the momentum of those before them. Politically, socially, and culturally they expanded previous paradigms and tactics, sometimes offering correctives to the preceding anthems. Through studied engagements with prior sounds and movements, these anthems were connected within a complicated and dynamic history of liberation acts among the African descended. "Ethiopia" set the stage for the modern Black citizen-subject in song with the others following in step, highlighting shared concerns and actively challenging and adjusting the perspectives that no longer met the needs of the intended communities. There are important differences between the pieces—politically, compositionally, contextually—yet their shared efforts to mobilize ground them as a genre within the pantheon of Black musics. The political imaginaries of these Black composers and performers were grown in concert with a global South advancing new strategies and collectivities in their battles with an atrophic colonialism. In recognition of their majority status, these political actors conceived of and enacted a musical project that was guided by what Vijay Prashad describes as an "internationalist nationalism," yet it still called upon a collective that was often, although not exclusively, organized by race.[33] The knowledges and best practices developed within and between radical internationalism and Black cultural traditions were translated and transferred to global communities through these anthems, making this constellation of actors, listeners, and publics vocal, rights-holding "citizens of sound."[34]

The anthems represented in *Anthem* are not the only ones produced by the African descended; there are other sonic texts that fit my theorization of the genre, but the six analyzed here were chosen for their connections to one another and intimate relationships to various social movements. Each chapter contends with the histories, communities, and performances that made the song a force within twentieth century Black political cultures and mobilizations. These are the anthems. Chapter 1 focuses on "Ethiopia (Thou Land of Our Fathers)," the anthem of the UNIA. The UNIA under Marcus Garvey sets the stage for the use of anthems as modern mechanisms of global affiliation and community building within the African diaspora. The regulated and formalized performances of "Ethiopia" ritualized the anthem within the organization, which grew to include hundreds of thousands of members across the diaspora and spawned national chapters in locations like South Africa, Canada, and the chapter's location of focus, Cuba. When one considers the multitextual and performative nature of its nation-building agenda, the UNIA is wholly situated within the Black arts renaissance of the 1920s, the decade of the organization's height. "Ethiopia" provides the evidence of a highly organized cultural wing within the UNIA even while its composition exposes the conflicts embedded within the organization around gender, in particular. Similar tensions are held in "Lift Ev'ry Voice and Sing," the canonized Negro National Hymn, anthem of the National Association for the Advancement of Colored People (NAACP), and focus of chapter 2. The UNIA and NAACP have been situated in Black literatures as opposites, contradictory in philosophy, reach, and practice. An examination of their anthems, however, draws the two organizations into close contact and highlights the shared impulse behind their differing agendas. J. Rosamond and James Weldon Johnson's "Lift Ev'ry Voice and Sing" became the mouthpiece for the NAACP in a moment of increased international recognition for Black art through the Harlem Renaissance, the growth of communism, and the expansion of various empires through war making. These conditions encouraged exchange among and between communities of color, and as the Depression dawned, "Lift Ev'ry Voice and Sing" became a tool within intercultural, international communiqués. A 1933 request to translate the anthem into Japanese manifests the ways in which politicized diasporas utilized sound as a tool of representation by sending blackness abroad in five-line staves.

The role of the solo artist in anthemic productions is introduced in chapter 3, which highlights the travels and refusals of Paul Robeson through his standard "Ol' Man River." Unlike those of chapters 1 and 2, his anthem was not formally adopted by a Black protest organization but instead was used by Robeson as a unifying text in multiple political struggles around the world. During the Depression, Robeson radically adjusted the text of the song—originally written for the musical *Show Boat* by Jerome Kern and Oscar Hammerstein II—and used it as the foundation for his repertoire of world folk songs sung in more than thirty languages. Blackness and labor are brought into stark relief within his anthem, which, in combination with his undeterred political speech in support of decolonization, peace, and civil rights, made him the target of intense public scrutiny and investigation. His recordings of "Ol' Man River" during the period of his passport revocation (1950–58) under McCarthyism announce his political project during the decade as his voice took flight in defiance of a growing surveillance state. The labor themes within Robeson's performances and activism are carried over into chapter 4, but they are analyzed at the local level as I trace the labor origins of the canonic "We Shall Overcome." Birthed in political performance during a tobacco strike in 1945, this anthem has suffered from inaccuracies and misrepresentation in the literature regarding both its organizational affiliation and its performers. Black women workers within an interracial Charleston local of the Congress of Industrial Organizations (CIO) were the leaders of the strike and literally composed and paced the pickets through their performances of the revised spiritual. Their defiance of societal, industry, and city segregation and creative mobilizations of Black cultural traditions announced the techniques of political protest that would organize untold numbers of the disenfranchised over the next two decades. The success of this job action was recognized first in the sounds that it produced—an anthem that would be carried to the hills of Tennessee, out into the Civil Rights Movement, and eventually to a world in coordinated struggle.

Black women's role in the long Civil Rights Movement is further interrogated in chapter 5 through its transition into the Black Power Movement. Nina Simone's voice bridged this change in "To Be Young, Gifted and Black," a genre-bending piece inspired by her late mentor, Lorraine Hansberry. The Congress of Racial Equality (CORE) anthem grew from a diverse repertoire of civil rights and feminist anthems produced by Simone throughout the decade, which, when read in combination, signal her political awakening and evolution in domestic and world affairs. Her political conversion was but one of her changes over the decade as her queer voice rose up to speak and sing on issues including women's rights and colonialism. Her engagement with a world corps of Black musics led her into conversation with figures such as South African songstress Miriam Makeba, whose delivery of "Nkosi Sikelel' iAfrika" announced the liberation of a number of African nations during the high tide of continental decolonization. Before its use as a Pan-African text, the song began its life as the anthem of the embattled ANC, the organizational focus of chapter 6. The multilingual composition of "Nkosi Sikelel' iAfrika" facilitated its broad usage and adoption throughout the 1960s and 70s in Africa and its performance by the Amandla cultural ensemble of the ANC in exile amassed a broad range of supporters and sympathizers worldwide, who began to apply the pressure necessary to topple the apartheid regime. The anthem is a continental experiment in resistance and solidarity that is reformed and tamed in the postdemocracy moment in South Africa, signaling the final stages of twentieth-century Black resistance through song.

The resonance of these anthems in the post–Civil Rights decades is discussed in the Conclusion, which also examines the last Black anthem of the twentieth century—Public Enemy's "Fight the Power." The move to hip-hop at the end of the century brings the politico-performative and compositional aesthetics of Black music full circle and signals a complicated, albeit possible, future for the anthem genre beyond the organized mass mobilizations that once characterized Black social movements. Although most of the organizations discussed within *Anthem* have faded from public view, their historical legacy is still heard through excerpts, remix, or code. As melodically organized political speech in performance, Black anthems continue to sound struggles over identity, power, and representation within a contemporary world order structured by legacies of slavery, genocide, and Western domination. Although it has limits, music, as a three-dimensional document, practice, and experience, still exists as a method for new political performances and futures. It is my hope that *Anthem* will assist in compelling the new sounds that inspire and mobilize the making of "a world in which it will be safe to be different."[35]

1

From Race to Nation

"Ethiopia" and Pan-African Pageantry in the UNIA

[T]o organize Negroes we have got to demonstrate; you cannot tell them anything; you have got to show them; and that
is why we have got to spend seven years making noise.
—Marcus Garvey

It was the thirteenth of August 1920, nearly two weeks into the month-
long International Convention of the Negro Peoples of the World held
in Harlem, New York. The stage was emblazoned with the colors of
red, black, and green, and the two-thousand-member audience sat in
eager anticipation of their entrance. On that day the Universal Negro
Improvement Association (UNIA) announced its human-rights platform for the protections of the Black race. Titled the *Declaration of
Rights of the Negro Peoples of the World*, the manifesto was designed to
broadcast the formation of and agenda for 400 million Negroes worldwide and was, on this day, given a rigorous and vibrant rendering by the
newly appointed provisional president of Africa, Marcus Garvey. As the
oratory closed, his breath hanging from the final line of the *Declaration
of Rights* ("These rights we believe to be justly ours . . . "), the audience
took its cue and boldly affirmed its solidarity when it "sprang to its feet
and sang most fervently the new anthem of the association, 'Ethiopia,
Thou Land of Our Fathers.'"[1] This recital was their moment of exultation and collective advance, signaling the introductory chapter of their
ascent into the world corps of nations.

The anthem, "Ethiopia (Thou Land of Our Fathers)," in performance
was the evidence of citizenship on the lips of UNIA members. Like the

Declaration of Rights, it was a defining text of the organization that ushered its performers into complex conversations and practices of race and nation, thereby becoming a centrifugal element and catalyst for a plethora of politico-cultural activities and symbols used to unite the "scattered of Africa." Culture was developed and mobilized within the organization by a cast of religious leaders, organizers, and musicians—including, notably, the anthem's co-composer and UNIA musical director Arnold Ford—as a strategy to build identification and solidarity among and between Afro-diasporic communities. This previously unknown combination of racial politics and performance made the UNIA the most adroit race organization of the immediate post–World War I order.

The UNIA practiced what performance scholar Honor Ford-Smith terms an "ecology of cultural production," which provided Black men and women the space to develop, distribute, and control their own representations. This process, "combined with cultural critique and audience education," made up a matrix of arts and performance whose didactic purposes propelled the organization forward.[2] A crucial centerpiece to this cultural project was the UNIA anthem, "Ethiopia (Thou Land of Our Fathers)," a text that launched the impressive platform of the organization even as its composition and performances around the world exposed the dangers of its gendered rhetoric. With this song serving as a mouthpiece for the organization, international divisions flourished from Canada to Australia, but nowhere more densely than in Cuba. As Black bodies traveled the globe following World War I, so too did the UNIA, and its performances forever altered the expectations, ambitions, and projects of the African descended and their protest organizations.

Black August: Building and Defying Convention(s)

By the time of the August 1920 convention the UNIA was more than six years old. Founded in Jamaica in 1914 by printer and race man Marcus Mosiah Garvey and his soon-to-be wife, Amy Ashwood, the UNIA taught thrift, dedication, and simple ambition to its followers.[3] This early stage of the organization was characterized by a resistance to political participation—a position deeply influenced by Garvey's relationship to the teachings of Black American leader Booker T. Washington.[4] A 1916 trip to the United States, in which he witnessed the nation's unique brand of Jim Crow, changed Garvey's perspective on politics and impressed upon him the necessity of a strong race program based in the political desires of Afro-diasporic communities. As the message and spectacle of the 1920 convention demonstrates, both Garvey and the organization quickly adjusted their political philosophies in order to respond to the growing racial antagonisms within the United States.

The UNIA's new Black world was launched from Liberty Hall. Dedicated on July 27, 1919, Liberty Hall was a nod to the building of the same name in Dublin, Ireland, which was a recognized site of rebellion during the Irish War of Independence.[5] The shared name of the two locations highlighted the organization's global perspective and encouraged visitors and members alike to imagine the UNIA struggle as an extension of existent nationalist movements. Liberty Hall therefore beckoned individuals invested, or at least interested, in a mobilization-centered approach to Black activism and served as a welcome site for visitors and UNIA members from around the world. The hall's location in Harlem, the "Black Mecca," offered additional incentives to the African descended. It was not only a densely populated Black section of the city, where Black men and women developed and enjoyed relatively safe public spaces, but also the hub of Black culture and protest, housing the offices of the UNIA and National Association for the Advancement of Colored People (NAACP), and forming the landscape for the labor militancy of A. Philip Randolph and Chandler Owen's socialist *Messenger* magazine. The Harlem Renaissance writers, musicians, and performers of the 1920s set a brilliant stage for the upcoming events of the blooming UNIA.

While Garvey harbored a "long-held belief in the unification of art and propaganda as the keenest instrument of progress," his vision was not universally held.[6] Debates within the infant UNIA hinged on questions of the relationship between performance and politics. As historian Colin Grant notes, "[E]ven before the fundamental building blocks were put in place, the ideological stress lines were beginning to show" between Garvey and his colleagues and culture was a sticking point that reflected the tensions of both performance and nation within the organization. The collective questioned, for example, "if meetings were to culminate in rousing renditions of the national anthem, should it be 'God Save the King' or 'The Star Spangled Banner'?"[7] By the time of the Liberty Hall purchase, the fault lines among the UNIA organizers appeared to be resolved. The organization had incorporated, and a decision on its sound had been reached.

The answer was the anthem "Ethiopia." Composed in 1918 by Benjamin E. Burrell (coauthor of the lyrics) and Arnold J. Ford (lyrics coauthor and composer), the song was informed by their profound sense of obligation to the furtherance of a Black nation. Both men were, at the time of composition, members of the UNIA-NY and used the organization's militaristic rhetoric to accomplish their goal of providing the Black nation with its musical accompaniment. The lyrics of "Ethiopia" demonstrate the efforts made by the two men to mobilize their singing audience:

> Ethiopia, thou land of our fathers,
> Thou land where the gods loved to be,
> As storm cloud at night suddenly gathers
> Our armies come rushing to thee.
> We must in the fight be victorious
> When swords are thrust outward to glean;
> For us will the vict'ry be glorious
> When led by the red, black and green.
>
> CHORUS
>
> Advance, advance to victory,
> Let Africa be free;
> Advance to meet the foe
> With the might
> Of the red, the black and the green.

With this rallying text, the UNIA sounded its position on Western colonialism in Africa and announced its impending project of reclamation. The text draws on heavily militaristic prose in order to manufacture a sense of power and emotional connection to the cause in the face of a dismal political reality and extended battle ahead. The early decades of the twentieth century continued the radical post-Reconstruction exclusion of Black political participation in the United States; from 1901 to 1929, there were no Black elected officials in the Senate or House of Representatives and local Black officials were scarce in communities north and south of the Mason-Dixon Line. Beyond the United States, the Black world lived and struggled under distinct and dispersed regimes of colonial domination. In the face of this radical exclusion, Black men and women played an exponentially larger role within their communities and used those spaces to not only investigate and respond to contemporary issues but also imagine, again and again, alternatives to them. "Ethiopia" reflects this future vision. The claim that "for us *will* the vict'ry be glorious" assumes success in an undetermined future—a utopia that is visible only because of Black people's remembrance and knowledge of an idyllic past condition, located in Ethiopia, the "land where the Gods *loved* to be." Landscapes of milk and honey were long since gone for Black subjects; "Ethiopia" predicted that the Black future of possibility could be made manifest only in the moment of a violent reversal of contemporary power relations: the Black man reclaiming his rightful place as leader of Africa. This power struggle was, as the exclusively male imagery attests to, incomplete; as I will soon discuss, the gender hierarchies that structured power on a global scale also abound within "Ethiopia." Although the UNIA was both revolutionary and progressive, it often remained, like so many of its contemporaries, stubbornly antiquated in its approach to gender and the role of women within its ranks. Women are not explicitly acknowledged in the past of "Ethiopia" or its future vision, thereby falling into the rhetorical and temporal gap of the anthem even as the Black nation's heterogeneity is put on display.

The internationalism of "Ethiopia" echoed the bustle of the UNIA, which by 1918 developed a language of diaspora to identify the organization's work and character through its global political aims and diverse membership. The New York branch alone boasted members from Caribbean, African, and Central American nations, and the myriad cultural tropes within "Ethiopia" mirrored that diversity. Drawn from the mystic and religious imagery of Psalms 68:31, the anthem privileges the Egyptian princes whose deliverance will allow "Ethiopia [to] soon stretch out her hands to God."[8] Through this vision, "Ethiopia" brought to the modern UNIA membership a resonant, biblical perspective on liberation and redemption from the cradle of civilization. This is the history that ordained Black victory and, in the hands of the UNIA, would usher the Black nation into its formative position as global redeemer. The text enforces its use as a nationalist tract by incorporating a call to the race ("Advance, advance"), a common goal ("Let Africa be free"), and a unifying symbol ("the red, the black and the green" of the UNIA flag). The spiritual core of the race in Ethiopia and the symbols of Africa's reclamation—the flag, the armies—project the "we" that the UNIA hoped would soon be realized.

The song's music adds an important layer of meaning to an already compelling and complicated text. The composer was Arnold J. Ford, the man responsible for many of the fantastic productions of the UNIA. Born in Barbados, Ford was a prominent fixture within the culture industry of the organization. A leader within New York City's Black Jewish circles, former military man, and trained musician, he offered many talents to the organization. Beyond his travels and experiences, his diasporic perspective is evident in his choice of a militant Jamaican missionary tune as the frame for the Exodus narrative within "Ethiopia."[9] Written in B-flat major, the anthem closely follows the notation and harmonic progressions of the Western tradition. Four-part harmony opens the piece with a short quarter measure in common time quickly leading the voices to a IV chord half note on "fathers" in measure 3. All four voices proceed together in harmony until a punctuated accompaniment entrance in measure 17 announces the gender break in measure 18. The men introduce the line, "Advance, Advance to Victory," while the women join in measure 19. This musical notation has social consequence as the chorus sings men into positions of leadership within the nationalist project while the women follow. This compositional element was not the only signal of gender stratification within the anthem or the larger UNIA. The gender break within the music, however, was a consistently replayed device of difference within a composition that eventually returns to four-part singing with "Let Africa be free," a communal exclamation highlighting the necessity of a combined effort in the rescue of Africa from the hands of oppressors.

Beyond its composition, it was the instructional elements and standardization of its performance across the organization that highlighted the hierarchies within the UNIA. The groundwork for these practices was laid at the International Convention of the Negro Peoples of the World. The 1920 event was described as opening "in a blaze of glory," and music was its spark.[10] The variety of music used by the UNIA was a formal process regulated by leaders in the organization and the inaugural convention was the place where the rules and regulations were devised and implemented. Delegates from twenty-five countries plus a participatory audience large enough to necessitate the use of Madison Square Garden discussed and debated the status and future of Black subjects globally, with a particular focus placed on Africa. From this gathering emanated the *Declaration of Rights of the Negro Peoples of the World*. Composed of twelve complaints and fifty-four demands and proclamations, the declaration attempted to outline the common condition of Negroes internationally, document the opinions of the convention participants, and set forth a platform for the actors of the movement with the express purpose being to "state what [the Negro race] deem their fair and just rights, as well as the treatment they propose to demand of all men in the future."[11]

The document is compelling for its comprehensiveness and multiple purposes. Its use as a representational record for the race as well as a rubric for the members of the UNIA ensured that the *Declaration of Rights* had a depth that was absent in other of the documents produced by the organization's contemporaries. The UNIA argued that the entitlements of the Black race exceeded the jurisdiction of any nation and were therefore a matter of human rights. Included within its articulation of rights is the privilege of expression. The organization recognized the importance of culture in advancing its agenda and used music, in particular, to promulgate the UNIA and its claims to nationhood; declaration 40 resolves that "the anthem, 'Ethiopia, Thou Land of Our Fathers', etc., shall be the anthem of the Negro race."[12] Originally written and adopted in the nascent stages of the U.S.-based UNIA, "Ethiopia" held a prominent position in the local events and international advances of the organization. Section 58 of the UNIA *Constitution and Book of Laws* states that "[t]he Anthem of the Association shall be played or sung at all public meetings or functions or whenever appropriate at the opening or closing of such meetings or both."[13] In tandem, the declaration and constitution wrote "Ethiopia" into the very structure of the nation and UNIA—two distinct bodies made contiguous through the anthem. As ethnomusicologist J. Martin Daughtry argues, "[T]he enforced ritual dimension of anthems elevates them above the level of mere propaganda."[14] The UNIA, in fact, argued that the performance of the anthem was a necessary part of political and civic participation within the Black nation; it reinforced doctrine and cohered the membership/citizenry. If, as other scholars have suggested, the UNIA was ordered by a Black masculinist performance of storytelling and ambition, then its anthem was the most consistent element of its organization.[15] The demand to sing drew individuals into the function of the nation and organization by uniting them in common cause politically and musically, as they used their harmonies as a practice that could liberate them. In this respect, the formal adoption and ritualization of "Ethiopia" signaled its role as a method to build citizens of both the UNIA and the Black nation.

The composition and performance of "Ethiopia" model the types of anxieties that exist within nationalist constructions, namely anthems. These songs are intended as public expressions of unity, an ambitious concept and practice under anyone's direction that inevitably falls short of its goal. "Ethiopia" exposes these hazards and imperfections at the previously mentioned gender break in measure 18. The lead that the men take in the singing of the anthem is structural: it is written into the composition and performance instructions for the song, officially configuring women as those who trail behind. This performance element is on display within the song as well as the documents that regulate the operation of the anthem within UNIA events. The *Constitution and Book of Laws* demands that "while ['Ethiopia'] is being played all persons shall stand. The men shall stand with uncovered heads except in uniform. Uniformed men in obedience to military regulations will stand at attention or salute."[16] The pomp and circumstance that the UNIA is known for, and that compelled the anthem's performance, was not unique to the organization. Cultural studies scholar Michelle Stephens argues that these performances "mirrored for the imperial world the racial and masculinist features of their own imperial and state ideologies."[17] The fantastic displays in the streets of Harlem and elsewhere in the Black world under the banner of the UNIA were spectacular, but instead of displaying an equally accessible and participatory Black power, they exposed the privileged masculine impulse of the organization and its mission. "Ethiopia" in performance helped to codify an already existent male-centric militarism within the UNIA through the specific acknowledgment and regulation of men's activities.

The gendered prescriptions for the performance of "Ethiopia" underscore the tensions within the construction of diasporic citizenship. The demand that "all *persons* shall stand" brings women into the fold of the nation through song, yet the absence of a specific right of performance within the instructions for the anthem marks women as both invisible to the process through an undifferentiated universality and crucial to its success through their participation. Even universality does not provide sufficient enough haven from gender difference however; gender theorist Simone de Beauvoir articulated the implicit gendering of universal categories, saying, "In actuality the relation of the two sexes is not quite like that of two electrical poles, for man represents both the positive and the neutral, as is indicated by the common use of *man* to designate human beings in general; whereas woman represents only the negative, defined by limiting criteria, without reciprocity."[18] The repetitive and ceremonial aspect of the anthem's performance forced women to negotiate their roles within the universal category of "persons" as well as their distinct difference from the men whom they sung alongside. Historian Ula Taylor argues that race women like Amy Jacques Garvey, Marcus Garvey's second wife, enacted a "community feminism," which "resembled a tug-of-war between feminist and nationalist paradigms but it also provided a means of critiquing chauvinistic ideas of women as intellectually inferior."[19] This "tug-of-war" by Jacques Garvey and, undoubtedly, the UNIA's foremost organizer, Henrietta Vinton Davis, as well as others, is embedded within "Ethiopia," and its institutionalization brought these tensions and many others to the fore through its efforts to organize the Black world.

"Ethiopia" existed as the central sound text within the UNIA but was buttressed by a number of others that served to highlight the distinct character of the organization. The organization's introductory hymn, "From Greenland's Icy Mountains," models a traditional hymn technique, dating back centuries. Four-part tonal harmonies form the core of the piece, with piano and/or organ accompaniment to fill in the traditional chord progression. Ford also relied on this technique within "Ethiopia" and his larger repertoire. His dedication to this style was facilitated and reinforced by others within the leadership of the organization. Garvey unabashedly promoted Western ideals in the work of his cultural producers, in particular UNIA musicians. In 1922 the UNIA press organ the *Negro World* ran a six-part series titled "The Negro and Music," in which UNIA Band leader William Isles discussed music within Negro culture. He argued that slave songs or spirituals—which were taking concert stages by storm in this period—were a form not in keeping with the contemporary Negro because "[t]he soul of this new Manhood Race of ours rebels against such utterances."[20] He believed the permanency of the slave song in the repertoire of Black Americans to be evidence of the death of creative potential in the community. By briefly tracing the musical genealogies of Greece, Scotland, and England, he reasoned that like that of Europe, the art of the Negro race would ascend with their humanity. This humanity, as his previous comment demonstrates, was a product of its time and was gendered first as male, although the universal again haunts the project under the heading of "Negro." Although Negro ascension was aligned with a European trajectory, Isles noted that "the Negro will not be able to attain the height of his musical ambition until he has created for himself institutions which are so essential to his progress in this line of endeavor."[21] Here he articulated a strategy for Black empowerment that combined art with separate community-serving political institutions; in so doing, he made one ambition dependent on the other, thereby fortifying the cultural imperative of the UNIA and ensuring the centrality of musicians like Ford to the successes of the Nation.

Like Isles, Rabbi Ford (as he was often called) closely followed Garvey's ideology of nationhood and lifting up the heroes of the race. Garvey's lessons demanded that his followers reject the songs of other cultures and instead "[s]ing your own songs and recite your own praises that glorify your own race."[22] The repeated use of the word "own" in this phrase is more than an identification for those doing the "sing[ing]," "recit[ing]," and "glorify[ing]"—it is also a claim of rights over the "songs," "praises," and "race" that organized the UNIA. Ford was a central actor within both the articulation and copyright of these beliefs. He assembled and institutionalized these claims through his publications, namely the *Universal Ethiopian Hymnal*, a collection of twenty-one hymns. Originally published in 1920 by the Beth B'nai Abraham Publishing Company of New York, the hymnal went through at least three editions between 1920 and 1922. Ford's constant reexamination and reworking of the hymnal made it a dynamic element within the UNIA, one that changed and conformed to meet the demands of its audience (or congregation). The production of a hymnal by a political organization offered some provocative advantages but also exposed the shaky foundation on which the organization's rhetoric was built. As a traditional religious tract the *Universal Ethiopian Hymnal* was able to play on the expectations of perseverance and faith, which served to organize the UNIA membership and the Black race more broadly into a collective group seeking deliverance. The secular mission of the UNIA, however, meant that the brutalities that they sought deliverance from were not resolved in heaven, but were struggled for and won on earth through the efforts of women and men, not God. The on-the-ground movements of the UNIA relied on a degree of cohesion among its constituents that was bolstered and compromised by cultural elements like the anthem and the hymnal, and it is this internal struggle and its material evidence that compromised the welfare of the organization and its aims.

The *Universal Ethiopian Hymnal* drew on canonical texts of the Western hymn tradition such as "Blest Be the Tie," but the vast majority of the hymns were composed and/or arranged by Ford and spoke directly to the goals of the organization. UNIA philosophy and rhetoric permeated every aspect of the program, from its documents and oratory to the clothes that people wore. Ford played a considerable role in this production—the performance of his music was a gauge of the organization's health. As a Black tradition without a literacy requirement, music enabled the UNIA masses to participate in the dissemination of the organization's message and to mediate their own desires and ambitions through their performances. The organization's motto, "One God, One Aim, One Destiny," was the title of hymn 7. The final verse reflects the importance of the motto as the chorus sings,

> O glorious day of peace on earth
> And goodwill to man to man,

> Soon must we herald in thy birth,
> Decreed since Time began.
> "One God," for war and strife must cease;
> "One Aim," that all be free,
> "One Destiny," that love and peace
> Be Man's eternally.

The UNIA's ideal of "One God" was particularly significant to the success of its nationalist agenda. Recognizing that the religious affiliations of the membership spanned many traditions, Ford straddled an ideo-rhetorical line in his use of the word "God," which served as a catchall for the figurehead of a number of faith practices. In that, he supported Garvey, who argued, "We, as Negroes, have found a new ideal. . . . We Negroes believe in the God of Ethiopia . . . the One God of all ages."[23] The collectivity imagined and used by Garvey here through his use of "we" is both an aspiration and an instructional device; it did not fully exist, although its reiteration worked to transform his audience into actors within its building.

As a "Black Jew," Rabbi Ford exemplified the gulf between the ideal of inclusion and its practice. He used music to mediate his relationship to the UNIA, his faith, and his communities and bring them into conversation with one another. "One God, One Aim, One Destiny," for example, used the story of the resurrection of Christ as well as the name of Allah in service of the organization's ideals. Ford's religious identification served as a counterpoint to the Christian overtones of the organization and signaled another layer of difference within an organization that struggled to attain an uncompromised "we." He led one of the more recognizable groups within Harlem, Beth B'nai Abraham Congregation, which was also the publisher of the *Universal Ethiopian Hymnal*. Though small in numbers, Harlem's Black Jews occasionally drew the attention of the surrounding community and news outlets. Urban historian Roberta Gold argues that the Black press primarily documented impartial accounts of the community in recognition of the fact that "from a black perspective, the link between black and Jewish identity was not novel but familiar, tapping long traditions in African American religious and political thought."[24] Indeed, the hybridity of the Black Israelite religion, which religion scholar Jacob Dorman argues had origins in "Pentecostal churches and its secret knowledge drawn from Freemasonry, Jewish Kabbala, and African American conjuring,"[25] was a perfect demonstration of the efforts made by Black populations to create alternative realities while still relying on shared histories and traditions of struggle.

The relatively unremarkable nature of the Black Jewish circles in Harlem was attributable, in part, to their location and relationship to Garveyism. In her early 1930s study of Black Jews, anthropologist Ruth Landes went so far as to describe Garveyite nationalism as "an essential matrix" of the Harlem landscape in which they worked.[26] The rhetoric of economic advancement within the UNIA, for example, offered one point of convergence between the groups, who sought to not only amass capital but also foster pride and independence among Black men and women, and ensure that their particular needs were met. Like the UNIA, the members of Black Jewish organizations were also overwhelmingly immigrant and working poor. Their shared investment in questions of access, wealth, and liberation facilitated the exchange of members between Jewish circles and the Garvey movement, and even if they were not dues-paying or participatory members of the UNIA, the two groups crossed paths at Liberty Hall where Black Israelites often held their own events and lectures. The practice of diaspora therefore was evident in both organizations. Black Jewish leaders often migrated to New York from locations within the diaspora, including Ford from Barbados and Rabbi W. M. Matthews from Saint Kitts. Judaism was already an exercise in diaspora, as was their engagement with the Afro-diasporic tradition of Ethiopianism, which the UNIA and its anthem drew upon and contributed to. It is this "bricolage" of culture and performance among and between similarly positioned communities, including the "chanting of Hebrew, the observance of dietary laws, and the swaying motions of prayer,"[27] and multiple engagements with a global phenomenon of religion and dispossession, sacrifice and alienation that frames the diasporic vision of these Black Jewish groups and aligns them with the UNIA. Black Jews understood their racial condition in tandem with religious persecution, and the two positions fed one another, leading to a unique perspective on the nature of racism and intolerance in the world and a shared commitment to political activity. Considering his intimate relationship with Garvey and the UNIA, it is not surprising that Ford's congregation seems to have been invested in issues of social justice. In December of 1925, Beth B'nai was featured in the (New York) *Amsterdam News* after a victory in the city court. Their landlord sued the congregation over allegations of a default on rent. Ford was able to provide documentation of his payments, and the "court rebuked the realty firm . . . for dragging the church into court." This "rebuke" by the court acknowledged the religious formation of Ford's congregation by calling it a "church," yet the term is imprecise and attempts to mainstream, or make accessible, an otherwise complicated group. It is clear that Ford labored within the court to make his congregation legible. He described that Beth B'nai "has a large membership of people who were born Jews." He also took the opportunity to demonstrate his "Hebraic training [when] he spoke in Yiddish to Justice Panken."[28] This performance of alternative affiliation by Ford was likely used as a way to not only authenticate his faith identity but also demonstrate a more complex blackness within the limited and limiting space of the U.S. courtroom.[29]

Beyond the shared philosophical and strategic elements, it is the *Universal Ethiopian Hymnal* that most intimately ties the Black Jews to the UNIA, as Ford used it with both the Beth B'nai Congregation and the UNIA. The act of anthology by Ford through the hymnal brought an added level of significance to the project. Anthology is a method of mapping and containment, compiling evidence in service of facilitating pointed dialogues within a corps of thinking and, in some cases, acting. Musical anthologies serve as a sonic treatise that can be "considered to be reflective of the laws of their domain,"[30] and the hymnal was an organizing text within the UNIA. It included the anthem "Ethiopia" as well as other pieces that reinforced the social order of the UNIA through a reaffirmation of the organization's motto ("One God, One Aim, One Destiny") and testaments of allegiance to Garvey ("God Bless Our President"). Through its dynamism, the *Universal Ethiopian Hymnal* encouraged a religious engagement with Garveyism, formalized and ritualized performance, and made music a central method of organizing the message, and therefore the members, of the UNIA.

The annual conventions, which brought together thousands of Black women and men from across the world, took great advantage of Ford's music. His songs were popular due to their notable musicality, yet it was the ability of the music to reinforce the ideologies of the convention that made it a crucial component of the program. "Ethiopia" in particular served as a mantra through its repetition during events of solemn remembrance and pitched exultation. The annual conventions in fact were the premiere sites of performance for the organization, offering artistic and political space for the race. This fusion was demonstrated in Ford's music, which was increasingly mobilized within the post-1920 UNIA musical pageants. The convention was described as "without exception, the greatest state social event that has taken place among black people in the last three hundred years," and the announcement and conferral of the UNIA court in 1921 solicited a number of exited responses from its viewers.[31] The first Mrs. Garvey, Amy Ashwood, described the convention's lavish court ceremony:

> The Hall was transformed into a magnificent tropical setting, with lighting effects, appropriate music being played. Each Dignitary was timed to arrive according to his rank, and an anthem or appropriate music played until he was seated. . . . Young ladies were presented, and honours conferred on persons who had served the Race faithfully and well. Titles were: Knight Commander of the Nile, Distinguished Service Order of Ethiopia, and the Star of African Redemption. After the ceremonies, supper was served; guests were seated according to rank. Then followed the Grand Ball, with all the courtliness of training, natural gift for dancing and love of music.[32]

It was Ford who provided the "appropriate music being played" at the reception and the accompaniment that followed each dignitary's procession into the hall. As this reading demonstrates, music was a central part of the event from beginning to end. Ashwood Garvey paints a portrait of an elite function complete with the bells and whistles that the UNIA was known for: the music, symbols, and pageantry of a rising nation.

Even in the face of criticism from contemporaries like Owen of the *Messenger*, Garvey's "insatiable appetite for ceremony" proved important for the success of the organization.[33] These symbols of prestige were deliberately meant to inspire the membership. The *Negro World* reported on the event:

> [U]nlike social functions held in the past by Negro associations, fraternal and otherwise, [it] was not an empty display of grandeur, but an occasion of far-reaching import to the Negro race in that it was a manifestation of the tremendous possibilities within the black people of the world for their future development along industrial, economic, political and social lines, and significant of their determination, through the instrumentality of the Universal Negro Improvement Association and its subsidiary branches, to put over completely the program of the redemption of Africa and absolute emancipation of the race from every form of oppression and injustice by which they are now beset.[34]

This hearty endorsement of the evening's activities was a testament to the power of what had formerly been considered auxiliary elements within political organizing. This witness debunks the myth that the music, titles, and processions of the UNIA were "empty displays of grandeur" by arguing that these performances created meaning in the lives of the members and their communities. The Black August parade brought witnesses from far and wide and was described by the child of a UNIA officer as "an exciting thing to see."[35] This enthusiasm was generated not simply in response to the spectacle but also in recognition of the "manifestation of the tremendous possibilities" of the Black race. According to the author above, it was only through the UNIA that "absolute emancipation" became feasible. Garvey promoted these activities, but it was through Ford that they were realized.

The performative tactics of the UNIA were profound enough to reverberate beyond the Black community and into the political left. Recognizing Garvey's success in the deployment of these acts, the Communist Party (CPUSA) considered borrowing from the UNIA reserve. After the 1921 UNIA convention, the *Communist* paper wrote,

> The Negro has a great love of display, show, pomp, ostentation, brass bands, mysticism, decorations, buttons, social frivolities and military display. (In this regard it is only fair to say that he is not alone.) These contraptions catch his imagination and act as an inducement for organization as nothing else can at the present time.[36]

This astute observer was correct in noting that these complicated displays were "inducement for organization" in the UNIA. Although somewhat pejorative, these comments highlight progressive movements' recognition of performance as a unique front from which to struggle for justice. While the early CPUSA counted only a small number of Black members, the UNIA boasted thousands and used music to reinvent a century-old ideology that propelled a Black political agenda into the modern age.

Music of the Masses: Organizing the UNIA

Nationalism was the form that the modern Black political agenda took and was therefore the motivating philosophy within UNIA formations: it both compelled the activity of the organization and organized it. The protections and comforts afforded by nationalism were pronounced in 1918, the year of UNIA incorporation in New York. The ravages of World War I in both the global and national arenas offered an appropriate backdrop to Garvey's program. His grounding in Black Nationalism however was not an entirely modern phenomenon. Black Nationalism is an ideology with roots in the theological and philosophical traditions of nineteenth-century Black America. Garvey entered prominently into the discussion in the last decade of what scholar Wilson Jeremiah Moses designates as "the golden age of black nationalism" (1850–1925). Garvey's moment in the sun of Black Nationalist discourse was a revision of the nineteenth-century version described by Moses as "absolutist, civilizationist, elitist, and based on Christian humanism."[37] Led by figures such as Alexander Crummell and Henry Highland Garnet, the early Black Nationalists broke ties with the abolitionist intellectuals of the period whose paternalistic ambitions often did more to preserve social stratification than to dismantle it. As historian Sterling Stuckey argues, Garnet's insistence that slaves fashion and fight their own battles exhibited a "degree of resourcefulness of intellect [by enslaved Africans] virtually unheard of in Northern abolitionist circles of the time."[38] This break with the abolitionist tradition proved their ideas distinct in the strategy for the emancipation of African captives in the Americas. Garnet's project was built on the promises of American democracy through the U.S. Constitution and highlighted U.S. revisionism rather than international solidarities.[39] His nationally bound strategies for liberation were ripe for sharing and challenge as the new century dawned.

Although it built on the themes of Black independence exhibited by Garnet and others, Garvey's stage of Black Nationalism showed "relativist, culturalist, proletarian, and secular" tendencies.[40] His focus on the Black working class was distinctive, yet his biggest break with the nineteenth-century tradition of Black Nationalism may have stemmed from his turn away from an orthodox Christianity. Crummell and Garnet were both Christian ministers with a profound dedication to the theological tenets of Black Nationalism; Garvey's interest in religion was first and foremost a tactical one, and it had limits. He openly acknowledged that he was "not one of those Christians who believe that the Bible can solve all the problems of humanity. The Bible is good in its place, but we are men. We are the creatures of God. We have sinned against Him, therefore it takes more than the Bible to keep us in our places."[41] Instead of a strict theology reliant on delayed liberation, Garvey chose to build on slave traditions that placed no barrier between the sacred and secular or between the spiritual and temporal world. As cultural historian Lawrence Levine noted, "[F]or Garvey religion was not an otherworldly affair; it taught ethical and practical principles that needed to be acted upon in this world."[42]

What unite these disparate incarnations of Black Nationalism are the conditions at the core of the ideology. Black Nationalism grows out of the experience of slavery—a system (especially as practiced in the United States) that destroyed ethnic differences between the enslaved through the universal condition of bondage.[43] Political theorist Cedric Robinson argues that twentieth-century Black radicals hailed from Africans who were "predominantly recruited from the same cultural matrices, subjected to similar and interrelated systems of servitude and oppression, and mobilized by identical impulses to recover their dignity. And over the centuries, the liberation projects of these men and women in Africa, the Caribbean, and the Americas required similar emergent collective forms in rebellion and marronage [and] similar ethical and moral articulations of resistance."[44] Black Nationalism is different from other types of nationalisms because its adherents are united neither by a common language nor by geography but rather, as Robinson outlines, by shared oppressions and the resistances to it. Through these processes and projects the enslaved gathered a communal sense of identity. Indeed, Moses states that Black Nationalism "has been nationalism only in the sense that the entire race has a collective destiny and message for humanity comparable to that of a nation."[45] The knowledge of a shared past and the idea of a collective destiny became the platform for Garvey's message to Black Americans and other diasporic subjects in the post–World War I period. His impact in this endeavor would be so thorough that "the golden age" that Moses speaks of would effectively end with Garvey's incarceration in 1925.

From this message of a collective fate Garvey derived his platform, which sought to convert existent Black religious sensibilities into an agenda based in the material world. In the UNIA, success and pride replaced piety and morality as the building blocks of a nationalist religion.[46] Historian and anthologist Robert Hill observes that the traditional religious potential of the UNIA membership was "converted into a new spiritual inspiration through Garvey's advocacy of the metaphysic of success,"[47] which is represented in Garvey's pragmatism and insistence on the cultivation of symbols and ideals specifically for Black people, such as a Black God and Ethiopia, which he described as the Black man's Palestine. Archivist and historian Randall Burkett articulates the necessity of these symbols to Garvey's Black Nationalism:

> The rituals, symbols, and beliefs appropriate to the UNIA would grow out of and build upon a shared experience of slavery and of racial discrimination, as that experience was interpreted in the light of a transcendent goal: the uplift of the Negro race and the redemption of Africa. They stood as symbols of national solidarity that endeavored to bind all men and women who willingly accepted the designation "Negro" into a single people whom God had specifically chosen for the task of building up a nation in Africa.[48]

UNIA symbols provided a method toward the consolidation of a "national solidarity" among Black people globally. Their arts program offered "a coherent and compelling way of looking at God, man, and the world, and at the meaning of black experience in Africa and America."[49] Members therefore were able to connect with the organization in innumerable ways, touching everything on the spectrum from the mundane to the mystical, and their participation, through symbols like the anthem, reaffirmed the centrality of the project to their lives. From that moment on, Garvey's greatest success stemmed from "his superb articulation of what many of his followers had long believed and acted upon in quiet dignity and strength: that blackness was nothing to apologize for; that black men and women shared a common proud heritage; and that the future was by no means hostage to white people."[50] The effect of this semireligious doctrine influenced the entire membership, regardless of internal gender struggles, and was summed up by long-time UNIA member Estelle James, who believed that the organization gave people like herself "something to live for. You even had something to die for if necessary."[51]

It was not necessary for Garvey to preach a conventional religious message—he had others to do that work for him. Ford enters into this discussion as one of the primary architects for the UNIA's faith program. His songs brought into harmony religious traditions and Garvey's secular vision of redemption from the quotidian racism of Black life. His *Universal Ethiopian Hymnal* was the major text for the services of the UNIA, and its songs combined textual and sonic guidance. All of the hymns in the hymnal end with the customary "A-men"/IV-I chord at the end of the last verse, signaling not only the end of the song on the tonic but also the end of the prayer with "Amen." As documented previously, these hymns were political tracts, and their prayerful ending of "Amen" was therefore both a petition and a proclamation. Ford's mimicry of the Christian liturgical style through the hymnal produced a comfortable space for those members accustomed to a religious service, yet his adaptation of lyrics within that traditional song technique promised instead, "Her children's shackles clanking fall / And freedom fills the air / With one accord they list the call / The Son of Man is here."[52] This "Son of Man" was Marcus Garvey, who replaced the Son of God as the shepherd of the downtrodden. As heavy-handed as the Garvey philosophy and imagery were within these songs, they nonetheless had the effect of materializing an alternative space for the production of powerful Black men and women. Through these songs Ford was able to show Black communities their reflection in the product of the UNIA.

While the ritual established by Ford and other leaders helped to expand Black citizenship practices, it also regimented and institutionalized them. Antiguan, Episcopalian, and UNIA chaplain-general George Alexander McGuire produced a series of stylized pieces for the organization including the *Universal Negro Ritual* and *Universal Negro Catechism*, both written between 1920 and 1921. These texts developed an infrastructure and protocol for UNIA meetings in the interest of uniformity across the multicontinent organization. For example, McGuire was the architect of the "order of service," which on Sunday evenings proceeded in this way:

> [Open] with the processional hymn "Shine on, Eternal Light," one of many hymns written for the UNIA by its musical director, Rabbi Arnold J. Ford. This was followed with recitation by the UNIA chaplain of Psalms 68:31: "Princes shall come out of Egypt; Ethiopia shall soon stretch forth her hands unto God," the most oft-repeated Biblical passage heard in Liberty Halls around the country. Next came the singing of the official opening hymn "From Greenland's Icy Mountains," which expressed, among other things, the organization's commitment to the Christianization of Africa. This was followed by recitation of the official motto of the UNIA: "One God, One Aim, One Destiny." After the Lord's Prayer came a series of formal prayers by the chaplain for the work of the UNIA and for its leaders. A sermon, or at least some brief remarks by the chaplain, was almost invariably a part of the program, followed by the business meeting. The program closed with a benediction and a recessional hymn—either "Onward Christian Soldiers" or the UNIA's national anthem, the "Universal Ethiopian Anthem."[53]

This description highlights the ritual involved in the organization's services and the multiple elements used to enforce the UNIA message. It is clear that music was an integral part of branch functions, and, like the passage from Psalms, it served as instruction. Ford's songs book-ended the service; they functioned as a welcome and a parting call to arms, inviting individuals into the fold and then motivating the membership to continue the organization's work outside of the hall.

The UNIA recognized early that the on-the-ground work of Black self-determination would be protracted and require mass mobilizations due to the likelihood of violence. In 1924 the *Negro World* reported McGuire's convention speech, "What Is That in Thine Hand?," delivered at Liberty Hall. In it he argued, "Destiny does not imply a blind fate. . . . It is destined by Divinity that in a nation and government of his own, in his motherland, Africa, the Negro shall enjoy liberty and happiness with a civilization and religious worship of his own, without hindrance from any other race or government." Here McGuire argues that this ideal, while inevitable ("destined"), would have to be struggled for. McGuire demanded action based on the unique possibilities and talents possessed by his audience. He argued that Black people held in their hands the rod of "Political Destiny," "Commercial and Industrial Achievement," and "Spiritual Freedom," and, like the rod of Moses, that rod should be used to "divide the Red Sea before us, and in the morning of victory again employ it for the confounding of our helpless pursuers."[54] This rod was not simply an empty metaphor—it was a weapon to be used to strike the enemies of the Black nation. In this moment, violence was understood as an impending reality, and the members organized accordingly.

Ford again entered prominently into this equation. In addition to being a trained musician, he was a former military officer, and he used both skill sets to further the UNIA program. In 1899, while still in Barbados, Ford joined the musical corps of the British Royal Navy. After his service on the HMS *Alert* and further independent travel, he landed in New York City, where he joined the Clef Club Orchestra under the tutelage of celebrated Black American conductor-musician James Reese Europe.[55] Europe's trajectory as a U.S. musician and race man intersects with Ford's in fascinating ways. Born in Alabama in 1880, Europe, like Ford, grew up playing multiple instruments. In addition to his musical acuity, he was recognized early on for his organizational ability and leadership potential. Between 1902 and 1903, Europe left his second home of Washington, D.C., for the bright lights of New York City. While there he switched from violin to piano and joined the booming musical comedy genre as a pit musician. Between 1904 and 1910, he became a leading figure in Black musical theater, making professional and personal relationships with other formative Black entertainers including Bert Williams, Bob Cole, and the chapter 2 figures J. Rosamond and James Weldon Johnson. According to historian Karen Sotiropoulos, these Black artists merged artistic and political ambitions, thereby "manipulat[ing] the stage mask" in order to place "the performing world within the framework of race progress."[56]

Europe's repertoire and later leadership positions model this process. In 1910, he was a founding member and elected president of the Clef Club of the City of New York. The club was intended to function as a trade union and booking agency for Black musicians who faced discrimination in hiring. As a member, Ford benefited from the professional and social networking of the club while also absorbing the uplift ideologies and organizing strategies of the all-Black business. In 1913 Europe left the Clef Club to establish his own Tempo Club, yet as World War I mounted, his focus adjusted to consider race within a global dimension. With a belief that "a national guard unit could become an important organization of benefit to the entire [Black] community," Europe joined New York's first regiment of Black National Guardsmen in September 1916.[57] By December, he was given the job of developing the best band in the U.S. Army. The initiative was in sync with the mounting UNIA model: a belief that Black men (in particular) could be recruited into service through music and other cultural opportunities. The Army officials in New York intended to bring more Black men into the Army through Europe's band. Newspaper ads read:

ATTENTION!!!

Negro Musicians of America

Last Call   Golden Opportunity

IF you want to do your *duty* in the present crisis.

IF you are not in a financial position to give your services as a private volunteer.

IF you would serve should you be able to make a living wage for your family.

IF you are a First Class Musician.

IF you have dreamed of belonging to a famous Military Band.

IF you have longed for the time you could devote All Your Time to your music.

IF you want to belong to a regiment whose officers are sparing no means to make their regimental band the Best In The World.

IF you want to be in a band that in the time of Peace will devote its time to Concert Tours.

Then Wire Or Call

LT. James Reese Europe, care of 15th Regiment, N.Y. Infantry, Harlem River Park Casino, 127th Street and 2nd Avenue, New York City.

>P.S. There Are Only a Few More Vacancies Left, and the Regiment
>Goes to Camp, Sunday, May 13th.
>
>So Hurry! Hurry! Hurry![58]

An opportunity to serve through music was an enticing prospect for many African-descended men from the United States and Puerto Rico. Europe's offer of a living wage combined with an opportunity to travel was proof enough of the band's efficacy in providing upward mobility. In addition to this, many Black leaders of the period favored Black participation in the war as a demonstration of patriotism and means toward equality at home. In this moment Ford found for himself another call to arms. Taking with him the fervor and dedication to racial uplift, music, and militarized defense exhibited by Europe, he entered the ranks of the UNIA-NY.

Notwithstanding the horrors of World War I, the early UNIA recognized a danger greater than the Central Powers of Eastern Europe; white supremacy, lynchings, and disfranchisement topped their list of threats to democracy. The 1917 riot in East St. Louis, Illinois, was an instance of particular brutality and terror. Taking place over multiple days, the violence that erupted there—with an estimated one hundred plus dead and hundreds more injured—devastated the national Black community. Although racist violence burned slowly in the city, the ember of hostility was lit on May 28 when participants at a local labor meeting accused the recent southern Black migrants of taking their jobs. A series of violent incidents over the next two days fanned the flames of animosity, and by the afternoon of June 2, the Illinois National Guard was enlisted. Offered little or no protection, the Black community burned into the next day, when the active rioting ceased. This event sent chills throughout the nation, in particular among the race organizations. The NAACP led eight thousand participants in a silent protest march in Harlem that demanded an end to discrimination against and aggression toward the Black community. Garvey, however, would not be silent on the issue. Titled "The Conspiracy of the East St. Louis Riots," his July 8, 1917, speech took aim at the mayor of East St. Louis, Fred W. Mollman, as well as U.S. democracy. Describing the events as a massacre rather than a riot, he recited a historical progression of violence against the Black community in the United States: "At one time it was slavery, at another

time lynching and burning, and up to date it is whole[sale] butchering."
For Garvey East St. Louis was not an isolated incident but one representative of U.S. democracy: "This is a crime against humanity; it is a crime
against the laws of the nation, it is a crime against Nature, and a crime
against the God of all mankind."[59]

The significance of the massacre extended beyond Garvey's individual preoccupation; his speech on the event signaled a turn away from
his ideo-political base in Jamaica to a grounding in the conditions of
the Black United States. Without losing a diasporic frame, the UNIA
now envisioned the end of U.S. racial violence as the key to Black liberation on a global scale. Using East St. Louis as a prime example of the
nation's racial politics, Garvey tailored the organization's platform into
a reflection of his belief that "[t]here is no strength but that which is
destructive, because man has lost his virtues, and only respects force."[60]
By stressing the necessity of defense, Garvey not only addressed his
contemporary condition as a Black man under white supremacist
democracy but also forecasted a future for the Black race that put the
white West on notice. In 1919 he announced, "It will be a terrible day
when the blacks draw the sword to fight for their liberty. I call upon you
400 million blacks to give the blood you have shed for the white man to
make Africa a republic for the Negro." Less than one year after the end
of World War I, Garvey met Western aggression with his own, arguing
that a Black offensive would require the Negro race to "build battleships
and raise armies."[61]

To service the future Black nation, Garvey and other UNIA leaders
began to construct a social order in the United States that would later
be transferred to Africa. Hill notes that "Garvey intended that the legislation and elective offices created during the [1920] convention would
form a veritable government in exile for Africa, marking a fulfillment
of his ambition to engage in the practice of statecraft and create the
symbols of black nationhood and sovereignty."[62] His Knights, Ladies,
and Generals would form the backbone of a Black state. Ironically (and
devastatingly), Garvey's models in this endeavor were the European
nations currently holding the African territories that he sought to liberate. Himself a colonial subject of the British Crown, Garvey ideal-
ized the authority and discipline of the Western powers and sought to
replicate them in blackface. His admiration for and adoption of certain

Western practices exposed the inherent tensions and precarity of Garvey's project, as well as its potential for demagoguery. Literary scholar Erica Edwards argues that a belief in the singular divinity of charismatic Black male leadership has overdetermined the narratives of modern Black social movements, and this is undeniably true of the UNIA under Garvey.[63] Yet his vision for liberation—even if it uncritically centered him and his authority—resonated within the Black world and compelled tangible results, including the formation of national defense through the paramilitary Universal African Legion (UAL), an arm of the UNIA that also highlighted the ordered and ritualistic components of the organization. Ford's unique talents in music and militarism were employed again in his position as instructor for the UAL. Exclusively composed of men, the group became an embattled site of nationhood within the broader organization and served as one of the primary vehicles through which a new nation would arise.

The manhood debates that swirled throughout the nation in the wake of World War I were particularly stark in the Black community as the New Negro ideology developed to combat American racism.[64] This ideology, which argued for the necessity of Black political incorporation and the importance of Black excellence in arts and education for the positive progression of the race, demonstrated both the potential of and the insidious intragroup divisions within the category of "Negro." The New Negro was the politico-intellectual umbrella under which the Harlem Renaissance was enacted and understood. Marked by the publication of Howard University professor Alain Locke's edited collection *The New Negro* in 1925, the Renaissance was a watershed moment in the public exhibition of Black art and culture that facilitated the displays offered by the UNIA. There were, however, disruptions and challenges to the ideology's performance and the ambitions of its architects, namely W. E. B. Du Bois and Marcus Garvey. The blues women—Bessie Smith, Gertrude "Ma" Rainey, and others—were the stars and the outcasts of this Black arts explosion. They challenged a number of the tenets upholding the New Negro ideology, including its compulsory heterosexuality, focus on bourgeois aspirations, and the centrality of manhood and militarism. The intersectionality of their identities and its performance led to their demonization by most New Negro intellectuals, even as they became household names within larger cultures of Black popular entertainment. As Angela Y. Davis writes, "[B]ecause women like Bessie Smith and Ida Cox presented and embodied sexualities associated with working-class black life—which, fatally, was seen by some Renaissance strategists as antithetical to the aims of their cultural movement—their music was designated as 'low' culture. . . . Consequently, few writers . . . were willing to consider seriously the contributions blues performers made to black cultural politics."[65] These women were some of the musicians and entertainers whom Ford composed against; not only were their musical styles read as "low culture," but their inflammatory gender performances of independence and queer sociabilities threatened to dismantle the distinct spheres of gendered power and influence constructed by the UNIA in Black streets and homes.

The pervasive practices of the gendered New Negro ideology in combination with Garvey's agenda of racial separatism made the male groups of the UNIA incubators for experiments in uplift strategy and armed defense. These men were made into incredible displays of Black masculinity through a distinct and public performance of militarism; the uniforms with tassels and belts, striped banding at the cuff, and the "gleaming swords" discussed in "Ethiopia," fixed the audience's gaze as the men moved in lockstep through the Harlem streets during UNIA events. This commanding and powerful male presence was part and parcel of a national obsession. Materializing as it did during World War I, the fascination with the military was national in scale, but as important as it was, the UAL was more than visual stimulation for Garvey. For him, strong race men would lead the race toward their goal of building a commanding Black nation; as he wrote in 1925, "It is because we have studied history that we of the UNIA have started toward empire."[66] As history teaches, the work of empire does not come about through peaceful means, and Garvey prepared his members for that eventuality.

With Ford at the helm, it is not surprising that the UAL had its own music, titled "Legion's Marching Song." This accompaniment to the impressive display of uniformed Black men was itself of military quality, with a text that follows the tenets of the march genre.

> We are coming, oh Mother Africa,
> We are coming to avenge your wrongs,

> We are coming, oh yes, we are coming,
> We are four hundred millions strong.[67]

The repetition of the words "we are coming" grounds the verse in a steady beat, which is necessary for the consistency of the military march—both physically and musically. Each line offers seven to ten syllables, making the accompanying music easy to standardize. The repetition also serves as a warning for those who might impede the progress of the 400 million Black women, men, and children whom the UAL represented and protected; "we are coming" references bodily movement, both in the streets of Harlem and overseas as thousands of Black women and men crisscrossed the Atlantic. The imagined "infestation" of foreign Black bodies alongside those who demonstrated in Harlem shook the foundations of U.S. democracy. Recognizing his influence and successful employment of their methods and ideologies, the federal government began surveillance of Garvey and his followers after World War I. While ultimately devastating for the organization, the government's investigation offered little deterrent to the day-to-day projects of the UNIA, especially because many of them centered on culture—a political strategy that is difficult to combat. Garvey recognized "the emotional power that makes nation-statecraft so influential" and preoccupied himself with the adoption and adaption of other successful nationalisms for his service.[68] As with the naming of Liberty Hall, the UNIA unabashedly reclaimed the strategies and tactics, symbols and rhetoric, of other nations and movements for their own purposes. The employment of these practices and ideas by Black people posed a danger for the existing power structure because they used accessible and familiar national icons to build an opposing empire.

"Ethiopia" figures prominently within this project as the most conspicuous and pervasive text to adopt the form and the function of other nationalisms. The quality of that adoption, however, extends beyond its designation as an anthem. The sound of "Ethiopia" intimately connects it to the accessible and familiar icons of the majority society, namely "The Star-Spangled Banner." Measures 33 and 34 of "Ethiopia" use two chords in variation: measure 33 starts with an augmented I on a half note, transitions to a V dotted-quarter note, and ends on the I on the last eighth note of measure 33 and the three count hold in measure 34 (see Figure 1.1). This ending not only mirrors the chord progression of the "The Star-Spangled Banner"—a song often performed in B-flat major—but also follows a very similar rhythm, despite the time signature difference. While "The Star-Spangled Banner" is performed in 3/4, its ending of a dotted-quarter, eighth, quarter, and dotted half note is very similar to the ending of Ford's composition (Figure 1.2).

Ford ingeniously employs "The Star-Spangled Banner" as a signifying text that configures a complicated symbiosis between the UNIA's Black nation and the superpower United States. The march syncopation of "Ethiopia" highlights the song's intended use within the Black nation and plays on the militarized origins of "The Star-Spangled Banner." This march also signals the pace at which the Black nation moves, not in retreat from the white United States but in active pursuit of its resources, influence, and power. The melody of "Ethiopia" offered the UNIA a tried and true method of engagement and mobilization: it delivered the sound of a powerful nation (the United States) into the ears of Black citizens transitioning from a race to a nation. This strategy was buttressed by the performance of various national anthems alongside "Ethiopia" at UNIA events around the world. As multiple performance descriptions demonstrate, "The Star-Spangled Banner" was a frequent visitor to the Black nation.[69] UNIA divisions in Canada also performed the British national anthem, "God Save the Queen," during their programs.[70] This practice did not entirely debunk Black American and Canadian patriotism but instead built upon it as a referent and redirected its energies toward the growth of a Black nation that would be equally positioned (if not culturally superior) to the United States and/or Canada. The deliberate pairing of "Ethiopia" with other national anthems by the UNIA built upon entrenched national systems of allegiance and citizenship in order to facilitate a similar loyalty for the UNIA and its emergent Black nation. By catering to the existent nationalisms of their international membership, the UNIA acknowledged the many affiliations and identities of their supporters and expanded their political reach further into diaspora.

Branches with Roots: Blackness and the UNIA in Cuba

The relationship between Black protest organizations and liberation fights globally was a hot-button issue for the U.S. federal authorities.

Figure 1.1.
Sheet music, "The Universal Ethiopian Anthem," measures 31–37. Words by Benjamin Burrell and Arnold J. Ford, music by Arnold J. Ford, ©1920. Source: From the private collection of Randall K. Burkett

While often exaggerated, claims made by government informants offer insight into the fears of U.S. officials when confronted by international and, perhaps more significantly, cross-racial collaboration and organizing. On more than one occasion, the UNIA was reported to operate in collusion with other radical groups, particularly those engaged in nationalist movements.[71] The diverse organizing practices of the UNIA developed a strong contingent of followers in the United States, but its import for Black people did not end in New Orleans, Washington, D.C., or even New York City. Local branches emerged all over the African diaspora. No single country outside of the United States produced more UNIA branches than Cuba. Of the forty-one countries with UNIA branches in 1926, thirty-five of them offered eight branches or fewer—at the top of the list stood Cuba, with fifty-two.[72] Locals developed in San Manuel, Puerto Barrios, Guantánamo, Ingenio Rio Canto, Ciego de Ávila, Jobabo, Santiago de Cuba, Guaro, Jatibonico, Morón, Manatí,

Figure 1.2.
Sheet music, "The Star-Spangled Banner," measures 19–34. Words by John Stafford Smith and Francis Scott Key, music by Francis Scott Key, ©1814. Source: J. W. Studebaker, Our Country's Call to Service: A Manual of Patriotic Activities through the Schools (New York: Scott Foresman, 1918)

Delicias, Cayo Mambí, and other parts of the country. By 1921, the *Negro World* was reporting exciting news from Cuba with headlines reading "UNIA Charter Unveiled in Puerto Padres" and "UNIA in Banes, Cuba Forging Ahead."[73] In his description of a "Rousing Sunday Night in Havana," B. G. Alfred described that "[s]ince the organization of the Havana branch of the UNIA by Mr. Louis LaMothe a few months ago, the interest of the members has been at the very highest." This interest on the part of Black migrants and Afro-Cubans led Alfred to comment, "There can be no mistaking the part the Negroes in Cuba will play in this serious game for a FREE and redeemed AFRICA."[74]

Much of the exposure offered to the Cuban branches was provided by the "Sección en Español" (Spanish Section) of the *Negro World*. Beginning in March 1921, this section of the paper, edited by M. A. Figueroa, reported the happenings of branches all over the Spanish-speaking Caribbean as well as Central and South America. Cuba again held a place of prominence in this section. The first edition, on March 19, ran the Cuban National Anthem, "El Himno de Bayamo (The Bayamo Anthem)," by Pedro Felipe Figueredo. The anthem was written on the eve of the Ten Years' War between Cuban nationalists and Spain (1868–78), and its lyrics offer all of the inspiration needed to urge on a pulsating, independent nation:

> To the combat make haste, Bayameses,
> Your own country regards with proud ambition;
> Break the chain that for bodies Inquisition
> While all Honor and Liberty cry.
>
> Ye desire not in fetters to live
> With offront and opprobium galling;
> List the bugle, attention, is calling
> Quick to arms all ye valliants now fly.[75]

This text is a mirror image of "Ethiopia." Both employ conventional tropes of service and sacrifice in order to motivate and honor those whose fighting made (or will make) their postrevolution reality possible. Much like Garvey's employment of Western statecraft methods, the language of both of these pieces emerged from the national icon assembly line of the West. What is important about the language is not what is said so much as how it is said and what remains unspoken. While "El Himno de Bayamo" is more explicitly gendered in its acclaim for the men of Bayamo ("Bayameses"), the calls to militarization in defense of the motherland and the glorification of those who rise to the challenge are shared between the two anthems and situate the nationalist project of Cuba alongside that of the UNIA. In this scenario, the prominence of the organization's institutional presence was managed through the close alignment of their cultural and gendered vision for freedom with that of Cuban nationalists.

The presence of "El Himno de Bayamo" in the organization literature is again an example of the UNIA using established national symbols to bolster its position as an open, diverse, and representative organization. Like UNIA's use of "The Star-Spangled Banner" and "God Save the Queen," the inclusion of "El Himno de Bayamo" in UNIA paraphernalia

played to the sympathies and allegiances of an already embattled population. The murders of high-profile national heroes like Antonio Maceo
during the course of the war were made public as deterrents against
further uprisings, yet Maceo was made an international hero in the process, and the anthem celebrated his sacrifice by enshrining all service
men within its sounds.[76] By printing this piece in the *Negro World*, the
editors not only extended their international reach through an overture
to their Spanish-speaking members and leaders but also acknowledged
the heroes of Cuba who in the 1920s would face a new foe.

The end of the Ten Years' War was ratified with the signing of the
Pact of Zanjón in February 1878, but the Cuban War for Independence
raged on. U.S. intervention led to the Spanish-American War in 1898,
in which the United States acquired a number of territories, including Cuba, Puerto Rico, and the Philippines. From this moment on U.S.
influence in Cuban politics, economics, and culture grew steadily. U.S.
participation in the establishment of the first Republic of Cuba in 1901,
largely to the exclusion of the Afro-Cubans and peasants who fought
for the nation's independence, allowed U.S. businessmen to flood the
country with funds for companies whose overproduction of sugar during World War I stifled the diversification of the nation's economy. By
the 1920s, U.S. films, sports, and art were prevalent in the country, as
Cuba became the playground for restless northern consumers. In
response to what some viewed as another occupation, "a nationalistic
literature, journalism and music scene developed" in Cuba.[77] It is within
this period of revived nationalism that the UNIA made itself a fixture in
the sociopolitical project of a nascent Cuban nation.

According to historian Frank Guridy, a "Harlem-Havana nexus" or
"trans-local space" developed in Cuba during the early decades of the
twentieth century and demonstrated a swell of exchanges between Black
artists around the world.[78] Blues poet and intellectual Langston Hughes
found "the heartbeat and songbeat of Africa" in Cuban dancehalls and
streets as he toured the country and met with Cuban artists like poet
Nicolás Guillén.[79] The UNIA triumphantly entered the country as a
resource for this young, vibrant community and marketed the Sección
en Español to them as the primary clearinghouse for UNIA culture and
politics. The diffusion of information served at least two purposes: it
helped to standardize the locals, and more important, it connected the

work of nation building by the organizational hub in New York to the efforts of the international branches. As the discourse of a Black nation progressed, the connective tissue of that rhetoric made its way into the programs of the Cuban branches. In the December 3, 1921, edition of the *Negro World*, Figueroa authored "Nuestra Raza" (Our Race). In it he argued that pessimists were the greatest obstacles to the organization, the nation, and the potential and progress of the Black race in this "age of activity." After outlining a UNIA campaign to gain 2 million new members in 1922, he wrote, "Let us transform our towns, villages, and cities to the elements of our race, until we reach the world's 400 million Negroes to sing this new hymn."[80] What followed this message was a Spanish translation of "Ethiopia." Here Figueroa employs the music of the movement as the method of engagement with and organization for the Spanish-speaking contingent of the UNIA membership. Its prominence within the landscape of the page—indented and centered within his paragraph—draws the reader's eye and becomes the anchor for his calls to the Spanish-speaking contingent of the race. The song figures here as an institutionalized performance piece and universal platform from which the members could struggle for justice internationally. From this moment on the Sección en Español was full of Cuban branch programs, from Sunday school events to meetings with dignitaries, and many of them paid tribute to the UNIA anthem.

The Cuban divisions of the UNIA had varying degrees of visibility and success with local authorities. The growing U.S. presence and entrenched Spanish colonial conditions of racial stratification set the terms for Black life in the country, especially within politics. In locations with an already hostile racial environment, locals worked in secrecy or fear due to perceived or experienced police and government suppression. Some branches, however, were able to develop a favorable relationship with local Cuban leaders outside of the UNIA. These scenarios were vividly described in the pages of the *Negro World*. Lady vice president of the Oriente branch Clarice G. Walters described the surprise and fanfare that greeted the governor in her chapter: "[A]n announcement was made that the Governor was at the door; it was exactly 12PM. The High Commissioner immediately ordered the entire membership to stand and the Lady President led off with the national anthem of Cuba, followed by the Ethiopian anthem, while he conducted

His Excellency and escort to seats on the platform." At this meeting the governor received a lush sonic greeting composed of the salutations and rituals of Cuba as well as those of the rising Black nation. For this UNIA local the two anthems went hand in hand, extending a precedent established thousands of miles away in Harlem. After settling into his seat of distinction, the governor spoke of the branch's perception within his area: "I was informed some time ago about the association; I was told that it is a political organization, but I never worried myself about it until today when I was again informed that a Cuban is identified with it as its leader and that he is making fiery speeches to excite the Cuban Negroes. So I decided to come here for myself." The governor concluded his remarks by offering any protections necessary for the success of the branch, a use of power that would ensure a level of safety for this exposed community. He later made a significant symbolic gesture when during another performance of "Ethiopia" he stood with the rest of the membership.[81] Within this scenario, the combination of the anthems served to stem reactionary critiques of the members' patriotism while also encouraging communication between communities that might otherwise consider their interests in conflict. The two anthems in performance here, therefore, had the effect of both igniting the freedom dreams of the membership and taming the insecurities of the watching authorities.

Despite favorable reviews in the pages of the *Negro World*—a paper with a pronounced agenda—the importance of the UNIA to the racial and political infrastructure of Afro-Cuban communities is debated. One scholar described the organization as quasigovernmental in the lives of the Black population, offering fraternal and political support to Black workers in particular.[82] Black laborers in Cuba, however, were not necessarily citizens of the country; like that to so many other countries in Latin America, migration to Cuba from other locations for labor opportunities was important to the country's economy. Sugar plantations in Cuba received large numbers of Jamaican workers, and while the migrations were hotly contested by some domestic labor organizations, the influx of workers continued. At the moment of Garvey's 1921 trip to the island, as many as fifty thousand Jamaicans may have resided in Cuba. Named Jamaiquanos, these workers and their families were considered by some as the reason for UNIA success in Cuba, although as the Oriente chapter shows Cubans were at the helm of some branches. Indisputably, Jamaicans made up a large proportion of the UNIA members in the country. As a population with essentially no political protections, Jamaican workers were at the mercy of any and all political systems in Cuba. The UNIA in that context was essential for the defense of the workers and their families.

Trade and industry conditions across the African diaspora hit workers and families hard as agricultural recessions and war changed the economic landscape of the world. Garvey's program for financial independence presented itself as a compelling option for those around the world struggling to make ends meet. King Sugar was the original mainstay of the economy in the British Caribbean, producing by the 1860s hundreds of thousands of tons of cane. Despite sugar's continued importance in providing employment on the island, historian Winston James shows that sugar production in the British Caribbean was quickly losing its hold on the world market, causing the flight of thousands of Jamaican men and women. By the first decades of the twentieth century, Cuba stepped in to recover the dwindling exports of islands like Jamaica and became the leader in Caribbean sugar, generating just under 75 percent of the regions' total output.[83] With surprising rapidity, a new agricultural sector developed in Jamaica to replace sugar: the banana trade. Originally introduced to Jamaica in the sixteenth century, bananas did not become a staple of the island's economy until the late nineteenth century. By 1900, banana production was the primary export, introducing new consequences for the workers who were primarily located among the poorer and darker classes. As the trade grew, power and wealth came to be concentrated in the hands of one U.S. businessman, Lorenzo Dow Baker. Increased pressure on the workers for lower wages effectively removed any sense of independence that the peasant class had managed previously. While the economy boomed, the laborers suffered increased scrutiny from suppliers who manipulated the Gilded Age systems devised by John D. Rockefeller and Andrew Carnegie. The big business land grab of Baker's Boston Fruit Company (and later United Fruit) squeezed the peasantry out of the market and out of any hope for independence. They increasingly became a part of a large machine that, according to historian Thomas Holt, "render[ed] the formerly independent peasant cultivators a virtual proletariat."[84] With the decline in sugar production and hegemony of Baker's bananas, it is not surprising that Jamaicans were the largest group of migrants out of the Caribbean in the late nineteenth and early twentieth centuries.

Garvey was a product of this out-migration. Trained as a printer, he left Jamaica to explore education and labor opportunities around the world. Garvey toured London, the metropole and hub of the British Empire, and colonial sites in search of societies in which he might labor and grow community institutions. He spent a number of years pursuing these goals in Central America, where West Indian immigrants formed a Pan-Caribbean bloc more sizeable than any other immigrant population. As "third country nationals"—British subjects working in Hispanic republics under the authority of multinational corporations—these laborers were afforded few if any juridical protections or rights.[85] Garvey's early organizing efforts in Central America took advantage of his skill as a printer; after settling in Límon, Costa Rica in 1910, he became editor of *La Nación* and used the newspaper to publicize injustices committed against West Indian immigrants. From there Garvey moved on to Panama, where he similarly agitated for equal pay and treatment for West Indian workers. A whirlwind tour of Honduras, Nicaragua, Ecuador, Columbia, and Venezuela followed.[86] As Garvey attempted to build an infrastructure for his budding racial program, which relied heavily on a progressive race-labor dialogue, he took advantage of and modeled a particularly West Indian radicalism, described by James as developing from a "peculiar civilization" within the Caribbean that allowed greater access to education and its pursuit throughout the world.[87] This is the tradition that also produced the migrants to Cuba and their organizations of defense.

Nonwhite Cubans had traditions of organizing dating to at least the nineteenth century, forming various collectives based on shared conditions of marginality and struggle. Called *cabildos*, these "mutual aid societies" were, according to Cuban writer and ethnomusicologist Alejo Carpentier, composed of members from various Black nations—a pan-ethnic, pan-national Black society. For fear of reprisal, these groups made sure to outline their function as one of aid and "recreational and leisurely pursuits." In highlighting the latter function, they were able to offer pageants, dances, and other celebrations, thereby continuing the ritualistic and linguistic traditions of Afro populations in Cuba—some indigenous—without detection. Other organizations, called *ñañigu-ismo*, offered a more inclusive membership, incorporating non-Afro populations as well.[88] These practices continued in the twentieth century with other of-color organizations, including the short-lived Partido Independiente de Color. Organizing based on color was stamped out by multiple ordinances and societal conditions, including the U.S. presence during the late nineteenth and early twentieth centuries and the damning Morúa Law of 1908, a regulation that prohibited organizing based on race. Named for the Afro-Cuban politician Morúa Delgado, this law sealed the fate of Afro-populations as those with little or no political participation or security.

This reality often led Cuban UNIA locals to divorce their activities from any explicit racial mission. In some instances, "the UNIA was registered with the Cuban authorities as the 'Universal Improvement Association and Communities League,' avoiding the words 'Negro' and 'African' used in the original name." As the country continued to bend to the will of the United States, it became increasingly difficult to satisfy the demands of a multiracial society, and some race-based organizations in Cuba succumbed to what amounted to a gag order. Scholar Jorge Giovannetti describes that "generally, the Cuban divisions of the UNIA portrayed themselves to state officials as organizations that would not pose any 'danger' to the Cuban society in general, and to the elites and government officials in particular." Whether this position proves tacit or coerced agreement with the government is up for debate, yet it is clear that the political terrain of the nation was uneven. Some divisions were bold in their language. In 1922, the Camagüey branch of the UNIA registered its association under the full name in Spanish, offering evidence of the significance of race to those leaders and, perhaps, their desire to more fully align with the U.S.-based UNIA.[89] In 1929, however—during the decline of the UNIA in the United States due to surveillance, persecution, and Garvey's 1927 deportation—a still functional and visible Cuban division in Las Villas was investigated by the regime of President Gerardo Machado and forcibly closed due to Machado's concern over his reputation with Afro-Cubans and, more significantly, their access to state power.[90]

The complicated relationship between the heterogeneous Cuban population and the Afro-immigrant populations involved more than the insecurities of individual politicians. The Cuban population was largely composed of white Cubans (mostly of Spanish heritage), Afro-Cubans, and mulattoes. The possibility for interracial cooperation on the island was tenuous prior to the presence of the UNIA; once the organization came to the island, it facilitated some conversations while ending others. Early on, a letter to the editor of the *Negro World* questioned whether or not solidarity could be expected of white Cubans. The author, living in New York City, wondered aloud whether or not the Negroes had "any right to expect any moral or financial support from the Cubans" in their endeavor for freedom.[91] Some Cubans said yes. While acknowledging the discrimination practiced by some Cubans against Black people, one Afro-Cuban man announced, "I always consider Jamaiquanos, Cubanos and Haitianos to be all sons of Africa, and as far as I am concerned, there is no distinction made, and it should be in the heart of every Cuban to treat them as a fellow brother."[92]

The Afro-Cuban presence in UNIA branches and the threat of their active participation in it was palpable; indeed, as Guridy highlights, it was precisely the potential of the UNIA to mobilize Afro-Cubans and mulattoes that sent Machado to their doorstep.[93] Yet there was also a vocal population who rallied against Garvey's race-based program. Some believed that the UNIA in Cuba would introduce racial antagonism where it otherwise did not exist. Others believed that "blacks in Cuba should ask for nothing based on race but rather on their condition of being Cuban." This belief was particularly popular with the lower economic classes of Cuba, among whom the African descended were concentrated. Cuban historian Tomás Fernández Robaina argues that despite an engagement with the elements of Garveyism, "Cubans did not see Garvey's approach as applicable to themselves. Cuban blacks showed little interest . . . in the Return to Africa program or in raising collective black consciousness about the racial question."[94] In spite of resistance to Garvey's "Race First" program, locals appeared all over the country.[95] Garvey's 1921 trip to Cuba brought a flurry of attention precipitated by his arrival on the *Yarmouth*, the first ship of the independently Black-owned Black Star Line enterprise. His reputation preceded him through the pages of the *Negro World* in both the English and Spanish editions that flourished in the country during the 1920s. As was the case in the United States, many more Cubans than simply members of the UNIA read the paper. Despite a potential disidentification with the idea of Africa as homeland, the cultural products of the UNIA were central elements of the Cuban programs described in the *Negro World*, especially "Ethiopia." The anthem, with its references to the "land of *our* fathers" and "for *us* will the vict'ry be glorious," bound the locals to the broader project of a collective racial independence through nationhood. Ultimately, some members of the Black community realized that "[i]t was difficult to ignore the fact that while black Cubans had asked for nothing based on their blackness they also obtained nothing as blacks."[96] This conundrum would produce continued debate over Garvey and his organization in the country.

Cuba was a location of great consequence for the success of the global organization, and although not unusual, disputes within and between divisions and the government compromised the UNIA's reputation in the country. If there was trouble in Cuba, a country with hundreds (if not thousands) of members, the member base of the entire organization suffered. While Garvey and the other leaders in the United States were hesitant, if not averse, to challenge the Cuban government, they took a large step forward for the success of their Cuban branches when they enlisted the Afro-Cuban leader of Havana Division 24, Eduardo V. Morales, to be high commissioner to Cuba in the 1920s. He was a well-respected administrator for the Cuban branches and served as the first, and often last, line of defense for the Afro populations. In this regard he was integral to the sustainability of the branches. In a report for the *Negro World*, Ethelbert Blackwood wrote from Cuba that "[i]t is almost certain that [Morales's] time is being taken up doing something to help poor Negroes from being il[l]-treated by the Cuban police, or from some of the cruel barabases [*sic*] here, and all these things have got to be done at his own expense."[97] One of his most admirable (and commented upon) attributes was his dedication to the idea and practice of an African diaspora. He was known and reported to not make distinctions within the race based on national identity; to him, all were members of the Black nation, and that fact surpassed the national identities of Cuban, American, and so on. An article by H. F. Campbell summed-up Morales's position when it headlined, "UNIA Not Organization of Africans, Haytians or 'Jamaiquanos,' Morales Tells Habana Hearers."[98] His investment in a pan-ethnic, pan-national blackness made him a perfect ambassador for the organization whose work was the consolidation of a race into a nation.

While the UNIA worked through Morales and others to demonstrate their commitment to international locals, Cuban locals worked hard to maintain a connection to the U.S.-based organization. Cuban members wrote into the *Negro World* to report on local events that often demonstrated the cultural contributions of their branch. Rob Blake wrote in with a description of a Sunday school cantata performed by the children of the Banes chapter. He wrote, "The Negro children who gather there at 3 o'clock every Sunday are instructed not only in the Scriptures, but every effort is made to stamp upon their infant minds the fact that they are as good as children of any other race, and that color does not determine the scope of their intellectual abilities. *Every Negro child in Banes knows the Ethiopian national anthem*, and, as can be plainly seen, Garveyism has already made its mark in their young lives."[99] Music in this account was the transmitter of race pride—a piece of culture that traveled with the local children from church to home and back again. In performance, "Ethiopia" was the vehicle that allowed for the divisions of the UNIA to draw or, in the case of the Oriente local, to build new members and connect their local struggles for rights and access to the transnational vision of Black triumph fostered by and promoted from the headquarters in New York City. The significance of the anthem to the UNIA branches, in Cuba and elsewhere, reveals music's function within the formation of transnational Black solidarities. While Black leaders and national government officials alike challenged the UNIA, its size disclosed the strength of its strategies. Ultimately, other twentieth-century Black movements showcased their indebtedness to the organization when they copied the style and method of the UNIA through their own special sounds.

* * *

The composition and performance of "Ethiopia (Thou Land of our Fathers)" as an anthem set in motion the modern development of a Black nationalist project of performance that informed the practices of the protest organizations that followed in its wake. No longer could Black music be understood as simply background noise or even accompaniment; through Ford and the UNIA, it was a mobilized political practice that trained its performers for dual membership within a local organization and a diasporic citizenry. The anthem, however, also attuned its singers to another axis of difference beyond race—namely gender—within the organization and surrounding movements for Black social and political justice, critically undercutting the organization's claims to inclusivity and unity. The density of the anthem as a transnational representation of the complicated negotiations within cosmopolitan Black communities was maintained through its strategic use by another race organization and UNIA contemporary, the NAACP. The NAACP's anthem eventually eclipsed "Ethiopia," but not without first contending with the power of the UNIA and the complicated internationalisms that ultimately exposed its own failures and practices of difference.

2

Extending Diaspora

The NAACP and Up-"Lift" Cultures in the Interwar Black Pacific

The Negro's gift of music has been almost entirely over-
looked . . . yet, it is the magic thing by which he can bridge
all chasms.
—James Weldon Johnson

In 1919 Reverend Henry Curtis McDowell, his wife Bessie Fonvielle
McDowell, and their daughter arrived in Portuguese-colonized Angola.
They were sent by the American Board of Congregational Missions, and
their goal was to establish a ministry station run exclusively by African
Americans. By 1922 their task was accomplished with the development
of the Galangue Mission. During the meteoric rise of Garveyism, this
couple had managed one of the major philosophical tenets of the Universal Negro Improvement Association (UNIA)—they "returned" to
Africa and developed a small community where Africans and African
Americans lived together. Despite an opportunity to be the poster children for the Garvey program, Reverend McDowell rejected him and
his agenda outright. Believing Garvey to be an imperialist, he wrote,
"Should Marcus Garvey and his crowd . . . come into possession of this
part of Africa, it would be a sad day for natives. A black exploiter is as
despicable as a white exploiter." Their refutation of Garvey in service
of a social welfare project of uplift was evident in more ways than their
religious service to the native population. It was also witnessed in the
ways in which they represented themselves and the diaspora. In 1930
the Galangue Mission celebrated fifty years of foreign missions. During the course of the celebration, the choir, under direction by Bessie

McDowell, sang James Weldon and J. Rosamond Johnson's "Lift Ev'ry Voice and Sing" in Ovimbindu, the local language. Reverend McDowell praised the performance and wrote to supporters in the United States, "Galangue has made the first step, so far as I know, in making ["Lift Ev'ry Voice and Sing"] the international anthem."[1] By using "Lift," the McDowells placed themselves and their mission inside the political and social project of America's most influential civil rights organization, the National Association for the Advancement of Colored People (NAACP).

It is not surprising that the McDowells chose "Lift Ev'ry Voice and Sing" as their song. By the 1930s, Garvey and the UNIA were a fading memory in America. His 1927 deportation effectively dismantled the broad-based movement that so many had worked to build. In this moment, the NAACP stepped in to recuperate the political energy of the Black community and use it toward their project of racial uplift. With "Lift Ev'ry Voice and Sing" as their anthem, the organization moved away from a Black nationalist frame toward an agenda of social welfare and interracial political campaigning to be recognized the world over. The use of "Lift" at the Galangue Mission may have been the first use of the song internationally, but it was certainly not the last. Another opportunity for translation and global community building through "Lift Ev'ry Voice and Sing" would soon appear, and in the process the concepts and practices of diaspora would be expanded and contested. As James Weldon believed, the "Negro problem . . . is and always has been a series of shifting interracial situations" negotiated by the African descended in every location in which they are present or, I would add, imagined.[2] The anthem's travel to Japan was one such negotiation that evidences the spread of Black protest traditions in excess of the nation and documents Black music as a global archive that labored to develop robust radicalisms and diasporas of political thought and performance during that generation's Great Depression.

Histories of Origin: The Brothers Johnson and "Lift Ev'ry Voice and Sing"

The history of the NAACP reads as a catalogue of Black leadership in the twentieth century. From its roots in the Niagara Movement of 1905 through the decades of a progressive U.S. Civil Rights Movement, the names W. E. B. Du Bois, Walter White, Rosa Parks, and Roy Wilkins serve as a genealogy for the NAACP and document but a few of the many icons of modern Black intellectual and activist practice. A pioneering scholar, militant advocate, and humanitarian, Du Bois is perhaps the most crucial figure in the history of the organization. As a founding member, he conceived of a program that was inclusive and broad in scope. The race men who met in Buffalo, New York, and closed ranks as the Niagara Movement adopted a constitution with numerous ideals that ultimately laid the groundwork for the principles of the NAACP, including the "freedom of speech and criticism, abolition of all caste distinctions based simply on race and colour, recognition of the principles of human brotherhood as a practical present creed, a belief in the dignity of labour, and [the] united effort to realize these ideals under wise and courageous leadership."[3] With the addition of white liberals in 1909, including reporter Mary White Ovington, pacifist and publisher of the *Nation* Oswald Garrison Villard, and Columbia University professor and pragmatist John Dewey, the NAACP was born.[4] After the founding of this organization "New York became again the centre of the organized forces of self-assertion of equal rights and of insistence upon the impartial application of the fundamental principles of the Republic, without regard to race, creed, or colour."[5]

Although very well intentioned, the NAACP often fell victim to its own ideologies. The organization prided itself on the stature and unimpeachable character of its leaders and members, thereby modeling a project of "racial uplift" that emphasized morality and education as the means to equality. Historian Kevin Gaines locates two separate periods of racial uplift in the Black community. One period, antebellum through the end of Reconstruction (1877), revolved around a "liberation theology" measured by "a personal or collective spiritual—and potentially social—transcendence of worldly oppression and misery." This idea of uplift vigorously championed education as the means toward freedom and was continued in the post-Reconstruction project directed by Black elites. For many of them, "uplift came to mean an emphasis on self-help, racial solidarity, temperance, thrift, chastity, social purity, patriarchal authority, and the accumulation of wealth." This new emphasis on "class differentiation as race progress" reinforced the economic divide plaguing the country during the industrial and gilded eras and served to splinter the Black community by drawing into conflict the practices of class distinction and the ideal of racial solidarity. Gaines argues that the uplift paradigm was as much about class as it was about race: "[E]lite African Americans were replicating, even as they contested, the uniquely American racial fictions upon which liberal conceptions of social reality and 'equality' were founded." In the first decades of the twentieth century these ideas became ubiquitous; the Black elites valued a "bourgeois morality whose deeply embedded assumptions of racial difference were often invisible to them." Instead of rejecting the popular American idea of "the Negro problem," many Black elites' "orientation toward self-help implicitly faulted African Americans for their lowly status," thereby reifying a stereotype that plagued the entire community.[6] The closely associated "politics of respectability," as historian Evelyn Brooks Higginbotham describes them, dictated not only class and racial functions but also gender relations.[7] With its emphasis on bourgeois normativity, the NAACP helped to shape and maintain these divisions. This symphony of identity debates permeated the daily experiences of Black people with the negative racial dogmas of the nation often unknowingly reinforced by the leading race organizations of the time.

In spite of its contradictions, the NAACP developed a culture early on in its history that made it a force to be reckoned with, artistically, socially, and politically. Its major press organ was the critically acclaimed magazine the *Crisis*. Under the leadership of Du Bois, the magazine was simultaneously a creative arts publication of poetry and short stories as well as an instrument for membership growth and political propaganda. First published in November 1910, the *Crisis* reached over thirty thousand readers within six years.[8] As an international periodical, it served to bring people of various cultural conditions together; messages of the Black North were delivered to the South, and news of the Black American condition traveled to an international audience. W. C. Handy, known as the Father of the Blues, wrote in his autobiography of the reach and importance of the magazine: "In the first mention of my work in the columns of *The Crisis* about 1915, a letter reached me from an African trader in Sierra Leone. He was on the subscriber's list of *The Crisis*." The trader whom Handy referenced was interested in entering into "some relations whereby we [in Africa] may avail ourselves of your music."[9] This example highlights the function of the *Crisis* as more than political propaganda—it also facilitated various community identifications through cultural exchange. Culture within the organization was a determining factor in its reception and popularity through the publication of writers such as Langston Hughes and Jessie Redmon Fauset and visual artists like Aaron Douglas. In addition to the *Crisis*, it was the music of the movement—the sound that resisted printing—that served to unite the cultural and the political in the lives of its participants. The song that inspired the masses of the NAACP was James Weldon and J. Rosamond Johnson's "Lift Ev'ry Voice and Sing."

The adoption of "Lift Ev'ry Voice and Sing" by the NAACP is a history with little clarity. Some sources locate its adoption in 1919, others in 1920. According to the documentation left behind, it was not until February 1921 that philanthropist and chairman of the board Joel E. Spingarn appointed a committee to brand the national NAACP with a song. Approximately seven months after the UNIA adopted "Ethiopia," Black Swan founder Harry Pace, Spingarn, and James Weldon Johnson gathered to find its equivalent for the NAACP.[10] While the committee discussion of the song's adoption is missing, texts outlining its influence and importance are abundant. Mary White Ovington may have played an early role in its adoption. Expressing her sentiments on anthems a decade later, she wrote,

> The writing of a national song is a very difficult task. During the [Civil] [W]ar many people tried a hand at it. The only successful song of this type that I recall, however, is "America the Beautiful," written by Katharine Lee Bates, many years later. But since 1900 there has been a noble national anthem that few white people know about. The words are by James Weldon Johnson, the music by his brother, Rosamond Johnson. The colored people sing it everywhere, in church and school, at meetings of organizations. Yet there is nothing in it that is not suitable to many groups in the nation. The music is glorious, the words majestic.[11]

Ovington described here a sonic color line between "colored" and white people as demonstrated through the knowledge and performance of "Lift Ev'ry Voice and Sing." Black people are argued to "sing it everywhere," while it lingers in obscurity for white people. Ovington conceded the special knowledges and cultural practices of Black people as well as her insider status, since she was aware of the song in spite of being white. Her mission however is not to praise the "glorious" and "majestic" song for its influence in Black America but to provide a cultural translation for a white audience who is blind to its existence. Far from passing judgment on white people for their ignorance, Ovington instead provides a discovery narrative that attempts to rework national dialogues on race and patriotism through a song with "nothing in it not suitable to many groups."

Prominent NAACP supporter Rabbi Stephen Wise of the Free Synagogue in New York echoed Ovington's description of "Lift Ev'ry Voice and Sing" as a "national anthem." He was so moved by his experience of the anthem on a trip to Atlanta that in 1928 he sent Johnson a testimonial for him to share with the song's publisher, Edward B. Marks Music Company. He wrote to Johnson that "['Lift'] is sturdy and bracing, and what a national anthem should be—a collective prayer." He continued to lavish praise on the anthem:

> The "National Anthem" by J. Rosamond and James Weldon Johnson, text and music alike, is the noblest anthem I have ever heard. It is a great upwelling of prayer from the soul of a race long wronged but with faith unbroken. I wish that "Lift Ev'ry Voice and Sing" might be substituted for some of the purely martial and unspiritual so-called national anthems [that] are sung by the peoples. It is a rare combination to have a text as fine as this, set with great beauty to song.[12]

The complicated layers of this statement to the Marks Company—a Rabbi arguing for the wide adoption of a Judeo-Christian inspired text, a white man praising the work of Black artists over white composers, and the wishful substitution of the "Negro National Anthem" for (what one can assume is) "The Star-Spangled Banner"—demonstrate the attempts of the brothers Johnson to expand the reach of their anthem, which was, by 1928, still absent from the national lexicon of symbols. As I will show, James Weldon harbored ambitious dreams for his hymn and strategically lobbied the Marks Company in order to positively respond to the many requests for the anthem from around the world. The fond recollections of "Lift Ev'ry Voice and Sing" by Ovington and

Wise speak to the ability of the song to transcend its beginnings in a specific time and place.

Like that of so much of Black music, the genesis of "Lift Ev'ry Voice and Sing" was locally situated in response to the needs of a particular community. As the 1899 anniversary of Abraham Lincoln's birthday approached, a group of young men in Jacksonville, Florida, gathered to plan its celebration. James Weldon was approached to offer an address, and after accepting he decided to write a poem in commemoration. Failing in his attempt at the project, he instead turned to his classically trained musician brother (John) Rosamond for assistance, and together they "planned to write a song to be sung as a part of the exercises. We planned, better still to have it sung by schoolchildren—a chorus of five hundred voices." James Weldon described the unfolding process:

I got my first line: Lift ev'ry voice and sing. Not a starting line; but I worked along grinding out the next five. When, near the end of the first stanza, there came to me the lines:

Sing a song full of the faith that the dark past has taught us.
Sing a song full of the hope that the present has brought us.

the spirit of the poem had taken hold of me. I finished the stanza and turned it over to Rosamond.

In composing the two other stanzas I did not use pen and paper. While my brother worked at his musical setting I paced back and forth on the front porch, repeating the lines over and over to myself, going through all of the agony and ecstasy of creating. As I worked through the opening and middle lines of the last stanza:

God of our weary years,
God of our silent tears,
Thou who has brought us thus far on our way,
Thou who hast by Thy might
Let us into the light,
Keep us forever in the path, we pray;
Lest our feet stray from the places, our God, where we met Thee,

> Lest, our hearts drunk with the wine of the world,
> we forget
> Thee. . . .

I could not keep back the tears, and made no effort to do so. I was experiencing the transport of the poet's ecstasy. Feverish ecstasy was followed by the contentment—that sense of serene joy—which makes artistic creation the most complete of all human experiences.[13]

From this catharsis stemmed one of the most celebrated songs of the next fifty years. By changing the composition from a poem to a song, Johnson acknowledged the necessity and power of collective performance. The use of plural nouns—"our," "us," "we"—prioritizes and privileges assembly and places the history of Black struggle and victory in the hands of a collective. Rosamond's composition in four-part harmony concretizes the necessity of cooperation in the success of the song's vision and performance. Their piece, which began as "an effort made under stress and with no intention other than to meet the needs of a particular moment," became that which surpassed all else in his repertoire. James Weldon ultimately believed that "nothing that I have done has paid me back so fully in satisfaction as being the part creator of this song."[14]

The text of "Lift Ev'ry Voice and Sing" exhibits literature scholar Richard Long's contention that James Weldon's "early verse was a species of propaganda, designed sometimes overtly, sometimes obliquely, to advance to a reading public the merits and the grievances of blacks."[15] Through "Lift," James Weldon highlighted the shared conditions experienced by Black people and championed the strength and resolve of the collective to persevere through them.

> Stony the road we trod
> Bitter the chastening rod
> Felt in the days when hope unborn had died;
> Yet with a steady beat
> Have not our weary feet
> Come to the place for which our fathers sighed?
> We have come over a way that with tears has been watered

> We have come, treading our path thro' the blood of the
> slaughtered
> Out of the gloomy past
> Till now we stand at last
> Where the white gleam of our bright star is cast.

In his recounting of a bloody past, James Weldon suggests that it is through song—lifting our voices to sing—that the Negroes in America most potently articulated their plight and their triumph. His recent success as a poet (with the 1899 publication of the dialect poem "Sence You Went Away") was translated in "Lift Ev'ry Voice and Sing" into a sonic literacy, which mitigated against the structural mis/undereducation of Black people in the post-Reconstruction United States. Through adjusting the method of delivery from text to sound, James Weldon ensured that the historical progress that he championed would have a structure, a pace, and a deeper and longer-lasting resonance than his individual address or poem may have allowed.

The gestures in "Lift Ev'ry Voice and Sing" toward a historiography of Black struggle in and through music are consistent throughout Johnson's larger body of work. His oft-cited masterpiece "O Black and Unknown Bards" (1908) charts a premodern genealogy for Black cultural politics:

> O black and unknown bards of long ago,
> How came your lips to touch the sacred fire?
> How, in your darkness, did you come to know
> The power and beauty of the minstrel's lyre?
> Who first from midst his bonds lifted his eyes?
> Who first from out the still watch, lone and long,
> Feeling the ancient faith of prophets rise
> Within his dark-kept soul, burst into song?
>
>
> What merely living clod, what captive thing,
> Could up toward God through all its darkness grope,
> And find within its deadened heart to sing
> These songs of sorrow, love and faith, and hope?

How did it catch that subtle undertone,
That note in music not heard with the ears?
How sound the elusive reed so seldom blown,
Which stirs the soul or melts the heart to tears?

You sang far better than you knew; the songs
That for your listeners' hungry hearts sufficed
Still live,—but more than this to you belongs:
You sang a race from wood and stone to Christ.[16]

Music, for Johnson, was the historical artifact that best articulated the pain and glory of this oppressed race. As the "dark-kept souls" groped toward a brighter alternative, music captured the truest emotions of the community and became the first act of resistance to bondage. His bards reconfigure the practices of Black leadership by using performance as the strategy of defiance and defense, singing "a race from wood and stone to Christ." This passage in particular distinguishes music as a tool of Black Atlantic modernity; his bards were the actors within cultural theorist Paul Gilroy's "counterculture [to modernity] that defiantly reconstructs its own critical, intellectual, and moral genealogy in a partially hidden public sphere of its own."[17] This piece, written as a commemoration of the composers and performers of slave spirituals, is used as the epigraph to the Johnson brothers' first *Book of American Negro Spirituals* (1925), which demonstrates through the songs that it praises the path of Black people from "slave ship to citizenship."[18]

Musically, "Lift Ev'ry Voice and Sing" exhibits components of the spirituals so diligently anthologized by the Johnson brothers. Relatively simple melodic lines and strong chord accompaniment mimic the reliance on the oral tradition in Black music (versus a literate tradition). Rosamond uses his accompaniment and vocal harmonies to highlight the meaning of the text. The first measure of the vocal line is a half measure and offers a running start to the A-flat major key signature, with the text "lift ev'-ry" notated by three eighth notes in the 6/8 time signature. While the song was written in 6/8, its performance follows a 12/8 phrasing, placing it alongside the Black gospel tradition, which, as I will discuss further in chapter 4, was growing in dynamic ways at this very moment. This quick introduction leads the vocalist to a strong tonic chord on the downbeat of measure 2. The melodic emphasis lands on the word "voice" with "and sing" (measures 10 and 11) following as long notes (dotted quarter notes). The basic line follows:

meas. 9   ♪   ♪   ♪   meas. 10   ♩·   ♩·   meas. 11   ♩·
"lift   ev'   -ry   voice and   sing"

This is the dominant rhythm that follows throughout the text in four-part harmony until the listener reaches a moment of unison in measure 24 with the text "sing a song full of the faith that the dark past has taught us." This portion of the song is carried in a full-bodied unison in the middle to low vocal range. In the following line, "sing a song, full of the hope that the present has brought us," "song" is emphasized with a flat sixth as the tempo quickens into a crescendo and returns to four-part harmony at "brought" with a fermata (untimed hold) at "us." The flat sixth introduces the listener to the changes from the "dark past" to the hope of the present and the return to a collective four-part is one of deliverance as singers and audience revel together in what "the present has brought us." To hold the "us" on a fermata signals its eternal construction, the ways in which Black people will be held together forever, outside of time. Following the hymn tradition, Rosamond ends the piece with a dramatic, prolonged seven chord that resolves into the major I, placing victory and harmony at the end of his piece.[19]

The composition of "Lift Ev'ry Voice and Sing" emerged from a profound insight in which James Weldon realized "the importance of the American Negro's cultural background and his creative folk-art" and, perhaps appropriating the theory of Karl Marx, began to "speculate on the superstructure of conscious art that might be reared upon them."[20] He and Rosamond soon decided that this grand "superstructure" could not be built nor properly nourished in their native Jacksonville, and the brothers descended on New York City with every intention of building a career in musical theater. Considering James Weldon's investment in the political ends of artistic innovation he could not have arrived at a better time. He noted that "[b]y 1900 the Negro's civil status had fallen until it was lower than it had been at any time following the Civil War," leading the race to be "surrendered to Disfranchisement and Jim-Crowism, to

outrage and violence, to the fury of the mob."[21] In response, Black artists, particularly those of the musical stage, conceived of and enacted
an agenda of supreme artistry in order to advance the race, and these
were the men whom the Johnson brothers came to know and collaborate
with while in New York: comedic musician Bob Cole, duo Bert Williams
and George Walker, comedian Ernest Hogan, art composers Will Marion Cook and Harry T. Burleigh, and poet Paul Laurence Dunbar. This
group of "post-slavery Black composers—i.e., those born before 1900"—
were, according to musicologist Lucius Wyatt, "nationalists in the sense
that they consciously turned to the folk music of their people as a source
of inspiration for their compositions."[22] In so doing, they developed
multidimensional representations of Black people to compete with the
primitivist, native, and minstrel stereotypes that characterized American
popular theater and culture. According to literature and performance
scholar Daphne Brooks, this cohort used their hyphenated identities to
construct a "kind of Afro-diasporic alienation effect," thereby engaging in questions of "how and in what ways to articulate the dissonant
multivocality of black identity in performance space."[23] The Johnson
brothers modeled this preoccupation with voices, identity, and performance through "Lift Ev'ry Voice and Sing," a sonic text that complicated
representations of Black people's relationship to and enactments of history and citizenship. By adjusting the images and sound of Black people
within the context of a booming national leisure culture, historian Karen
Sotiropoulos argues that James Weldon and his contemporaries became
the "artistic arm of race leadership at the turn of the century."[24] Their
"love for the race," as Walker described it, led them to "feel that in a
degree we represent the race and every hair's breadth of achievement we
make is to its credit."[25] His sentiments reflect the paradigm of uplift institutionalized by the NAACP and other race organizations of the period,
materializing it as both organizing frame and performative act.

The methods of resistance employed by Black performers, composers, and writers, including "parody—inversion, reversal, and 'signifying,'"[26] were intended to mean something to those who viewed their
performances. Whether it was through a critique of the Black elite or
derision of white racism, these compositions and performances created
a bridge between the quotidian and the utopian for Black citizens. This

turn-of-the-century period is therefore essential for the study of Black politico-cultural formations and highlights James Weldon's unique role in them. During the course of his seven-year career with J. Rosamond and Bob Cole in Cole & Johnson, James Weldon produced over two hundred songs and expanded his intellectual and artistic horizons by entering prominently into the political sphere. A devout Republican, James Weldon used his political ties to move about the western hemisphere after ending his professional affiliation with Cole & Johnson, in the process developing a complex perspective of power and difference on a global scale. In 1906 he accepted a federal position as consul at Venezuela (1906–9) and later Nicaragua (1909–13), where he likely overlapped with the enterprising and migratory (although then unknown) Marcus Garvey. While in Nicaragua he also married his longtime sweetheart Grace Nail and continued writing, publishing his classic _Autobiography of an Ex-Colored Man_ anonymously in 1912. A twist of electoral fate that same year beckoned James Weldon back to New York as contributing editor to the oldest of New York's Black newspapers, the _New York Age_. From this position, Johnson would "become visible as a national race leader" through columns that offered his social and political philosophy.[27] His reputation with the _New York Age_ was precisely the platform needed to gain the attention of the burgeoning NAACP.

James Weldon's role in the organization took off in 1916 when he was an invited participant in the first Amenia meeting, an interracial conference at the New York estate of liberal philanthropist Joel E. Spingarn. Dedicated to "questions relating to the Negro," this event included early NAACP leaders, including Du Bois, and occurred at a moment ripe with change; the escalation of war in Europe called into question the extent to which the United States would intervene. This riddled international landscape was the backdrop to domestic anxieties over the mass movement of Black bodies from South to North as well as from South and North to the West. The Great Migration of African Americans from the South during World War I generated new understandings of family, work, and survival within and from without the Black community. By the time of the signing of the Treaty of Versailles in 1919, over 400,000 Black southerners had come north to work in war industries and other industrial jobs vacated by white servicemen.[28] In this moment of increased international crisis and unparalleled national movement, the Amenia Conference "took its place in the list of important events in the history of the Negro in the United States."[29]

Obviously impressed by James Weldon, Spingarn quickly followed the conference with an invitation to join the staff of the NAACP. Johnson recalled that Spingarn's offer "was in line with destiny," and with a strong sense of fortuitousness on his side he accepted the position of field secretary, a new position within the organization created by the Board of Directors in 1916.[30] Johnson's primary goal was to grow the membership. Low in funds and low in numbers, the NAACP struggled in its early years to build a reputation. What effort was made in that arena was due to the only tool at their disposal: agitation. Similar to the early work of the UNIA, the NAACP used public meetings, the *Crisis*, pamphlets, and any other open forum available to spread their message. The odds were against Johnson as the only paid staff person with the explicit job of traveling to gain membership.

In 1916, there were sixty-eight local NAACP branches across the northern and western United States. Three additional branches in the South—in New Orleans and Shreveport, Louisiana, and Key West, Florida—added up to a total membership of 348. Johnson decided to attack the organization's weakest area; to the surprise, and in some cases horror, of other staff and board members, Johnson proposed to embark on an effort to organize the South. As he told it, "[I]t was my idea that the south could furnish numbers and resources to make the Association a power." This understandable course of action was met with resistance; some believed that organizing in the South would cause a division within the organization, so much so that that its imperatives would have to change. They argued that greater latitude in decision making was best achieved free from the challenges of additional southern locals. Johnson felt differently and harbored

a deep conviction that the aims of the Association could never be realized by only hammering at white America; I felt convinced that it would be necessary to awaken black America, awaken it to a sense of its rights and to a determination to hold fast to such as it possessed and to seek in every orderly way possible to secure all others to which it was entitled. I realized that, regardless of what might be done *for* black Americans, the ultimate and vital part of the work would have to be done by black America itself.[31]

Johnson's perspective undoubtedly was influenced by his southern background and hopes for the Black populations there. He ultimately won over the board and commenced with a southern project in which he developed pamphlets and speeches outlining the association's purpose, how to open a branch, and how to govern it. While the fruits of his labor in the South were mixed, he did achieve a sizeable base of support, and by 1919 there were 131 NAACP branches in the U.S. South.[32]

During his tour of the South, Johnson encountered individuals who, while not necessarily knowledgeable of the NAACP, knew of him—through his popular songs, Broadway fame, and writing. Quite often however it was "Lift Ev'ry Voice and Sing" that built the acquaintance between Johnson and his southern constituency. The oral traditions of the South made his anthem a prominent cultural text prior to its adoption by the NAACP, demonstrating the organization that already existed in the South. Johnson corresponded with southerners like Mrs. Effie T. Battle, a student-teacher living in Boston, who claimed to have "taught [the] National Negro Anthem to thousands of Negro children in Dixie."[33] Her statement evidences the underappreciated work of women—especially southern women teachers—who offered Johnson and the NAACP their greatest resource: word of mouth. By teaching and performing the anthem in the 1910s and '20s, they also carried the seeds of Black political organization, which would grow and connect them to the national organization upon adoption of the anthem by the NAACP in 1921. "Lift Ev'ry Voice and Sing" had the southern presence that the NAACP lacked, and its performance at association functions built upon two decades of memories prior to the NAACP's arrival. As sociologists Ron Eyerman and Andrew Jamison document, the memories associated with music are often as significant as the music in the contemporary moment because they remain as a "potential way to inspire new waves of mobilization."[34] In this regard, Black southerners already had a relationship with Johnson, and the NAACP's adoption of this piece that had so long been a part of southern culture was an inviting and mobilizing feature for future members.

In spite of its wide reception, "Lift Ev'ry Voice and Sing" was not above questions, critiques, and in some cases outright skepticism, and the resulting exchanges between Johnson and the listeners and performers of the anthem document its impact on the performance practices, identity, and political formations of twentieth-century communities. Miss Captolia Dent, musical director at Paine College in Georgia, asked about the performance of the piece. In 1932 she wrote, "Will you please inform me as to whether persons singing [the] last stanza of [the] National Negro Hymn should slightly bow heads?" Johnson replied, "Let me say that the last stanza of the Negro National Hymn is, as may be plainly seen, a prayer, so it would naturally not be out of keeping to sing it with slightly bowed heads, though I do not think that need be deemed necessary."[35] Miss Mabel Anderson of the Civic Melody Chorus in Ohio asked a similar question: "There has been considerable controversy both pro and con regarding standing when singing, 'Lift Every Voice and Sing.' Please inform me the proper thing to do." By the time of this 1934 correspondence, Johnson had a reserve of experience with the song in performance. He wrote back to Miss Anderson, "I may say that my observation in various parts of the country has been that it is generally sung standing."[36] Here, Johnson offers his "observation" rather than his authoritative instruction as coauthor, allowing the customs of the Black community to dictate his answer to this question of performance. Through this position, Johnson acknowledged that the song belonged to the race, not to him, and that it had autonomously developed customs above and beyond his imagination.

Some of the questions leveled at Johnson revolved around the song's composition. Mrs. Lisbon C. Berry of North Carolina exposed her many encounters with the song when she wrote in 1933, "I am writing you today to ask just how you intended the last verse of 'Lift Every Voice and Sing' to be sung. Some I notice sing it very softly others very forcefully. Will you please tell me just how *you* prefer it[?]" In a fashion befitting of a composer-poet, Johnson replied, "In singing the last stanza of 'Lift Every Voice and Sing,' the first six lines should be sung softly; the next two lines, the long lines, should be sung with a gradual crescendo; and the last three lines should be sung fortissimo."[37] Unlike the previous correspondence, this response shows Johnson taking ownership over the song as he outlines specifically what he would like to hear from its performance. In this exchange Johnson used his instructions to translate for the performers and audience his knowledge that within the song's final "fortissimo" stanza "the American Negro was, historically and spiritually, immanent."[38]

The language used within the correspondence received and sent by Johnson fails to pinpoint the exact terminology by which "Lift Ev'ry Voice and Sing" was understood. While others, including performers as well as his NAACP colleagues, used the term "anthem," Johnson was consistent in his description of the song as a hymn. Hymns are sacred texts, written as praise or prayer, and are often religious in nature, offering adoration to deities or their personification. While often contained within the purview of the church or other religious organizations, hymns are not without political import; they are organizing tools that manage services—the literal space of a religious gathering—and compel service—an action demanded by the songs themselves, whether the action is singing or charity. In this way, Johnson's use of the word is not so much a rebuttal to the category of anthem—those songs that organize citizenship practices—as much as it is a restaging of "Lift Ev'ry Voice and Sing." His use of the word "hymn" does not evacuate the song of its function for the race, nor does it debunk the song's nationalist impulses since he regularly employs the language "Negro National Hymn"; this wording instead demonstrates the work of the anthem above and beyond the edicts of any single organization and represents the hyphenated identity of African Americans by setting "Lift" up as a companion to "The Star-Spangled Banner," not its challenge. He did not, however, restrict others' interpretations of or expectations for the song within the lexicon of Black performance texts, thereby allowing the category of anthem to remain attached to the song for many decades to come.

The nuance of language encircling "Lift Ev'ry Voice and Sing" and its significance as a living document of the Black experience did not dissuade its detractors from leveling critiques; on the contrary, the anthem's prominence encouraged them, and their responses exposed the virulence of racialized citizenship within the United States. In 1934 Mrs. L. H. Tyler of Ohio dismissed Johnson and wrote directly to the publisher of "Lift," Marks Music Company:

> I wonder if you could give me a little information regarding a song copyrighted by your company?

The song "Lift Every Voice and Sing" by J. Weldon Johnson. You have in parenthesis "National Negro Hymn," what is meant by this? When a group are singing this song is the audience expected to stand as they do when singing the "Star Spangled Banner"? This question has been discussed pro and con in our little City, where a group of Negroes have a chorus directed by a white leader and the audiences have been asked to stand. Some question the authority of this. Would appreciate your opinion on it.[39]

This letter addresses the questions of authenticity, reception, and universality that orbited around the use of "Lift Ev'ry Voice and Sing" as an anthem. Her comments challenge the cultural practices employed by Black people in their efforts toward self-determination within a national body politic of their own design. Her denial is represented first by the fact that she addressed her comments not to either of the Johnson brothers but to their corporate publisher. The dismissals continue within the text, which reflects the entrenched ethnic particularity of U.S. nationalism. She begins by calling attention to the relationship between "Lift Ev'ry Voice and Sing" and "The Star-Spangled Banner," a piece that was officially declared the U.S. national anthem only three years prior to her correspondence with Marks.[40] Like "Lift," "Star" was used for decades before its official adoption and was an ubiquitous element within performances of U.S. patriotism. It is clear in her address that she did not believe the two pieces had equal standing and, more than that, that she understood them to be representative of two very different spheres within American society—one national (equated with universality), and one sub- or nonnational (equated with particularity). According to Mrs. Tyler, never the twain shall meet—not ideologically, socially, or even within performance. Standing during the presentation of "Lift Ev'ry Voice and Sing" would seem to desecrate the former—the *real* national anthem. In this scenario, "Lift Ev'ry Voice and Sing" posed an unwelcome challenge to this woman's racialized citizenship, in spite of the important collaborations and, at the very least, conversations that transpired after its performance in her "little City." In that location, musical performance was a litmus test for experiments in interracial cooperation. "Lift Ev'ry Voice and Sing" exposed the power dynamics that determined the nation's character, and despite numerous local battles over its use, reception, and performance, it traveled beyond the U.S. South and into the global arena, feeding other challenges and victories.

Japan's Muse: Afro-Nippon Relations and the Reach of Black Music

In 1933, James Weldon Johnson received a letter from Yasuichi Hikida, a Japanese immigrant to New York City. Hikida arrived in the United States in 1920 and quickly familiarized himself with the functions of Black American organizations, first among them being the NAACP. By the time of his letter, he was a longtime member of the association and had attended numerous events in Harlem, twice meeting Johnson at organization functions. He worked at the Japanese consulate in New York City for a brief period as well, foreshadowing the crucial synergies at play between his work with Black Americans and his work for Japan. Hikida took advantage of the extended Black activist channels in the city through friendships with NAACP leader Walter White and Puerto Rican intellectual and bibliophile Arturo Schomburg as well as by attending cultural events within the community, including a Paul Robeson concert at Town Hall. But it was his association with the NAACP that offered him his first acquaintance with "Lift Ev'ry Voice and Sing," by then known as the Negro National Anthem.[41] Hikida recounted this event:

> It was during the Springfield Conference of NAACP that I was impressed and thought so much of "Lift Every Voice." I heard the song many times before 1930, but it was at that time when I felt its great beauty and force; and thought its significance to the life of the American Negro. How, evening after evening . . . I enjoyed, and moved, and impressed [sic]! I thought [to] myself that it would be a wonderful thing to introduce the song to Japan.[42]

Hikida's letter outlined a plan, with Johnson's permission, to translate "Lift Ev'ry Voice and Sing" into Japanese. As expressed here, he recognized the song's "significance to the life of the American Negro" and was confident that a similar effect could be had in Japan. Hikida's belief that this song would be a factor abroad is a reflection of the cross-cultural and diasporic exchanges that the Harlem Renaissance of the 1920s helped to initiate and the Great Depression of the 1930s reinforced worldwide.

The work of developing Afro-Japanese relationships was in motion for many years prior to 1933. Historian Reginald Kearney argues that between 1900 and 1945 "black intellectuals, who differed sharply from one another regarding domestic goals and strategies for black advancement, were in basic agreement that Japan's achievements on the world scene were good for peoples of color everywhere."[43] African American leaders W. E. B. Du Bois, Mary Church Terrell, Booker T. Washington, and Walter White were among those sympathetic to or active in the causes of the Japanese in this period. Marcus Garvey was awed by the military prowess of the Japanese and imagined their crucial role in the fight for Black liberation.[44] After the Japanese victory in the Russo-Japanese War of 1904–5, Japan was seen as a contender in global power struggles, and the fact that the Japanese were of the "darker races" of the world offered them approval and respect within the Black community. While the amount of support they garnered in the Black community is difficult, if not impossible, to quantify, Kearney argues that "prior to Japan's attack on Pearl Harbor, a great many, perhaps most, African Americans had only positive impressions of the Japanese and their achievements."[45]

These "positive impressions" were translated into on-the-ground advances in the Black freedom struggle. Collaborative ventures between Japanese and Black organizers and activists sprung up across the United States during the 1930s, but as historian Ernest Allen, Jr. documents, the Midwest was a particular bastion of interracial radicalism. He argues that the "pro-Japan penchant of Missouri blacks was characteristic of African American thought of the era: an unfolding of messianic nationalist sentiment occasioned by the hard times of the Great Depression and a populist-based admiration for Japan," which attracted "tens of thousands of black Missourians to the pro-Japan movement."[46]

Black organizations were in large part responsible for the extension of diaspora to include Japan and other "Asiatics" through creation myths and messianic visions. The Nation of Islam (NOI), founded in 1930, was a principal coordinator of this project. Leader Elijah Muhammad taught that Black people were "members of the Asiatic [Black] Nation," a condition of existence that "referred to all the people to the south and east of Western Europe and all people who were believed to have ancestry among these peoples." Furthermore, Elijah Muhammad preached that all of Africa was a part of the "Orient" or Asiatic Nation.[47] While cultural and religious emulation guided much of the orthodoxy of the Asiatic Black man espoused by the NOI, Muhammad's prophecy that "white civilization would be destroyed by the Mother Plane—a giant circular plane—built by Allah in Japan," demonstrated admiration for the military and technological might of Japan as well.[48] It is through the evidence and imaginary of both its power and culture that Japan was welcomed into the fold of the African descended. With "tens of thousands of African Americans" embracing what religious historian Nathaniel Deutsch calls a "pan-Asiatic racial identity" in the early decades of the twentieth century through the NOI and other organizations, Hikida's translation represented a natural extension of the relationship that had evolved in the political and cultural spheres between Black Americans and the Japanese.[49]

Hikida recognized that it would be no small task to translate the song into a vernacular Japanese while still maintaining the intentions of its American usage. He confessed, "I discovered that I had sadly mistaken for this assumption when I came to the point of the translation of 'Lift Every Voice.'" He outlined to Johnson that he "faced a black Wall [sic] in this translation" and included other concerns as he moved forward with the project: "1. It must be translated as music as well as song; 2. It never before was introduced to Japan[,] so it will make a precedent and must become standered [sic] version; [and] 3. Therefore it must be not only good translation, but must be the best translation."[50] Hikida seemed preoccupied with the details of the project, but for good reason. His letter demonstrates his awareness that there was something at stake in whether or not he was successful—failure in this project might damage communities and relationships beyond his association with Johnson or the NAACP. Hikida's attention to the issue of translation exposed a necessary obsession with language. Indeed, "the practice of translation" described by literary scholar Brent Edwards "is indispensible to the pursuit of any project of internationalism, any 'correspondence.'" As an always-already fraught enterprise, translation within diaspora must do battle with "unavoidable misapprehensions and misreadings, persistent blindnesses and solipsisms" and the tyranny of difference.[51] As an outsider to this "practice," Hikida demonstrated an appropriate amount of concern as the translation moved forward.

To facilitate the language difficulties, Hikida enlisted the talents of Reverend Koh Yuki.[52] Described as "one of the most important and active committee [members] of [the] newly published Japanese Hymnal[,] which has been used and will be used by almost all Christian Churches in Japan in years to come," Yuki was well suited for the task of the translation, particularly in its combination with music.[53] Upon its completion, Yuki wrote, "I feel confident to announce . . . my Japanese version [of "Lift Ev'ry Voice and Sing"] as one of my masterpieces."[54] While his translation altered the text to accommodate Japanese phonics and syntax, the music remained the same, thereby leaving the song's core structure unaltered. Although its publication was directed at a Japanese audience and for Japanese performers, maintaining the identical harmonies and chord progressions of the U.S. version would be the glue that bonded this piece to the traditions of the African American community.

Hikida understood that the decision to translate "Lift Ev'ry Voice and Sing" must be measured by its weight within Black U.S. histories as well as its future impact in Japan. He announced to Johnson, "To attempt such a difficult work with my limited knowledge, [would] be an insult not only to its author but to fo[u]rteen million American Negroes."[55] Music was the text tying Johnson to "fourteen million Negroes" and the best medium for this negotiation between the Black United States and Hikida's Japan. It is important to notice that Hikida's request was not for the establishment of an NAACP branch in Japan. The anthem excelled in areas that the formal NAACP did not; it embodied the organization, camaraderie, and political vision that one might expect of an NAACP chapter while also presenting the added advantages of easy transport and the dynamism of performance. Of all Johnson's achievements it was his accomplishments in music that served to resonate within and potentially mobilize alternative national and cultural imaginations.

Hikida's choice of Black music as his method of political translation underscores a unique negotiation of Japan's history of engagement with the West. Recognizing the exercise of ideological authority by the Western nations, Japan long kept a safe distance; prior to the opening of consular relations with the United States in 1854, Japan practiced a strict seclusion policy. The next one hundred years of Japan's history were marked by internal disputes and battles for power as well as aggressive expansion into surrounding nations. In the twenty years between 1895 and 1915, Japan's military boosted the country's reputation and colonial holdings; victories over China and Russia "not only extended its empire . . . but also vaulted [Japan] into the ranks of the world powers."[56]

The recession that followed the World War I economic boom witnessed widespread disorder; in 1919 alone, there were 497 labor disputes, coupled with hundreds of tenancy quarrels as well as anti-Japanese demonstrations held by students in Korea and China, while the U.S. Japanese Exclusion Act, which radically curtailed the numbers of Japanese immigrants to the West Coast, was instituted in 1924.[57] The worldwide economic Depression of 1929–30 "heightened demands that Japan abandon its unproductive policy of cooperation with the Western powers and act independently and forcefully in foreign affairs." The military again played a decisive role in this move away from diplomacy; state violence, political assassination, and a withdrawal from the United Nations were the symptoms of what the "Japanese regard as the phase of fascism in their country."[58] This oppressive military state exacerbated the conditions that would lead to Japanese participation in World War II and an exodus from the country of nearly 37,000 to the United States between 1920 and 1940.[59] It was at the very beginning of this turbulent period that Hikida traveled to the United States.

As Hikida and other Japanese men and women traveled west, Black Americans were traveling east. One of the contributing factors to the positive reception of the Japanese by Black people were the "first-person reports" offered by the Black intellectuals and reporters who maintained a healthy engagement with Japan in the first decades of the twentieth century.[60] Du Bois was a central interlocutor in this enterprise. "For more than three decades," writes Kearney, "his interpretations consistently sought out the positiveness in the policies of the government of Japan."[61] His documented perspectives must be understood as negotiated speech; he walked a political tightrope with regard to Japan, which in this period initiated intense domestic surveillance and violence as well as the invasion and occupation of neighboring nations. It is clear that Du Bois's celebration of Japan stemmed from his investment in a world without white rule; he consistently highlighted Japan's stature as the only Eastern nation to successfully and uncompromisingly reject the authority of the West. The treatment that he experienced during his travels in Japan—events facilitated in no small part by the ever-resourceful Hikida—was employed as evidence proving that there existed "a certain bond between the colored peoples because of world-wide prejudice."[62] Because of this "bond," Du Bois wrote that Black people should not only see themselves as aligned with Japan, but also join their efforts for global racial justice since they were the only colored nation powerful enough to topple white supremacy.

Du Bois's colleague James Weldon Johnson also engaged with Japan in his early days with the NAACP. At the end of World War I he joined the Japan Society, believing, like his solicitors, that "there is no question about the importance to the United States of good relations with Japan."[63] Ten years later he had more intimate contact with Japan and its culture. During the fall of 1929, he was part of a delegation headed for Kyoto under the banner of the American Council of the Institute of Pacific Relations (IPR), a nongovernmental organization founded in 1925 and interested in discussing relations between the nations of the Pacific Rim.[64] Largely composed of philanthropists and academics, this delegation represented the organization at the third biennial conference of the IPR. Aboard the steamship from Seattle, Johnson encountered strangers who expanded his understanding of Eastern Asia, but the personal acquaintances were simply companion to the visual encounters. Upon reaching the shore, Johnson was awestruck at the elaborate scene he viewed: "I judge there is no experience more fascinating for the American or European traveler than the first landing in Japan. Strange lands there are many, but I surmise that in none, other than Japan, is found such perfection of strangeness—strangeness which at once excites the sense of wonder and satisfies the sense of beauty." While Japan seemed unfamiliar from the sea, once on land Johnson received the type of reception he was accustomed to as a popular U.S. figure. After being surrounded by half a dozen Japanese reporters—"as enterprising and insistent as their New York or Chicago brothers could be"—he was interviewed and photographed. Almost immediately, he was asked about the Negro condition in the United States and the efforts of the NAACP, which led Johnson to remark, "[T]hey were surprisingly familiar with the aims and work of the organization."[65]

This familiarity and interest in the Negro condition was not an isolated event. While in Kyoto, Johnson continued to be recognized as a Negro American race leader. He was asked for autographs, original poems, and other memorabilia. The most significant requests took shape as entreaties for help. The conditions described in these pleas offer compelling accounts of the experiences and desires shared between the Black and Japanese communities. One such account came from Masao Kajimar of Shimonoseki City. In a letter to Johnson shortly following the IPR trip to Japan, Kajimar wrote,

> I am a Japanese boy—fifteen years old. I am a boy who express[es] agree-ment [with] your opinion—for the black race agitation. I have been deeply sympathise [sic] with them in their situation, on hearing. [sic]
>
> I am glad you came [to] Japan to attend the meeting. Because, vener-able Mr., I . . . put myself in your agitation. I think, to do so, is that I will extremely satisfied [sic], reason why[,] I am a Japanese. I pray that you make me associate with you, and you lead me to your agitation. If you admit my entreaty, I will do my best for your agitation.[66]

This appeal not only demonstrates knowledge of Johnson and his work for racial justice but also hints at the education and feelings of solidarity possessed by some members of the Japanese public with Black life and politics. While he maintained a focus on the Black American commu-nity, Johnson understood the necessity of using his political work and art to address the common state of all those abused by white oppres-sion.[67] Of his trip to Japan, he remarked, "[T]he truth that came home most directly to me was the universality of the race and color problem. Negroes in the United States are prone, and naturally, to believe that their problem is *the* problem. The fact is, there is a race and color prob-lem wherever the white man deals with darker races."[68] This "race and color problem," more famously described by the like-minded Du Bois as "the problem of the color line," proved more and more complicated as the Depression deepened and fascism gripped the world.[69]

Profits and Propaganda: The Limits of Cultural Exchange in the Expanse of War

The global backdrop of a threatened second world war infused the exchange between Johnson and Hikida with no uncertain amount of significance and urgency. Yet in advance of its eruption, it was the domestic context in the United States that provided the greatest potential for violence through the ongoing national efforts to squelch labor and Black radicalism. As cultural historian Robin Kelley impeccably documents in Birmingham, Alabama, the Depression brought to the fore extreme formations of formal and informal white vigilantism and violence. In its wake, Black resistance mounted and through a unique alchemy of ideology, auxiliaries, and tradition there developed an indigenous "culture of opposition" among Black working people.[70] Johnson's art helped to increase the reserve of cultural tools available to Black people nationally and, if Hikida was successful, internationally. This project of translation demonstrated the reach of Black cultural labor but also the bulwarks inhibiting its creative and political potential. As the anthem gained prominence, the music industry actually resisted Johnson's intentions for "Lift Ev'ry Voice and Sing," compelling unintended consequences for this act of Afro-Nippon solidarity.

In his letter to Johnson, Hikida was confident that "Lift Ev'ry Voice and Sing" would make a difference in Japan: "I do not know whether at the time you wrote the song [if] you actually for[e]saw the importance of it to the life of [the] American Negro today. I do feel . . . this translation of 'Lift Every Voice' into Japanese will bring a significant result in years to come."[71] In part, the success of the song would be its communicative effects beyond language and location. He reminded Johnson of the foundation for this association between the Black American and Japanese communities—the tie that transcends the boundaries of language and geography—the bonds of race, when he wrote, "I do not know how many languages the song is already translated [into], but I am sure this will be the first time to be translated into a l[a]nguage of a colored race."[72] As I discussed in this chapter's introduction, Hikida's was not the first translation, but his request was certainly distinct. Despite the miscommunication and misinformation that he acknowledged to exist between the two races, Hikida believed that "this translation will eventually contribute an important factor to create a sentiment and promote [an] understanding of [the] American Negro among [the] Japanese." He offered an illustration for this process should the translation move forward:

> During my trip to the South, many Negroes told me that they wished to
> make a trip to Japan—someday. I advised them to do so by all means—
> but not someday, at certain day [*sic*], say for instance, in 1940 when we
> will be the host to the Olympic game. Suppose you send some American
> Negro athletes to that game[,] which possibility is already proved, and
> many of you go to Japan, then, what better way can you think of to wel-
> come you there than by singing "Lift every Voice" in our native tongue?[73]

Johnson's reaction to the "perfection of strangeness" that awaited him
in Japan during his visit of 1929 surely would be no match for arriving
to such a welcome as Hikida described. After reminiscing on Johnson's
humble beginnings in Jacksonville, Hikida wondered, "Who dared to
have thought that that shanty building could [have] nurtured a soul
which would tie fo[u]rteen million souls together? And at the one-
thirds mark of the present century, by acc[i]dent, or by providence if
you call, going to tie these souls to seventy-million Asiatics?"[74] This was
the challenge that Hikida placed in front of Johnson at the end of his
letter. Would Johnson, through "Lift Ev'ry Voice and Sing," take up the
mantle of a pan-Afro, Japanese public? Unfortunately, Johnson alone
could not decide the answer to that question. Hikida's vision of Afro-
Japanese solidarity would face another moment of jeopardy as the
logistics of the enterprise became increasingly arduous in America.

In addition to his own concerns with the translation, Hikida faced
an uphill battle with the Edward B. Marks Music Company, the publisher of "Lift Ev'ry Voice and Sing." Starting with their copyright at the
turn of the century, the Marks Company kept close reigns on the piece,
often denying the most elementary of requests. By 1933, dozens, if not
hundreds, of individuals and groups were turned away by the Marks
Company. From requests to print the hymn in Sunday school bulle-
tins to small school performances, the company worked to protect its
interests. John Irwin, associate at the *Epworth Herald* of Chicago, hoped
to use "Lift" in a hymnal for the organization's summer camp. After
contacting the Marks Company in 1932, he wrote to Johnson, "[W]e
were informed that they did not grant to anyone the right to publish
and print the words or music, in whole or in part of any of their copy-
righted publications." Irwin then stated a compelling case for easing
the permission rights: "It seems to us that such a policy for handling

this splendid song is a very great limitation of its possible usefulness. To have groups of young people all over the country singing this great song ought to be one way of helping them to share the aspirations of the Negro race."[75] Johnson responded to Irwin in agreement but conceded that the "refusal to grant you permission is not by any means unique. A great many applications for permission to reprint the hymn have been received within the last ten or fifteen years, but the publishers, feeling that it would reduce the sales of the hymn in the form in which they publish it, have consistently refused."[76]

The copyright practices of the Marks Company exposed the gulf that existed between Johnson's intentions for the song and the profit imperatives of the music business. "Lift Ev'ry Voice and Sing" was, by the time of this correspondence, set apart within Johnson's repertoire, and its unique identity as an anthem made it a "valuable piece of property," not because of its potential to generate income (as the Marks Company imagined) but instead because it promoted the noblest aspirations of Johnson and the NAACP: interracial cooperation, democracy, and justice.[77] To materialize "Lift" as "property" exposed it to the whims of the marketplace, an already tortured and precarious location for goods and services during the Depression, especially those produced by and for Black people. This designation also assumes ownership, whether to the Marks Company or to James Weldon and J. Rosamond Johnson. As the performance of "Lift Ev'ry Voice and Sing" by Black communities and its adoption by the NAACP shows, neither of these claims to ownership was entirely legitimate, nor was either complete.

Johnson was again contacted for reprint rights over the same hymnal project discussed by Irwin. Johnson confessed to Marks that "I would hardly give it consideration except for the fact that it comes from a man of such wide influence, Mr. Will W. Alexander, Executive Director of the Commission on Interracial Cooperation in Atlanta." Writing on behalf of Irwin, Alexander hoped to use his reputation to bring about a different resolution. Johnson now took a more proactive approach with the Marks Company and outlined the stakes associated with this particular reprint: "It may be worthwhile considering that this would be a step toward introducing the anthem among white people in the South, something which as yet has not been done, and that such a step may lead to a further nationalization of the song."[78] The effects outlined here by Johnson are significant. An adoption of the anthem by the white South could have significantly boosted the effectiveness and popularity of not only the authors and publisher but also the NAACP and its progressive platform for racial justice. The organization was still struggling in the South, and the shared cultural practice of performance through "Lift Ev'ry Voice and Sing" had the potential to dramatically increase the size of the organization and its ability to work interracially.

While championing the practical considerations of this request, Johnson's letter to Marks also provocatively suggests the role of cultural production within nation formation; he acknowledged that the song had multiple uses and that the work of "Lift Ev'ry Voice and Sing" was exponentially larger than its service to the NAACP—if given the opportunity, the anthem could represent the nation. This comment, taken alongside the earlier discussed evocations offered by Ovington and Wise, begins to demonstrate how centrally configured this text was within Black life and culture. To imagine that "Lift Ev'ry Voice and Sing" could be successfully nationalized speaks to Johnson's vision for a principled U.S. political culture based in the histories, struggles, and sounds of the African descended. Unfortunately his enthusiasm was not contagious. In a statement dripping with paternalism, Marks replied, "While I have carefully read Mr. Alexander's letter and just as carefully taken into consideration your recommendation, I regret to state that I do not consider it to the best interests of either Rosamond, yourself or myself to grant this permission." Exposing the true foundation of his rebuttal, Marks noted, "[W]hat people receive for nothing, they will not purchase."[79] This tension between doing the work of racial justice and adhering to the mandates of the music industry continued to plague "Lift Ev'ry Voice and Sing."

Possibly expecting more of the same from the Marks Company, Johnson early on encouraged Hikida to contact the Marks Company about the translation, and he did as well. On November 1, 1933, Johnson wrote to Marks, "I have written to Mr. Yasuichi Hikida, who lives at Bedford Hills, New York, and advised him that he had better write to you and make an appointment and then come down to the city and talk this matter over. I still think that we can afford to be easy in the matter and facilitate them as much as we can while protecting our own rights in placing the hymn before the Japanese nation."[80] Again, Johnson was forthright about his position on the issue—Hikida's situation should be afforded ease. His genuine excitement for the project was earlier articulated to Hikida when he wrote, "I am impressed by the plan and enthusiastic about it" despite the "stupendous task involved."[81] In his correspondence with Marks, however, Johnson was careful to balance his animation with a nod to the desires of the company. Hikida too worked diligently to remove any extra obstacles to the task of translating "Lift Ev'ry Voice and Sing." He was proactive, contacting the Library of Congress about musical reproduction rights and also sharing with the Marks Music Company a copy of the international copyright agreement between the United States and Japan. It appears as though his work paid off: by the end of 1933, the process had moved forward. Whether Marks's decision to give the go-ahead was tied to a profit motive or other reasons is unclear. Whatever the reason, Johnson was confident that Marks "is as desirous as I am of seeing the hymn published and used in Japan."[82]

The interaction between Johnson and Hikida was scant in the years following this exchange over the anthem. There was no communication between the two men in 1934. In 1935 Hikida wrote to Johnson with the primary interest of gaining his opinion on his new manuscript titled "The Canary Looks at the Crow," a report on the Black American condition through the eyes of the Japanese. While the manuscript gained little traction with publishers, something within it encouraged Johnson to comment, "I do not consider that Japan needs to make a defense, and certainly she needs no apology to be made for her."[83] This statement echoes the sentiments of other Black Americans who felt camaraderie with the colored nation, although it also hints at Japan's increasingly embattled position in the lead up to World War II. Japan's continued annexation of Korea heightened what was an already precarious balance in Japanese rhetoric between global racial solidarity and virulent nationalism. While he may have discussed these political maneuvers with Johnson, the literature between the two men shows that Hikida was primarily invested in bringing to evidence the translation. His inquiry with Johnson in December 1935 included a note that read: "I just heard today from home that the translation of LIFT EVERY VOICE AND SING will be published in the January issue of the best magazine in [the] Japanese musical world."[84] Quite enthusiastic about the prospect, Hikida promised to avail Johnson of the magazine's arrival. After lamenting the absence of the magazine in other correspondence, Hikida eventually stopped mentioning it altogether, and it faded from the historical record without having made its way to the United States.

Although Johnson never saw the finished product published in Japan, the translation was eventually realized. In September 1936 *Ongaku Sekai* (Music World) published "The World of Black People and The World of White People from the Perspective of Yellow People: Introduction of National Negro Anthem," by Yonezo Hirayama, the pen name of Yasuichi Hikida. The article included an image, a copy of the sheet music with roman lettering produced by Koh Yuki, and introductory remarks by Hikida.[85] The first feature of the article that strikes the reader is the illustration. On the right-hand side of the title page is a hand-drawn minstrel character that runs nearly half the length of the page. Sporting a top hat, signature blackface distinguished by exaggerated light lips, and long shirt and pants, the figure is posed next to the text in an angular marionette position (see Figure 2.1). It is not clear if Hikida or the publisher decided to include this image. In either case it is shorthand that orients the reader toward some engagement with blackness. The ready-made trope of the black minstrel, sans comment or critique, offered easy associations between the Black body and performance, a perilous cohabitation when filtered through the imagery and stereotypes grown from minstrelsy. As Eric Lott describes, "[B]lackface allowed the minstrel to play in the fantasy and fears of blackness while at the same time having complete control over them."[86] The international success of Al Jolson's 1927 film *The Jazz Singer*, in which he praised his "Mammy" in blackface, enlivened the lingering ghosts of minstrelsy for a Depression-era audience. The damaging effects of this performance were replicated in the *Ongaku Sekai* translation, which was originally meant to advance and "promote [an] understanding of [the] American Negro among [the] Japanese." It is not clear if the minstrel who adorned the article's title page is a white man in blackface or a Black man in blackface, a critical distinction that is made no more clear by Hikida's commentary.

Hikida begins his introduction with a discussion of "proletarian literature" in the United States. Citing authors such as Theodore Dreiser, William Faulkner, and Upton Sinclair, Hikida argues that the

Figure 2.1.

Detail of illustration from
Ongaku Sekai (Music World),
September 1936, p. 91. Source:
Courtesy of the College of Music
at the Library of Tokyo, Tokyo,
Japan

contemporary works of the 1930s revealed "the exploitation and persecution of Negro workers by white capitalists in the Southern state[s]."
At this moment he mentions the only Black author in his catalogue,
NAACP leader Walter White, whose novel *The Fire in the Flint* details
southern lynchings. Hikida's relationship to Black people and their
cultural productions is used within the text to prove his authenticity and authority: "I have been staying in [the] U.S. for more than ten
years . . . studying Negro literature. I translated Mr. Walter White's *The
Fire in the Flint* in order to introduce him to Japan." His next venture in
this arena was the publication of "Lift Ev'ry Voice and Sing," which he
pursued "in order to give good reference of the study of Negro literature and music in Japan."[87]

The histories and cultures of the African descended in the United
States are woefully absented from Hikida's introduction; instead he

chose to substitute vague descriptions of emotion for substance. He wrote, "When you read Negro literature or sing Jazz [sic], you have to remember one thing. If you do not know the lives of Negroes and understand how and why they expose their emotions, you will not be able to write about nor sing about the naked truth of Negroes' lives."[88] His emphasis on a three-dimensional engagement with Black communities is well warranted, yet his introduction does nothing to help his largely urban Japanese audience understand the "lives of Negroes," nor does it entirely situate "Lift Ev'ry Voice and Sing" as the opportunity for the magazine's readers to do so. It is only in his description of the anthem in performance that the reader receives a sense of the power of this music: "When Negroes sing this National Anthem, [they] are in a trance, and are dreaming of a free country in a profundity, they truly find solace in the song."[89] It is significant that Hikida maintains the identity of "Lift" as a national anthem. It highlights for his Japanese audience the importance of the text to Black Americans and their music traditions but also implicitly registers the song as a negotiation of the nation's established symbols and, by extension, its performances of unity.

The final statement within Hikida's text ties his Japanese audience to the possibilities held within "Lift Ev'ry Voice and Sing"; he wrote, "If the Japanese people, who is the leading nation of Asia, understand and sing the National Negro Hymn, thirteen million American Negroes will see it as an epoch-making event and have great joy."[90] Why a performance of "Lift" by the Japanese would be "epoch-making" for American Negroes is never articulated, but the possibility engendered by that vision draws together two differently embattled communities through a song that had the potential to facilitate a cross-cultural exchange with powerful repercussions for political solidarities in a decolonizing world.

Within a few years of his last letter to Johnson, Hikida had the opportunity to see and manipulate the effects of "Utae Takaru Jiyu no Uta" in Japan.[91] In the wake of the 1941 attack on Pearl Harbor, Japanese nationals within the U.S. mainland were interned. At the time of his detention, Hikida was said to have "hundreds of pounds" of information on Black Americans in his possession.[92] This evidence no doubt facilitated his swift departure from the United States. Intelligence gathering on this scale caused alarm for the U.S. government because it was a technique of cross-racial leftist organizing; less than a decade earlier, interracial organizers with the Pacific Movement of the Eastern World also were described following their arrest as having "suitcases filled with records of lynching incidents, newspaper clippings concerning the Scottsboro case, and other literature."[93] Similar items likely composed the many pounds found on Hikida. While he was forcibly removed from the site of his research, his work in the United States would not be in vain; he went back to Japan and became the authority in Afro-Japanese relations. The title was well deserved; "perhaps no Japanese worked more diligently [than Hikida] to foster a bridge of understanding between the people of Japan and American blacks."[94]

During the War effort in Japan, Hikida was responsible for significant intelligence gathering including the publication of *Senji Kokujin Kosaku* (Wartime Negro Propaganda Operations) in January 1943.[95] His distrust of "the filter of a white media" encouraged him to direct the Black propaganda machine during the war, which he used to great effect.[96] Playing on the racial divisions exacerbated by the failures of U.S. democracy, Japanese propagandists differently used race as a way to divide and conquer during the War. As Joel Berreman described in 1948,

> The American treatment of colored peoples was kept continually in front of us. Every discriminatory practice in the armed forces, in defense industries, in social and economic relations, was seized upon [by the Japanese]. . . . Discriminatory laws against Negroes, Orientals, and Mexicans were repeatedly cited, as well as imperialistic practices of the Western powers throughout the world. In contrast with the Allies, Japan was pictured as champion of all colored races, fighting to free them from white domination and enslavement.[97]

International reporting from Tokyo of the 1942 Detroit race rebellion that developed in response to the desegregation of the Sojourner Truth Projects as well as the consistent attention paid to the violence and discrimination facing Black service men provided compelling evidence to support the Japanese assertion that Americans could never be purveyors of freedom as they claimed.[98] This position was supported by the NAACP, which argued, "a Jim Crow army cannot fight for a free world."[99]

The Japanese propaganda used in response to the Allies was often as deceiving and exaggerated as any coming out of Washington or London, yet Japanese efforts fundamentally changed the course of imperialism in the twentieth century. Historian Gerald Horne argues that wartime Japanese propaganda forced the Allies, namely the United States and Britain, to reconsider and revamp their efforts among their domestic populations and colonial holdings; Japan's position as an Axis enemy power that defined itself as the champion of the colored race hastened the critique of and retreat from white supremacy in the United States and British Empire.[100] This dismantlement was the project that Hikida shared with his comrades in the United States during the Depression and that which returned with him to Japan. He participated in the search for a new racial reality, a solidarity that might be communicated across difference and he found his method through "Lift Ev'ry Voice and Sing."

Considering Hikida's labor in translating and publishing the anthem, it is not a stretch to imagine that it may have been a part of Japanese war propaganda. Had the nearly 200,000 Black soldiers who served in the Pacific theater of operations heard and/or used "Lift Ev'ry Voice and Sing," they would have held company with other Black GIs around the world. World War II veteran and former U.S. senator Ed Brooke narrates his experience of "Lift Ev'ry Voice and Sing" in tandem with his service:

> When I finished high school and moved on to Howard University, I continued to sing and hear "Lift Every Voice and Sing" at small and large gatherings on and off campus. The stirring words of James Weldon Johnson and the soul-gripping music of his brother J. Rosamond Johnson stayed with me when I served with the brave enlisted men and officers of the Negro 366th Infantry Combat Regiment in Italy fighting in World War II in a segregated U.S. Army to preserve world freedom and liberty. When the morale of our troops was low, as it often was, we sang our Negro National Anthem. It sustained us and helped us to carry on.[101]

The morale fostered among the Black soldiers through the singing of "[their] Negro National Anthem" was surely experienced by other soldiers during wartime, and it may have been facilitated by the efforts of the Japanese. The vision that Hikida expressed to James Weldon Johnson in 1933, which included a welcome for Black women and men through the singing of "Lift Ev'ry Voice and Sing" in Japanese, was but a prelude to the possible reality of a radio broadcast of the Negro National Anthem over "enemy" airwaves.

It may never be known whether "Lift Ev'ry Voice and Sing" was used in Japan's wartime broadcasts, but the legacies of Afro-Asian solidarities advanced by Johnson, Hikida, and others are pronounced.[102] When World War II ended and the Axis coalition dissolved, these Afro-Asian political alliances were revived and continued to link African Americans and the "darker nations" in collective response to the hegemony of the white West.[103] A conspicuous and resonant narrative of political ingenuity through music facilitated these coalitions, growing the base and ushering in new techniques of performance and solidarity.

* * *

The transnational impulse imbedded within the Johnson-Hikida exchange exploded post–World War II as the NAACP grew its legal defense division and its anthem "Lift Ev'ry Voice and Sing" continued to be performed in the United States by actors whose coalitions looked abroad for encouragement and inspiration. With a level of urgency and organization previously unknown, the postwar world was ripe for the dismantling of state-sponsored oppressions as the colonized and disenfranchised demanded their rightful access to the practices of democracy resolutely espoused by their native and adoptive lands and fortified through war. The dawning of decolonization in Africa and elsewhere led to the increased movement of Black men and women from colonial holdings to the metropole and invited dense communication networks, constitutive of texts both written and performed. From the ashes of violence and in the wake of new technologies of labor and surveillance emerged an anthem that forsook the rigidity of institutionalization in order to follow these populations and represent them in locations around the world. The singular talents of the anthem's vocalist, combined with the strategies and struggles of Black and laboring people throughout the Atlantic, constructed and mobilized a new front in global productions of justice.

3

Songs of Free Men

The Sound Migrations of "Ol' Man River"

I'll sing . . . all over this great land until my people are free.
—Paul Robeson

"We know about this struggle," wrote Paul Robeson. His comments, written during World War II, brought into stark relief the conditions that threatened the practice of freedom on a global scale, and he articulated them through a communal language ("we") balanced by his own experiences and knowledges: "We know what oppression means. We have all experienced it. I was in Spain. I saw the people's struggle against Fascism. I was in Germany. I know that Hitler would make me a slave forever."[1] This danger, palpable at the time of his writing, stirred him to action. In addition to writing, he spoke and performed at a number of events in support of GIs that also addressed the concurrent issue of civil rights. In 1942, he appeared at "Labor Salutes the Armed Forces," at the Central Park Mall in New York City. Sponsored by the Congress of Industrial Organizations (CIO), the program included tributes to various divisions of the U.S. Armed Forces, "the interned workers," China, the Soviet Union, and "the fighting French."[2]

The threat of fascism during World War II was enough to mobilize the most ardent of peacemakers, including Robeson, who traveled in order to commune with the soldiers in the European theater of operations. As he mentioned in his article, he was in Spain working alongside the Loyalists and in Germany singing for U.S. soldiers. In 1945 he, along with his musical partner and accompanist Lawrence Brown, embarked on a tour with the newly established United Service Organizations (USO). According to a 1946 souvenir book, "The day after his arrival he gave his first concert, and by plane and staff car squeezed in 32 appearances in Germany, Czechoslovakia and France. He was greeted by some of the largest GI audiences ever assembled in this theatre, as his programs appealed specially to soldiers. Some of the towns visited were Munich, Nuremberg, Berchtesgaden, Garminsch, Pilsen." This whirlwind tour facilitated an already established presence and reputation in Europe, and it was, as always, music that facilitated the connection. His large audiences registered their approval in city after city with the "favorite GI songs prov[ing] to be 'Water Boy' and 'Ole Man River.'"

The use of this last song by Robeson throughout his career charts his growth as a politically oriented artist and citizen of the world. Beginning with his 1928 run in the musical *Show Boat* to the end of his life, Robeson infused the song with the contemporary currents and political significance of the struggles for civil rights and self-determination in the workplace. He stands among a cohort of giants whose use of culture distinguished them in the eyes of those whose challenges they represented on the stage and screen. "Ol' Man River" was the clarion call in Robeson's crusade for civil and human rights, becoming his signature performance text within social movements ranging from Wales to Indonesia. In his strategic employment of this song in response to myriad conditions of oppression, Robeson made "Ol' Man River" an anthem and became a leader and mentor within a post-Depression era of musician activism. By speaking and singing in universal cadences, Robeson conjoined the issues of race, labor, and internationalism in the vibrant political culture of the Black Popular Front in the 1940s and 1950s and used performance to defy the geographical and political borders of U.S. imperialism and influence.

Continuity and Change: "Ol' Man River" and the Black Folk Canon

Robeson's first interaction with "Ol' Man River" was through his performance in the musical *Show Boat*, yet his relationship with the musical that made him a star was a tortured one. *Show Boat*, based on the wildly popular novel of the same name, tells the story of a showboat on the Mississippi River in the late nineteenth and early twentieth centuries. Main characters include showboat captain Andy Hawkes, his puritanical wife Parthenia Hawkes, and their rambunctious and later starlet daughter Magnolia (Hawkes) Ravenal. The supporting cast is made up primarily of showboat entertainers and workers, including the Black kitchen duo Joe and Queenie.[3] When Robeson was offered the part of Joe in the original run of the musical in 1927, he declined, citing scheduling conflicts. "Ol' Man River," the musical's soon-to-be standout hit, was dedicated to Robeson by composer Jerome Kern, which made his pass on the part even more pronounced. As theater scholar Scott McMillin documents, the earliest known script for the musical entirely centered on Robeson as actor, singer, and personality, making his withdrawal from the role the precursor to radical changes within the show.[4] *Show Boat*, however, went on to be a huge Broadway success with Jules Bledsoe, the prominent Black baritone, in the role. Despite a well-received performance, Bledsoe was passed over in the European tour. When the production moved to London in 1928, producer Florenz Ziegfeld again offered Robeson the role, which he accepted. He won over London director Alfred Butt when he agreed to sing "Ol' Man River" a total of three times during the performance instead of the original one. This small role was described by his wife Eslanda Goode Robeson as "ridiculously easy," yet she saw the potential in the "song hit of the show," and so did Robeson.[5] He wrote to his musical partner Lawrence Brown that "I sing only one song—'Ol' Man River,' but it runs through the show and I get three good spots for it. I'll get a lot of publicity, and it might make London concerts easy."[6]

Other components of the musical beyond Robeson and his early fame as a singer served to make the musical a success. *Show Boat* is recognized as a production that changed the way that patrons viewed musicals. According to musicologist Geoffrey Block, "Before *Show Boat* and for a long time thereafter operettas were generally set in exotic locations filled with people most audiences were not likely to meet in everyday life." *Show Boat*'s "early Americana . . . began to replace fictitious European places as suitable locales."[7] The locale used in the musical was the mysterious and romantic Mississippi River, a construction of *Show Boat* novelist Edna Ferber. Ferber was born and raised in the North, and her description of the southern United States and its people was largely based on prominent racial and class distinctions as well as its history of slavery, which was dramatized in numerous novels of the time including *The Man in Gray* (1921), by Thomas Dixon.[8] Block's assertion of the importance of location is supported by the musical—using the U.S. South as the site for the novel and musical made it accessible to a broad population who might feel out of touch with the settings in popular European musical theater. The fascination with slavery as a condition of the Black United States is palpable throughout *Show Boat*. Cultural studies scholar Hazel Carby argues that "slavery haunts the literary imagination because its material conditions and social relations are frequently reproduced in fiction as historically dynamic; they continue to influence society long after emancipation. The economic and social system of slavery is thus a prehistory . . . a past social condition that can explain contemporary phenomena."[9] Whether in service of eradicating contemporary racial inequalities or further entrenching them, this literature continued to engage the U.S. public in slavery and its effects. Both the novel and musical add to the literature as they demonstrate the social depravity of the Black United States in a way that freezes Black subjects in time—a liminal sociopolitical space within the temporality of the novel, which spans fifty years, from the 1870s to 1920s.

Despite Ferber's argument that "'Show Boat' is neither history nor biography, but fiction," its depictions of Black people were based in comfortable associations that offer an assumption of fact for the reader through their familiarity.[10] Indeed, Ferber "wrote badly about black people";[11] for example, her imagination ran amok as she described the characteristics of a Black kitchen worker: "A simple, ignorant soul, the black man, and a somewhat savage." She continues with a phenotypic description of the man as he responds to the captain's wife in anger: "A red light seemed to leap then from the big Negro's eyeballs. His lips parted in a kind of savage and mirthless grin, so that you saw his great square gleaming teeth and the blue gums above them. Quick as a panther he reached down with one great paw."[12] The "big eyeballs" and "gleaming teeth" of this Black man-beast are recognizable because they are drawn directly from the minstrel stage, a practice very much alive in U.S. theater in the period. By the time of the musical *Show Boat*, it was not only white actors who performed within this genre of blackness—Black musicians and actors began their own blackface reviews. Artists like Bert Williams and Bill "Bojangles" Robinson performed and made their fortunes under cover of burnt cork.[13] Even as a politicized Black musical theater tradition developed on Broadway through the efforts of James Weldon Johnson and others—most prominently with the 1921 production *Shuffle Along* in which Robeson played a small role—minstrelsy and its commodity vestiges continued to pervade popular culture on stage.

The notion that Black people are inherently and indiscriminately musical offers another prominent stock characterization in Ferber's novel, which, in part, made its transition to the musical stage an easy one. Numerous instances describe "the mellow plaintive voices of Negroes singing on the levees and in cabin doorways as the boat swept by." Magnolia in particular seems to be fascinated with Black people due to their musical prowess. She "learned to strut and shuffle and back-and-wing from the Negroes whose black faces dotted the boards of the southern wharves as thickly as grace notes sprinkle a bar of lively music."[14] But it was in her relationship with Joe that she found the most satisfaction because it was from him that she learned the spirituals, the songs that made her stardom possible. Scholar Bethany Wood argues that the musical erases the gender critique of Ferber's novel, especially through the character of Magnolia, who balances Victorian tradition with modern perspectives, thereby "represent[ing] Ferber's ideal of American womanhood."[15] While Wood convincingly details instances of gender challenge embedded within the novel, she fails to acknowledge how that ideal is intimately (although, perhaps, unwittingly) formed by Black culture (especially music) in both the novel and musical. Joe is the muse for Magnolia's performances: "Jo[e], the charming and shiftless, would be singing for her one of the Negro plantation songs, wistful with longing and pain; the folk songs of a wronged race, later to come into a blaze of popularity as spirituals."[16] The "later" period that Ferber mentioned was upon her as the book was published, and it was Paul Robeson who most dramatically made that cultural revolution viable. His 1925 concert tours with Lawrence Brown were solely composed of Negro spirituals. The connectedness of the text with the reality that Robeson offered unfortunately ended there. The racial dogmas of the novel continued in its translation to a musical as both relied on comfortable associations (of the U.S. and Black South) to induce a shared sense of history—a national unifying text lived over and through the bodies of Black people.

A 1928 recording of "Ol' Man River" exhibits a number of the pejorative constructions and performative obstacles within the song. Beginning with a signal of the old South through a banjo introduction, the song then brings in an animated orchestral accompaniment for Robeson's *moderato* vocal line, which would later be adjusted in his solo performances. He sings the original Hammerstein lyrics that, within the context of this recording, are not as pronounced due to their quickened pace. There is an additional vocal line provided by a male singer with a slight voice, who adds the lyrics, "Don't look up and don't look down / You don't dares make da white boss frown / Bend your knees and bow your head / and pull dat rope until you're dead." This labor invective is offered by a voice that is peripheral to the staging that privileges Robeson, making his soundings less recognizable, sonorous, and valid. Any critique within the production therefore collapsed through competing narratives and the levity of accompaniment provided by the Paul Whiteman Orchestra. Whiteman, whose orchestra was composed exclusively of white musicians, considered himself the "King of Jazz" in this period. His role in this production of "Ol' Man River" added a whole new dimension of meaning to the lyric, "Niggers all work while de white folks play."[17]

Robeson's concerts prior to 1927 stand in stark contrast to his role as Joe. While this reality caused him conflict, it was great boon for the production. A reviewer of a solo concert offered one year prior to his run of *Show Boat* asserted Robeson's quality as a performer when the reviewer stated, "His voice is exceptional for its racial quality, which means a lusciousness rarely to be found outside the throats of colored men and women. Added to his vocal qualifications, he has a fine intelligence and a deep understanding of the songs he is giving, this last something that is so often lacking in singers who try to give the spirituals."[18] In addition to his repertoire, it was the tone and quality of Robeson's voice that distinguished him as a performer, marking him as distinct within a cacophonous performance industry. As I will discuss in more detail later, his voice as a technology developed into a powerful tool within his later political agenda. His growing artistic prominence in the moment of *Show Boat*'s ascendance brought an identifiable dignity to the role of Joe that was otherwise absent. The language used in the show to describe the Black community not only was offensive but also subscribed to a system of dialect that racially isolated the Black characters in the show. Dialect in the text of "Ol' Man River," written by Oscar Hammerstein II, is represented throughout the song. The first line of the song reads,

> Dere's an ol' man called de Mississippi, Dat's de ol' man dat I'd
>   like to be.

The dialect demonstrates a particular version of blackness out of sync with the "fine intelligence" of Robeson, a Phi Beta Kappa scholar at Rutgers University and Columbia Law School graduate. Hammerstein's dialect not only distinguishes Black from white in the musical but also serves to contain the Black characters in their *natural* state as uneducated and simple laborers and confidants.

The musical composition offers no haven from the false constructions of blackness in the text. Hammerstein's frequent collaborator, Jerome Kern, was the song's composer and similarly used sonic tricks to identify Joe in the musical. "Ol' Man River" is written in the key of C major (CM); with no accidentals (flats, sharps, and naturals), it is the least complicated key for the student of music because it requires recognition of minimal notation and is limited to only the white keys of the piano. All of Joe's musical entries are in this key, marking Joe phonically and making him the human equivalent of the unadorned CM key—plain and bare. The composition changes in measures 25 to 33 to a solid chord accompaniment with prevalent augmented chords leading the ear to anticipate the tonic (I). The lyrics of this section offer listeners their only insight into Joe's anger at his condition:

> You and me, we sweat an' strain, Body all achin' an' racked wid'
>   pain.
> "Tote that barge!" "Lift dat bale!" Git a little drunk An' you
>   land in jail.[19]

The preponderance of accidentals in this section highlights its difference in purpose for the character and feel for the audience, yet Joe's righteous indignation would not last. Beyond these two lines, the CM/I returns and so does Joe's apathy. He settles back into his position of defeat, quietly acknowledging his personal fears and his admiration for the carelessness and blissful ignorance of old man river. This is what the listener has been waiting for: the I and the return of Joe to a state of wretchedness.

Robeson's uneasiness with the musical did not dissipate during his run with the show. With such wide exposure and so many questions circulating around his person—both personally and professionally—Robeson made the decision to use his platform to continue his tradition of individual concerts. These performances gave him the opportunity to continue spreading the rich art of the spirituals that served as crucial counterpoints to the representations of blackness in *Show Boat*. In this endeavor he would need his good friend and collaborator Lawrence Brown. Brown became aware of Robeson's frustrations with the musical early on. Eslanda wrote to Brown that "Paul is sick to death of 'Show Boat' and will kick up his heels with glee when its [*sic*] over."[20] The monotony of the role undoubtedly contributed to his frustrations with the musical. In this situation, Robeson's respite became the concert stage. The tours that followed Brown's arrival in London caused a stir and added to the duo's popularity, leading one reviewer to comment that Robeson was "the finest musical instrument wrought by nature in our time."[21] It was the spirituals alongside "Ol' Man River" that best exhibited his talents. During his tour, Robeson continued his reliance on Negro spirituals in concert but added a group of "Plantation Songs" inclusive of a Stephen Foster set: "Poor Old Joe," "My Old Kentucky Home," and "Old Folks at Home."[22] Compositionally and culturally, this set exists in distinction to the pieces composed by Brown and Harry T. Burleigh, Black composers and arrangers often used by Robeson in concert. It also falls outside of the critical anthologies of spirituals designed and published by James Weldon and J. Rosamond Johnson during the 1920s. The inclusion of Foster in Robeson's concert programs for this period gives some indication of the slippery terms under which spirituals were defined.

In a December 1931 performance at Royal Albert Hall in London, Robeson sang "Were You There" by composer/arranger Harry T. Burleigh, "Goin' to Ride up in de Chariot" and "Steal Away," arranged by Brown, and finally "Ol' Man River" by Kern.[23] The inclusion of "Ol' Man

River" in the set of spirituals perpetuated the common belief that it was indeed a Negro spiritual. Despite a superficial effort, this "pseudo-spiritual" was not based in the oral and musical traditions of Black America like the work of Burleigh and Brown.[24] Burleigh, who is often acknowledged as the leading composer/arranger of Negro spirituals, offered this definition of the form:

> The Plantation Songs known as "Spirituals" are the spontaneous outbursts of intense religious fervour, and had their origin chiefly in Camp meetings, Revivals, and other religious exercises. They were never "composed," but sprang into life ready-made, from the white heat of religious fervour during some protracted meeting in camp or church, as the simple ecstatic utterance of wholly untutored minds, and are practically the only music in America which meets the scientific definition of Folk Song. It is a serious misconception of their meaning and value to treat them as "Minstrel" Songs. Their worth is weakened unless they are done impressively, for through all these songs there breathes a hope, a faith in the ultimate justice and brotherhood of man. The cadences of sorrow invariably turn to joy, and the message is ever manifest that eventually deliverance from all that hinders and oppresses the soul will come, and man—every man, will be free.[25]

In this description, Burleigh outlines the expressive quality and social consequence of the spirituals. The intensity and "fervour" that he notes as hallmarks of the music contradict the staid process by which "Ol' Man River" came into being. It is considered an art piece, composed (not arranged) by a popular songwriter. The message of the spirituals, which offer "faith in the ultimate justice and brotherhood of man" with "cadences of sorrow [which] invariably turn to joy," are nowhere present in Hammerstein's lyrics. Joe ends the song as despised and broken as he began—a victim of an inescapable cycle of disappointment and defeat.

It is the message of eventual deliverance and freedom that distinguishes Robeson's later repertoire from this early hodgepodge of pieces. Brown contributed significantly to this change as well as the development of the spirituals canon. He was particularly invested in fieldwork, often engaging in close contact with rural Black populations in the South, and he built his repertoire of arranged spirituals from this research. Robeson credits Brown with convincing him that "our music—Negro music of African and American derivation—was in the tradition of the world's great folk music."[26] Robeson indeed rebelled against the oft-claimed "childish simplicity" of the spirituals by arguing their place within the global folk canon.[27] Robeson and Brown's budding internationalism through the world's folk music makes their choice of a spirituals set inclusive of Kern contradictory, socially and phonically. Robeson was a rigorous student of music who understood composition and the ways that varying musics fit together across genre and culture. He later wrote, "Continued study and research into the origins of the folk music of various peoples in many parts of the world revealed that there is a world body—a universal body—of folk music based upon a universal pentatonic (five tone) scale."[28] This tonality stands in stark contrast to the CM key of "Ol' Man River." The four songs in combination were odd bed fellows; not only was "Ol' Man River" missing the history and sacred substance of the Negro spirituals, but it was radically different in tonal formation from the great canon of folk music of which Robeson was a champion.

It is a provocative exercise to imagine that Robeson performed "Ol' Man River" along with the spirituals set in order to highlight its deficiency. A reporter for the *Montreal Daily Star* wrote in 1935 that Paul Robeson's voice "brought out all that was good in the *imitation* songs—'Old Man River,'—the best of them . . . but it showed up their inferiority to the real thing."[29] This reporter noticed the distinct differences between the songs, going so far as to call "Ol' Man River" an "imitation." The song was described by another reporter in Northern Ireland as of "suspect quality," and the shortcomings of "Ol' Man River" in style and message would soon encourage Robeson to rethink its importance to his repertoire.[30] By the time of the film version of *Show Boat*, "Ol' Man River" had faded from the documentation of Robeson's individual performances; between 1936 and 1940, it is absent from his concert programs.[31] This does not mean that it was not performed. The song was still his trademark in many ways; one reporter highlighted its significance by writing that "Ol' Man River" is "the song that to Robeson is what the prelude is to Rachmaninov."[32] While vanishing from the written program, the song often appeared as an encore. This adjustment represents a considerable shift in his performance strategy. One concert account reported the dramatic effects of a Robeson program absent "Ol' Man River": "So we come to that shrill treble voice in the gallery which expressed the wish of other members of the fairly large audience—a cosmopolitan one, by the way, with many in formal attire—when it requested 'Old Man River.'"[33] This demand would continue throughout Robeson's career. In 1942, a woman identifying herself as Kissye left a handwritten note on the back of his concert program that read, "Paul dear- Every one [sic] wants 'Old Man River.'"[34] As I will discuss, the absence left by "Ol' Man River" on the program allowed Robeson to expand his concert repertoire alongside his revolutionary political vision.

As the amendment in the program suggests, Robeson's investment in the song changed over time. Removing it from the official program allowed Robeson the flexibility to decide whether to perform the song or not as the audience and circumstance dictated. This experimentation in his programming coincided with his rising investment and consciousness in politics and world affairs. Black audiences in particular facilitated the change in Robeson's approach to the song; many Black patrons and reviewers of *Show Boat* were understandably upset with "Ol' Man River," mounting protest in printed venues well past the musical's twentieth anniversary.[35] Journalist and public intellectual J. A. Rogers reported on the London performance for the Black newspaper *Amsterdam News* in New York. He shot the musical through with questions of authenticity when he wrote that the lazy yet good-natured Negro represented by Robeson through his character Joe was a stereotype "that exists more in white men's fancy than in reality."[36] The musical's perpetuation of Black servility caused some to mount a public, organized protest over the song's lyrics through the Black newspapers. The opinion section of Baltimore's *Afro-American* discussed the issue:

When newspapers last week reported that Oscar Hammerstein 2nd had no intentions of changing the words of "Ol' Man River" as suggested by Paul Robeson, the AFRO suggested that he might as least eliminate the word "darky." Said Mr. Hammerstein: "This is not my word but is the invention of some singers. The modern lyrics in 'Ol' Man River' as used in the recent production of 'Show Boat' is 'colored folk work on the Mississippi.'"[37]

Theater scholar Todd Decker has catalogued academic and activist critiques of *Show Boat* and its racial politics from 1948 to 2005.[38]
Stunningly, he absents Robeson's vocal role in the demands for revision prior to 1948, thereby omitting evidence like that provided by the
Afro-American writer. As a text at odds with the Black folk music canon
as well as Robeson's political identity formation, "Ol' Man River" was
primed for a revision. This realization by Robeson demanded that he
move beyond the original intention and usage of the text and join in
the efforts to make the piece a progressive reflection of the Black United
States and a declaration on the changing landscapes of the world.

Diaspora at Work: Robeson's Changing Worldview

Robeson's social and political journey in the 1930s offers insight into his
decision to remove "Ol' Man River" from his concert programs during much of the decade. This period exhibited Robeson's willingness
to expand his acting and musical portfolios in unconventional ways as
new pieces became a part of his repertoire. Biographer Martin Baum
Duberman highlights the early 1930s as a moment of intense change
and enthusiasm in his personal growth: "Newly vocal on themes that
had quietly engaged him intellectually for years, his excitement grew,
and he began an energetic effort both to broaden his own insights
through formal study and to incorporate his emerging new perspectives into his concert work and his future plans."[39] By highlighting the
social and political changes that took place in and around Robeson, a
more nuanced vision of his time abroad develops; this period was not
a hiatus for Robeson—it was a period of growth and development in
revolutionary diasporic politics.

New geographies and affiliations played significant roles in Robeson's evolving consciousness. While in London staging *Show Boat*, he
decided to make that city his home for the next decade. He argued that
his reasons for staying were much like those of other Black U.S. expa-
triates. For him, "London was infinitely better than Chicago has been
for Negroes from Mississippi."[40] This location would serve as more than
a professional haven for Robeson—while there his politics also under-
went a dramatic shift. As a child in New Jersey and North Carolina he
witnessed Black laboring conditions in the U.S. South, but his time in

London birthed his great political investment in labor and the conditions of the working class on a global scale. In his book of essays *Here I Stand*, he acknowledged that "[i]t was in London, in the years that I lived among the people of the British Isles and traveled back and forth to many other lands, that my outlook on world affairs was formed."[41] Beyond the concert stage and society affairs, there was something else in the landscape of the city that did not involve the bourgeoisie—an alternative culture that availed to him a unique part of the country where he could be among "the common people." This group became so integral to Robeson's worldview that their acquaintance meant that he might live the rest of his life in England.

Dreams of a permanent relocation across the pond, however, would not last. As Paul and Eslanda studied—he independently and at the School of Oriental Studies at London University and she at the London School of Economics—they increasingly came to know London as the metropole and "center of the British empire."[42] That realization brought them closer to the African students who were organizing in London and abroad for greater Anglo-African cooperation and understanding, decolonization, and a unified Africa. Through these efforts Robeson developed a relationship with the West African Students' Union (WASU), an organization founded in London in 1925 by Chief Ladipo Solanke of Nigeria and Dr. Herbert Bankole-Bright of Sierra Leone. Historian Gabriel Olusanya explains that the organization's success stemmed from multiple sites of relative power held by the students, ranging from geography to class: "Because of its strategic location in London[,] the heart of the British Empire, and because it comprised the leading educated elite of the day and because of its contact with leading men in all walks of life in Britain, the WASU was able to exert constant and effective pressure on the Colonial Office for political advance in British West Africa."[43] Beyond its impact on the British government and other African students, WASU served a critical role in Robeson's understanding of Africa and the conditions of colonialism. He began to study African languages and cultures and incorporate this work into his artistic repertoire and political activity. Linguistic experimentation and his efforts at translation allowed Robeson to build connections across difference and geography.

Robeson was a cultural icon of growing prominence, and his assistance and outspoken nature on African struggles shone a light on anticolonial mobilizations as well as his own identity formation. By 1935 his cultural politics led him to unapologetically "think and feel as an African." This realization was not a passing fancy—it was instead "the most momentous thing in [his] life," and it drew the attention of a diverse audience of workers, artists, activists, and officials.[44] His new identity compass, in combination with his growing involvement with African decolonization, solicited the ire of British authorities. Robeson argued that "there is a logic to this culture struggle, and the powers-that-be realized it before I did. The British Intelligence came one day to caution me about the political meanings of my activities. For the question loomed of itself: *If African culture was what I insisted it was, what happens then to the claim that it would take 1,000 years for Africans to be capable of self rule*[?]"[45] Robeson was a prominent actor within the "culture struggle" that he described, yet it was due to the surveillance of MI5 that he came to recognize the centrality of his voice and the cultural productions of the African descended within the pursuit and practice of liberation. In this respect, his power partially derived from its attempted suppression. This intervention on the part of the British would be only the first of his many encounters with state surveillance.

It was in the 1930s—during the height of collaboration between WASU and the British Labour Party[46]—that Robeson jumped into the efforts of the African organization and those of labor.[47] The confluence of African struggle with that of labor was not simply an ideological exercise in collaboration—it was a practical concern. Port cities in England and Wales were homes for many African migrants through their service and work on ships and docks. According to historian Laura Tabili, approximately one-third of the 200,000 men in the British seafaring workforce in the first half of the twentieth century were "coloured [men] from East and West Africa, India, the Caribbean, and the Arabian peninsula."[48] These men were so prominent in British cities in the 1930s that "most of the 250 extras in the [1935 Robeson] film [*Sanders of the River*] were blacks recruited from English port towns who had been born in Africa."[49] Workers from Liberia and Sierra Leone composed a large portion of the Black workforce on the docks, particularly as day laborers. African men were appealing to British employers because they were "specifically engaged to perform work deemed unsuitable for white seamen in the tropics. In addition, African labour was cheaper."[50]

These laboring men were those who most affected Robeson's experience in England and Wales. He spoke with fondness of acquaintance with "another class of Africans—the seamen in the ports of London, Liverpool and Cardiff."[51] As he continued to study and witness the African experience, his passion for African independence and cultural production grew.

The cultural impact that these workers had on Robeson was a significant part of the bond that he developed with them. The atmosphere of the dock induced "a cohesiveness that embraced both workplace identification and language" among the workers.[52] With frequent trips back and forth to Africa, the African dock community maintained a connection to their homelands while continuing to decipher and navigate their presence as colonial peoples in Britain. Their passages constructed "alternate public spheres," which is theorized by cultural studies scholar Paul Gilroy as a part of diasporic existence that seeks to maintain particularism and solidarity while investing in a new society.[53] Travel was a crucial element of this project. Literary scholar Gretchen Gerzina argues that "travel itself acted as the safer domestic space, conferring at least a temporary freedom akin to that in which nonenslavable people found ease and community."[54] Travel therefore was a libratory practice, one greatly influenced by the ebb and flow of labor.

Because of their movements and preservation and sharing of cultural practices, African workers helped to characterize and marshal alternative formations of Black identity; "they were in the foreground of an international black community that found cohesiveness in the notion of an African original 'home,' expressed in the terminology of racialized solidarity made possible by their mobility."[55] Robeson's time on the docks offered him firsthand experiences with these men, and through this contact he came to know more than stories of the African condition—he also produced a quasi-genealogy for his African identity. Of his time in London he wrote, "I would go out and meet the sailors on the docks, and we became very good friends. I was struck by the fact that they were very much like our own people in the south. I met a youth from the Kolibar—and he sang: 'Ye annin.' And I said, I have heard that before." This encounter for him "was not a question of words alone, but it was the story of my own race."[56] Cultural exchange solidified a bond that Robeson already believed to exist, and music became the critical link that offered him insight into a shared history. These workers not only expanded his identification with Africa and African people but also challenged him to experiment with world ideology through his study, activism, and repertoire.

Working people caused a revolution in Robeson's thinking about comparative politics and diaspora. During the 1930s his politics changed from a race identity and reliance on "cultural pluralism" in the early part of the decade to a "revolutionary internationalism" largely facilitated by his engagement with African workers who, in their capacity as carriers between different diasporic locations, produced opportunities for intelligence gathering and dissemination around the world.[57] Communication with various African countries, the West Indies, Central and South America, as well as the United States facilitated a conversation between diasporic populations over racial conditions globally. Seamen and other workers transported periodicals including the Black U.S. newspaper the *Chicago Defender* and the internationally circulated communist *Daily Worker*, which maintained a high level of information despite colonial efforts at censorship. As historian Penny Von Eschen argues, print journalism was a spark in international challenges to oppression and "provided the vehicle for the creation of [an] imagined diaspora and unified intellectuals and activists across the globe."[58] Robeson used this information and its networks to continue in the Black Radical Tradition through concerts and performances aimed at challenging systems of power.

During the course of his stay in Europe, Robeson used the stage and screen as his political platform. After his run with *Show Boat* ended in 1929, he took numerous dramatic roles that demonstrated his commitment to advancing African and African American history and culture.[59] In 1936, on the heels of his very public involvement in the defense of Ethiopia after its invasion by Italian fascist Benito Mussolini, Robeson starred in the play *Toussaint Louverture* by Marxist-socialist intellectual and activist C. L. R. James. *Toussaint*, a play in three acts, is based on the heroics of Toussaint Louverture, the most iconized leader of the Haitian Revolution (1791–1804). Robeson played the namesake, a role that further connected him to the political imagination and radical histories of the diaspora. His acquaintance with C. L. R. James also facilitated that bond. James was by 1936 a well-known radical, having spent his early political days in Trinidad under the tutelage of labor leader and captain

Arthur Cipriani and writing for the Trinidad Workingmen's Association journal the *Socialist*. After arriving in London in 1932, he traveled the many corridors of local politics, including that of the Labour Party, but historian Robin Kelley argues that "it was as a budding Trotskyist and supporter of the Independent Labour Party that James entered London's hotbed of Black anti-colonial and Pan-Africanist politics."[60] This collective included James's childhood friend and early Black communist George Padmore and leading Pan-African scholar Duse Mohammed Ali. According to Von Eschen, these men represented for Black Britain

> a tiny, close-knit community of intellectuals who had formed longstanding and dense relationships—social, intellectual, and political—that transcended personal and ideological differences. This group of transplants from colonial societies—who still maintained strong ties to their homelands and were aware of the burgeoning trade union and anti-colonial activities there—grasped the vulnerability of colonialism and predicted its collapse over the next decade. In analyzing, interpreting, and helping to shape this process, they creatively reshaped the leftist politics of the 1930s.[61]

While these men often published on and organized around issues of import to diasporic politics and culture, Robeson must be counted among them as a practitioner of culture. His particular contribution in this period was still demonstrated most thoroughly in his art.

Three years after *Toussaint*, Robeson added another hero to his acting portfolio; this time he portrayed the Black American labor icon John Henry in the 1939 musical of the same name by Roarck Bradford and Jacques Wolfe. Recent scholarship has unveiled many of the mystical layers of John Henry that were once obscured.[62] A northerner, he was born in Robeson's home state of New Jersey in 1847. In 1866 he was convicted of theft in Virginia where post–Civil War officials administered harsh and protracted jail sentences under the Black Codes.[63] His ten-year sentence in the Virginia Penitentiary guaranteed him a position on a railroad chain gang, placing him side by side with the new steam-powered drills that threatened to end the necessity of workers on the job. The brutal realities of mechanization, race, and punishment in the U.S. South burden Henry's story with pain and the continuing failures of Emancipation.

The lore that has developed around him however—his stature, his strength and determination in besting the steam drill, and his beautiful voice—stands as testament to the importance of heroes in the development of class identity. He became a hero for workers around the country, and the music born to honor him—the "hammer songs"—is the record of his legacy. Labor and culture are dramatically brought to life in these songs, and Robeson performed many of them, including "John Henry," arranged by Hall Johnson, and "Hammer Song," arranged by Lawrence Brown. Released in 1943 in a series titled *Six Negro Folk Songs*, "Hammer Song" pays tribute to Henry as an icon and representative for the working masses. In the song, Robeson sings, "Dis am de hammer, kill John Henry, say, Kill John Henry, can't a-kill me." This protest against dying at the hands of a demanding boss resonated across industry and time and is a haunting rebuttal to "Ol' Man River." The last line of the song champions the symbol of the laboring masses, saying, "Dis ole hammer rings like silver, say, rings like silver, shines a-like gold."[64]

In addition to the labor and working-class themes in his stage and film work, Robeson used the post–*Show Boat* moment to make labor a permanent fixture of his musical repertoire. As mentioned earlier, the absence left by "Ol' Man River" on his concert programs offered space for new pieces that would reflect his political evolution. In 1942, Robeson began to perform the labor classic "Joe Hill." This ballad is dedicated to the man of the same name—an immigrant, itinerant laborer, union organizer, and musician. After being found guilty on contested charges of murder, Hill died in 1915 at the hands of a Utah firing squad. He became an international icon and martyr of labor, particularly the radical Industrial Workers of the World, with his famous line, "Don't mourn—organize!" Robeson's version of the song was an alteration of the original text by Earl Robinson (of "Ballad for Americans" fame). The original version said, "Where workers strike and organize, Says he, 'You'll find Joe Hill'"; Robeson's version incorporated a broader humanity beyond organized labor's strikes and union campaigns when he sang, "Where working men *defend their rights*, It's there you'll find Joe Hill."[65] This rendition extends the too-often limited goals of organized labor and embraces a broader civil rights position; through this emphasis, Robeson conjoined the labor history of the piece with the contemporary challenges of race. A reviewer of a 1943 Robeson concert acknowledged the transcendent elements of the song when he wrote, "There was Joe Hill, an American song of a legendary labor hero which is so perfect a thing in its artless simplicity that it takes on a universality beyond its text."[66] Indeed, Robeson's rendition was infused with the spectrum of his political commitments, which encompassed a global majority composed "of the working peoples of every land."[67] "Joe Hill" intimately connected Robeson to the struggles of the working class as he sang it for unions and many others in the era of the Congress of Industrial Organizations (CIO).

Race was not the only condition of difference that concerned Robeson. Although not as prominent, nationality and gender were also considered political elements within his oeuvre. He addressed both conditions in a 1935 article for the London *Daily Herald*. Robeson's close bonds with "those who have lived in a state of inequality . . . workers, European Jews, women . . . those who have felt their status, their race, or their sex a bar to a complete share in all that the world has to offer,"[68] did not allow him to only engage male workers or excise all other locations beyond his European sphere of influence. While his surroundings in Britain offered tangible example of the power of labor and organization, a radical change in the face of labor was also occurring across the pond. An explosion of worker activism and organizing in the United States caused headlines in 1935 when the Committee for Industrial Organization formed as an offshoot of the American Federation of Labor (AFL). During the 1920s, the U.S. trade union movement suffered crushing blows as the right to organize was stripped away and small unions died at the hands of highly organized industry moguls. Paternalistic company unions stepped in to absorb residual demand from workers, while the AFL was argued to rest on its haunches. Leaders of large unions began to speak up in response to the assaults on labor. While the government was a prime target of their criticism, the outdated models of the AFL drew their fire as well. Sidney Hillman, John L. Lewis, and others argued that a new day in labor had dawned; as mechanization developed in the first half of the twentieth century, a new style of work developed as well. No longer was a majority of the U.S. working class skilled—they were now largely unskilled and working in the mass production sites of meatpacking and processing, car factories, textiles, and electronics. While their philosophy was not radically different from that of the AFL, these leaders now called for a strategy and industry-wide program of industrial unionism—a program envisioned by the leaders to address the humanity of the workers, not simply wages and hours.[69] The CIO's reception among workers as an alternative to the stodgy, old-time ways of the AFL proved nothing but antagonistic to the relationship between the two groups, effectively sealing the rift, and in 1938 the once AFL-affiliated Committee of Industrial Organization gave way to the independent Congress of Industrial Organizations. As the organization grew, so too did a radicalized and increasingly interracial working class who made the U.S. landscape a viable space for the politics of Paul Robeson.

In 1940 Robeson returned to the United States and to *Show Boat*, this time performing his famous role in a Los Angeles revival production. After many years in Europe studying and engaging world politics, his return marked a change in his approach to performance. This transformation was most dramatically recognized in the changes he made to his *Show Boat* standard. In the same year as the L.A. production critics began to document a change in the lyrics of "Ol' Man River." The *New York World Telegram* reported that his Carnegie Hall performance of "Ol' Man River" was "fitted up with some anti-war verses."[70] The *Wisconsin State Journal* reported with more precision, "In 'Ol' Man River,' he altered the lines a bit. For 'tired o' livin'' and feard [*sic*] o' dyin',' he used 'I must keep fightin' until I'm dyin.'"[71] A reporter in Hartford noticed, "The encores included 'Old Man River' (with 'you have a little grit and you land in jail' substituted for 'you get a little drunk and you land in jail')."[72]

Robeson in fact completely overhauled the text, and in doing so he owned the song in a way that few performers are capable of. Where Black American stevedores once sang "Niggers all work on de Mississippi / Niggers all work while de white folks play," as the introduction to Robeson's solo in the musical, Robeson now imagined the conscientious African dockworkers whom he met in Liverpool and Cardiff as his chorus. These real men replaced the shuffling, self-deprecating men of both Ferber and Hammerstein's imaginations and inspired Robeson to make the song one of protest. His revisions included the following:

> *Original*: "Dere's an ol' man called de Mississippi / Dat's de ol' man dat I'd like to be"; *Robeson*: "There's an old man called the Mississippi / That's the old man I *don't* like to be"

Original: "Git a little drunk An' you land in jail"; *Robeson*: "Show a little grit And you land in jail"[73]
Original: "I git weary An' sick of tryin' / I'm tired of livin' An' skeered of dyin'"; *Robeson*: "But I keeps laughin' Instead of cryin' / I must keep fightin' until I'm dyin'"

As Robeson knew all too well, he could rarely offer a concert in which "Ol' Man River" was not requested. In this situation, these changes to the text were imperative; the new lyrics made the song the central etude within his program for social justice.

The political salience of the song is recognized in Robeson's many performances of it after his return to the United States. In 1942 he offered a concert at the Municipal Auditorium in Kansas City. The recital "which progressed through the first half with the utmost harmony and good humor," quickly regressed into "an atmosphere of tension and ill feeling . . . when Paul Robeson, the principal artist, announced from the stage that he was continuing the concert under protest against racial segregation" in the venue. He regretted the interruption in the performance but made his reasons clear: "I have made it a lifelong habit to refuse to sing in Southern states or anywhere that audiences are segregated. I accepted this engagement under guarantee that there would be no segregation." It was only through the persuasive arguments of local Black leaders that he agreed to finish his performance. After a group of Russian folk songs, he sung the "'Jim Crow' song, to verses of unmistakable racial protest, and he sang it with stronger feeling than he had put into any other number."[74] His encore, performed for a discernibly smaller number of patrons than his first selection, was his final statement on the night's events: "Ol' Man River."

Robeson's radical revision of the song continued to receive attention as the social and political landscape of the world changed. In 1949 a reporter commented on Robeson's choice of words by saying, " . . . and finally 'Old Man River,' in which he interpolated lyrics which probably would have thoroughly astonished Oscar Hammerstein."[75] The new "Ol' Man River" designed by Robeson, while potentially causing conflict with Hammerstein II, was his legacy to an entire generation who survived the Depression only to be met with war. A member of that generation fondly recalled Robeson and his song:

Probably the youth of America may not remember the man or any of his songs, that the older ones will fondly recall, such as the never-to-be-forgotten "Old Man River." . . . A lasting tribute to "Old Man River" as people here in London often think of Robeson, is that for many years people of color objected to some of the lyrics in the song as a slur to Afro-Americans, and it was left to Paul to do something about it. Whenever he sang "Old Man River," he deleted the objectionable words, and made a substitution, and today the song is being sung with the same words that he substituted.[76]

By the time of this tribute, "Ol' Man River" was an anthem, a song that resituated the role of Black culture within global justice movements and their representations. In changing the lyrics, Robeson simultaneously extinguished its exaggerated dialect and adjusted the political message of the song to accommodate his growth as an activist and Black world citizen. His transformation of the text was so complete that by 1950 he could declare, "Like Ol' Man River, I plan to keep fighting until I'm dying—or until my people are free" without any sense of irony or need for clarification.[77] At Robeson's hands, old man river had been transformed from a weak, pitiable Black man to a righteous iconoclast and global freedom fighter.

Stage and Soapbox: Robeson's Cold War Performances

Robeson came back to the United States in the 1940s a hero. He made a name for himself in the arts communities of Europe, was an antifascism activist, and developed strong political networks that would become increasingly important in later years. His classic, "Ballad for Americans," written by Earl Robinson, made him a national celebrity in 1939 and an icon for the richness of U.S. diversity and cooperation. Recognition for his work on behalf of humanity came often, whether from small community collectives or international political groups. In 1945 the National Association for the Advancement of Colored People (NAACP) honored him with the Spingarn Medal, which was yearly awarded in recognition of the "highest or noblest achievement by an American Negro during the preceding year or years." Robeson received his award with the citation, "For his distinguished achievements in the theatre and on the concert stage, as well as for his active concern for the rights of the Common Man of every race, color, religion and nationality."[78] This strong endorsement from the leading U.S. civil rights organization of the period was well deserved, yet as the decade progressed, the praise once heaped upon Robeson would decline as the Cold War politics of the post–World War II moment grew. Within two years of this award, his star fell. Republican Senator Joseph McCarthy (R-WI) spearheaded a national hysteria over communist influence in government, media, and Hollywood, leading some to argue that his 1947 assent to public office in the Senate signaled a second Red Scare.[79] The transition into the second half of the century proved socially and politically tenuous for the aging left and other radicals who ideologically grew alongside communism in the 1920s and '30s.

It was exactly at the moment of McCarthy's ascent that Robeson made a daring announcement. During a 1947 concert in St. Louis, he announced that he was leaving the professional concert stage in order to fully dedicate his time to political work. This hiatus would allow him to engage in the activities that had sustained him during his time in London: public speaking and concerts in support of sociopolitical causes including the anti-apartheid struggle. This period of political work began that very day as he joined the picket lines of the NAACP at a local Jim Crow establishment. This certainly was not the first of his political engagements. Ten years earlier he, along with his mentor W. E. B. Du Bois, had been instrumental in the formation of the Council on African Affairs (CAA), an organization that worked "to provide a sound basis of accurate information so that the American people might play their proper part in the struggle for African freedom."[80] The organization also expressed more aggressive ambitions encompassing "the political liberation of the colonized African nations, and improved economic and social conditions on the African continent."[81] Robeson served as chairman of the organization for many years in addition to serving as an ambassador during his art hiatus. It was under the banner of the CAA and like-minded organizations that he traveled to speak and perform during the late 1940s and 1950s.

The conditions that gave rise to his career hiatus reflected the political terrain that existed while he traveled in Europe during the 1930s. Again it would be working people and the members of the African diaspora who would gain his greatest attention and support. Robeson reflected on that day in St. Louis saying,

I announced that I would put aside my formal career for the time being
to enter the day-to-day struggles of my people and the working masses
of this country. I meant the struggle for our daily bread—such battles as
I had been part of on the picket lines on the Mesabi iron ore range, with
the auto workers in Cadillac Square, the gallant tobacco workers in Winston-Salem, the longshoremen, cooks and stewards in San Francisco, the
furriers, electrical workers and a host of others.[82]

These workers and many others became Robeson's colleagues and compatriots during one of the most challenging periods of his life. As he
worked to maintain a base of support for the causes he championed,
he received mixed reviews across the country. Trade unions, anticolonial organizations, and civil rights groups largely embraced Robeson,
but the broader public, under the sway of McCarthyism, would in 1949
resort to violence in order to silence him and his fellow artists.

In August Robeson experienced a tailor-made horror at his concert
in Peekskill, New York. Originally organized by People's Artists, Inc.
as an opportunity to raise money for the Harlem branch of the Civil
Rights Congress, the concert headlined Paul Robeson with other artist participants including folk icon Pete Seeger. In the midst of McCarthy's America, Robeson's advocacy for relations with the Soviet Union
overshadowed the intentions of the performance, and organized mobs
were unleashed to intimidate and ravage his comrades. The first performance, scheduled for August 27, 1949, was called off due to preemp-
tive hostilities. In spite of constant assertion that the violence was in
response to Robeson's politics, the reaction by rioters offered a deeper
reading than an anticommunist politic. Racial and ethnic epithets and
slurs were launched at would-be attendees to the concert. The Ku Klux
Klan and sympathizers in the area burned a twelve-foot cross at the
Peekskill concert site. The racial dimension of the hatred at Peekskill
was not lost on the Black community, as outrage registered across the
nation and the world. In the fashion of a war correspondent, concert
attendee and journalist Leslie Matthews of the *New York Age* wrote,

This is being written a few short hours after my departure from the Hell
on Earth that was Peekskill, NY, this Sunday before Labor Day, 1949. I
still hear the frenzied roar of crowds, the patter of stone against glass and

flesh. I hear the wails of women, the impassioned screams of children, the jeers and taunts of wildeyed youths, I still smell the sickening odor of blood flowing from freshly opened wounds, gasoline fumes from autos and buses valiantly trying to carry their loads of human targets out of the range of bricks, bottles, stones, sticks. I still feel the violence, the chaos, which permeated the air. I still hear, smell, and feel Peekskill.[83]

The events of Peekskill spread like wildfire nationally. Conflict flared again over the issue of communism and its relationship to the Black community in the United States. While many in the community worked diligently to refute the idea of Black communists and communist sympathizers, Peekskill aroused in some a need to rally to the defense of Robeson. On September 10, less than a week after Robeson had successfully performed the second concert in Peekskill, the *New York Age* again commented, "No Negro since Marcus Garvey has so projected himself into the eyes of the public as has Robeson during the scant few months he has actually been in the center of the world stage. . . . This is the first time since Frederick Douglass that Negroes have been presented a lion-hearted man who takes action instead of writing letters. . . . It has excited admiration in the minds of hundreds of thousands who can hardly pronounce 'Communist,' let alone belong to that party."[84] This journalist courageously writes Robeson back into Black protest culture when so many, from within and without the community, worked to discredit and expel him. By placing Robeson within this lexicon of Black leaders—alongside Marcus Garvey and Frederick Douglass—the author challenges the audience to imagine Robeson's acts as a continuation of a long-standing radical tradition within Black American political activism and discourse. These comments also establish Robeson's role within the diasporic tradition of these two men who throughout the nineteenth and early twentieth centuries worked in Latin America, the Caribbean, and Europe to address and raise awareness of the despised conditions of Black people during and after slavery.

Robeson's success at the second Peekskill concert stemmed from his belief in democracy and dedication to freedom of speech and expression. He responded to hecklers at the second Peekskill performance by saying, "This is my answer," and then proceeded to sing songs of nations, cultures, and peoples in struggles against tyranny and oppression. Pete

Seeger described that Robeson sang for an hour, with a highlight for him being "'Ol' Man River,' from 'Show Boat,' which he was famous for."[85] While men stood at his side to protect him from rocks, gunshots, and other assaults, Robeson proceeded to sound the voice of freedom and justice in the midst of a violent mob estimated at one thousand people. This response was purely Robeson; culture had long been his weapon of defense, and he wielded it with unparalleled precision. The concert was ultimately bittersweet; while Robeson overcame the shouting and violence, he also became aware of the forces that worked to end his career at any cost. Peekskill effectively ended any positive mainstream press associated with Robeson or his concerts and was the event that organized his entrance into the Cold War; it was a blueprint for the types of violence and censorship that he would be subjected to throughout the next two decades of his life. With the events of the concert still lingering in the public imaginary, Robeson attempted to move his peace projects forward.

His political agendas and career suffered the greatest setback in 1950 when his passport was revoked. As members of the white and Black communities debated his politics during the period of revocation (1950–58), Robeson adjusted to his national captivity by focusing his political energies on the conditions of the Black working masses in the United States.[86] The international sphere was never far from his mind, however. He was very clear about the true reasons for the denial of his right to travel. During the course of his famous 1956 appearance before the House Un-American Activities Committee (HUAC), he declared,

> Could I say that for the reason that I am here today you know, from the mouth of the State Department itself, is because I should not be allowed to travel because I have struggled for years for the independence of the colonial peoples of Africa, and for many years I have so labored. . . . The other reason that I am here today is again from the State Department and from the court record of the Court of Appeals, that when I am abroad I speak out against the injustices against the Negro people in this land. . . . That is why I am here. This is the basis and I am not being tried for whether I am a Communist, I am being tried for fighting for the rights of my people who are still second-class citizens in this United States of America.[87]

Far from simply addressing the court in response to his own circumstances, Robeson presented testimony, theater scholar Tony Perucci argues, that "mobilize[d] performance to challenge the produced crisis culture that underwrote the postwar racial capitalist practices of the U.S. at home and abroad."[88] His ability to build commonality and conversation between the Black populations of the United States and Africa, as well as the world's laboring masses, drew the fury of the United States. Under pressure from continued racial discrimination, censure, and violence, the 1939 patriotism engendered by Robeson through his performance of the critical (yet praised) nationalist song "Ballad for Americans"—convincingly argued by cultural historian Michael Denning as the anthem of the Popular Front—gave way to the resounding legacies of Hammerstein's "Ol' Man River": racism, Jim Crow, and suppression of labor.[89]

It is in this moment of Robeson's domestic incarceration by the state that "Ballad for Americans" failed to signal a progressive United States. Only ten years after its composition and performance through the Works Progress Administration and Robeson's lush rendition on CBS radio, the song no longer contained the stamina of an organized and embattled working class struggling across racial and national lines. Both "Ballad for Americans" and Frank Sinatra's "The House I Live In" (also brilliantly revised and performed by Robeson) are argued by Denning as Popular Front "pleas for racial and ethnic tolerance," yet "Ballad" holds special significance "as a synecdoche for the extraordinary flowering of the historical imagination in Popular Front fiction, film, music, and art."[90] This flowering was trampled underfoot by McCarthy through his HUAC trials, leading Robeson and his comrades to reevaluate their political ties and commitments. This change is evident within his repertoire; in the early 1940s Robeson regularly performed excerpts of "Ballad," but by the end of the decade it was no longer found in his recitals. This absence, like that of "Ol' Man River" a decade earlier, signaled the changing political and social composition of Robeson's interests and audiences. Yet unlike with "Ol' Man River," Robeson did not revise "Ballad" for performance—it was simply abandoned. It was no longer acceptable for Robeson to "plea[d]" for the conciliation that mobilized his political communities ten years earlier. He instead sonically reinvented the scenarios described in Show Boat in order to demand the change that a world under fascism could never offer. In 1945 the U.S. War Department defined fascism as the "pitting of religious, racial and economic groups against one another in order to break down national unity." Taking stock of its presence domestically, the War Department continued, "[N]ative fascists have often been anti-Catholic, anti-Jew, anti-Negro, anti-Labor, anti-foreign-born . . . [and] deny the need for international cooperation."[91] More than "Ballad for Americans," Robeson's "Ol' Man River" organized the receiver to understand difference as structurally embedded, rather than located in individual bodies. His revised anthem—with its clear articulation of the labor-race conflation and global condition of suppression—was a response to the visions of Popular Front progressivism that were never fulfilled, becoming a sonic representation of an ongoing Black Popular Front.[92] Descriptive of the coalition of Black churches and fraternal, civic, and social organizations, the Black Popular Front can be understood through leaders such as Robeson who continued to have a labor focus and international view of struggle in the Black community well into the 1950s. Their artistic and political platforms therefore provided for the continuance of a crucial dialogue among and between various social and political groups and agendas.

Robeson extends the legacies of traveling Black orator-activists such as Marcus Garvey, Frederick Douglass, and Ida B. Wells, from the nineteenth and early twentieth centuries into the Cold War era when travel was not a right for U.S. citizens but instead a privilege to be offered and revoked at will. Robeson's performance practices consistently challenged the modern border's "powerful governmental desires [of] security and mobility" through a diasporic and global perspective in his repertoire and political activity.[93] His defiance of the British authorities through his assertion of African culture compromised the security of the British Empire during the 1930s and the ability of that empire to manage space and the bodies within it. Robeson's position as a U.S. subject served to further expand the potential for a revolution of the African descended, especially considering his import as a musician and film star. By employing multiple sonic, cultural, and political tools, he was able to build a career beyond his time in London in which he chose when to speak, with whom, and at what time, with only strategic consideration offered to the many confinements at work around him.

One of Robeson's greatest transgressions was that he played with, manipulated, and disregarded the borders of his position as a Black American. He was a "bad nationalist," which literary scholar Brent Edwards describes as "a subject who doesn't *perform* nationalism, who doesn't follow the protocol, who doesn't register."[94] His rejection of nationalism places his anthemic project outside of the rubric theorized and pursued by Garvey, whose "Ethiopia (Thou Land of Our Fathers)" was meant to call into being a definable and exclusive nation that would solicit particular citizens for inclusion. Robeson's defiant citizenship refused to be tokenized or contained by borders and instead sought a complex humanity that lingered on the periphery—a space for the African descended that gave way to diaspora through an identification with blackness as a condition of affinity and camaraderie beyond knowable signs and signals such as homeland, language, and appearance. The migratory actors within diaspora were constantly negotiating their relationship to one another, to their nations, and to those locations in which they settled, those adoptive countries where difference was violently read through the body. This knowledge ensured a contentious relationship between Black bodies and those who profit from and seek to control them.

Robeson's containment was not an isolated incident. The international domination of Black bodies through travel restriction was a prominent tactic employed by colonial powers throughout the African world. Black populations in Rwanda and South Africa continued to encounter intranational travel restrictions well into the late twentieth century, and the violence that attended anti–Pass Law demonstrations, like the Sharpeville Massacre of 1960 (discussed in chapter 6), exposed the fear of Black mobility. Robeson was keenly aware of these diasporic conditions through his own study and work with the CAA and its newsletter *Spotlight on Africa*, which often discussed the struggle of Africans in tandem with those of the African descended in the United States. In "Africa and the Commemoration of Negro History," Robeson argued that economic exploitation was the root of African and Negro exploitation. When that system was destroyed, so too would the myths and misrepresentations that stem from it, leading to a world in which "no one will dare speak of white supremacy or Negro inferiority."[95] Through the work of Du Bois, Robeson, and others, *Spotlight* exposed the strategies of white rule shared between empires and demonstrated for CAA members and readers the conjoined nature of Black oppression. This reality made for impressive coalition building at the local and national levels and encouraged many within the international arena to follow in kind. Even on "house arrest," Robeson was one of the most vocal among this mobilized international public—so prominent, in fact, that his records were banned on South African radio.

Robeson's case strikingly demonstrates sociologist Radhika Mongia's argument that "the passport not only is a technology *reflecting* certain understandings of race, nation/nationality, and state but was central to *organizing* and *securing* the modern definitions of these categories."[96] Within the period of Robeson's revocation there existed a heightened international sensitivity to race relations within the United States. Deployments of military agencies to various locations in the U.S. South offered visual demonstration of the national practice of racial codification but also implicitly referenced the rapidly changing landscapes of a world struggling toward liberation. Robeson made these links explicit within his performances and speeches; his critiques of U.S. escalations of war in Korea, racism and segregation across the United States, and maltreatment of workers in the United States, Panama, and the United Kingdom in particular made public topics of issues that the U.S. State Department otherwise considered a family affair. Robeson's family, however, was not constituted by a national border, and therein lay his danger. By revoking his passport, the State Department attempted to blur "the vocabularies of nation and race" and reconstitute Robeson's identity by making him first a national subject.[97] Robeson's chosen identity as an African and his continual demonstration of "his people's" unequal access to the riches and rights of the nation defied the singular and militarized nationalism ordered by the United States. Because of this transgression and defiant citizenship the State Department withdrew his federally sanctioned mobility.

With the foreign arena out of physical reach, Robeson developed a series of political and performance strategies that challenged the surveillance and detention apparatuses of the Cold War United States. One of his most robust national alliances was with the National Negro Labor Council (NNLC). Formed in 1950, the NNLC developed as a protective and progressive organization for Black workers within the AFL and CIO.

Their investment in culture demonstrated an agenda that went far beyond the bread-and-butter issues of trade unionism. While employment, wages, and other classic union issues were a part of the program, the NNLC's fight was two pronged: the fight for Black people *and* for labor. As historian Mindy Thompson notes, the beliefs and practices of the NNLC "expressed the militancy and courage of the working-class. Their use of culture, their respect for the heritage of Black people, and their programmatic conceptions expressed their high understanding of the history and nature of Black oppression."[98] In combining a Black liberation agenda with organized labor, the NNLC sought to revolutionize both spaces. Culture was viewed by the organization as a front on which to achieve this goal. The third convention of the NNLC called for "[a] heightened fight for the right of Negro cultural workers and for a closer integration of Negro culture with the Negro people's freedom movement."[99] Ewart Guinier—a respected Black trade unionist and intellectual—and his New York Labor Council put this statement into action through multiple events in the city. He was clear about the centrality of culture and its producers to a successful movement for justice and the NNLC's culture expert, Paul Robeson, played a major role in that production. At the 1951 convention, Guinier acknowledged him and his contributions:

> Not all of us are fortunate enough to be able to have Brother Robeson appear at our Council endeavors. You know that he want[s] to wherever he goes, and he has. As a matter of fact, when I travel around the country for my union [UPW-CIO] I find in many localities that the Negro workers say—"The best organizer that we have is Paul Robeson, because when he comes to town the Negro workers turn out to greet him and we get an opportunity to get together with them." Well, we must see that we develop many more Paul Robesons among our men and women by giving them the opportunity to come forth culturally.[100]

Here Guinier highlights Robeson as an organizer—the individual who brings workers into communion with one another around a more perfect vision and then mobilizes them in service of it. Through its investment in the radical potential of culture and its practitioners, the NNLC provided social and political sustenance to Robeson during a period of intense isolation.

While his speeches, writings, and interviews continued to further his political agenda, performance remained Robeson's greatest province of influence. Concerts for the NNLC in Detroit, Cleveland, and New York City helped to sustain his visibility and career while detained in the United States. In 1952, he toured under the banner of the United Freedom Fund sponsored by the NNLC, CAA, *Freedom* magazine, and the Committee for the Negro in the Arts. During the course of this tour, Robeson met with workers around the country, visiting numerous Negro Labor Councils and union rallies. He also performed in some high-profile concerts that brought him international recognition in spite of his inability to travel. Enterprising union and political leaders developed new opportunities for him to perform, in the process challenging the authority of the U.S. government. During his eight years of national captivity his sound migrations were launched. These performances allowed Robeson's detained voice to take flight to other culturo-national spaces of possibility; the two performance sites most demonstrative of this method were the Peace Arch at the U.S.-Canadian border (1952) and the 1955 Asia-Africa Conference in Bandung, Indonesia.

State Department officials succeeded in restricting Robeson's access to international audiences and comrades, but their actions also developed a counteraction, which manifested itself as a series of creative subversions and libratory practices in Robeson's domestic travels, networks, and performances. In early 1952 Robeson was invited to perform at the annual convention of the Mine, Mill and Smelters' Workers Union (Mine-Mill-CIO) of British Columbia, Canada. Although his passport was seized, the trip to Canada posed no concern to the union or to Robeson and his associates; at that time, no U.S.-born citizen was required to possess a passport to cross into Canada from the United States, ensuring for all those involved that Robeson would be allowed easy passage to his destination. On January 30, Robeson's security motorcade approached the U.S.-Canadian border in the state of Washington, where they stopped to check in with the Immigration and Naturalization Service (INS) before crossing. Robeson recalled, "Then the representative of the American State Department called me in, and nervously informed me that though no passport was needed, a special order had come through forbidding me to leave the country. If I did, it might mean five years and a fine!"[101] The shock and outrage demonstrated by parties on both sides of the border precipitated the growth of an international and multiyear movement to highlight Robeson's persecution, and it began that day at the border.

The original plan devised by the Seattle CIO included a taped broadcast that would then be mailed to Vancouver.[102] In the meantime, however, an illegal international telephone feed was set up by the International Brotherhood of Electrical Workers between Robeson in Seattle and the convention in Vancouver. Robeson's larger-than-life voice rang out from the loudspeakers of the convention hall as he apologized for his absence, argued for his right to travel in order to continue speaking and performing in response to the struggles of oppressed people, and sang the songs that continued to build his artistic reputation abroad. The excitement generated from Robeson's "telepresence" was enough for labor leaders on both sides of the border to plan for the next event, a concert on the border.[103]

The first Peace Arch concert was staged in Blaine, Washington, in 1952 with limited resources but an abundance of enthusiasm and participation from local organizations and fans. Robeson offered only one stipulation for his participation in the event: that ticket prices be limited to one dollar so that Black people and workers could attend. This pricing made for crowds estimated at twenty-five to thirty-five thousand people on the Canadian side of the border alone. While the sheer number of people in the audience rivaled the attendance of many of his previous concerts, even in his heyday, the conditions of this performance were unlike those of any other that he had experienced to that point. The amplification and staging of this concert demonstrated the importance and difficulty of sound technology within Robeson's production of transnational solidarity. Taking place in an open-air venue with a limited history of live performance, the Peace Arch concert required special accommodations. Robeson was set up on stage with the most crucial of technologies at his disposal: a microphone. In the late twentieth century the microphone regained its rightful centrality within the production of Black music (along with two turntables), yet its importance in this venue decades earlier was heightened as Robeson sought to reach a massive number of listeners who were located in two different countries.

This concert became an opportunity to do more than hear Robeson; Mine-Mill advertised the event as an "opportunity to register . . . protest against the United States government."[104] The explicitly political nature of the event ensured a Canadian public ready to receive Robeson's position on world affairs. The combination of a radical politic with worker-friendly ticket prices ensured a large and diverse crowd whose sympathies and politics were ripe for Robeson's message of freedom. His performance included a dedication of "Joe Hill" to Mine-Mill, in which Robeson added and amended verses, performing a total of eight (compared to five in other recordings). Additional verses included, "'In Salt Lake City, Joe,' says I and standing by my bed, 'they framed you on a murder charge.' Says Joe, 'But I ain't dead.' Says Joe, 'But I ain't dead.'" and "'Joe Hill ain't dead,' he says to me, 'Joe Hill ain't never died; where working men defend their rights Joe Hill is at their side. Joe Hill is at their side.'" He also made more potent the lyric "Says Joe, 'What they *forgot to kill* went on to organize'" by changing it to "Says Joe, 'What they *can never kill* went on to organize.'"[105] These amendments to the song—which by this point was a part of his repertoire for ten years—highlight Robeson's respect for the insider knowledge of his audience. Where in other performances he curtailed the verses, he offered the unabridged version in Blaine. His increased involvement with and sensitivity to labor was by this point fully articulate.

In addition to "Joe Hill," Robeson included a Negro spiritual that had long been a part of his repertoire: "No More Auction Block." The prominence of this piece in the concert proceedings was evidenced by the fact that it was the only song in the set to receive an introduction by Robeson. In it he details a brief history of slavery in the United States and the continuing consequences and tyranny of the system on Black citizens. He also highlights those freedom fighters who made abolition possible, namely Frederick Douglass, Harriet Tubman, and Sojourner Truth. He argued that these freedom fighters "might have sung this next song—*must* have sung it."[106] Robeson's creation of this genealogy primed the audience to see him as a continuation of that tradition specifically through the performance of this song. By 1955, Robeson had performed "No More Auction Block" for thirty years, and he used it to highlight and reinvent Black people's present racial condition through the sounds of the past. "No More Auction Block" was a platform from which he could tell to an international audience the timeless story of Black struggle over oppression.

Robeson used "Joe Hill" and "No More Auction Block" to prepare the audience for the grand finale—the glue that holds the history of labor in tension with that of the African diaspora—"Ol' Man River." His performance of the song differed significantly from previous performances. As Lawrence Brown begins the piano accompaniment, Robeson enters, "That ol' man river, that ol' man river, he must know something but don't say nothin'" in a slow, bluesy tone with more exaggerated slurs and slides than were common in other performances of the song. This beginning is not the official entrance; his performance of the song at the Peace Arch dismisses his standard first line, "There's an ol' man called the Mississippi. / That's the ol' man I don't like to be." This act is Robeson again reading his audience. His experimentation with speed and method in the song slows the tempo to match the import of the message that he's offering. The microphone was central to the success of this message making; sound studies scholar Mark Katz argues that "performing for the microphone . . . require[s] moderating one's technique in a variety of ways." Robeson's alternative entrance and blues-influenced tonality and phrasing would not have been legible without the assistance provided by the mic. Through it Robeson was able to offer, like the crooners described by Katz, "a sense of intimacy between artist and audience, collapsing the technologically imposed distance that would seem to preclude such a relationship."[107] He ends the song with a *molto adagio* phrasing in which he crawls through the line "But I keeps laughin', instead of cryin'. / I must keep fightin' until I'm dyin'." This slow, deliberate phrasing of "Ol' Man River" refused the accelerated gait of contemporary political development, in which U.S. legislation and the rights that they guarantee were open to reckless usage and interpretation. In that way, both his unhurried voice in Canada and his body positioned at the border interrupted the progress of a hysterical U.S. nationalism that threatened to permanently impede the practice of democracy, both domestically and abroad.

Robeson's Peace Arch performance was an experiment in accessibility. His choice of location, hodgepodge of stage and set, and demands that all tickets be affordable to working people ensured that the event would not be hindered by his inability to travel, the imperfect performance apparatus, or the limited resources of his intended audience. Three years later, Robeson was still detained in the United States and negotiating his ability to speak, only now his audience consisted of millions, and the increased number of borders separating them seemed insurmountable.

In 1955, the Asian-African Conference of Non-Aligned States met in Bandung, Indonesia, near the capitol city of Jakarta. Twenty-nine newly independent nations met there to discuss the ends of colonialism and the futures that lay ahead. Indonesian President Sukarno welcomed the delegates and in his remarks appealed to their commonalities: "We are united by a common detestation of colonialism in whatever form it appears. We are united by a common detestation of racialism. And we are united by a common determination to preserve and stabilize peace in the world." According to social historian and theorist Vijay Prashad, it was these elements, not any "intrinsic cultural or racial commonalities," that united those represented at the conference.[108] While unity was a conceptual framework and practical aim for the participants, the attendees grappled with the many divisions that existed among them, and those divisions began with the roster of countries participating in the conference. While some nations declined involvement in observance of their relationship with one of the major powers, others were not invited due to their political regimes of violence and terror (viz., South Africa). The United States was not an invited nation, and it demonstrated itself to be particularly antagonistic to the participation of its individual citizens, especially its Black citizens. The federal government labeled the conference "offensive and dangerous" and further described it as "a confirmation of the resistance to American strategic interests in Asia."[109] Beyond economic concerns, U.S. officials worried that the nation's image abroad would be damaged if race in the southern states became a discussion topic at the conference. The U.S. presence at the conference, then, was fraught, and for Black Americans it offered a space of both potential camaraderie and isolation.

Black American leaders responded differently to U.S. noninvolvement at Bandung. Adam Clayton Powell, Jr., a standing congressman from New York, announced, despite considerable protest, that he was attending the conference on his own dime. He believed, as he told President Dwight Eisenhower, that Africa was "the emerging continent for the immediate future." In this respect, Powell thought it not only his right but also his duty to travel to the conference in order to meet with representatives of these emergent nations. While in Bandung he engaged in diplomatic conversation with Zhou Enlai, premiere of Communist China, and met regularly with Indian prime minister Jawaharlal Nehru. He made a triumphant return to the United States after his "pilgrimage to a new Mecca" and was greeted with a standing ovation upon his reemergence in Congress. This partial conversion of his peers within government was a distant second in intensity when compared to his own metamorphosis. He wrote in his autobiography,

> Bandung had completely changed my thinking. It made me over into an entirely new man. Before the Bandung Conference I could have been called, with some justification, a nationalist. Nearly everything I had done was aimed at obtaining more rights for the Negro people. After the Bandung Conference I came back to find the America of 1955 hungrily desiring a partnership with this new Afro-Asian bloc, and to find that such a union was blocked by the crass stupidity and ignorance of our State Department. I knew then that something drastic had to be done, and a great change took place in my own thinking; my perspective changed.
>
> Whereas previously I had though of civil rights in terms of rights for Negroes only, I now thought of civil rights as the sole method by which we could save the entire United States of America.[110]

Although still largely U.S.-centric, Powell's epiphany hinted at a belief already held by a number of prominent Black figures: that it was necessary to engage Africa and Asia as models of progressive cultural and social politics. W. E. B. Du Bois had long been a supporter of the "Afro-Asian bloc," as a benefactor to emergent artists inspired by African traditions, through travel and lecture in Africa and East Asia, and as a leader of the Pan-African Congresses occurring in the first half of the twentieth century. Du Bois was unable to attend the Bandung Conference due to his own passport revocation, but his comments on its significance were unequivocal. In the newsletter of the CAA he wrote, "[I]n another half century the colored world is going to date the beginning of its integrity, unification, and self-conscious progress on the great Pan-Colored meeting of 1955."[111]

Du Bois's pupil, Robeson, still under detention in the United States, creatively intervened at Bandung.[112] He was invoked when Powell "took it upon himself to rebuke Robeson" and decry reports of racial stagnation in the United States as "Communist propaganda."[113] Powell's statements were refuted by the absence of both Du Bois and Robeson at the conference, yet despite being unseen, Robeson was heard at Bandung. His speech for the conference praised the proceedings and declared the right of these countries to independence: "[T]he Asian-African Conference signal[s] the power and determination of the peoples of these two great continents to decide their own destiny, to achieve and defend their sovereign independence, to control the rich resources of their own lands, and to contribute to the promotion of world peace and cooperation."[114] His comments reflect his alignment with the conference attendees and their principles of cooperation, yet it is his music that demonstrates his truest affinity for and engagement with the populations in attendance. In addition to his speech, Robeson sent along a recording with three songs to be played: the Negro spiritual "No More Auction Block," the peace ballad "Hymn for Nations," and the anthem "Ol' Man River."

The Peace Arch performance was difficult, but the Bandung Conference offered ever more significant obstacles. There was no immediate border to sing across; this time, millions of miles of ocean and colonial territory separated Robeson from his intended audience. The only opportunity available to Robeson was to send a recording, a technology that he was readily familiar with. He was recorded live as early as the late 1920s and made a very lucrative career of it with a number of different companies. Yet by the time of the Bandung Conference, labels refused to record his songs. In response to this silencing, Robeson founded the Othello Recording Company in the early 1950s. With the assistance of his son Paul, Jr., Robeson endeavored to produce a limited number of recordings for fans around the world.[115] These productions existed outside of the dominant Cold War marketplace, which not only censored the content of the music but also forestalled access to the technologies that would make Robeson's voice audible to a global audience. By taking the means of production into his own hands, Robeson made the process more democratic and more accessible to grassroots political organizations, as these were his primary constituencies during the last decades of his life.

Robeson's efforts to produce his own music demonstrate how recording technologies attend the deconstruction of borders and subversion of institutions of power. Ethnomusicologist Peter Manuel's work on Indian popular music details how new media "accompany the evolution toward postindustrial societies wherein information of one kind or another is the most valuable resource and product."[116] Knowledge sharing and knowledge accumulation impact identity formation, facilitate transnational conversations, and are intimately related to the development of social movements. These are exactly the types of processes that motivated Robeson's artistic and political work during this wave of decolonization. By reaching beyond the borders of the United States through sound, Othello Recording and its products were configured within a global flow of cultural products, which, literature scholar Pamela Caughie argues, "made it increasingly necessary to think of identity in other than nationalist terms."[117] Othello was developed precisely because the nation employed what economist Jacques Attali has theorized as a "technology of listening in on," inclusive of "eavesdropping, censorship, recording, and surveillance," in order to refuse the manufacture and dissemination of Robeson's political soundings.[118] In this scenario, his DIY recordings from studios around New York City were intended to defy the nation through their production and escape to eager receivers around the world.

The recording that Robeson sent to Bandung was an accompanied manifesto used at the conference as the technology through which he might speak. Through his recording, musical culture developed as a mediating tool, a way in which difference could be traced (as genealogy) and contended with (through practice). His selections mapped the history of his politics and sound, grounding his performances within a broader, Janus-faced rehearsal of sonic rebellion. The first piece was the Negro spiritual "No More Auction Block," which Robeson described in his 1952 Peace Arch performance as the song that "comes from the very depth of the struggle of my people in America."[119] The use of this song again in Bandung demonstrates Robeson's constant attention and return to the cultural foundations of his craft, as well as the continuing resonance of Negro spirituals in his political work. He followed "No More Auction Block" with the peace ballad "Hymn for Nations," which begs, "Build the road of peace before us, build it wide and deep and long /

Speed the slow, and check the eager, help the weak, and curb the strong / None shall push aside another, none shall let another fall, / march beside me, oh, my brothers, all for one and one for all."[120] Bandung's emphasis on disarmament and international peace found resonance in this text that similarly served to represent Robeson's long investment in an end to war. The final track of the recording, "Ol' Man River," was, by 1955, received as an anthem of the disenfranchised and oppressed. Robeson's opening remarks to the conference—"Heartfelt greetings to all of you, peoples come from the shores of the Ganges and the Nile, the Yangtse and the Niger, nations of the vast Pacific waters"[121]—hinted at his presence among them through the imagery of his iconic song that sought to connect the fluid geo-histories of the participants to the Mississippi River/United States from which he labored.

Robeson's singing voice betrayed his physically situated body through its flight; as he (in body) struggled against his imposed national detention in the United States, his voice was located where be believed it ought to be: in the Third World, a constellation of desires, hopes, dreams, and objectives that, according to Prashad, is not a place but a "project."[122] Robeson's dismemberment—body in the United States, voice in Indonesia—is a function of his passport revocation but also reflects the colonial condition of fragmentation famously theorized by revolutionary intellectual Frantz Fanon.[123] It was through these similarly experienced conditions of state violence and oppression that Robeson/singer could imagine a universal humanity/audience and conjure it through his performances. The Bandung stage of Robeson's career was a torturous one, filled with no uncertain amount of danger, yet it was also a hopeful period as Bandung was in a sense a homecoming for Robeson; the personal relationships that he shared with attendees (including his longtime friend Nehru, whom he met while in London in the 1930s) and their collective investment in an end to colonialism built recognition without sight.

Robeson's culturo-political effectiveness in the absence of a physical presence in Bandung and elsewhere exposes the command of sound within political mobilizations. As heightened a spectacle as the Black body was within the media blitz of the post–*Brown v. Board of Education* moment, it too often functioned as a spectacle employed to meet the divergent needs of the movement and the state.[124] While news agencies attempted to capture the still life of a surging national mass, Robeson spoke and sung to a global majority as a living entity—literally breathing through speech and song—in order to organize the rage of their defeat and enliven their dreams of victory. The Civil Rights Movement that grew from the intense repression experienced by Robeson and others became a new platform for organizers and artists who looked to him as a role model, including singer-actor-activist Harry Belafonte, a self-described Robeson "disciple."[125] In 1958, the year of his passport reinstatement, he returned to London, where he was warmly received, but within five years he retired permanently from the public stage. Like many of the visionaries before him, Robeson suffered for his dreams of a better labor movement, a better United States, and a better world. But his political commitment to the rights of the common man everywhere never faded. As his life was near a close, he reminded his friends and family, "Though ill health has compelled my retirement, you can be sure that in my heart I go on singing:

> But I keeps laughing
> Instead of crying,
> I must keep fighting
> Until I'm dying,
> And Ol' Man River
> He just keeps rolling along!"[126]

* * *

In the hands of Paul Robeson, "Ol' Man River"—as sung to workers in Oakland, Detroit, Winston-Salem, Wales, and Spain—was a catalyst for a labor activism that incorporated culture as a protest strategy within job actions. This creative impulse, which had organized job rebellions among the enslaved for more than a century, entered prominently into the modern era of wage slavery while still carrying with it the legacy of sounds composed under the chattel system. During the post-Depression era it was the U.S. South—a complicated geography of social and labor regimes—that spawned a world anthem. Sonically grown from Negro spirituals and socially ordered by an entrenched Jim Crow disfranchisement, the song that organized the picket lines of tobacco workers on the eastern seaboard soon escaped by dreaming of a day, not too far in the future, when victory would belong to the workers.

4

Women's Work

"We Shall Overcome" and the Culture of the Picket Line

You think about that, it's almost like a prayer of relief. We didn't make up the song. We just started singing it as a struggle song.
—Lillie Mae Marsh Doster

Riding high on their international acclaim, Paul Robeson and Lawrence Brown performed a special concert for the Highlander Folk School in Washington, D.C., on May 10, 1942. Advertised as Robeson "in a program of Negro Folk Song," the event also included performances by Huddie "Leadbelly" Ledbetter, a well-known blues musician and figure of the Popular Front folk music circuit. Robeson's set included international folk songs such as the Irish "Oh, No John!" and Jewish "Chassidic Chant," but the grand majority of his songs exposed his deep investment in the songs of his people, the spirituals. His standards, "Go Down Moses," "Water Boy," and "Joshua Fit de Battle of Jericho," presented to the audience a lesson in Black folk traditions that emphasized liberty and freedom. The concert program offered no particular song titles for Leadbelly's set; instead, it referred to a group of "Negro Work Songs, Ballads, and Blues."[1] The emphasis on work in both men's repertoires is representative of their roots in the spirituals as well as Highlander's support of and strategic reliance on those traditions within their worker organizing programs. Within this nationally as-of-yet-unknown worker's commune in the hills of Tennessee, the lines delineating art and politics were blurred, often collapsing into each other as music, poetry, and drama vocalized the trials and triumphs of an aggrieved laboring class.

Robeson's participation in this event demonstrated his affinity for the laboring masses of the world, a diverse constellation of service and industrial, blue- and white-collar, men and women workers. However, his attendance also signals the growing importance of Highlander as an organization that furthered both labor education and art. As World War II ended, Highlander provided hope and sustenance to the frustrated, beleaguered, and in some cases hunted members of the labor movement. Just as Robeson's public life demonstrates, the radical anticommunist turn in the national political climate had the potential to devastate individuals and ravage entire organizations. In response to this assault, Highlander musical director Zilphia Horton looked to the workers for inspiration and organizing techniques. In the late 1940s she shared a budding worker and civil rights anthem that declares the ability of movement actors to withstand and overcome oppression. Grown from Black folk traditions, "We Shall Overcome" rose to prominence as the anthem of the Civil Rights Movement but began its political life as a freedom song in a labor battle on the southeastern seaboard. The complicated narrative of the song's birth in civil rights struggle begins in the histories of a failed Reconstruction in the U.S. South, but its transformation and usage provide compelling evidence of the unique regional organizing strategies of Black people and the resilience of their cultural formations.

Black women were central actors in both the ferocity of the strike that birthed the political usage of "We Shall Overcome" and the transition of the song from a strike ballad to a civil rights anthem. The 1945–46 tobacco strike in Charleston evidences the political import of the song, and a closer look at the women of the strike, as workers and cultural producers, demonstrates the critical role that Black women industrial workers played in the politics of movement building during the transition from a waning U.S. labor movement after World War II to a burgeoning U.S. Civil Rights Movement in the mid-1950s. Black women were a significant percentage of the tobacco industry's workforce and as such constituted an important interest group whose numbers could be organized to effect various work and community outcomes. The Black women of the Food, Tobacco, Agricultural, and Allied Workers of America (FTA) Local 15 used the factory as a space to act upon various sociopolitical issues and solidarities across gender and racial lines. As the 1945 strike gained momentum and public recognition, Black women continued to assert their right to fair work environments and equal citizenship through a ballad that they carried from the streets of South Carolina to the hills of Tennessee.

From Field to Factory: Race and Labor in Song

The historico-musical lineage of "We Shall Overcome" travels a long, and at times obscure, passage from its roots in Negro spirituals to its usage as a labor ballad. While the sacred and secular are often in conflict, the mid-twentieth-century use of an antebellum religious song fits squarely within the larger canon of Black protest music. Musicologist Brandi Neal outlines that there were methodological as well as social reasons for the adoption of certain songs into the mounting Black American freedom movements: "Elements of black sacred music, simple and repetitive melodies and texts and universal themes, facilitated the adaption of sacred hymns and songs. . . . [A]dditional functions of the black church, for example to serve as socioeconomic support to the oppressed black community in post-Civil War America, transformed social activism into a spiritual endeavor. It was inevitable that sacred traditions, namely music, aided social activism."[2] The role of the Black church in the Civil Rights Movement is indisputable; the prominence of Black religious figures such as Reverend Martin Luther King, Jr., Reverend Ralph Abernathy, Reverend Fred Shuttlesworth, and others highlights this point. However, the music of the movement, by and large, did not originate with these leaders of faith, nor did they solely carry it. Indeed, as musician-historian-activist Bernice Johnson Reagon outlines, "The church provided the structure and guidance for calling the community together; it trained the singers to sing the old songs and gave them permission to create new ones; [and] it *sometimes* produced real leaders, in its ministers, deacons, and church mothers."[3] The church then was an incubator for political activism, but as this description attests, its major agents were not necessarily the titled members of the church but the often-unnamed singers and musicians who used songs identified with particular faith communities and adapted them to other avenues of Black life, including trade unionism. Because of their grounding in methods of resistance to slavery, songs such as "Onward Christian Soldiers" gained new credence as a mechanism of political defense beyond their original religious use.

In the transition from slavery to freedom, Black people, according to historian Lawrence Levine, "assigned a central role to the spoken arts, encouraged and rewarded verbal improvisation, maintained the participatory nature of their expressive culture, and utilized the spoken arts to voice criticism as well as to uphold traditional values and group cohesion."[4] The twentieth-century continuation of this tradition is witnessed through the use of Negro spirituals, whose musical adaptability and attachment to histories and methods of struggle made them central elements of social justice organizing within Black communities.

The political landscape of the South in the New Deal era and the decade following was a determining factor in the continued use of the spirituals as a mode of opposition. The U.S. South in the late 1930s and 1940s was manacled to the idea of white supremacy in all things social and political, instituting the de jure and de facto practice of Jim Crow as a means of managing those divisions. Political disfranchisement, educational inequity, and employment discrimination made the post-Depression era South a fraternal twin of the pre-Emancipation South. As historian C. Vann Woodward wrote, "In so far as segregation is based on these assumptions [of Anglo-Saxon superiority and African inferiority], therefore, it is based on the old pro-slavery argument and has its remote ideological roots in the slavery period."[5] South Carolina offers a particular view of these ideological forces at work. Psychiatrist Robert Coles wrote in 1972 that "[n]o southern state can match South Carolina's ability to resist the claims of black people without becoming an object of national scorn."[6] Multiple factors contributed to this alchemy of repression, including radical segregation in all things social, labor stratification, and the dominance of a white supremacist Democratic Party. Between 1900 and 1944, only white Democrats were elected to state offices in South Carolina.[7] "White primaries" were held in the state into the 1950s, effectively precluding Black participation in elections on any substantive level. In their ability to control the political life and by extension the social hierarchies of Jim Crow, South Carolina politicians ensured that their state would retain the types of institutions that seventy-five years earlier had developed and maintained slavery in the U.S. South.

With sociopolitical conditions in South Carolina replicating those of a slave state, the spirituals spoke directly to the contemporary political struggles of African Americans. While some within the Black

community disparaged the spirituals due to varying investments in fully
acculturating to a modern, popular, and middle-class post-Emancipation
U.S. landscape, many praised the songs as a reflection of Black rigor and
ingenuity. Scholar and activist William Edward Burghardt Du Bois made
special note of the spirituals in his foundational text, *The Souls of Black
Folk*. Published in 1903, his "polyphonic montage" offers autobiographical material interlaced with Black society and politics under Jim Crow, all
of which is prefaced by chapter with an excerpt of musical notation.[8] Du
Bois notes the significance of this music, all of them spirituals, in the final
chapter, "The Sorrow Songs": "They that walked in darkness sang songs
in the olden days—Sorrow Songs—for they were weary at heart. And so
before each thought that I have written in this book I have set a phrase,
a haunting echo of these weird old songs in which the soul of the black
slave spoke to men." These "weird" melodies of the enslaved were for Du
Bois the penultimate achievement of the United States and its service to
world culture: "[S]o by fateful chance the Negro folk-song—the rhythmic
cry of the slave—stands to-day not simply as the sole American music,
but as the most beautiful expression of human experience born this side
the seas. . . . [I]t remains as the singular spiritual heritage of the nation
and the greatest gift of the Negro people."[9] Du Bois's contention that these
songs are the "sole American music" makes their placement within social
movements all the more impactful through identifying that there is both
a racial and national culture at work in the employment of these songs.
Within the context of struggles for justice, the adapted spirituals were the
cries of a minority group sounded through a national music.

While the spirituals were a national treasure, Du Bois was clear that
the songs could not be disarticulated from the conditions, experiences,
and exceptional knowledges of their producers. He outlined that there
are three unique characteristics that the Black race offers to America: "a
gift of story and songs—soft, stirring melody in an ill-harmonized and
unmelodious land; the gift of sweat and brawn to beat back the wilderness, conquer the soil, and lay the foundations of this vast economic
empire two hundred years earlier than your weak [white] hands could
have done it; the third, a gift of the Spirit."[10] The combination of music,
labor, and spirit that Du Bois described is revealed in the cultural and
social practices of both enslaved and free Africans in America. Under
slavery, the spirituals combined these three elements in very practical

ways. The use of the spirituals in enslaved communities highlights the spiritual and religious sentiments of the music while also document-ing the toil that organized the public world of the captives. Musicolo-gist Samuel Floyd, Jr. outlines the significance of work to the tradition of Negro spirituals: "The songs of black boatmen . . . were ascendant during the period of slavery. The calls, cries, and hollers of field workers and rivermen had been widespread, central, influential, and indispensable in slave culture from the beginning." From the documents and recordings available, musicologists surmise that the early work songs of the slaves "were characterized by regular meters and rhythms, contained grunts and moans as part of their expressive vocabulary, and made use of over-lapping call-and-response techniques." These rhythmic and melodic cries and hollers sometimes were "verbally articulate and communica-tive; at other times, they were wordless. But *meaning* was always pres-ent and was always communicated."[11] These songs and calls of the work-ers were part and parcel of the laboring practices in Black communities because they maintained an expressive quality constitutive of melody for pleasure, rhythm for work pace, and meaning for critique and resistance.

The element of rebellion in the spirituals transferred into the mod-ern era of industrial capitalism where wage slavery replaced the tortures and bondage of chattel slavery. As industrial unionism developed in the 1930s it was met with a new organizing challenge as waves of African Americans moved from the rural South to the urban industrial cen-ters. Organized labor's use of the spirituals, and its modern cousin gos-pel, grew with the advent of the Congress of Industrial Organizations (CIO) in 1935 and served to facilitate interracial organizing through the development of hybrid cultural practices within locals. Black work-ers, many of whom remained in the South in spite of opportunities in northern industries, brought the fervent rebelliousness of the spiritu-als to their job actions with the organization. Historian Philip Foner documents that "when Negro tobacco workers in Richmond went on strike in 1938 under the leadership of the CIO, they burst forth with the spiritual 'We Shall Not Be Moved.'"[12] This demonstration highlights both the necessity of music in Black protest cultures and the flexibil-ity that the CIO local allowed these workers in their attempts to gain equality in the workplace through protest. The spirituals continued to offer deliverance from the cruel realities of earthly existence, but within the labor movement their expression of liberation was tied to the protest actions of the workers on the ground. "We Shall Not Be Moved" thereby expressed "the attitude of all black workers who now received the opportunity to join the labor movement through the CIO."[13]

The work of cultural historian Brenda McCallum highlights the integral nature of gospel music to unionism in the one-time industrial mecca of Birmingham, Alabama. Black men in steel and other industries responded to the segregationist policies of their employers by forming gospel quartets to carry the union message. In addition to its political imperative, the culture of these quartets "developed within and grew out of what Archie Green has described as a 'traditionalizing circle' and was demonstrated through a complex of oral narratives about associational life—camaraderie on the job, solidarity in the union, and fellowship in church."[14] Singing songs such as "This What the Union Done" and "Union Boys Are We," these men integrated the radical potential of the union with the religious ferment of the gospel developing a hybrid space of political possibility through music. Calling it the "gospel of unionism," McCallum described that

> [it] served as a legally and culturally sanctioned basis for social action and reform and provided relatively safe and noncombative strategies and modes of protest that were particularly effective in the Jim Crow South. It was within the image of a Christian and democratic mission of unionism that the seemingly dichotomous values of spiritual fellowship and hope for material gain could be merged. Southern black workers' narratives and songs began to address social problems as well as spiritual problems; they were used to praise the gospel of unionism, with an implicit message of social protest. Pro-labor gospel songs thus served, concurrently, functions that were both oppositional and conservative.[15]

In this scenario, the union was a "secular church" with the songs becoming a part of the sermon that attempted to balance, or at least negotiate, the competing prerogatives of sacred and secular, employment and protest. The ability of these singers to integrate the union message with the cultural practices of the Black workers made the union a location of fellowship, further inducing Black participation and investment in workplace organizing.

Throughout her expansive repertoire on the songs of the Civil Rights Movement, Reagon discusses the use of what would become "We Shall Overcome" by Black workers in South Carolina. In her dissertation on the subject, she presents a South Carolina ensemble singer named Mrs. Janie Hunter, who sang "I Will Overcome" in Johns Island, outside of Charleston. Hunter recalled, "I have been singing that song for a very long time, and we think it was nothing then, until equality come and we did overcome." On its origins and transmission among the Black community she acknowledged the importance of oral traditions: "It is a Black song. They [Black singers in her community] didn't like the songs from the books; they learned it from the old people."[16] Here Hunter signals the song's presence within the histories of her community ("a very long time") and its performance aesthetics ("they didn't like the songs from the books"). By using alternative community pedagogies ("they learned it from the old people"), this Sea Island community was capable of expanding the reach of its performance models into nearby Charleston, where Black women workers on the picket lines used it and contributed to the song's evolution.

The many textual revisions of what we now know as "We Shall Overcome" highlight its growing militancy in the years leading up to the Charleston strike. While "I" has traditionally had a "communal aspect in black music culture,"[17] the change in the lyrics by the members of the Food, Tobacco, Agricultural, and Allied Workers of America (FTA) from "*I* will overcome" to "*we* will overcome" highlights, for a broad audience, the importance of collectivity in the project for freedom. The alteration of the line "we *will* overcome" to "we *shall* overcome" happened after the Charleston strike by workers at the Highlander Folk School (HFS), yet both versions point toward the certainty of redemption. The use of the word "someday" offers a vision into a future of brighter possibility, but this vision is not based on blind faith in things unseen—it is instead grounded in the action surrounding the performance of the song, whether that be on the picket line or in the jails that housed demonstrators during the Civil Rights Movement. The movement taking place in the contemporary moment is a large part of the potency of the lyric because it offers the tangible condition of struggle within a specific time and place. Whereas spirituals under slavery often relied on delayed redemption in heaven, "We Shall Overcome" rose to prominence within the context of a lived labor battle in which the workers understood that their victory would be here on earth.

The growth of "We Shall Overcome" into an anthem began in the spirituals but developed in part through the Black gospel tradition. Textually, the song is a derivative of Charles Albert Tindley's composition "I'll Overcome Someday," published in 1900. Tindley is recognized as the "progenitor of Black-American Gospel music." Born a slave in 1856, he taught himself to read while he worked as a laborer in Maryland. By 1900 he was a recognized public speaker on the verge of becoming pastor to a large congregation in Philadelphia. More than his oratory, however, it was his musical compositions that made him a recognizable fixture in Black faith communities. Despite being musically illiterate, Tindley made his mark on Black hymn traditions by deviating from the white composers whose style had marked the field. According to musicologist Horace Boyer, Tindley's style was punctuated by his "concentrat[ion] on [biblical] texts that gave attention to such important concerns of black Christians as worldly sorrows, blessings, and woes, as well as the joys of the after-life," emphasis on the pentatonic scale with "blue thirds and sevenths," and his allowance of "improvisation of text, melody, harmony, and rhythm" in his pieces.[18]

Most often, Tindley's lyrics reflected the conditions and struggles of his community and were applicable to the everyday situations of his parishioners and other Black Christians; in that way, his texts were thoroughly modern and could easily be translated into mobilizing texts for social or political issues. The delivery and performance of Tindley's lyrics are central to this effort because he had "a penchant for writing 'sing-a-long' choruses, choruses so exciting or moving that congregations join in the singing."[19] Such was the case with "I'll Overcome Someday."

> I'll overcome someday,
> I'll overcome someday;
> If in my heart I do not yield,
> I'll overcome someday.

The relationship of this text to "We Shall Overcome" is unmistakable—Tindley's chorus sets the foundation for the anthem known today. The change in meter from the original 3/4 to 4/4 for "We Shall Overcome" is important; 4/4 is the most basic of meters for musicians, hence its designation as "common time." This distinction allows for greater participation from new learners or the musically untrained, and the even number of beats per measure allows for ease of use during marches and other physical movements where pace is measured, such as on a picket line. The label of "common" also adds rhetorical significance to the song's usage in labor and civil rights organizing; it is both an acknowledgment of the quotidian nature of Black struggle in the United States and an ironic refutation of Black people's music and protest activities as common. Despite the difference in meter between "I'll Overcome Someday" and "We Shall Overcome," the short phrasing and repetitive chorus in A-A-B-A style induce audience participation in the performance of the song, thereby making it a communal project ideal for group protest and action. Tindley's hymns were not composed or performed in a rollicking Black musical style, yet his compositions became functional texts as central to the development of a twentieth-century Black spirituality as the Chicago creations of the "Father of the Gospel Blues" Thomas Dorsey. It was therefore the *practice* of "I'll Overcome Someday" that elevated it artistically and politically.

Neal argues that in addition to its references to early Western hymns "O Sanctissima" and "Lord Dismiss Us with Thy Blessing" and close relationship to "I'll Overcome Someday," "We Shall Overcome" is also shaped by the spiritual "No More Auction Block," also known as "Many Thousands Gone."[20] This piece is an important component of the sound and practice of Negro spirituals; its descriptions of a new Black identity that defies the institution of slavery made it a protest piece first during the era of Reconstruction.

> No more auction block for me, no more; no more.
> No more auction block for me, many thousands gone.

"No More Auction Block" held particular currency in the age of unregulated industrial wage labor, yet it gained popularity in the years following Emancipation due in large part to the performances of the Fisk Jubilee Singers, a collective of young Black singers at Fisk University who traveled around the United States and abroad to raise funds for their struggling school. They became ambassadors for the college as well as the Negro spirituals and in the process "constructed an aura of seriousness around their activities and projected the memory of slavery outwards as a means to make their musical performance intelligible and pleasurable."[21] This effort facilitated the recurrent use of slavery in twentieth century sociopolitical discourse and set the stage for solo Black concert singers such as Paul Robeson and Marian Anderson who made "No More Auction Block" and other spirituals a regular part of the classical vocal repertoire.

Neal and Reagon both suggest that the closest melodic relation to "We Shall Overcome" is the gospel hymn "I'll Be Alright." This song, also developed through oral traditions, became a part of the Black musical lexicon by the turn of the twentieth century largely through its prominence as "the root song that was standard repertoire in many traditional Black Baptist and Methodist churches in the United States."[22] With little exception the two songs are identical in their rhythmic and melodic structures.[23] Other authors have speculated on the author of the melody in the modern version of "We Shall Overcome,"[24] but it is clear that both "We Shall Overcome" and "I'll Be Alright" owe their most tremendous debt to a collective process stemming from the oral traditions of the Black community. As I will discuss later, questions of ownership are important, yet Black history demonstrates that within the projects of music and social movement making, the most advantages are gained when the individual (voice) is sacrificed in service of the collective.

The move from a hymn and religion-centered approach in Black music to a protest tradition is located in the technical particularities of the songs as well as their use. Reagon argues that freedom songs fall into two basic categories: adapted songs with a new purpose (as expressed primarily through new lyrics) and topical songs developed primarily for a movement, cause, or event.[25] The first category encapsulates most of the Black songs used within protest cultures of the first half of the twentieth century. The collective process through which these songs come to life is the first, and most important, element of their success. Minister Wyatt Tee Walker accentuated this element in his study of Black church music: "It was the music of the slaves more than anything else that gave them a sense of community. Everyone could participate, and the Spiritual form and performance were nonexclusionary."[26] This process induced collectivity through the intimacy of performance and picked up on a tradition of cooperation that was the basis for African survival under slavery and, in 1940s Charleston, the success of the workers on strike. When those on the picket line sang, a swell of hope would develop as members participated in naming their desires and dreams for whoever would listen.

Legacies of resistance to slavery reinforced the on-the-ground investment in a social justice approach to music making in Black communities, but in 1945 this history was also buttressed by influences from Popular Front folk music and performers. Reagon's own investment in music as a political tool led her to build a relationship with one of the most recognizable figures in American folk music, Pete Seeger. His influence as a part of the Almanac Singers, Weavers, and later People's Songs made him a pioneer in the use of music as a way to imagine and create a better world. Founded in Greenwich Village, New York, in the same year as the Charleston strike, People's Songs was a collective of musicians, educators, and trade unionists who, according to historian Robbie Lieberman, believed that "popularizing folk and topical songs would return the folk heritage to people, educate people about important issues, and encourage creativity and activism."[27] This belief was informed by many years of political activity around issues such as war, labor, and racism. Reagon attributes some of the popularity of "We Shall Overcome" to Seeger and his networks but is clear that "[i]t was not only Seeger . . . but Seeger chained to a struggle by the physical and musical presence of some of [the Movement's] most radical organizers" that made the song and its performances a triumph.[28] In that case, the song had no foundation or appeal outside of the struggle that it was used in service of and those who made it possible. It is not Seeger or even Highlander, then, but instead the Black women workers and their conditions in the Charleston FTA strike that must first be acclaimed.

Protest and Laughter Too: The Strike at American Tobacco Company

By 1945 the labor movement struggled to maintain its once lauded Popular Front cohesion. Loyalty oaths and no-strike clauses sustained the national American Federation of Labor (AFL) and CIO during the war effort, but the dramatic decrease in war production and the rapid return of soldiers in need of work depressed the once-stable wartime economy. In response, strikes broke out across the country. Sensational newspaper headlines emerged declaring, "Over 70,000 Workers Idle in U.S. Strikes."[29] Truck drivers in Chicago, rubber workers in Akron, and auto workers in Detroit struck for better working conditions and updated contracts. The work actions spread throughout the U.S. Empire as Puerto Rican sugar workers struck under the Confederación General de Trabajadores (General Confederation of Workers) for new contracts and the Federación Libre de Trabajadores (Free Federation of Workers) for union recognition.[30] As service men entered the cities to break the strikes, war rhetoric was used to support the aggressive tactics of federal and local authorities. During the truck driver strike in Chicago, city official Ellis T. Longnecker announced at a press conference, "The same army that beat [Adolf] Hitler will beat this strike." He then threatened all drivers younger than thirty-eight years of age with the possibility of draft if they failed to return to work.[31] This type of local and national repression and intimidation was common, yet strike actions accelerated nationally and showed the resolve of the workers in their efforts to control their labor conditions. While a majority of the domestic strikes occurred in the North, the South had its fair share of job actions, and the booming tobacco belt on the southeastern seaboard was a ripe location for worker activity.

The tobacco industry's development and production in the post–Civil War South made it a site of growth for businessmen and trade unionists alike. Tobacco developed as a cash crop in the late nineteenth century. Between 1880 and 1890, brightleaf tobacco grew into a significant source of revenue in South Carolina.[32] Despite an initially meteoric rise, tobacco had numerous rises and falls within the state's economy. Historians Eldred Prince, Jr. and Robert Simpson note that "[t]he growers' tragic tendency to overproduce compounded by their lack of solidarity made them vulnerable to a highly prejudiced marketing system."[33] As the industry mechanized around the turn of the century, small farmers lost their investment if they refused to join in the ominous tobacco monopolies like that of James Buchanan Duke of North Carolina, who set a standard for emergent businessmen across the nation. With a regional tobacco empire brewing, Duke moved to New York in order to build a tobacco base in the North. Instead of fighting his competitors

[handwritten margin note: Tobacco monopoly broken up]

in North Carolina, he followed John D. Rockefeller's lead and bought them out. From these purchases, Duke formed the American Tobacco Company (ATC) in 1904.[34] Also like Rockefeller, Duke's business activity was being watched. During the 1911 antitrust trials under President Theodore Roosevelt, ATC was divided into fourteen smaller companies.[35] This division furthered competition and escalated the economic highs and lows of the industry. The precariousness of the market would continue to plague tobacco even while mechanization offered new opportunities and new international markets.

Prosperity returned to the tobacco industry in the 1940s and '50s in large part due to the centrality of tobacco to the war effort. During World War II the demand for cigarettes skyrocketed both domestically and abroad. The popularity of ATC's Lucky Strike brand cigarettes offered some buffer from the inevitable rise and fall of the tobacco market; tobacco leaf prices doubled between 1940 and 1946, but domestic sales of Lucky Strike increased by 32 million units in 1946 alone.[36] Domestic consumption reflected attempts by families to cater to their relatives in the war through care packages and other gifts. The prominence of the cigarette as an easy and portable tobacco product made the economy of Charleston and other tobacco cities grow exponentially.

The extension of wealth within Charleston had its limits, however. The economic and material conditions of Charleston's Black community in the 1940s had seen very little gain in the decades since Emancipation. In 1946, the National Urban League (NUL), an interracial, nonpartisan organization working for African American rights, visited the city for four weeks in order to document the social and economic conditions of the Black community. Working in conjunction with the Charleston Welfare Council, the NUL collected data on education, politics, and labor. They reported that infant mortality in Charleston was nearly two times as high for Black children as it was for white children. Local political organizations did not work interracially; in the rare instance that cross-racial cooperation was solicited, the sole interracial group in Charleston welcomed "discussion of non-controversial subjects" only. The focus of the NUL report, and the greatest evidence offered to explicate the gross discrepancies between Black and white in Charleston, was labor. In accordance with the national trend, the number one occupation for Black women in Charleston was domestic service. Black men primarily worked as laborers in factory and field. Black women and men were systematically denied opportunities for city jobs and professional positions, including law enforcement. As of 1946, there were no Black men on the police force[37]—evidence of employment discrimination and an indication of the vulnerabilities to legal and extralegal violence faced by Black Charlestonians.

The white public's perception of Black workers within industry fed the belief that they were ill suited for professional positions. Managers and business owners in Charleston overwhelmingly commented to the NUL that Black workers' "[a]ttendance [was] poor and below average." Their highest compliment described Black performance on the job as "fairly satisfactory except on Monday after pay day." There was a silver lining within some service industries, however. Increasingly, Black workers joined the small but steady stream of trade unionism in Charleston. During the 1940s, Local 1422 of the International Longshoremen's Association (ILA-AFL) and Local 78 of the Bricklayers Union (AFL) were all Black, with the exception of white managers on the docks. Despite their numbers and organization, the extent of Black participation in citywide union coalitions and politics was limited. The Central Labor Union was a local coalition of labor organizations with an exclusively white membership. As a federation of workers, it was largely responsible for the public maintenance and representation of labor in Charleston. Black workers attributed their absence in the organization to differential treatment within local labor based on race.[38] As a consequence, Black workers had neither access to nor faith in the Labor Union, exposing a rift among the ranks of Charleston labor.

In the midst of segregated locals, the FTA set a different standard. The international initially established itself in the South under the United Cannery, Agricultural, Packing, and Agricultural Workers of America (UCAPAWA-CIO), an organization that developed during the Great Depression of the 1930s and, according to historian Vicki Ruiz, worked on the West Coast to "incorporat[e] large numbers of Mexican, black, Asian, and Anglo food processing workers under its banner."[39] Their project in southern tobacco was to debunk the racially exclusive Tobacco Workers' International Union (TWIU-AFL). UCAPAWA hoped to organize the interracial tobacco industry, which relied on large numbers of Black workers, a majority of whom were women.

Recent UCAPAWA wins in other parts of the country helped the organization to gain ground in the South. In 1942 they won a contract for the P. Lorillard Plant in Ohio and later established themselves across northern tobacco plants in New Jersey and Pennsylvania.[40] Their success then carried over into the South. Local 22 in Winston-Salem, North Carolina, gained organizing rights from R. J. Reynolds Tobacco Company in 1943, with a contract following the next year. This drive was successful in a number of ways. Historian Robert Korstad describes Local 22 as "the prize local in what was arguably the most diverse left-led union in the country."[41] The local developed leaders among the Black community and encouraged Black women in particular to take an active leadership role in the union. Moranda Smith, a member of Local 22, was a leader in the local and became the first Black woman on the executive leadership of any U.S. trade union. In 1944 UCAPAWA became the FTA. This change, which sought to incorporate more workers in various industries, signaled the promise of the union's efforts to organize tobacco in the mid-1940s.

Taking advantage of labor unrest in the mid and late stages of U.S. involvement in World War II, the FTA spread on the southeastern seaboard. Charleston Local 15 became a major player in that project and the company took notice. By 1940 ATC implemented a public relations strategy that took readers inside the employer-employee relationship at the Charleston plant. In July ATC published *The American Tobacco Company and Its Service to the Public*. This document intended to paint a picture of industrial bliss and positive relations in order to dismiss the concerns of the workers and their union. "One of the greatest assets possessed by our Company is the fine relationship between its management and its people," they asserted. *The American Tobacco Company* provided numerous reasons for why this relationship was so pleasant:

> Because it is the policy of the Company to deal with its employees in matters pertaining to wages, hours and working conditions through representatives selected by its employees. Because we believe in paying—and do pay—fair and liberal wages. . . . Because we believe in and maintain a reasonable work week and a reasonable work day. . . . Because we provide clean and pleasant working conditions and a healthy environment in our plants. . . . And, finally, because we believe in the utmost

freedom of discussion between the management and its employees, or their representatives, towards the settlement of any problems that may arise.[42]

According to the company author, small numbers of employee representatives offered sufficient voice for the workers, with everyone bargaining in good faith. Despite this assurance, ATC acknowledged that it met with representatives of the TWIU, the segregated local, and renewed agreements with the union for 1938, 1939, and 1940.[43] With large numbers of Black workers laboring in the tobacco plants, an alternative was desperately needed if organized labor was to make its mark in the southern tobacco industry. That alternative was the UCAPAWA (FTA), which gained recognition as the workers' bargaining unit in Charleston in 1943.

The FTA's program of industrial unionism included bringing Black workers into leadership positions, thereby exponentially increasing the numbers of organized workers in the plant. Local 15 organizer Stephen P. Graham noted that it was the Black workers—who composed, in his estimation, 95 percent of the union membership—who carried the union battles.[44] Black workers brought with them particular experiences and grievances as they navigated the workspace. In October of 1945, Black women at the ATC cigar factory in Charleston held a sit-down strike in protest of the firing of a male colleague. According to published reports, the unnamed Black man was fired due to "charges of familiarities with negro [sic] women workers, who were under the supervision of white forewomen." Upon investigation of the matter with the accused, he denied the charge, and the woman in question said "she knew nothing of the affair." President of Local 15 Reuel Stanfield said that the incident had exposed "a bad state of affairs. The girl in the case is all upset and the man's wife is stirred up too. The women workers are afraid if they go back to work they might get in the same kind of a mix-up and the men don't want to take the chance of having scandalous charges placed against them."[45] This situation highlights the contiguously raced and gendered dynamics of this region and industry. Indeed, as Glenda Gilmore has shown, Black women challenged "the South" imagined by white southerners, a place with "fundamental social hierarchies that depended nearly as much upon fixed gender roles as they did on the privileges of whiteness."[46] Yet the Black women demonstrated their willingness to respond to racial attacks in the workplace. It is clear that this was not an isolated incident considering that the action staged by these Black women was described as the second in recent months.

The experience of Black workers—Black women workers in particular—is documented by more than their work actions. The company offered visual representation of the unequal working conditions in their public propaganda piece *Sold American!* Within the book-length tract, visual aids are used to explain the functions of the plant from tobacco harvest to final product shipping, yet these images reveal more than mechanical plant operations—they expose deep racial antagonisms and hierarchies of privilege within the factory. The types of work produced by ATC employees highlighted the necessity of organization in the industry:

> The majority of the workers, other than stemmers, employed in leaf plants are unskilled workers. These include "pickers" and "searchers," female employees in the stemming room who remove any foreign materials and stems which remain on the tobacco strips after the leaves have been stemmed. They also include "hangers," who place the tobacco on sticks before it goes into the redrying machine, and general laborers, who move the tobacco from one part of the plant to another and pack it in hogsheads. The great majority of all workers in leaf establishments are Negroes.[47]

Black women were the principal workers for the grand majority of the "unskilled" and "general" jobs described here. Through visual techniques of perspective and scenery, *Sold American!* provides the "photographic evidence"[48] of Black women's compromised and degraded positions within the company.

Figure 4.1 depicts the initial leaf processing station where the product is cleaned and reconditioned. This step is shown to be the exclusive province of Black women, who are dressed in clean yet ordinary street clothes with headscarves wrapped tightly over their hair. The only mechanization offered to these women is the conveyor belt that carries the raw tobacco at a steady pace; their labor is otherwise entirely manual, producing heaps of discarded stems all trimmed by hand. The photographer deems unimportant whose hands are laboring here. It is impossible for the viewer to see these women's faces in the photograph due to the distance between the photographer and the subjects and because the majority of the women in the photo have their backs to the camera. The long-shot angle of the camera offers breadth but no depth as we see the two dozen or so Black women bent over the conveyor belt and standing at the storage stalls while they stem, sort, and dry the tobacco. Viewers are given no signs and no clues about who these women are beyond the raw materials of their dress and racial appearance, a dangerous omission that allows too quick a dismissal of these precariously situated women. In this scene, the women are anonymous laborers whose only function is to offer evidence of the company's productivity and, presumably, the factory's integration.

In comparison, Figure 4.2 offers a look at the work of white women who require no headscarves. Despite being more closely associated with the industrial component of the company due to their proximity in the photo to cigarette-sorting machinery, their appearance with neatly coiffed hair, slim waists, and pressed uniforms highlights a distinct femininity. Black women's work with tobacco plants represented an immature and raw female subject (a contested and often racially exclusive category),[49] while white women's work with cigarettes at the end of the line of production demonstrated an evolved womanhood. Long gone were the turn-of-the-century fears over white women entering the workforce—this photograph illustrated for a midcentury audience that these young women were polished and well kept by the ATC. One of the women even sits during her job, a luxury unavailable to the Black women of Figure 4.1. The descriptive captions under each of the photos also place a positive subjectivity within grasp of the white women as they are offered titles such as "catcher" and "inspectress," while the Black women are given none. Their caption is no more than a description of the work being done, not who is doing it. Black women in this ATC document are thereby the unnamed and unacknowledged cogs in the wheel of production. In this context, Black women's demands at ATC necessarily combined elements of labor and social protest. Due to their large numbers and particular experiences, Black women's voices would continue to lead the call for justice in the actions of Local 15.

As Local 15 grew in numbers and became more organized, demands on the company began to mount and strike conversation brewed. One month prior to the Black women's sit-down action, the Charleston *News and Courier* reported that the local had called on the U.S. Conciliation Service to assist them in their demand for a fifteen-cent increase in hourly wages. It is likely that Black women workers took strength and momentum from the union's demand and used it for their own action that October. The wage demand by the union was only part and parcel of the program, however. While the negotiations continued, Local 15 President Stanfield announced, "[T]he union is launching a city-wide campaign to interest the people of Charleston in supporting the union's demand."[50] With nearly fourteen hundred workers eligible for the wage increase, it was vital that the local incorporate the broader community into the struggle and offer some education about their goals and organization. Toward that end, the union began an aggressive leafleting campaign in Charleston at the end of October 1945. This public campaign coincided with a full-fledged call to strike on October 22, 1945, which included approximately one thousand white and Black workers. They demanded a "wage increase [of 40 percent], a closed shop, six days sick leave, and improved working conditions."[51]

The strike quickly became a national affair through the coordination of strike activity among regional locals. A walkout occurred at FTA Local 186 in Philadelphia on October 15, followed by the strike announcement at Local 15, and finally Local 56 of Trenton, New Jersey, which joined on October 25. The locals were in contact for some time in order to secure a standard contract for all three ATC locals. In addition to the strike, the locals called for a national boycott of ATC products. A major target of the boycott was the popular Lucky Strike cigarette. Stanfield believed that "[w]ith the support of the CIO members nationally, we expect to cut the sales by about 3 million packages of Lucky Strikes per day."[52] Broad trade union support was witnessed in a number of ways. The Teamsters (AFL) vowed not to ship ATC products until the strike was over, and as I will soon discuss, the Charleston unit of the National Maritime Union (NMU-CIO) also proved to be an important ally to the FTA strikers.

In spite of the solidarities expressed by the three FTA locals with respect to a standard contract, different issues were discussed and

Figure 4.1.
Black women process the raw tobacco. Source: *Sold American! The First Fifty Years* (American Tobacco Company, 1954), 122.

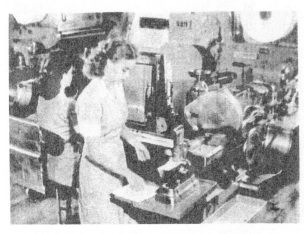

Figure 4.2.
White women manage the cigarette sorting machines. Source: *Sold American! The First Fifty Years* (American Tobacco Company, 1954), 127.

prioritized at each plant. In Philadelphia, their demands included a "no-discrimination clause in the contract,"[53] an item that the Charleston local would have been hard-pressed to make legible, let alone win. Issues of geography also were evident in the way that the locals positioned themselves within the industry. Stanfield acknowledged the North-South differential when he commented, "We think it is about time that the workers in the South were paid decent wages. That is what we are striking for and we think that a lot of people in Charleston, workers and business men alike, will support us, especially now that our president, Harry S. Truman, has told them that companies can afford to give them wage increases. The boycott will give them a chance to take definite action against low wages for the South."[54] Leveling the economic playing field between North and South was a project that the CIO invested in during the decade. Recognizing that the labor movement would perish without national uniformity, the program attempted to bring the depressed wage scale of the South on par with the higher scale of the North. Their major project in this endeavor, appropriately named Operation Dixie, was launched in May 1946 with 250 organizers and one million dollars.[55]

The success of Operation Dixie in the South is dubious. While their efforts brought much needed attention to the area, the discrepancy between the organization's philosophies and practices caused fissures and conflict. The post–World War II moment offered the opportunity to sail high on the winds of victory abroad but the political climate of the United States under McCarthyism suppressed the more radical component of the CIO. Labels of "un-American" and "communist" were hurled at the international, which struggled to defend itself. Interracial organizing was increasingly scrutinized as the largely white veteran population returned for their jobs and the CIO's political endorsement of southern Democrats did not help race relations within the organization. In order to straddle the line, Operation Dixie was clear about the fact that reaching out to Black workers did not mean an endorsement of social equality. Historian Ernest Obadele-Starks remarks that this limited view required a unionism that focused "on shared economic issues, rather than on broader problems of social equality, in order to be successful."[56] Interracial unionism therefore was a limited project in the South with little investment in or resources with which to struggle around issues of race or gender. This failure had profound effects on the South's economy, but the Local 15 drive offered hope in the early stages of the program's development. Their enthusiasm and stamina in Charleston made for an impressive test case on the efficacy of a southern CIO program.

As the strike gained public notice in Charleston, a program of divide and conquer was established by the local authorities. Black workers were disproportionately targeted for harassment on the picket line. In early November 1945 Stanfield commented in the local press that the

Black picketers were peacefully demonstrating and resented the police cursing them. Along with the cursing, a physical event occurred where signs were smashed. In response, Stanfield called for a larger picket line.[57] Ultimately, the picket line called for by Stanfield was composed of only two hundred picketers, a scant fraction of the twelve hundred that he originally hoped for. This situation may indicate race relations in the plant; picket line statistics offered by Stanfield nearly two weeks later revealed that there were approximately seventy-five white and two hundred Black workers marching in their segregated pickets.[58] These numbers show the determination of the Black workers but also suggest that the two hundred people who showed up in support of ending police harassment may have been composed primarily, or even solely, of Black workers. This picket did little to stem attacks and harassment of Black workers continued. At the end of November, a Black woman worker was arrested for "disorderly conduct." This amorphous and egregiously used category of criminality was disproportionately inflicted upon Black women.[59] Recognizing that the charges were ludicrous, her fellow workers rose to the challenge. Three white women workers testified that the charges against her were false, and she was released.[60] While imperfect, the union ignited some sense of solidarity across racial lines.

By January 1946, striker attrition and concern for those who remained was making news in Charleston. Headlines such as "Plant Manager Pleased at Cigar Output" and "Union Asks Public to Aid Strikers Here" called into question the union's proximity to victory.[61] Nationally, the federal Fair Employment Practices Commission bill, which demanded an end to discrimination in hiring, was filibustered in the Senate with Democratic Senator Richard Russell of Georgia claiming that if the bill were passed, Hitler could get a job in the United States ahead of returning GIs.[62] Back in Charleston, the picket lines were becoming contentious. Stanfield was arrested in January on disorderly conduct charges, adding another level of antagonism and structural uncertainty to the strike. The arrest was surely suspect, due not only to the precarity of the union and their activities within city politics but also to the nature of coverage offered by the local *News and Courier*, which was owned by a wealthy white Charlestonian who was, according to journalists Gene Roberts and Hank Klibanoff, "as conservative as they came."[63] This local archive must be taken with a grain of salt when recounting the events of the strike and requires a reading of silences in order to understand the unique position of the Black workers involved. What the *News and Courier* does not yield in its coverage is the fact that the spirit of those demonstrating was not lost in the flurry of attacks and setbacks. In order to maintain their drive, the strikers employed weapons outside of the average labor arsenal.

Music was a dramatic part of the picketer exhibition outside of the factory. Charleston was nestled in an area of the country where labor radicalism and Black music culture converged. According to cultural historian Michael Denning, "The tobacco towns of Durham, Richmond, and Winston-Salem that were the home of [a] black working-class left also nurtured the Piedmont's blues and gospel culture."[64] Following the oral traditions of the blues and gospel, the Black workers of Local 15 made "I/We Will Overcome" the prize piece of their demonstrations. Member Stephen Graham considered it the theme song of the union. He said, "As far as Charleston was concerned, we were the first to use it. . . . We would meet at one house and someone would say, boy I don't know how we are going to make it but 'We'll overcome someday.'" Another member, Isiah Bennett, relayed the song's influence: "Everytime [*sic*] we opened up a meeting we would sing a song. 'We Shall Overcome,' 'We Shall Not Be Moved.' . . . The song 'We Shall Overcome' originated on the picket lines, in the union halls and in the churches where we would meet."[65] The musical performance of solidarity by the workers was the glue that bound the picket line, union hall, and church together. The many different layers of interaction between the Black workers "together . . . formed a strong group identity, a bond that grew out of shared life experiences and their music expressed deeply felt emotions about their common condition."[66]

Music's powerful ability to compel further strike action and antagonize the employer and authorities was documented in Charleston; less than three months into the strike, "[t]he singing of union songs [was] stopped by order of the police department."[67] Various attempts like this one by the authorities to disrupt and forcibly end the strike were met with resistance. During the course of their strike, the FTA developed deep ties to another CIO union in Charleston: the NMU, a left-led interracial union that in the 1940s successfully lobbied the Merchant Marine to appoint its first Black captain, Hugh Mulzac.[68] The NMU in

Charleston showed similar determination in their support of the strike at ATC. Anthony Lucio, port agent for the union, offered preference for jobs aboard Charleston ships to NMU members who joined the FTA picket lines. The presence of the NMU brought an energy that was deeply appreciated.

The musical gag order imposed by the Charleston police was part and parcel of the public debate around the strike. An unsigned editorial in the *News and Courier* welcomed the silence:

> The CIO should be grateful to the city police of Charleston for putting a stop to the merriment and levity in the picket lines at the American Tobacco [C]ompany. The strikers are supposed to be in dead earnest, carrying the torch for deep convictions, marching toward the New Freedom. But there's little fun in these serious matters and the natural song that is locked in the hearts of the cigar-makers eventually had to burst out. The police action has brought them back to proper decorum, and alas, to the humdrum routine of workers on strike. Laughter is not for crusaders.[69]

On the surface, this editorial appears to agree with the policy of the police department, yet it also casts judgment on the "humdrum routine" of labor, exposing the complicated layers of the politics of performance. The author addresses not simply an end to song or an end to distracting sounds on the line, but instead the end of the "merriment and levity" that the music elicits. These emotions and their display—less than the sounds—are what the author exposes as the true concern with the workers' picket activity. In their "march toward the New Freedom," the workers found the "fun in these serious matters" and demonstrated that the solemn labor protest imagined by this writer was an objectionable model for Charleston workers and their unions. Lucio announced that the forced passivity of strike performance was "a violation of our civil liberties." In response to this attack, the FTA and NMU joined forces in the courts "to obtain the right to shout union slogans and sing union songs in the picket line at the tobacco plant."[70] This issue, however, would have deeper resonances than its impact on the strike. Little did the Charleston police know that the songs sung on the picket line by Black workers were reinforced by a history more powerful than their

demands for silence and that one song in particular, "We Will Overcome," would have a purpose and a future beyond Charleston.

The Making of an Anthem: Living Archives
and Contested Anthologies

As the strike moved forward, the union worked to expose the perspectives of the workers. Black and white women were vocal throughout the
strike process and became the representatives for the FTA nationally. On
the West Coast the union had a socially and politically generative relationship with women workers; Ruiz describes that "UCAPAWA [later
FTA] locals provided women cannery workers with the crucial 'social
space' necessary to assert their independence and display their talents.
They were not rote operatives numbed by repetition, but women with
dreams, goals, tenacity, and intellect."[71] Women's leadership in the FTA
was replicated across the country. Approximately eighty women of the
national union participated in a "tobacco strike parade" in front of the
White House in order to support the striking workers in Charleston,
Philadelphia, and Trenton.[72] The union organ, the FTA News, also offered
women ample discursive space in their coverage of the strike. Announcing "The Strike Is Solid," the FTA News in December 1945 quoted at
length six women workers, two from each plant on strike. Mary Turner
of Philadelphia Local 186 discussed the tactics used by the bosses:

> At the beginning of the war, the Company hired colored girls as cigar
> makers for the first time. At first we didn't want these girls in the plant.
> We were afraid they would work for lower pay. But then we saw that
> the bosses wanted to pit us against one another. They gave us different
> lunch hours, different wash rooms. During our organizing campaign,
> the stooges tried to make the Negro girls distrust the white girls. But it
> didn't work. We came to understand their game. And every time they
> tried to keep us apart—we just got closer together.[73]

Her assessment of these Jim Crow practices in the North points toward
a shared condition of racial and gender antagonism employed by the
company managers in order to divide and conquer the workers across
the three locals. Their ability to overcome these tactics as a collective

of women was informed by the culture of the union and the education that it provided to its members with regard to class oppression.

The two women quoted from Local 15 offered distinct perspectives on the reasons for their participation in the strike. Wiladean Blankenship, a white worker, commented,

> I wasn't in the union till 2 days after the strike began. Didn't even know what unions are about. The boss got up and made a speech, telling us we didn't have to join the Union; we could keep on working. But there was no work to do. All we did was sit around and laugh. I decided to go home and think about it, because, somehow, it all didn't seem right. I've been out on the picket line ever since.

Blankenship's strike experience is here narrated as a reasoned and dispassionate response to a boss whose alternative to the union was to "keep on working" even in the absence of work. Her assessment was noticeably different from that of her Black coworker, Irene Reid:

> Since our 5 [cent] raise, my take-home pay is $25 a week, but it isn't enough. I have to care for mother. Rent is $17 a month; insurance, $10. Groceries cost me $40 a month now. Then there's clothes and everything else. When I get a full supply of groceries one week, I have to cut down the next week, in order to keep within my budget. The colored girls in our plant get 2 or 3 [cents] less than the others. Before the war, only the lowest paid work was for Negro people. Recently, they've been spreading the word around that they were going to fire the colored girls.[74]

This description focuses primarily on the bread-and-butter issues of the Black women workers in the plant—practical considerations for a community in Charleston that struggled to live above the poverty line. While Blankenship's account describes a slow, calculated relationship to unionization, Reid's demonstrates a distressed need to protect and provide for her family and the jobs of her fellow women. These two perspectives are fairly representative of the quotes chosen by the FTA in its publication; of the six accounts in the article—three white women and three Black women—all three Black women mentioned finances in their account, while only one of their white colleagues did so. The article exposed the racialized considerations at play among the FTA membership nationally and the tensions that existed even within the solidarity of strike activity.

By early 1946, after nearly three months on strike, the workers in Charleston struggled with decreasing morale. The accumulated effects of the post-holiday slowdown in production, threats, limited income, and continued employer rigidity encouraged the workers to speak with their feet as attrition became one of the most pronounced obstacles facing the strike. In January the *News and Courier* reported a public plea from the union: "The appeal, signed by Reuel Stanfield, president of Local 15, Food, Tobacco, Agricultural and Allied Workers of America, CIO, stated 'our funds are running low. Our workers are suffering and need help badly. They will be forced to return to work, thereby causing all workers in the South and the nation to lose, if they do not get help quickly.'"[75] Stanfield's appeal demonstrated concern for the immediate circumstances of the workers in Charleston as well as the success of organized labor nationally. This was a necessary pairing of interests; Local 15's relationship with and strike activity alongside sister Locals 186 and 56 and their coordinated efforts with the Teamsters and NMU put into practice a national solidarity with the potential to significantly grow union strength and density across industries. A successful job action in Charleston therefore carried with it both local and national consequences.

While rhetorically powerful, Stanfield's statement exposed the desperation of the Charleston workers as they approached their fourth month on strike. City residents too began to grow weary of the strike. On February 1, Mary Notwen wrote a letter to the *News and Courier* editor in which she called the FTA strike a "total failure."[76] An attempted raid by the TWIU-AFL, public reports documenting the increased numbers of workers returning to work, and major union settlements in the automotive sector compelled the union negotiating committee to come to the table with ATC. On March 31, Local 15 ratified an agreement for a 15 percent increase in wages—an offer that the union had flatly denied six weeks earlier.

In the wake of the agreement, the public appeared to be silently thankful that the distraction had been eliminated. The *News and Courier* discontinued reports of the workers, offering no follow-up on the new conditions inside the factory, nor did reporters document any further the circumstances of the Philadelphia local that had not yet signed an agreement with ATC.[77] However, those invested in Charleston's Black community paid some final notice to the labor action. In its 1946 report, the NUL documented the end of the strike:

> During the period of the survey, the Charleston Tobacco Workers were on strike because of low wages. Before the survey was completed, the workers returned to their respective jobs with a 15% increase in wages and salaries—an increase of 8 cents per hour. It seemed, however, that the increase was not as great as was expected. The union attributed this to the lack of education and organization. The education of the workers was very low and they did not seem to understand the real meaning of organized labor. As a result, a portion of the workers returned to their jobs or crossed the picket line while the strike was in action and caused production to continue, even though on a small scale. The salary and wages ranged (prior to the strike) from 42 cents per hour minimum, to 47 cents per hour maximum. The increase ranged from 50 cents per hour minimum, to 55 cents per hour maximum. This is the major Congress of Industrial Organizations [CIO] local in the county. It has a reported total membership of approximately 1,200 almost 1,000 of which are colored.[78]

This description, which is heavily influenced by statements from union leadership, blames the workers for the collapse of the strike, placing their "lack of education and organization" at the center of the strike's failure to halt production at ATC. Considering that 83 percent of the union workers were Black (according to NUL figures), this judgment is surely a raced one that considers success only in terms of empirical evidence (numbers on strike, wage increases, etc.). Historian Robin Kelley's poignant observation that social movements are too often judged in terms of success and failure rather than the power of their dreams highlights the qualitative importance of worker resistance and encourages an engagement with the movement and its actors on its own terms.[79] This option was not immediately available to the Charleston workers; they received little or no public voice with which to narrate the strike events—at least not until members of Local 15 traveled northwest into the woods of Tennessee.

In 1946 and 1947 members of Local 15 traveled to Monteagle, Tennessee, to participate in workshops at the Highlander Folk School (HFS). These interracial groups were composed of FTA members from across the South. Individual unions were often invited to intensive sessions with Highlander, and for the 1947 FTA session, from May 11 through 24, the unions made sure to incorporate the music of their movement. The July *FTA News* bulletin printed a photo of a half dozen attendees to the session with a caption that highlighted the use of song in the training: "'Great Day, the union's marching' [sic] was one of the favorites in the after supper sings at Highlander Folk School, Monteagle, Tenn., during the two–week FTA term. . . . Here Washington O'Bannon, steward at Quaker Oats Local 19, Memphis, Tenn., sings a verse of 'Great Day' to be followed by the whole group in the chorus. Zylphia [sic] Horton of Highlander staffs [sic] plays accordion."[80] Encouraging the workers to sing was not only an act of empowerment and solidarity in the moment but also became a form of oral history as the workers learned the context of the songs and took them back to their locals across the South. Highlander was a major platform for the proliferation of southern movement songs during the transition from World War II into the Civil Rights Movement and as such became a living archive of movement culture and leftist strategy.

HFS developed in the 1930s as an institution that catered to and celebrated "workers with hand and brain." Its three-dimensional approach to worker organizing made it a clearinghouse for rising leaders within trade unionism, in particular the CIO. Founded by Myles Horton in the hills of Tennessee, HFS originally offered educational opportunities for regional workers and invested in local labor issues. In 1934 Highlander initiated a Worker's Council that developed the school's activities and voted on the implementation of labor organizing and community action projects. Shortly thereafter, Zilphia Mae Horton (then known as Zilphia Mae Johnson) arrived to work on the budding extension program, which sought to add national labor events and drives to the HFS agenda. As the focus broadened, so too did their tactics. The growing cultural program in the school was fed by Horton's background as a concert pianist and her investment in music as an organizing tool. The residential program established by HFS in 1938 became a test ground for the uses of culture in labor organizing.[81]

Music and drama were key components of the worker education program at HFS. According to historian Aimee Horton, "[M]usic and drama in the form of labor songs and labor plays were viewed in terms of how they could be used by local unions and the larger movement." HFS staff were determined "to teach students how to be play producers and song leaders—how to carry their songs and plays and those of other workers back to their locals, back into the movement." Through this focus, HFS served as an epicenter of cultural strategy. The workers too participated in moving the songs from HFS back into the movement: "Gathered from and inspired by the movement; sung, collected and taken back to local unions by many groups of worker-students and, finally, published in union-sponsored song books, [the movement songs] traveled across the South. . . . The process continued with the discovery of original strike songs on visits to picket lines."[82]

Visits to strike activity sites around the country provided Zilphia Horton with a rich archive of protest songs. The establishment of citizen schools across the South to train Black activists and community members in the practices of democracy (first among them voting) cultivated a mobilized Black citizenry and helped to proliferate the cultural practices that developed within those communities. Labor songbooks documented the school's reliance on song as a pedagogy that did not focus on teaching music as notation or theory, but instead, according to education scholar Terese Volk, "music [was] used to teach about labor and labor concepts."[83] It was therefore the practicality and applicability of music to daily conditions that made it an important reserve of information and transformation that could be *used*. The HFS songbook included the standout "We Shall Overcome." While the song is often associated with the school's high-profile names of Zilphia Horton, Pete Seeger, and Guy Carawan, the song's utilization in the 1945–46 Charleston strike is the event that brought the song to HFS; this fact, alongside its musico-political genealogy in the Negro spirituals, makes its genesis as a movement song truly grassroots. Yet, as I mentioned earlier, the oral traditions at work in its history also obscure its trajectory. Aimee Horton describes the development of "We Shall Overcome" this way: "[M]embers of a CIO Food and Tobacco Workers union in Charleston, South Carolina, changed its lyrics during a strike in 1945 and sang 'We Will Overcome' to maintain morale on the picket line. The following year two women from the union local attended a workshop at High-lander and taught the song to other students."[84] The identity of these two women is one of the greatest mysteries in the history of the song.

A Black woman named Lucille Simmons is mentioned in oral his-tories of the song as the picket line architect for "We Will Overcome," leading the singing and adaptation of its words to fit the occasion. In rare and tentative accounts she is referenced as the original teacher of the song at HFS.[85] Local 15 member Stephen Graham remembered that "Delphine Brown and Lucille Simmons would always lead ['I/We Will Overcome'] and when [they] put the words out we would all fall behind."[86] The April 1946 session at HFS was the first FTA leadership training school. At that event "[s]eventeen black and white tobacco, food-processing, and cottonseed oil compress workers from seven southern states attended."[87] This session may have included the two women whom Aimee Horton mentions; the two women may have even been Brown and Simmons. Less than one month after settling their contract, these women would have had a wealth of insight into grass-roots organizing and provided a sterling example of the role that music played in their struggle.

Myles Horton recalls the story differently, telling of white members of Local 15 who, while at HFS, attempted to recount the song to Zilphia Horton with limited success. If true, the difficulty of recollection faced by the white workers likely stemmed from the fact that they did not par-ticipate in the performance of the song on the Charleston picket lines.[88] Yet with the help of Zilphia Horton, the white members wrote a version of the song that became a part of her repertoire.[89] Who exactly taught the song to Horton and the participants at HFS remains unclear. What is certain however is the role that the song would have at HFS. Myles Horton recalled that "We Shall Overcome" was one of Zilphia's favorite songs and she used it often in HFS programming. The use of "We Will Overcome" in this space offered the song an opportunity to join in the pantheon of protest songs traveling around the country through grass-roots organizing.

It is unlikely that Charleston's white workers were able to recount the song at HFS without the assistance, if not leadership, of the Black women from the FTA. Myles Horton's recollection therefore must be read with a discerning eye that takes into consideration the community from which the song stemmed and that community's relationship to the strike in Charleston. As the leaders on the picket line and often within the cultural productions of their churches and communities, Black women were the bridge between the song's semiprivate usage in the Black community and its public launch into labor and civil rights organizing. It is the picket leader Lucille Simmons who was positioned best to effect this conversion and translation. As the song leader, she was able to manipulate the song's mechanics on the line, taking advantage of its "slow rhythmic pulse (sometimes referred to as short meter) [which] increase[ed] in tempo to a 'shout.'"[90] This style fit the pace of the picket line by beginning in a slow meter and gradually building in intensity as more voices joined the chorus. Simmons "used her immense vocal talent" and organizing skill to reconstruct the song to suit the purposes of the community on strike.[91] It is she who through her intimate knowledge of the song's sound, meaning, and power was capable of teaching it to the organizers at HFS.

Once the song was introduced at HFS, the staff centered it within their worker training and individual performances.

> Recognizing its emotional appeal, Zilphia Horton slowed the tempo, added new verses, and began singing and teaching it to HFS students and at various gatherings in the South. Pete Seeger learned the song from Zilphia in 1947 and revised it further, altering "we will overcome" to "we shall overcome" and including more verses during his concerts around the country. The song's popularity did not spread far beyond the school and a few folk singers during the 1940s and 1950s. Guy Carawan was introduced to the song by a West Coast folk singer named Frank Hamilton. Carawan helped give the song its contemporary format and taught it and other freedom songs at HFS workshops and civil rights gatherings throughout the South during the early 1960s.[92]

The musician-activists mentioned here—Zilphia Horton, Pete Seeger, Frank Hamilton, and Guy Carawan—are prominently configured within the histories of "We Shall Overcome" for three primary reasons: the privileges of whiteness, the production of song anthologies, and legal copyright protections. In highlighting the compositional revision of the anthem by Horton, the author quoted above offers an alternative origin narrative for the anthem without acknowledging that the work she attributes to Horton was in motion already, just on a smaller scale. Horton's whiteness, musical education, and institutional affiliation gave her a platform and level of legitimacy that the Black women of Local 15 did not receive. Similar conditions of privilege worked for the white men involved in the song's history. Seeger and Carawan continued to use the HFS model of taking the music of the workers to the people in the post-1955 moment when the Montgomery Bus Boycott signaled increased public attention and opposition to Jim Crow in the U.S. South. As I discussed in chapter 3, placing restrictions on mobility for the African descended has long been a strategy in social movement suppression. The fact that Seeger and Carawan were white men gave them the flexibility of travel unavailable to many Black women and men in the U.S. South. The continued migrations of the song grew its popularity exponentially and made it possible for the song to be sung at lunch counter demonstrations on the southeastern seaboard as well as in the jails of Georgia and Alabama.

"We Shall Overcome" was a mainstay of these political gatherings and events because its performance was an entrenched practice within movement circles. HFS played a large role in making its performance legible for the many activists who came through its programs as participants and staff, including Septima Clarke, Rosa Parks, and Martin Luther King, Jr. Continued travel to sites of movement organizing, like the 1960 founding of the Student Nonviolent Coordinating Committee (SNCC) in Raleigh, North Carolina, ensured that if the movement actors could not come to HFS, then HFS would come to them. In their capacity as song leaders and teachers within various, although overlapping, sites of civil rights struggle, Seeger, Hamilton, and Carawan anthologized the performance of "We Shall Overcome," in the process greatly accelerating its canonization within the movement repertoire.

Like with the cases of "Ethiopia" and "Lift Ev'ry Voice and Sing," publication facilitated the anthem's permanent placement within the sound of the movement. Guy Carawan publicized "We Shall Overcome" through a number of publications during the high tide of civil rights activism, including a two-volume set, the first of which was aptly named *We Shall Overcome! Songs of the Southern Freedom Movement*. Published in 1963, *We Shall Overcome!* is both a songbook and pictoral narrative of the movement. Still photos of devastated urban landscapes, smiling interracial groups of youth, and endless police violence punctuate the collection, which is organized thematically by protest action: sit-ins, freedom rides, voter registrations, and so on. The emphasis on the visual highlights the movement as action, not simply notes on the page. In his introduction Carawan pays tribute to the songs at the foundation of Black protest: "No other songs have been able to express so closely the feelings of the participants or have been so easily adapted to fit current situations as some of the old spirituals. When sung with anything approximating the old time style and spirit, they are unbeatable."[93] Here Carawan mentions the roots of the tradition through the spirituals, even as he refuses to name the "old time" context that birthed the sounds, namely chattel slavery, a structure of African oppression and survival that was regularly signaled by contemporary Black movement actors. Carawan's acknowledgment is not a substantive ethnomusicological or historical situating but serves instead as an approximation or shorthand for Black musical traditions that, despite their freeze-frame in his anthology, were dynamic and living more than a century after their origin.

This anthology is unlike the HFS songbook, which did not include musical notation; *We Shall Overcome!* includes vocal lines for soloists, and in some cases, a single group line. Carawan acknowledged that any attempt to capture these songs on the page is imperfect, and as such "the song versions given in this book should not be taken as absolutely definitive."[94] The anthology betrays this sentiment, however; it is exactly his position as a cultural broker within the Civil Rights Movement and his access to the communities who produced these texts that allowed him to publish these songs and portray his interpretations as authentic. The sociointellectual weight garnered by published texts validated his authority and that of the songs represented therein. In that way he was recognized as the educated collector who, not entirely unlike Carl Van Vechten of the Harlem Renaissance, was celebrated as an informant, translator, and expert on the cultures of those whose repeated repression made his project imaginable.

Carawan's collections, and others like it by Pete Seeger, were possible only because of his early claims to "We Shall Overcome" and other Black folk songs. In 1960, Seeger, Hamilton, and Carawan decided to take up the publishing of "We Shall Overcome," adding Zilphia Horton as a fourth songwriter posthumously (she died in 1956). In his narrative of "We Shall Overcome," Seeger describes, "My manager and publisher, Harold Leventhal, said, 'Pete, if you don't copyright this song, some Hollywood character will. He'll put new lyrics to it like, "Baby, let's you and me overcome tonight."' So Guy, Frank and I allowed our names to be used."[95] In allowing their names to adorn the copyright, Seeger, Carawan, and Hamilton claimed ownership over this multiauthored sound text, unwittingly assisting in the dismissal of the communities from which it originated. Some attribute this absence to memory loss. According to music journalist Hardeep Phull, "Lucille Simmons was left off simply because no one could remember her name at the time."[96] What he considers a simple oversight is one of the quotidian brutalities that, en masse, help to disarticulate Black women from the telling and documenting of history. Beyond the legal claims, the work produced by Simmons and the women whom she struggled alongside was silenced in the move to copyright a song that for nearly four months paced and announced their struggles for justice in Charleston. "We Shall Overcome" is an anthem precisely because it was tied to a movement for justice and fervently used by those most impacted as a method of protest at the site of struggle. This is the legacy that informs its worth as a future text within movement mobilizations and makes it a resonant project within HFS, Montgomery, and various other locations. Copyright has played a role in the erroneous histories of the anthem by cataloging and archiving those with access to managers and publishers, not the women—those "outlawed speaker[s] whose humanity is continually staked on [their] invisibility in political society"[97]—who used the music as a way to speak and be the impossible.

While the anthologizing of the anthem by these movement professionals made it a standard within civil rights affairs, "We Shall Overcome" resisted the fossilization of the canon and grew in unexpected proportion. Performance was the vehicle of contestation and the opportunity for various movement actors to signify on the song's roots in the spirituals and labor, while also using it to challenge the bourgeois, masculinist impulses that developed as the struggle was reduced to icons within the popular imaginary. In a 1964 recording of the anthem in Hattiesburg, Mississippi, a woman is the song leader of the rolling performance that never pauses. Even in the conventional breaks between verses, the voices of the participants (which are overwhelmingly female) rise up to fill the voids and speak to the violences of their moment, signaling both the extension of a long past of struggle and the endurance necessary to continue on. In this sonic history of the Civil Rights Movement, the anthem is present in the middle and at the very end of the collection, which is composed of amended Negro spirituals such as "Go Tell It on the Mountain" and "This Little Light of Mine," the favorite song of movement leader Fannie Lou Hamer.[98] "We Shall Overcome" is therefore embedded in this genealogy—it is both built upon a past foundation and the harbinger of a new future.

The importance of "We Shall Overcome" to Black social and political spaces in the long Civil Rights Movement is indisputable. A grand part of its significance is in the roots that it exposes—roots based musically in the spirituals, and politically in labor. The song is a great microcosm of protest traditions whose practices on the ground exhibit what religion scholar Jon Spencer describes as "song energizing protest and protest energizing song[,] generat[ing] a reservoir of courage, energy capable of propelling the group toward the mountaintop."[99] By all accounts, the mountaintop was not achieved for Local 15. Yet while the strike failed to produce the intended outcome, other immeasurable gains were made. The Black women of labor created social justice on the lines where none existed in the factory, and in spite of attempted censorship their songs resonated above Charleston, beyond the South, and into a movement that would radically change the political and social landscape of the nation and the world.

* * *

"We Shall Overcome" constructed a global movement audience that grew from the particular conditions and considerations of Black women industrial workers. Their rebellion against the hierarchies and isolation of wage labor impacted a new generation of women who picked up their techniques to build appending struggles. As the Civil Rights Movement widened, women continued to voice their alternative strategies of resistance to racial inequality, class oppression, and gender discrimination. Music as a method for announcement, camaraderie, and dissent maintained its presence in the movement repertoire. The twists and turns of domestic and international politics shook the foundations of Black struggle, as technologies of surveillance and war making again demanded new interventions and sacrifices. From this turbulent period emerged a Black woman troubadour who, with a little help from her friends, was able to synthesize competing agendas and articulate the pain and despair of a divided movement into a universal effort through an anthem that signaled the move from Black rights to Black power.

5

Soul Intact

CORE, Conversions, and Covers of "To Be Young, Gifted and Black"

I know my people need me and I won't let them down.
—Nina Simone

In a 1963 picture captured by members of the Highlander Folk School, Nina Simone grips the hands of the man and woman to her left and right while those around her sing (Figure 5.1). This tight space is one of performance, and although she was a solo artist, it was not hers alone. Simone is here sandwiched between two formidable Black activists whose careers would affect the advance and cultures of (inter)national politics: Marion Barry, Jr., who would later be mayor of Washington, D.C., and writer-activist-intellectual Lorraine Hansberry. While her comrades sing, Simone appears to be silent. Her gaze is directed toward an object outside of the group as she hovers between and behind both Barry and Hansberry. Behind her, actor and folk singer Theodore Bikel cranes his neck above her head to join in the communal performance. The interracial composition of the participants in tandem with the crossed arms that hug their chests while holding tight the hands of their neighbors signals that they are performing "We Shall Overcome." The photo documenting this "impromptu song session" at Bikel's home in Greenwich Village is not labeled with that anthem, however;[1] it is instead captioned by Simone's song, "To Be Young, Gifted and Black," which was penned six years after this photo was taken. This alternative caption suggests that while Simone may be silent within this snapshot

Figure 5.1.

Photograph, Avon W. Rollins, Lorraine Hansberry, Nina Simone, Marion Barry, Jr., John Lewis, and Ella Baker. Source: Courtesy of the Highlander Research Center.

of the day's events, she was not silent in the larger movement that it represents; she was, in fact, one of its authors and defining artists.

It was the people who surrounded her in this photo, especially Hansberry, and the others in the streets who made Nina Simone believe in the depth and power of her own voice. The first twenty years of her career were marked by rapid transition, as the world around her struggled against white domination in multiple arenas of the United States and abroad. The advance of the U.S. Civil Rights Movement and decolonization in Africa were haunted by loss, as leaders perished from disease and violence. In response, Simone constructed a music-politic that would both eulogize the dead and mobilize the living. She recognized the threat of violence that might attend her work and said, "[T]hey can try to kill me—I know they want to—but I'm not going to be quiet, *no way!*"[2] The defiance manifest here was a defining characteristic of her professional, artistic, and political repertoire, and she employed it in order to high-light the power of her message and to perform for the world the brav-ery of her comrades who faced pervasive danger in the Civil Rights and Black Power mobilizations that defined her generation. This period was the height of Simone's fame, making it impossible and, more important, undesirable for her to cower or hide; instead she used the stage as the meeting place for diasporic artists, activists, and audiences who gathered in order to commemorate, coordinate, and raise collective challenges. Like those musician-activists before her, her sound politics constituted new publics through the composition and performance of music.

Simone's aggressive touring schedule and subsequent record sales internationally make her art a global phenomenon, capable of influ-encing cultures within the diaspora and organizing world. Some of her songs state their international perspective explicitly. Her 1969 anthem "To Be Young, Gifted and Black" documents her investment in the political potential of youth in the struggle to defeat U.S. racism as well as oppression abroad. Described as Simone's "aspirations of the Black Power movement" by cultural historian Craig Werner,[3] this text would stand as one of her most important contributions to the legacy of the long (and international) Civil Rights Movement. Its use and adoption in organizing for civil rights in the United States cemented its posi-tion in the movement canon of arts and letters and acts as both a lov-ing memorial to the life and work of her mentor-confidant Lorraine Hansberry and a defiant celebration of and for the young people who through sit-ins, marches, and community organizing continued the fight of the many leaders gone.

Simone and her anthems are necessary players within the histories of Black resistance because her work documents the rise of a secular and popular consciousness within the movement and also situates the Black response to injustice in the form of a global collective that is sounded and re-sounded through her performances, thereby offering "a window into a world beyond liberal civil rights organizations and leaders and into networks of activist cultural producers."[4] "To Be Young, Gifted and Black" is a striking representation of this project because it articulates the transition from the civil rights activity of the 1950s and early 1960s to the Black Power methodologies of the middle to late 1960s and early 1970s. As she gained critical knowledge of domestic and international social movements and put that knowledge into play, Simone was institutionalized as a prized movement icon and troubadour.

"They Can't Hide from Me": Rights and Power from the Concert Stage

The brilliant constellation of artist-activists working in, with, and through the Civil Rights Movement is difficult, if not impossible, to enclose. The genre of these musicians covered the gamut from rock 'n' roll to classical. Perhaps no other artist bridged performative politics with such widely disparate musical genres as the unclassifiable Nina Simone. The mystery that surrounds Simone stems in part from her musical ingenuity and the ways in which she defied categorization. She commented that "[critics] want me to be a jazz singer or a blues singer; they just can't get that I don't have a category, I just sing what I feel and if it crosses the line then that's all right with me. I never want to be stuck in one place musically—it's not who I am."[5] Her ability to transcend (or completely ignore) boundaries carried over into other areas of her life, yet that which made her difficult to grasp also made her available to a diverse public. The lengths of her artistic reach and ingenuity exhibit the power and potential of Black music. As cultural historian Brian Ward maintains,

> African-American music has always been characterized by its willingness and seemingly endless capacity to fuse many varied, often apparently incompatible, influences into a succession of styles which have reflected and articulated the changing circumstances, consciousness and aspirations of black Americans; black Americans who have themselves been differentiated by class, gender and geography, and doubly defined by their immanent American, as well as by their more distinct African, heritages.[6]

Simone's acknowledgment of this variety within her repertoire allowed her to build artistic and political relationships with diverse individuals and organizations. She was among those architects who through art, organizing, and other avenues of intervention planned for the alliances that built the movement.

Her artistic hybridity was evident in her early pieces, which included musical theater, blues, and jazz standards. Simone used her knowledge and perfection of each genre to measure her "freedom" as she described it, a practice that she exhibited through various sonic and performative methods ranging from moans to cursing to piano virtuosity. Through her unique deployment of "experimental wanderlust" and "black feminist distanciation," she conceived of and displayed what literary scholar Daphne Brooks describes as "a performative sit-in" at her piano.[7] Especially explosive during her live performances, Simone's sit-ins represented the merger of her decades-long musical training with her minute-by-minute evolution as an activist. Early tributes to Duke Ellington and others linked her to an established musical trajectory, yet her constant musical about-face "amounted to formal disturbances that upset the order and cultural logic of 'protest.'"[8] Her music therefore modeled important organizing strategies, such as constant movement/evolution, flexibility, and unpredictability. It was her musical knowledges that most significantly impacted the movement and literally and figuratively set the stage for her political investments and performances that traversed time, technique, and medium.

Simone's radical methods of sound and performance modeled the strategies of revision that structured the transition from the Civil Rights Movement to the militancy of the Black Power Movement. In a world defined by the Vietnam War and the continued presence of inequality and violence in the United States, a younger guard began to question the rhetoric, pace, and tactics of their elders and mentors. The anthemic evidence of this transition was "To Be Young, Gifted and Black" (1969), yet Simone had five years earlier announced this sea change. Although both texts predate the formation of the Black Panther Party— the organization that epitomized these new radical activists—Simone's iconic "Mississippi Goddam" (1964) and "Four Women" of 1966 indicate the departure that Student Nonviolent Coordinating Committee (SNCC) activist Stokely Carmichael and others called for.[9] "Mississippi Goddam" was written in response to the assassination of Medger Evers and the Birmingham church bombing that killed four little girls. Simone described that in that moment "all the truths that I had denied to myself for so long rose up and slapped my face," leading her to understand "what it was to be black in America in 1963."[10] Written in only an hour, "[Mississippi Goddam] was my first civil rights song, and it erupted out of me quicker than I could write it down. I knew then that

I would dedicate myself to the struggle for black justice, freedom and equality under the law for as long as it took, until all of our battles were won." The shift in the use of her music for individual gain to community advancement signaled her deliberate entrance into the movement and it gave her great satisfaction: "I was proud of what I was doing and proud to be part of a movement that was changing history. It made what I did for a living something much more worthwhile."[11]

During a 1964 performance of "Mississippi Goddam," Simone announced that "this is a show tune but the show hasn't been written for it yet."[12] This lament is only partially true. There was an organized narrative linking her compositions and performances to the unfolding national rebellion, yet the Civil Rights "show" battled both the segregated performances of the nation and its own internal divisions. Simone's music and commentary from movement stages worldwide offered the critical counternarrative to the Jim Crow show as it developed in 1963 and 1964 in Alabama (which got her "so upset"), Tennessee (which made her "lose [her] rest"), and, of course, Mississippi ("Goddam!"). Her criticisms adjusted the timeline of and exposed conflicts within the U.S. Black liberation agenda, including a fundamental disagreement over the utility of nonviolence.[13] Simone confessed, "I wasn't convinced that non-violence could get us what we wanted."[14] That position is reflected in the song, which argues that those working against Black liberation would "die like flies," clearly revealing her rage at the events in Birmingham and her unwillingness to turn the other cheek in the face of such violence. She also questioned the movement's insistence on integration, singing, "You don't have to live next to me / Just give me my equality." This text highlights the unnecessary and potentially damaging conflation of integration with full access to citizenship by both the movement and its detractors; they were not one and the same, and to want or gain access to one was not necessarily to want or gain the other. The Black Power advocates of 1966 and beyond understood and contributed to this division and found in Simone's music an alternative method of articulation and archive of consciousness.

In the same year as the development of the Black Panther Party, Simone released "Four Women," a song that challenged the entangled oppressions of race and gender through the legacies of chattel slavery. In it Simone confronts the flattening of Black women into one-dimensional objects by addressing the intersectional identities of four distinct Black women, all of them representations of women who are at one and the same time real and imagined. Each character in the text has a direct link to slavery as a site in which Black women were mercilessly tortured, violated, and caricatured. A slow, methodical piano line and a single drum are the backdrop for her probe into these haunting figures: the deceptively plaintive Aunt Sarah, mulatta beauty Saphronia, and seductive provocateur Sweet Thing. In her last installment, Simone conjures her deep resentment and anger at the position of these women into a punctuated crescendo in her vocals: "My skin is brown / My manner is tough / I'll kill the first mutha I see / My life has been rough / I'm awfully bitter these days / because my parents were slaves." With a swell that amounts to a scream, she ends the piece, "What do they call me? / My name is Peaches!"[15]

The names of these women invoke a series of (mis)identifications for listeners that reflect the deep fissures and silences within African American women's historiography. Gender theorists and historians have done compelling work in order to situate the stock characterizations of Black women within a broader discourse of dominance and power in U.S. history. Literary theorist Hortense Spillers exposes these caricatures through her own subjectivity when she writes,

> Let's face it. I am a marked woman, but not everybody knows my name. "Peaches" and "Brown Sugar," "Sapphire" and "Earth Mother," "Aunty," "Granny," God's "Holy Fool," a "Miss Ebony First" or "Black Woman at the Podium": I describe a locus of confounded identities, a meeting ground of investments and privations in the national treasury of rhetorical wealth. My country needs me, and if I were not here, I would have to be invented.[16]

Simone's "Four Women" was the prelude to the formation of post–civil rights Black feminist organizations including the National Black Feminist Organization (1973) and Combahee River Collective (1974), and she used it to disarticulate her body and those like hers from genealogies of representational violence. Simone believed that "Black women didn't know what the hell they wanted because they were defined by things they didn't control and until they had the confidence to define themselves they'd be stuck in the same mess forever. ['Four Women'] told the truth many people in the USA—especially black men—simply weren't ready to acknowledge at the time."[17] Through Simone's truth telling, "Four Women" was, according to musicologist Tammy Kernodle, "one of the strongest pronouncements of black women's experiences in America since the recording of blues women in the 1920s and 30s."[18] Simone's continuation of that legacy through "Four Women" incites a discursive rebuke that owns race and gender while allowing that dualism to mean something different within the context of revolution.

Black women's and lesbians' "experience and disillusionment within [Black] liberation movements, as well as experience on the periphery of the white male left . . . led to the need to develop a politics that was antiracist, unlike those of white women, and antisexist, unlike those of black and white men."[19] This politics shaped the post-1968 moment of world revolution as these women demonstrated the radical reinvention of subjectivities outside of nationalistic and colonial designs.[20] Gender historian Kimberly Springer locates the beginning of an explicitly stated Black feminist movement in 1968 with the birth of the Black Women's Liberation Committee. The movement encompassed "the political and cultural realms of black feminists' activism including organizations, prose, essays, fiction, scholarly studies, films, visual arts, and dance," with major figures in this endeavor including Toni Cade Bambara, Ntozake Shange, and Michelle Wallace.[21] Missing from this list is Simone, whose work within the Civil Rights Movement and on the stage prior to 1968 signaled an adjustment of the place of Black women in both locations. Her "Four Women" prescribes Black women's subjectivity in accordance with the rising tide of pride and self-determination that pervaded both the women's and civil rights agendas. This task required that Simone revisit the history and legacy of slavery in the United States and not all were pleased.[22] Her recovery of America's dark past in "Four Women" spoke to an important turning point in the development of a Black feminist agenda and demonstrated her clear understanding that "[t]he fight for civil rights . . . had been around since slavery days, and the movement that I knew was the latest version of that struggle."[23]

The movement continued to reinvent itself, and Simone performed its genealogy on stage. Her anthem "To Be Young, Gifted and Black" solidified the transition from the Civil Rights Movement of "Mississippi Goddam" to the militant, and often nationalist, perspective of organizations like the Congress of Racial Equality (CORE), a long-time movement powerhouse that itself adjusted to meet the demands of Black Power. As historians August Meier and Elliot Rudwick document, CORE leaders of the post-1965 period "thought more in terms of power than moral appeals, thus adumbrating the popularity of the Black Power slogan."[24] This approach aligned them with some groups while estranging them from others. There were multiple civil rights groups in circulation in this period, each with its own interpretation of racial progress and victory, thereby developing a "competitive rivalry [that] galvanized the civil rights cause."[25] CORE was one of the most influential of that pantheon. Founded by James Farmer in 1942, CORE was an interracial organization that began its efforts in the U.S. North. With a largely white middle-class base, the organization worked to gain national recognition in the years prior to the landmark 1954 Supreme Court desegregation case of *Brown v. Board of Education*. Farmer was the formative figure in this end, gathering support from local white liberals and, slowly, the Black community. He had previous organizational experience with trade unions and the Fellowship of Reconciliation (FOR), a religious-pacifist organization invested in civil rights. Prominent members of FOR included Bayard Rustin prior to his role as confidant and advisor to Martin Luther King, Jr. and work with the March on Washington, and the theologian and labor advocate A. J. Muste who was also a prominent member of King's inner circle.[26]

Farmer was deeply influenced by the members of FOR, and their techniques offered a launch pad for his own ideas on racial justice organizing. Born in 1920 in Texas to a preacher and former teacher, Farmer spent his childhood in Holly Springs, Mississippi, where overt racial prejudice was a matter of course. As an adult he avidly dissected nonviolence and planned a public strategy for using its methods to eradicate U.S. racism. He told his father, "[F]or the time being, [FOR] [wi]ll sharpen our nonviolent swords in northern settings. When we go south, we'll be ready to face their bullets. If they have the jails, we have the bodies. No doubt, some of us will die. If we have to, we'll be ready."[27] This statement, uttered at the age of twenty-one, is an uncannily accurate portrait of the work ahead of him.

Despite his best attempts, Farmer was unable to bring FOR on board with his agenda. Instead he formed CORE in order to "impale racism and segregation on the sword of nonviolent techniques."[28] Desegregation struggles at a local Chicago restaurant, housing establishment, and roller skating rink, although not all won in a court of law, began to change public opinion on segregation—including recognition of its presence in the North—and the effects of civil protest. While World War II raged on, the newly established CORE struggled but was soon launched into the national spotlight by its participation in the Montgomery Bus Boycott of 1955. Designed in large part by union man E. D. Nixon and starring schoolteacher Rosa Parks and young minister Martin Luther King, Jr., the participants of the boycott launched a Black offensive in the South. Lasting just over a year, the boycott of Montgomery's public transit proved that Black people could and would organize to protect their rights, even in the stifling and violent U.S. South, and they would use nonviolence as their method of resistance. Six years later CORE centered nonviolence in the launch of their Freedom Rides, a program designed to fill the southern jails by resisting the Jim Crow practices of interstate travel. On May 4, 1961, a group of thirteen white and Black men and women gathered at a Greyhound bus terminal in Washington, D.C., to embark on their southern trip. As the riders made their way southwest from Virginia to North Carolina and beyond, the terror grew. The foul southern air was thick with the smell of blood as men and women, Black and white, were violated, beaten, and arrested, yet the nonviolent method was not abandoned. For Farmer nonviolence exposed rebellion as well as a "seductive gentleness" and highlighted the Black organizing arsenal as one of myriad strategies and levels of impact.[29]

Music was one method employed by CORE to respond to violence and engage the conscience of the nation. Farmer was able to articulate early on how music serviced the movement; he argued for the inclusion of Rustin in the strategic planning of the Montgomery Bus Boycott because he was a seasoned organizer, "an excellent singer and particularly skilled in leading group singing. Further, he knew the gospel songs, spirituals, and folk songs and could be very helpful in bolstering morale." Farmer was in contact with movement singers like Guy Carawan and took a note from their playbook by including within CORE's repertoire songs such as "We Shall Not Be Moved" and "Which Side Are You On?"[30] Throughout the 1960s, the organization maintained its reliance on music as a vehicle of protest. In 1962 CORE released *CORE:*

Sit-In Songs, a collection of revised spirituals, amended labor songs, and movement standards including "We Shall Overcome." The singers were young members of CORE, many of whom had been jailed in organization demonstrations. The liner notes for the recording offer some important insights into the connection between music and the movement. Author Robert Brookins Gore wrote, "These kids are out to change the world and you can tell it by the way they sing. When they sing 'We Shall Overcome' they aren't kidding. Listen to them and you can hear the sincerity in their voices."[31] Here Gore described music as an exposition of political and moral aptitude and intent. If you don't believe their actions, he demands that you believe their *sound*: "The real feeling of the freedom fight leaps out at you. You feel as though you actually belong to CORE, belong in the fight with these youngsters who are out to change the world." This change is manifested on wax, although it is not sealed or frozen in time; for Gore, its effects remain dynamic because "[t]his album puts you in touch with history in the making."[32]

While consumer activism has its limits, fund-raising for civil rights organizations was a perennial concern, and the sale of this recording was a major factor in the CORE fund drive for 1962. The dual function of music in the struggle, as both political strategy and money-making venture, was evident in more than recordings. CORE rallies and concerts enlisted the talents of jazz singer Sarah Vaughan, folk artist Joan Baez, Rat Packer Sammy Davis, Jr., singer-actor and activist Harry Belafonte, folk idol Odetta, and Simone. Musicologist Ingrid Monson notes that these fund-raisers "offered a dramatic forum in which northern audiences could hear directly from southern activists about day-to-day life on the frontlines of the movement." The concerts simultaneously benefited the organizations by giving them "the opportunity to reap the symbolic rewards of celebrity association with the struggle and create social spaces in which musicians and audiences could feel as though they were doing their part to aid the southern struggle."[33]

The necessity of continued struggle was evident as the nation buzzed with civil rights discourse and the surfacing of a cultural shift in Civil Rights Movement strategy. By mid-decade Black Americans were "suffused with a new militancy, a new sense of urgency . . . [evidenced by] the widespread use of deliberate mass jail-ins[,] a disposition to meet violence with violence, a tendency to package several demands together—to demand total integration rather than to work for one reform at a time—and the involvement of greater and greater numbers of people from all strata of the Negro community."[34] CORE's involvement in this revival of movement energy and potential is documented in their ability to fill jails across the South. While the "disposition to meet violence with violence" was coming from another source, these practices highlight the growing militancy of Black youth in particular and their cultural politics were adjusting to match their activist spirit.

Cultural practices were central to the challenges leveled at the established order from within the Civil Rights Movement as well as from without. Hair was particularly important. Chemical perms that straightened Black hair fell out of favor with the nationalist Black youth, who traded perms for naturals. The larger one's Afro, the greater respect one would gain in the movement because hair was inextricably linked to authenticity. Cultural studies scholar Kobena Mercer notes that because hair is shaped and groomed, it is socialized "making it a medium of significant statements about self and society and the codes of value that bind them, or do not." As a "sensitive area of expression" hair has the potential to demonstrate political agreement or disharmony. While acknowledging that styles such as the Afro and dreadlocks have in the contemporary moment lost some political salience due to their incorporation into mainstream culture, Mercer nonetheless argues that these styles can stand as "solutions to the ideological problematization of black people's hair" because "in their historical contexts, they *counter*-politicized the signifier of ethnic and racial devalorization, redefining blackness as a desirable attribute." Through demonstrating everyday life, "these black styles in hair and dress helped to underline massive shifts in popular aspirations among black people,"[35] including a move away from a singularly U.S.-based analysis of civil rights toward a radical humanitarian engagement with the Third World.[36]

Fashion was another forum of political expression. Just as the Black and Latino zoot-suiters of the 1940s used their aesthetic practice to propose alternative notions of the nation during World War II, Black activists, many of whom bridged the Civil Rights Movement with the nascent Black Power struggle, used their dress as a means to critique restrictive social categories. SNCC workers in the South were known to wear a "uniform" consisting of work shirts, dark pants, and denim coats. This ensemble demonstrated a closer affiliation with the working people of the South whom they sought to mobilize. As the decade of the 1960s progressed, a growing guard of the movement looked to Africa for cultural inspiration. African dashikis replaced Levi's jeans and African-inspired wooden and beaded jewelry replaced gold and gems. It was often these aesthetic and political rebels who came to cherish and identify with the project of Nina Simone because she too reflected this aesthetic revolution. By 1968 "[g]one were the wigs, replaced by an afro [*sic*]," and her performances in "African garb only added to the mystique." What some white audiences may have read as "mystique," her Black audiences read as pride. Simone took advantage of this disconnect in performance, at various points telling her audiences (often majority white) that certain songs "were for all you black folks out there." At other times she "called for all the black people in the audience to stand up—sometimes it was as few as two—and said, 'I'm singing only to you. I don't care about the others.'"[37] Labeled the "true singer of the civil rights movement" by Stokely Carmichael, Simone proudly rose to meet the challenge of the young vanguard of Black radicals, and for that she was respected and rewarded.[38]

At the height of Black Power, a reorganized and revitalized CORE institutionalized "To Be Young, Gifted and Black." The quest for equality was a long road that grew no shorter with the signing of the Civil Rights Act of 1964, and CORE adjusted accordingly. Between 1964 and 1966 the organization rolled back its demands for integration and belief in the exclusive use of nonviolence.[39] The post-Farmer CORE was in fact receiving criticism from other civil rights organizations for its political positions, which included lobbying for racially exclusive schooling.[40] The rebuke of integration made CORE a contentious body within the pantheon of organizations, but there was no absolute consensus within the movement. Simone herself believed that "[i]n a white man's world the black man would always lose out, so the idea of a separate black nation, whether it was in America or in Africa, made sense."[41] What she did not yet understand was that she would be central to this creation. In October 1971 CORE invited Simone to New York City for what she assumed would be a regular benefit. Upon her arrival, she was surprised to learn that she would receive a citation for her work in the movement. However, her citation was overshadowed by the honor that she received when the "hundreds of delegates" to the CORE conference resolved to adopt "To Be Young, Gifted and Black" as the Black National Anthem.[42] Thoroughly Black Nationalist in its pronouncements and objectives, CORE of 1971 concretized Simone's ability to represent them and their movement by announcing her song as their anthem. This act served to displace the decades-old use of James Weldon and J. Rosamond Johnson's "Lift Ev'ry Voice and Sing" as the Negro National Anthem. The change from Negro (National Anthem) to Black (National Anthem) highlighted the important identity contests that were waged in the fifty-year period between adoption of these two texts; that this new Black nation was radically different than any previous incarnation is evidenced by its anthem, which displayed a militant pride through its grounding in the contemporary mobilizations of the African descended. Yet Simone's adoption of the play by Lorraine Hansberry and her brief autobiographical narrative within "To Be Young, Gifted and Black" acknowledged the past even as it forecast the promises of the future. By 1971, Black men and women had an anthem to reflect their circumstances and announce a new era of cultural pride and political determination. Simone conceded, "I wasn't in the movement for personal glory, but this dedication made me very proud because it showed I was succeeding as a protest singer, that I was writing songs people remembered and were inspired by."[43] "To Be Young, Gifted and Black" did more than inspire; its heightened function as an anthem highlighted its didactic function within the Black nation and made it a powerful representation of the "freedom of collective animation" discussed by literary scholar Scott Saul.[44] Through its composition and performance, "To Be Young, Gifted and Black" signaled a new phase of Black liberation struggles in part built by the work and camaraderie of two unique women.

"Don't Let Me Be Misunderstood": Conversion and Global Camaraderie

In late 1964, Lorraine Hansberry was confined to a hospital bed in Massachusetts. Her cancer was advanced, although very few were aware of the severity of her condition. Despite her physical distance from her home base in New York, she was never far from the thoughts of her loved ones. She received numerous "get well" cards from friends, fans, and well wishers, including Roxie Roker Kravitz of television's *The Jeffersons*, *Autobiography of Malcolm X* collaborator Alex Haley, who encouraged Lorraine to believe in the power of the metaphysical, and CORE leader Weldon Rougeau, whose letter of encouragement read in part, "I know that [your] strength will keep you from despairing." One card in particular spoke to the fun-loving yet deeply intimate relationship that Hansberry shared with the sender. The front of the card reads, "Flat On Your Back?" and continues inside, "Keep Punching . . . Get Well Soon!!" This card, which encouraged Hansberry to keep fighting, was sent by Nina Simone. The adhesive marks that adorn the corners on the back of the card exhibit its importance to Hansberry as she likely affixed it to her hospital room wall in an attempt to make the physical space familiar and amenable to her rehabilitation. In the comments at the end of the card, Simone playfully teased her mentor when she wrote, "Anyway, what are you doing in the Baptist Hospital? You're not Baptist—look out or they'll convert you. Love, Nina."[45]

The potential for conversion jokingly mentioned by Simone in her get-well card serves as a framework for discussing the powerful relationship shared between the two women, who together struggled in the break between culture and politics, art and activism. "Conversion," according to Merrill Singer, "is not something that befalls the individual, but rather a social process in which he/she takes an active part,"[46] and Simone's activity was composed of a dense theory-praxis inspired by those around her. Simone's tribute to Hansberry after her passing was the iconic sound interpretation "To Be Young, Gifted and Black," itself an act of conversion with profound implications for how the Civil Rights Movement would represent itself internationally. While it was Simone who warned Hansberry of conversion by Baptists, it was Hansberry who had earlier converted Simone—an act that produced a movement intellectual and, ultimately, an anthem.

The picture used to begin this chapter captures the relationship shared by the two women; Hansberry is the one in front, holding onto Simone until she found her voice. By the time that the picture was taken, Simone was "follow[ing] the development of the civil rights movement" but conceded that "[i]t would take a special kind of friend really to pull me into the ideas of the Black Movement and force me to accept that I had to take politics seriously."[47] That friend was Hansberry, whose 1959 play *A Raisin in the Sun* became a Broadway phenomenon. Hansberry was born on the predominantly Black South Side of Chicago to an upper-middle-class family, and her exposure to civil rights activism began as a child when her family moved into a white neighborhood. With threats and violence impending, the Hansberry family took their case to court, winning a landmark housing desegregation ruling. As a young adult Hansberry continued to challenge racial and political conventions by writing for *Freedom*, a radical Black newspaper published under the direction of the embattled Paul Robeson and W. E. B. Du Bois. During her tenure with the paper, she wrote about developing Third World political struggles, including the so-called Mau Mau Rebellion in Kenya. Unlike other writers in the white and Black press who damned the uprising for its violence and unfamiliar cultural practices, Hansberry championed the Mau Mau for their ability to respond to the brutalities of British colonialism, even if they met that brutality with their own. Her keen awareness and insight into current events globally made her a bridge between diasporic activists; according to historian Fanon Che Wilkins, "Hansberry affirmed her political kinship with anticolonial insurgency by arguing that the sweep of national independence movements globally was inextricably linked to the political initiatives of black Americans engaged in similar, and sometimes overlapping, struggles for freedom, full citizenship, and self-determination." This broad agenda not only argued for an expansion of the U.S. civil rights lens to incorporate global struggles, particularly in Africa, but also demanded that Black Americans concern themselves with the shape of the postcolonial state. Her assertion that liberation would come to Black Americans and Africans alike was shadowed by the world that Black people globally would find in its wake: "Hansberry believed that gaining civil rights in the United States and obtaining independence in colonial Africa were two sides of the same coin that presented similar challenges for Africans on both sides of the Atlantic."[48] Her concern then was not a question of victory but one of how to rebuild Black communities on the other side of that inevitability.

Hansberry wrestled with that question in her daily life by engaging the movement in the United States and abroad through study, writing, and action. Of her relationship with Hansberry, Simone wrote, "Although Lorraine was a girlfriend . . . we never talked about men or clothes or other such inconsequential things when we got together. It was always Marx, Lenin and revolution—real girls' talk."[49] The mentoring relationship that developed between the two women models the traditions of Black women's kinship networks discussed by Black women scholars and writers like Hansberry's *Freedom* magazine colleague Alice Childress, whose 1956 novel, *Like One of the Family*, features the interior lives of Black women workers in New York City and their shared strategies of resistance. Afternoon discussions in the kitchens and communal spaces of Black women's homes were incubators for political discussion as they shared and critiqued the conditions of Black life—those quotidian brutalities that to the outside world often were unrecognizable but for the African descended exposed entrenched structures of power and difference. The discussions of Hansberry and Simone duplicated these traditions even as they approached the bourgeois salons of the Black middle class that had since the late nineteenth century brought Black intellectuals and artists from the United States into communion with one another over shared issues and texts and fostered exchange across the Atlantic.[50] In its hybridity—the down-home and the ivory tower— the space shared by Simone and Hansberry materialized the "real girls' talk" described by Simone and became the catalyst by which she understood herself as "a black person in a country run by white people and a woman in a world run by men."[51] This catharsis was the first conversion moment shared between the two women, and through it Simone changed. She would no longer be defined only as a musician; she was now attuned to her subjectivity, what it meant in context, and, through Hansberry's organizing and example, how it might be mobilized in the fight for Black liberation.[52]

"Mississippi Goddam" and "Four Women" epitomize Simone's early political awakening through which she gained a radical recognition of her blackness and gender identity. Like that of Hansberry, however, Simone's awakening found root in her childhood. Born Eunice Waymon in Tryon, North Carolina, during the Great Depression to domestic and part-time minister Kate and former musician, entrepreneur, handyman, and later minister John Divine, Simone recalled a pivotal moment in her youth in which her passion for music collided with the violence of racism. At the tender age of eleven she came face-to-face with Jim Crow at a piano recital in Tryon. As she took the stage to perform, she noticed her parents being escorted from their front row seats to the back of the auditorium. They "allow[ed] themselves to be moved," and no one "said anything, but I wasn't going to see them treated like that and stood up in my starched dress and said if anyone expected to hear me play then they'd better make sure that my family was sitting right there in the front row where I could see them." Her parents were brought back to their original seats and the recital began, but something about Simone was fundamentally different in that moment. She became more resilient and conscious as her "skin grew back again a little tougher, a little less innocent, and a little more black."[53] This was only the first of many disappointments that Simone would face during her lifetime in music; ultimately she realized that the music alone could not provide her the happiness that she longed for because it existed in a world that required revision.

Simone's transition and awakening in this moment—becoming "a little more black"—set the stage for the maneuvers that she would have to make as an adult performer. The move to "To Be Young, Gifted and Black" in 1969 demonstrates Simone's political evolution over a revolutionary decade marked in part by loss. The painful disorientation faced by surviving U.S. Civil Rights Movement actors after the murders of civil rights activists James Chaney, Andrew Goodman, and Michael Schwerner in Mississippi and the assassinations of Martin Luther King, Jr. and Malcolm X threatened to eclipse the gains of the 1964 and 1965 civil rights legislation. Simone felt this impact while she also battled a grief closer to home. Her intensely intimate relationship with Hansberry, which had awakened her to a level of consciousness and critical analysis previously unknown, was cut tragically short. On January 12, 1965, Hansberry passed away of cancer at the age of thirty-four. Her terminal illness, as well as the outrages that inspired Simone's "Mississippi Goddam," made plain how exposed and rightless Black people were. In a very real sense, the Birmingham church bombing and myriad other violences directed toward Black life demonstrated for Black people that nothing was sacred—not religion, not life. These imperiled conditions exposed the racism theorized by geographer Ruth Wilson Gilmore as "vulnerabilities to premature death";[54] this matrix of liability includes the poverty, undereducation, and ghetto segregation that Hansberry so often brought attention to. Simone carried with her Hansberry's knowledges and employed them in her own conversion practice as she reinvented Hansberry's posthumously released 1968 play, *To Be Young, Gifted and Black*.

Simone's sonic homage to her dear friend built upon the rich experiences that detail Hansberry's text. Compiled after her passing by her ex-husband and literary executor Robert Nemiroff, *To Be Young, Gifted and Black* (*TBYGB*) offers an experimental form of playwriting that combines pieces of a number of Hansberry's writings from the stage and screen, as well as compositions from newspapers, journals, public events, and personal correspondence. Although the play was "a small representative sampling" of Hansberry's genius, Nemiroff described it as Hansberry's "self-portrait" that seeks "to relate the artist to the person, and place the parts within the context of the whole in such fashion as to enable the words she left to tell her story without intrusion or comment, explanation or footnotes of any kind."[55] The prefatory notes to the volume offer the only appendages to her words, one of which was written by Nemiroff and the other by James Baldwin. Although she did not adapt *TBYGB*, Hansberry shines in the play. Her brilliance as a writer and thinker, dramatist and philosopher, is demonstrated in vignettes that juxtapose, for example, a portion of dialogue from her "epic effort," the play *Toussaint*, in which the plantation owner's wife Lucie dumbfounds him with the request, "Tell me—what is freedom . . . ?," with a personal note in which she described her emotional and physical health, lamenting, "It is so awful to live without envy of anything."[56] Pairings such as this disrupt the linearity of past to present and embed the play within multiple jagged displays of life and privilege where the audience is not spared confrontation with the questions and conditions that order our world, including the brutal realities of racism. Hansberry wrote, "*Despair*? Did someone say despair was a question in the world? Well then, listen to the sons of those who have known little else if you wish to know the resiliency of this thing you would so quickly resign to mythhood, this thing called the human spirit."[57] For Hansberry, this feeling of loss did not signal an existentialist crisis, as it did for contemporaries like Norman Mailer; literary scholar Cheryl Higashida argues that she rejected existentialism for its solipsism and a "concern that [it] would fuel the cold war backlash against diverse forms of liberatory [*sic*] politics."[58] Despair was not an end but a means; it was an inevitability that aroused in her the reality and persistence of its inverse: hope. She was invested in finding the processes that would make that transition easier, faster, more long-lasting. Because, as she argued, "each piece of [Black people's] living is a protest," it was imperative that one use one's unique talents to "*impose* the reason for life on life" so that one might "live because life has within it that which is good, that which is beautiful, and that which is love. Therefore, since I have known all of these things, I have found them to be reason enough and—I wish to live. Moreover, because this is so, I wish others to live for generations and generations and generations and generations."[59]

The resonance of and for life is paramount throughout *TBYGB*. As a posthumous project, it is not hard to imagine why. Yet her formulation of life throughout the play is not simply a request for breath, it is a dense articulation and practice that holds within it the dichotomy of despair and hope that fascinated both Hansberry and Simone. Simone's 1968 remake of "Ain't Got No/I Got Life" from the 1967 musical *Hair* offers one model of how life through the body ("I got my tongue, my chin, my neck, my boobies, my heart") is also constitutive of the possession of "my soul" and "bad times" and defiantly figures against a lack of wealth and social standing ("I ain't got no home / Ain't got no shoes / Ain't got no money / Ain't got no class").[60] *Life* or living, then, is, for both women, deeply connected to the world beyond the body but is not reducible to its material trappings. Both versions of *TBYGB* are organized around an examination of this interplay and necessarily engage it through a multitextual approach in and beyond the written word. Although known as a writer, Hansberry in fact requests that we use our ears; throughout the play she uses cues to heighten the sensory elements of Black experiences. Included within *TBYGB* is an exchange between a young Black woman (She) and a white male intellectual (He) at a cocktail party. Their argument and final reconciliation are mediated through Black music; at his insistence that she not "get folksy," She argues that Black people do not live in the clouds but on Earth— "How else could we come up with a song like 'Oh, Lord, I Don't Feel Noways Tired!'"[61] This song then consumes her, leading her into a private sequence in which music is the "bridge across the chasm" of communication and understanding. "It was made up of a band of angels of art," says She, who "saw Jimmy Baldwin and Leontyne [Price], and Lena

[Horne] and Harry [Belafonte] and Sammy [Davis, Jr.]. And then there was Charlie White and Nina Simone."[62] Young University of Wisconsin student Candace demands that her African paramour Monasse "Sing the anthem . . . again" and is herself possessed by Africa through song: "She had never heard African music that had not set her mad with the romance of her people, *never*. At the first rich basso boom, her heart rose in her bosom, her teeth set, her eyes widened, and Africa claimed her."[63] It is not a stretch to believe that Simone's "African-rooted classical music," as she categorized it, manifested a similar effect in Hansberry, deepening their bond and serving as inspiration in her prose and drama.[64] Hansberry's earlier demand that people interested in the question of despair *listen* plays off of Simone's demand in "Mississippi Goddam" ("Don't tell me. I'll tell you.") and announces a respect for the voices of the disenfranchised described here—voices that shouted, wailed, and sung in their attempts to peel away the façade of an egalitarian United States.

Simone's "To Be Young, Gifted and Black" ("TBYGB") is a continuation of Hansberry's project of identification and critique. Within their efforts to tell the stories of the African descended, both women also materialize the systems that made the world in which they lived. The despair represented in *TBYGB* is gestured toward in "TBYGB," first in its slow, methodical accompaniment. It is not mournful but manages to set a tone that encourages reflexivity through its melodic stillness, which incorporates moments of silence every couple of measures—a strategic pause in which the participating audience can reflect. Simone sings, "To be young, gifted and Black," followed by a two-beat pause. She follows the break by giving meaning to her previous statement: "Oh what a lovely, precious dream." Simone's use of the word "dream" is loaded with the history that it follows. Martin Luther King, Jr.'s "I Have a Dream" speech and the "American Nightmare" articulated by Malcolm X battle for space within both *TBYGB* and "TBYGB," as both men's beliefs are tested in practice. It was unclear in 1969 which vision would become reality. Simone's "dream," however, also provides the necessary balance to the frightening present; it is aspirational and encourages the listener to grow in the present ("open your heart to what I mean"). "TBYGB" was an organizing text that acknowledged despair but led the listener toward its alternative by drawing attention to the strength that already existed within them: "When you're feeling real low / there's a great truth that you should know: / When you're young, gifted and black / your soul's intact."

The instructional quality of Simone's "TBYGB" is the result of her political training as well as the structure provided by the original *TBYGB*. In using Hansberry's public speeches and writings, the play is able to reinforce the themes of her dramatic work with the lucidity of her lived convictions. One of the final scenes of the play stages an awards ceremony for the United Negro College Fund composition scholarship. In it, the character "Playwright" names her investment in that event and launches the phrase that moved a generation when she announced, "Apart from anything else, I wanted to be able to come here and speak with you on this occasion because you are young, gifted and black." She applauded the student-writers and encouraged them to use their talents in service of something greater than themselves:

> Look at the work that awaits you! Write if you will: but write about the world as it is and as you think it *ought* to be and must be—if there is to be a world. Write about all the things that men have written about since the beginning of writing and talking—but write *to a point*. Work hard at it, *care* about it. Write about *our people*: tell their story. You have something glorious to draw on begging for attention. Don't pass it up. *Use* it. Good luck to you. The Nation needs your gifts.[65]

This character's insistence that art be *used* also accounts for what it should be used in service of; she argued that they must tell the story of "our people," whose stories speak to not only the present at hand but also the future that will someday exist. Hansberry modeled this practice through art that she defined as realism; in an interview captured within *TBYGB*, she argued, "[T]he artist who is creating the realistic work imposes on it not only what *is* but what is *possible* . . . because that is a part of reality too. . . . [I]t requires a much greater selectivity—you don't just put everything that *seems*—you put what you believe *is*."[66] This belief system, which is fused to the practice of art, centralizes the truth of Black life and humanity within the "freedom dreams" sung by Simone, allowing us all to believe that "there is to be a world," as Playwright put it.[67] Hansberry's vision is intimately connected to the influence of her mentors, and through her art, and that produced by her comrades, she put the United States on notice that Black people's present was not finished—it had both a past and a future.

Both texts engage the future, although its utility lies less in its ability to signal temporality than practice. The play is infused throughout with fictional accounts, anecdotes, and personal correspondence that discuss conditions yet to come. In her response to Mailer's essay "The White Negro," Hansberry critiques "The New Paternalists" who "have mistaken the *oppression* of the Negro *for* 'the Negro.'" She ends by highlighting his tragic flaw: "Norman, write not of the greatness of our peoples—yours or mine—in the *past* tense."[68] She disrupts his narrative and its assumptions by insisting on a future, a radical position within the context of the Cold War and its attendant ravages in Vietnam. Her discourse here exhibited an Afro-futurism concerned with what cultural critic Kodwo Eshun describes as "the possibilities for intervention within the dimension of the predictive, the projected, the proleptic, the envisioned, the virtual, the anticipatory and the future conditional."[69] The "To Be" that the title of the play and anthem announced was both the prospect of identity and its making, thereby condoning growth, change, and innovation. The future is the space of opportunity and provides an organic focus for Simone's song, which she penned after seeing the stage play. The music for "TBYGB" is an animated yet measured soul tune that begins with a solo octave piano flourish by Simone, jumps to a staccato two-chord introduction, and then transitions into the vocal line brought in by a small chorus whose articulation of the word "black" is emphasized by a concise and crisp "k" at the very end, making it the most prominent word in the vocal line and, through its repetition, the song. The lyrics of "TBYGB," written by jazz musician and lyricist Weldon Irvine, Jr., reflect a strong awareness of and solidarity with the cultural practices of their contemporaries in the Black community who proclaimed, "Black is beautiful." With its unequivocal assertion of pride and the desirability of being Black, "TBYGB" is the Afro translated into music:

> Young, gifted and black.
> Oh what a lovely precious dream,
> To be young, gifted and black,

Open your heart to what I mean.
In the whole world you know
There's a million boys and girls
Who are young, gifted and black, and that's a fact.

The emphasis on youth in the text salutes the grassroots leaders of global liberation movements—namely the brave young people who put their lives on the line at the lunch counter in Greensboro, in the streets of Albany, Georgia, and on the buses in Birmingham; the youth of SNCC and Oakland who broke away from the nonviolent wing of the Civil Rights Movement; and those whose struggles abroad continued to dismantle centuries-old colonial infrastructures.

TBYGB salutes these young people by publicly supporting their tactics as well as their agendas, in so doing foreshadowing the turn to Black Power. As Hansberry wrote to white southerner Kenneth Merryman, "I think, then, that Negroes must concern themselves with every single means of struggle: legal, illegal, passive, active, violent and nonviolent. That they must harass, debate, petition, give money to court struggles, sit-in, lie-down, strike, boycott, sing hymns, pray on steps—and shoot from their windows when the racists come cruising through their communities."[70] CORE garnered notice on more than one occasion within *TBYGB*, the most prominent of which dealt with this very issue. In 1964 Brooklyn CORE organized a controversial "stall-in" in which they stopped traffic on the Triborough Bridge in protest of racial inequality and violence. A number of leaders, Black and white, opposed the strategy and spoke publicly against it. This moment exposed the dissension in the ranks of Black civil rights organizations; not only was the role of white people within Black organizations being questioned, but, increasingly, blackness was measured and defined by the individual's level of militant action.[71] In his article, "They USED to Be Colored," William Worthy argued, "Here at home, our idealistic preferences for non-violent solutions are rapidly becoming irrelevant." He praised the stall-in for "dramatically highlighting the mushrooming challenge by black nationalist youth to the white-ruled Black Establishment." After predicting the demise of the liberal, interracial CORE, he advocated for the development of an "all-Negro" organization and for more leaders like Isiah Brunson—organizer of the stall-in—who would "vigorously articulate a comprehensive program of social, economic and anti-colonial demands" so that the Black community could "forget about the sorry men who used to be colored."[72] Hansberry's comments on the protest did not proscribe directives, although like Worthy she critiqued "the sort of 'progress' our satisfied friends allude to"—like the landmark court cases won by her father—"when they presume to deride the more radical means of struggle." She supported the members of CORE by assuming ownership of the emotions that precipitated the action in question: "Fatuous people remark these days on [Black people's] 'bitterness.' Why, of course we are bitter." These "fatuous people" constitute a different public to whom she sends the brilliance of "Harlem" (1951), written by Langston Hughes, which begins by asking, "What happens to a dream deferred?" His series of provocative scenarios of resolution ("Does it dry up / Like a raisin in the sun?") ends with the query, "*Or does it explode?*"[73] Hansberry takes her readers to Harlem via Hughes in order to expose the evolution of Black political insurgency and its future via what Worthy named a "Negro underground."[74] With Hansberry's solidarity on display on stages across the country, it is not surprising that the newly positioned CORE would choose the sonic conversion of *TBYGB* as its anthem.

As the tumult of perspectives suggests, CORE was in a moment of transition. The new leadership was young and embattled, and the anthem spoke to their challenges and ambitions. It is these young people who own the future that has yet to materialize:

> There's a world waiting for you,
> Yours is the quest that's just begun.

The consistent emphasis on looking forward is momentarily unsettled in "TBYGB" by the reflections of a veteran Simone, who laments, "Young, gifted and black / Oh, how I long to know the truth. / There are times when I look back / And I am haunted by my youth." Hansberry's recollections within the stage play also are haunted by her past—a previous life intimately connected to the woman that she became. Sociologist Avery Gordon argues that "to be haunted is to be tied to historical and social effects."[75] The "changing same" described by Hanberry and Simone contemporary LeRoi Jones was discussed also by Simone, who made sense of her life's continuity in 1969 when she argued, "Yes, I'll always be changing. As I change, my material changes. Where my head is there my material is. [Yet,] you don't basically change your character. You grow, but you don't change your character. . . . What I always was is being reaffirmed in a deeper sense."[76] Instead of ignoring her lifetime of encounters with racism, sexism, and poverty or banishing those knowledges to the waste bins of history, Simone highlighted them in "TBYGB" as a haunting because they resonated beyond her particular experience and generation. These conditions were the substance of both women's experiences, and through them, the story of the nation was told. Their haunting finds resolution through exposure because "haunting, unlike trauma, is distinctive for producing a something-to-be-done."[77] Again, the "To Be" that both women were consumed with appears. Enter the youth; to them is offered the challenge to meaningfully engage the past/haunting while strategizing around what Hansberry described as the "the world that awaits you" and Simone calls "the quest that's just begun."

The future was propelled back onto Hansberry through *TBYGB*. Her sightedness predicted the changes that she did not live to see, namely the transitions from nonviolence to armed militancy, global "no-confidence" insurgency, and the growth of a queer liberation movement. Her visions lived on in her writing, its staging, and, through Simone, its sounds. The conversion moments shared between the two women over the period of their friendship is seen most dramatically in the extension of the play into an anthem—a reworking that made *TBYGB* portable and useful in a different way. Hansberry understood that there were more like her in the world, people who would take up the mantle of critique and dissent, who would sacrifice in service of their ideals. Simone was one of those people, and her anthem was the answer to Hansberry's final request in *TBYGB*: "If anything should happen—before 'tis done—may I trust that all comas and periods will be placed and someone will complete my thoughts—This last should be the least difficult—since there are so many who think as I do—."[78] The completion of Hansberry's thoughts through "TBYGB" signaled the move from her memory to what James Baldwin described as her "overpowering vision," from eulogy to imagination.[79] As civil rights turned to Black Power, the play and replay of Simone's final and, perhaps, most enduring anthem chronicled the new guards and new worlds that would arise on a global scale.

The Possibility of It All: Covers of CORE and Its Anthem

Simone's conversion of *TBYGB*, which she composed and performed to honor her friend and mobilize those who followed in her footsteps, required that she again marshal her unique talents through an instrument that was relatively new to her. Like that of Robeson before her, Simone's political and anthemic genius materialized in her inimitable voice. Manifested through conversion by friends and the violence of a world invested in difference, it became a strategic tool and technique that radically transformed her as a musician. She never intended to be a vocalist. In the early 1950s, Simone (then known as Waymon) was urged to build her musical career in Atlantic City, where she landed at the Midtown Bar and Grill. Reluctant, if not scared, to tell her mother that she would be playing piano in a bar, she reinvented herself as Nina Simone. This name change signaled a new persona and a new musician. As she played in Atlantic City, her repertoire began to fuse her canonical roots with her secular interests, combining "classical pieces, hymns and gospel songs . . . occasionally slipping in a part from a popular song." Her jazz instinct in improvisation was surely developed during this period as she used the music already at her disposal to invent completely new pieces and respond to the desires of her audiences. The grand transformation in her repertoire occurred at the demand of the bar owner. After complimenting her on her piano playing, he told her "tomorrow night you're either a singer or you're out of a job."[80] With no alternative, Simone became a singer.

The addition of vocals required a major adjustment in her repertoire and preparations each night. With no formal vocal training and little confidence in that instrument, Simone early on performed songs that allowed her to highlight the piano over her own voice. That strategy slowly faded away as she gained control over the production and uses of her voice; while both "Mississippi Goddam" and "Four Women" employ the piano in important ways, the instrument is ultimately a supporting character, with her voice as the star and method of deliverance. Her business acumen, which developed over time and allowed her some control over the manufacture and distribution of her voice, coincided with her political development, and from this merger she became envoiced in a way unimaginable. Simone's singing voice became the mechanism through which she would develop her artistic and political imprint in the 1960s and '70s. This voice marked the transition from Eunice Waymon to Nina Simone and brought with it all of the ecstasy and turmoil that would mark her later life. The process of becoming envoiced in Atlantic City was itself a conversion that led to libratory experiences and practices that would impact multiple generations of women.

Black women's speech was a troubled production within political and Civil Rights Movement networks; some were completely silenced, while others were disciplined to fit the prerogatives and serve the needs of others. As jazz vocalist and Simone collaborator Abbey Lincoln said of her own movement participation, "[B]eing female, you're not supposed to have too much to say. People used to say to me 'Anna Marie or Abbey, you talk too much.' Well, what can you do about that?"[81] Both Lincoln and Simone interpreted the attempts to quiet them as provocation to speak louder, and they joined with women in the movement who similarly spoke to power in new ways. In 1964, women in SNCC wrote the "SNCC Position Paper (Women in the Movement)." In the document, the women named issues of gender discrimination within the organization that made for unequal decision-making power in their day-to-day work.[82] This push from within the Civil Rights Movement directed, and at other times reinforced, the political projects of the movement artists; it was "as though musicians were challenged to prove their artistic worth and the excellence of African American music by the bravery and moral example of the Civil Rights Movement."[83]

Historian Ruth Feldstein argues that "Simone's public rage [in response to socio-political issues] was intentionally incendiary and emphatically unladylike, as far from the respectability of a classically trained female performer as one could imagine."[84] While "trained," Simone resisted the disciplining of class and gender conventions, and her transgressive identity performance was manifest three-dimensionally; her politics, body, and voice caused alarm. As I will soon discuss, Simone's dark skin already complicated the conditions of performance, especially within the recital of her anthem "TBYGB." Through her demand that she be read as beautiful—with her broad facial features, natural hair, and African-inspired ensembles—she refused to conform to white standards of femininity, and her affective gestures in performance, which were described by one reporter later in her career as "without guile, without charm," contoured narratives of powerful, declarative statements rather than questions or pleas, thereby refusing to produce the intimacy that mainstream audiences expected of their musicians.[85] Read as a "diva" and "difficult" by one promoter and audience member after another, Simone argued that these responses were a direct result of her insistence that she be paid adequately for her work and listened to because she was both an artist of the highest caliber and an educated citizen of the world.

Simone intentionally shaped her persona in this period for certain audiences, most especially Afro-diasporic populations and Civil Rights Movement workers. Historian, activist, and musician Bernice Johnson Reagon recalls, "Simone helped people to survive. When you heard her voice on a record it could get you up in the morning. . . . She could sing anything, it was the sound she created. It was the sound of that voice and piano. . . . Nina Simone's sound captured the warrior energy that was present in the people. The fighting people."[86] That sound was political, racial, gendered, and classed in ways that defied categorization and stretched the listening ear to place it within its context and social milieu. Indeed, that "warrior energy" was a constituent part of her voice and contributed to the incessant questions about its quality and tone. Comments by reviewers and listeners alike regularly questioned the gender of the voice that they heard, arguing, "She sounds like a man."[87] While this interpretation may be quickly dismissed as nonsense or lambasted as racist (neither position do I completely disagree with), I argue that it gestures toward another layer of her defiant performance. The fact that Simone had perfect pitch demands a reevaluation and second listen to her sound, as this condition underscores how meticulous and concise she was in the use of her voice. The control that she held over her sound, which was connected to her ears as well as her throat, lungs, and diaphragm, means that its production was deliberately employed to deliver the model of perfection that she heard in relation to the world around her. Her pitch was intimately connected to the entire sonic landscape of which she was part, from the notes of her piano to the sounds of the streets outside. In this way, her perfect pitch conjoined her musicianship with her citizenship and made her sound even more knowledgeable and descriptive than musicians whose ear is attuned only to their immediate environment. There is a queering of her gender performance through her voice that is available only through the process that Reagon describes. Simone's "voice on a record" betrayed the otherwise straightforward gender presentation that she displayed on stage, and through that sonic transgression, she was capable of further troubling the myriad racial and gender politics that she critiqued within her songs. The "sonic black womanhood" described by Brooks was therefore differently articulated and understood in Simone's recordings than her live shows,[88] and the fact that she was "one of the most pirated performers ever" means that her voice was itself a method of contestation, crossing lines of gender and legality through its (un)condoned replaying around the world.[89]

Cultural production gave Simone the freedom and the platform to use her voice in ways unavailable to so many other Black women. With the release of "TBYGB" in 1969, however, she joined an already vibrant chorus of Black women's voices across the country in response to Hansberry's play. Its release occurred five years after the Birmingham bombing, but it was no less adjacent to a world in turmoil. The previous year had witnessed eruptions of global violence in Paris and Mexico City, while the dual crisis of a spreading war in Vietnam and continued racial tyranny in the United States led to student demonstrations around the country and urban riots in response to the assassination of Martin Luther King, Jr. Simone, who no longer had Hansberry to lean on, channeled her crisis into her sound. Through "TBYGB" she was able to commiserate with the many others who loved Hansberry: not only their shared comrade James Baldwin but also the scores of men and women who flocked to see *TBYGB* off Broadway. Civil rights icon and Paul Robeson mentee Harry Belafonte backed the original production, which "tour[ed] 41 states in an unprecedented three-year tour."[90] In 1971, one of the play's actresses, Camille Sands, wrote an article for the *New York Times* in which she described the show's reception in Detroit. She described that the company "as Black artists expressing the Black experience, accepted [the audience's] laughter easily and gratefully in recognition, and the joy, joy, joy of recognition was almost overwhelming." Various moments during the play brought out visceral reactions in the audience, facilitating intimacy and mutual gratitude: "At Lorraine Hansberry's words, 'I was born Black and female,' there was an explosion of applause and vocal acknowledgement of 'What It Means.'" Hansberry's words are the mirror image to Simone's earlier recognition of her blackness and gender identity, demonstrating how both women understood their bodies in relation to their art/work. The enthusiastic endorsement of Hansberry's play by a primarily Black audience acknowledged and shared in the power of her words as well as her lived experiences. The Black Power arts scene continued to recognize the dynamic relationship between audience and performer/writer by drawing all event participants into its realism, a style earlier discussed by Hansberry as a combination of "what *is*" and "what is *possible*."[91] Sands commented that the emotional response by the audience to *TBYGB* allowed for the "crossing over of my people from shadow into substantial Black, the hollow gray places having been filled by their knowledge and acceptance of themselves."[92] This didactic exchange continued in the project of *A Raisin in the Sun*, which, according to Baldwin, exposed for the first time in American theater "so much of the truth of black people's lives."[93] *TBYGB* also shared a relationship with the works of Black Arts writers Amiri Baraka and Larry Neal, who after *Raisin* continued to reinvent the relationship between theater and Black communities in the mid-1960s, as well as the forthcoming and explosive play of 1975, *For Colored Girls Who Have Considered Suicide When the Rainbow is Enuf*, by Ntozake Shange. Hansberry's posthumous contribution to the project of Black theatrical storytelling was the evidence of ongoing representational shifts in Black identity and consciousness.

The events of the late 1960s and early 1970s encouraged radically different notions of what "substantial black" meant within Black communities and their freedom struggles, with negotiations of identity ranging from the moral to the aesthetic. It was in the period of a heightened Black Power and militant cultural nationalism that Nina Simone's converted "TBYGB" found its place as a secular anthem. Released as a single in November 1969, the song was the standout of her 1970 album *Black Gold*. The cover of the album offers one interpretation of a substantial blackness through a unique remodeling of the silhouette by Simone (Figure 5.2). The striking juxtaposition of color—black and an orange-gold—perfectly sets off the large Afro and contours of her face, here in black. Yet the blackness of her face is not an abyss or an absence—it is instead filled with musical notation. This image represents what those who knew Simone already were aware of: that she was indeed composed of music—that the arpeggios and rests, flats and sharps, whole notes and fermatas that composed her scores also structured her DNA. Within the interplay of colors the notation also provides evidence of her belief that her music was intelligible only because she was Black—indeed, the notation and the sound that it organized could be deciphered only in the midst of her color-blocked environment because it was on and in her dark skin, from her body, from her culture. Were her deep black color to disappear, so too would her music, into the homogenous and uniform background. Her profile on this album cover remixes the "shadow" described by Sands into a "substantial Black."

Neither version of *TBYGB* was content to wallow in the past, or remain static in the present. In his review of the play, music journalist Nat Hentoff remarked, "The kaleidoscopic fusion of autobiography, invention, intentions, doubts and affirmation immersed my daughter and me not in a memorial but in a thrust of spirit that kept us both, for a while after we left, silent and thinking about possibility."[94] The possibility pondered by Hentoff and his daughter was the hoped-for response; Hansberry's three-part play invites these types of meditations and uses her body and experiences, and those of the community around her, as a platform from which they might be launched. Simone's nearly ten minute (con)version on *Black Gold* does a similar work. Recorded live in 1969 at the New York Philharmonic Hall, "TBYGB" sings the praises of the African descended and becomes Simone's method for making her "soul intact," as she exorcises her personal haunting on stage. The song is prefaced by comments for her muse Hansberry, whom, Simone is confident, the audience knows already: "Of course you know who she *is*," she says and follows her resultant soft chuckle with "dig that." Simone highlighted the play in her comments, telling the audience that it is being performed downtown, thereby making an explicit link between the two pieces while also honoring Hansberry's labor even after her passing. Simone conjures Hansberry in that moment, saying that she "comes alive more everyday" due to what is being written and said

Figure 5.2.
Nina Simone, *Black Gold*
(RCA Victor, 1970),
cover.

about her. Simone foreshadowed the end of her song in performance, not because it will be any less powerful or necessary at a future date, but because "very soon now, say, maybe four or five weeks, I won't be able to sing ["TBYGB"] anymore for each time I do it she comes a little closer and I miss her a little bit more." Simone did not yet know that her song would be enshrined within a Black movement canon as an anthem; here, she is able to relate to and imagine the production only by way of its muse. Through the composition of the song and its performance, Hansberry still lived and was ushered to her rightful place on stage by Simone through her dedication: "So, for her, while she's here with us and she approves, 'To Be Young, Gifted and Black.'"[95]

Simone's deep appreciation and love for Hansberry is witnessed in the song's composition, but it is through its performance that Simone draws the attention of her listening public back to the movements of Black people who, she argued, "need all of the inspiration and love that they can get."[96] Arguments for Black equality, like this one, from the concert stage "evoked racially specific kinds of fear" that showcased the interplay of white consumption and anxiety.[97] As the blackface performances of the mid-nineteenth and early twentieth centuries demonstrated, Black culture and its approximations were used by whites to "play in the fears and fantasy of blackness."[98] This method of release was unavailable to would-be white consumers of Black Power because they no longer had complete control over the bodies, representations, or narratives offered on stage. Black artists worked diligently to own their spaces of performance and employed various techniques in order to make that possible. Simone took advantage of her performance platform by acknowledging racial divisions, but instead of exposing the white members of her audience—who were often the majority—she draws attention to and brings closer the Black members. As she said during the 1969 performance, "[To Be Young, Gifted and Black] is not addressed primarily to white people, though it does not put you down in any way. It simply ignores you." She ends her introduction by provocatively requesting that her primarily white audience *not* buy her recently released RCA 45, saying, "So since this house is full and there are 22 million Blacks in this country, I only want 1 million to buy this record. You understand?"

"TBYGB" resonated within Black communities around the country and solidified Simone's status as icon. Her call to "unify us" and catalog of iconic Black freedom fighters including "Martin," "Lorraine," and "Langston" made the song a representative of the political cultures brewing in the wake of the 1968 urban uprisings. The off-Broadway production of Hansberry's play from which the song was born, as well as the rise of Black Power aesthetics, propelled Simone's phrase into the mainstream, with one Black journalist reporting that it "is so moving in its content that it ranks with Rev. Jesse Jackson's inspirational 'I am somebody.'"[99] The phrase catapulted the song into heavy rotation on Black radio. In early January 1970, "TBYGB" was number 3 on the top 10 chart in the Black newspaper *New York Amsterdam News*; by the end of that month, it was number 1, ahead of the Jackson 5 hit "I Want You Back."[100] "TBYGB" ultimately reached number 8 on the national rhythm and blues charts and even cracked the pop chart at number 76. Its defiant and unabashed announcement of Black beauty and achievement alongside its popularity on the charts primed it for use by members of an increasingly international Black Power vanguard.

The choice of "TBYGB" as the Black national anthem highlights Simone's standing within the protest traditions of the Black United States, where she managed a "level of involvement . . . unmatched by any of the major figures of Rhythm & Blues in the early-to-mid 1960s,"[101] as well as the currency that she managed to amass as an ambassador for Black America abroad. She had a special relationship to Africa that modeled for Black Americans the types of connections that could be had with the peoples and lands of the embattled continent. Her investment in and engagement with Africa intimately connected her Black Power ascendance to a growing and mobilized "Third World Left." Simone embarked on her first trip to Africa in December 1961, when she traveled to Lagos, Nigeria, to participate in a two-day festival for the American Society of African Culture (AMSAC) along with a group of thirty-three Black artists and intellectuals, including Langston Hughes and folk singer Odetta.[102] Hughes was the narrator and emcee for the event and announced to the African communities in attendance, "We have come through the air and across the ocean—seven thousand miles, to exchange with you *our* gifts, to exchange with *your* artists *our* art, and to give you, this audience, in all humbleness and love and sincerity our talents." This "exchange" was fueled by the long-standing diasporic ambition of return: "In a sense, we feel we are coming *home*, to our ancestral home, back to the roots of our culture. . . . We come back to you, the land from which our forefathers came—to this great continent in its mighty march toward the future—we come to bring you our music and our songs."[103]

Simone continued to exchange with African musicians for the rest of her career, and her collaborators included Nigerian drummer Michael Babatunde Olatunji and South African singer Miriam Makeba, who will be discussed further in the following chapter. Their camaraderie and the sounds that emanated from it meant that Simone would continue to return to Africa, physically and sonically. After the 1961 festival she described, "I knew I'd arrived somewhere important and that Africa mattered to me, and would always matter. The people of Lagos never made me feel anything other than welcome but it wasn't Nigeria I arrived in—it was *Africa*."[104] This "Africa" was indeed an introduction of importance and would become more vibrantly three-dimensional for her as the decade progressed, leading her into the Black Power moment of radical activist flight and exile. In July 1969 she was a participant in the Pan-African Cultural Festival in Algiers, Algeria, a country that had only seven years prior achieved independence from France.[105] Organized by the Organization of African Unity (OAU)—a continental body dedicated to African sovereignty, quality living standards for African people, continental unity, decolonization, and international cooperation[106]—the Pan-African Cultural Festival served as more than an artistic celebration; it also highlighted a new, albeit short-lived, hub of the Black Panther Party. A little less than a year after he fled the United States under threat of imprisonment for a San Francisco shoot-out with police, Black Panther Eldridge Cleaver was reunited in Algiers with his wife and Panther activist Kathleen Neal Cleaver during the month of the festival. Other Panthers and revolutionaries joined in the festival and reunion, including cofounder Bobby Seale, David Hilliard, and Kwame Turé (formerly known as Stokely Carmichael), who was in exile in Guinea.

In the wake of the Pan-African Cultural Festival, the OAU proclaimed that "[n]ever before, had African culture and arts given such a brilliant display of their richness, variety and genius. Above cultural and artistic achievements, this First Festival was the triumph of African solidarity and purpose, the triumph of AFRICANITY."[107] The "Africanity" described by the OAU was a postcolonial construction that built upon previous Afro-diasporic consciousness movements including *Négritude*, a theorization of African arts and culture shaped by Senegal's Leopold Senghor and Martinique's Aime Césaire in the 1950s, even as it picked up on U.S. civil rights victories and signaled contemporary upheavals. By the time of the Pan-African Festival, the urban U.S. sounded like brass and rhythm guitar as the popular soul-funk anthem by James Brown, "Say It Loud (I'm Black and I'm Proud)," reached number one on the rhythm and blues charts. "Say It Loud" offers many of the bells and whistles of a protest anthem; unapologetically prideful lyrics and a catchy hook along with a funk beat make it an attractive song for mobilized youth cultures. The song also related contemporary struggles with those of the past when Brown declared, "We've been buked and we've been scorned / We've been treated bad, talked about as sure as you're born," a clear reference to the spiritual "I've Been 'Buked and I've Been Scorned," popularized by Mahalia Jackson during her performance at the 1963 March on Washington. Despite its adoption in popular discourse and its chart success, Brown removed "Say It Loud" from his stage set within a year of its release. According to him, the song had run its course. Ward editorializes that "there was arguably as much racial politics in the list of dances on the fade-out of ["Say It Loud"] as in the main body of the lyrics, with their obvious, if effective, 'we'd rather die on our feet, / than keep livin' on our knees' sloganeering."[108] The message-power of Brown's song should not be summarily dismissed—particularly in light of its use to rally a distraught Black community in the wake of King's assassination and its attendant "build it, don't burn it" vernacular—but Ward is right to question the song's effectiveness in Black political organizing. Up until that point, Brown rarely participated in the on-the-ground struggles of civil rights organizations. He further drew the ire of Black communities for his pro-U.S. posturing during his State Department–sponsored trip to Vietnam and his early 1968 release "America Is My Home," which argues that material accumulation is equality.[109] The pressure that he received from the Black community to respond to contemporary political circumstances ultimately crystallized in "Say It Loud." In this instance, Brown was the one organized, yet no conversion transpired. His performance of "Say It Loud" lasted only as long as its chart success.

Brown's absence of leadership was filled my Simone, whom radical SNCC activist and author H. Rap Brown called "the singer of the Black revolution."[110] Simone's decade-long involvement in Civil Rights Movement mobilizations, in combination with her extensive repertoire of standards and anthems, made her an icon of the Black Power generation and provided compelling evidence to support the dual importance of the art *and* artist in the work of the long Civil Rights Movement. "TBYGB" and Simone accomplished what "Say It Loud" and Brown could not: they represented and modeled the ethical superiority and diversity of the movement communities, thereby mobilizing a diverse global counterpublic of dissenters who relegated to myth the manufactured apathy and naïveté of Black youth. This cadre of young individuals rallied and congealed as a group around the joys and terrors of blackness, exhibiting a complicated engagement with race and its performance. Hansberry too contributed to the dynamism of Black identity and its representation, as *A Raisin in the Sun* and *TBYGB* show. Simone was an iconoclast within Black culture who also served as a medium for Hansberry, for the anthem was "given" to her, as she described it, to then "give to the kids by [Hansberry]."[111] The intimacy and dedication of artistic transfer and mentoring modeled here made Simone's anthem deeply personal, deliberate, and enduring in ways that the fleeting, albeit explosive, performances of Brown could not, or would not, approach.

Simone's unique ability to be grounded in and by the Civil Rights Movement while also gaining popular success is what, in part, led to the wide exposure of "TBYGB," which took on another life beyond its use by CORE. During the early 1970s it was covered by a number of popular Black artists, including Donny Hathaway and Aretha Franklin. Hathaway's version was released in 1970 on his first studio album *Everything Is Everything* and was placed on the track list after his hit jam session "The Ghetto." There is a natural flow between the two texts, as the former, an instrumental, is only rarely punctuated by vocals and the chant, "the ghetto." The congas bring the diaspora into harmony with the sounds of U.S. urban enclaves and build on the growing cacophony of rhythms that develop by the end of the song. This acceleration, punctuated by hand clapping, leads the listener to his storefront church for the final track of the album: "TBYGB." Hathaway's rich baritone, an electric piano accompaniment, and a slower pace and steady beat structure highlight the anthem. Simone's momentary breaks are smoothed out in Hathaway's rendition, which encourages the listener to sway in motion with his timing and lyricism. He uses a call-and-response format reminiscent of the Black preacher, beckoning "Can I get somebody [to] help me?" This call is met by the first introduction of a female chorus (more than 5 minutes into the 6:41 song) who follow his line, "To be young, gifted and black," with a drawn out loop "is where it's at."[112] His choice of female chorus is a counterpoint to Simone's use of The Swordsmen in her 1969 release and balances an otherwise masculine scene, as Hathaway plays preacher to a listening audience/congregation.

Aretha Franklin's cover similarly plays to the church as she draws on her many years of service as the daughter of a preacher. Appearing on her 1972 album of the same name, "Young, Gifted and Black" provides a differently gendered soundscape as she sings throughout the introduction of the song with a female chorus.[113] This homogenous soundscape is punctuated only by piano accompaniment and electric organ as the women crawl through the song, until 1:43 when a break introduces a solo piano escalation leading to the tonic chord of the song and entrance of the drums with a faster rhythmic soul pulse that mimics Simone's original syncopation and breaks, unlike Hathaway's fluid, unbroken melodic line. Franklin follows this alternate beginning with an improvised call-and-response to the other vocalists, while she wails "keep your eye on the future!"[114] Franklin's version is a melding of the Simone and Hathaway approaches; it begins by riffing off of Hathaway and his use of gospel-style antiphony yet retains the special coding of Simone's original through its lyrics and eventual move to her syncopated vocal delivery.

Covers "typically retain the essence of the melody and lyrics (for a song) but may greatly very in other dimensions," thereby providing "an intertextual commentary on another musical work or style."[115] Lyrical retention is certainly evident in the Hathaway and Franklin versions, yet their ingenuity is found in their reworking of the composition through gospel traditions that far surpass Simone's original. However, the melodic and compositional differences do not fundamentally alter the song in purpose. Engineer Daniel Ellis contends that in "pop music, the main purpose of recording a cover version is typically to investigate a more-or-less radically different interpretation of a song."[116] Hathaway and Franklin are in some ways constrained in their interpretations by the song's use as an anthem, which canonized Simone's performance as *the* standard for musicians and listeners alike. The familiarity and significance of the text in performance did not dismiss the ingenuity and innovation inherent to Black musical performance, but it certainly evidences the push and pull of anthemic solidarity as each new version, indeed each performance, brings different interpretations to bear on its moment of articulation. While the sound varied in their covers, the purpose behind them was aligned with the original composition, offering evidence of the pervasive cultural currency associated with "TBYGB." Both artists seek through their versions to place themselves within the Black consciousness of the period. Hathaway was the newcomer, the rookie, whose choice of "TBYGB" on his debut album exposed his early attempts to foreground a radical engagement with Black communities through sound. Franklin on the other hand was already a seasoned performer, having achieved chart success with the feminist anthem "Respect" (1967), "(You Make Me Feel Like) A Natural Woman" (1967), and "Think" (1968), among others, prior to her release of "Young, Gifted and Black." Her cover similarly indicates a desire to connect with Black communities, although this piece stands just outside of her already established repertoire, which was composed primarily of "middle-of-the-road" pop-soul tunes and covers by the likes of Burt Bacharach. Her interpretation then serves as a venture into a politicized blackness that was previously underdeveloped in her recordings. Both artists found success in their efforts; Hathaway went on to be a crucial soul performer and composer during the 1970s, while Franklin later was labeled the "Queen of Soul," a royal title comparable to, although not quite as provocative as, Simone's "High Priestess of Soul." With these sonic reinforcements, CORE's anthem continued to appear in Black mobilizations and documents throughout the decade.

"TBYGB" was the last anthem conjured by the High Priestess, but it continued to reverberate due to the efforts of these artists and others during her exile from the United States after 1970.[117] The resilience displayed by her anthem offered an appropriate end to the decade that proved to her who she could be and what she and her people could accomplish in the world. The movements that she helped to build displayed a dynamic engagement within communities of color over liberation and justice, thought and practice, both nationally and internationally. Simone was an interlocutor between art and politics within these struggles and used the stage and the studio as her locations of protest, while her voice was the method of deliverance for her message and her freedoms, as they circulated through the cultures of diaspora and built on the legacy of those who came before her. With the motivation and instruction of her friends and mentors, she realized and confirmed for others that "though it be a thrilling and marvelous thing to be merely young and gifted in such times, it is doubly so, doubly dynamic—to be young, gifted *and black*."[118]

* * *

By 1970, the cross-continental currents of revolution were backed by the winds of victory. Decolonization in Africa, starting with Ghana in

1957, meant that an entirely new world was opening up for the African descended, manifesting the postcolonial stage that Hansberry tirelessly imagined. Even in the midst of these victories, one country held particularly tight the reins of settler colonialism and globally relished in its particular brand of Jim Crow segregation, which in its colonial tongue was called "apartheid." The white powers of South Africa produced one international spectacle of violence after another, murdering native populations by the thousands and forcing thousands more into exile. Like Paul Robeson before her, Simone argued the vile and fascist nature of the apartheid regime, while in the struggle she also supported her friends who were taking increasingly high-profile positions in the dismantling of the South African behemoth. From this collective developed a project that announced Black strength even as it contended with the diversity of its members and philosophies. From locations across the globe an anthem was performed in order to sound the final stage of a battle burdened by history but emboldened by precedent.

6

Sounds of Exile

"Nkosi Sikelel' iAfrika" and ANC Ambassadors

Who can keep us down as long as we have our music?
—Miriam Makeba

Carnegie Hall was like a second home for Nina Simone. She performed there on more than ten occasions, each time as a more accomplished and higher profile artist. Yet it was her May 1961 show that marked an early "milestone" in her career and made an indelible mark on her personal life. The event was a benefit for a Harlem church, and despite her misgivings about religion she obliged their request. It was there that she made her first acquaintance with a woman who would become a close friend, confidant, and mentor: Miriam Makeba.[1] Hardly a household name at the time, the young Makeba made her first popular appearance in the United States in 1959, the same year that Simone burst onto the blues and jazz scene in New York City. Makeba was mentored and supported early in her international career by artist-activist Harry Belafonte, the man responsible for organizing a number of civil rights benefits during the decade. His influence offered tremendous opportunities for Makeba, who was able to plug into existent Black arts networks with relative ease. It is within this orbit that she met and befriended Simone and began a decades-long friendship that would alter both women's lives and those of their audiences, and highlight and challenge the perceptions and practices of each woman's native land.

Diasporic anthems originating elsewhere profoundly impacted the Civil Rights Movement in the United States and the solidarities that developed on a transnational level. The circuitry of music propelled political understandings of Jim Crow in the United States and apartheid in South Africa onto a global stage, where musicians played a formative role in unveiling these conditions and composing their responses. Their artistry was the method of exposure, and for these acts they faced incredible consequences. Makeba used her platform as a performer to critique and destruct the apartheid apparatus from sites around the world, and for that she was exiled from South Africa. Before she was a part of an international civil rights vanguard, before she was Mama Africa, she was a young singer thrust into the political fray of a struggling country whose future ultimately lay in the hands of those like her who were removed forcibly from the national body, including the touring cultural ensemble Amandla and its parent organization, the African National Congress (ANC), a political body formed in 1912 and banned in 1960. This moment of rupture for the organization coincided with Makeba's banishment and moved the organization toward a strategy of violence as they navigated the cultures of exile. The uses of the ANC anthem, "Nkosi Sikelel' iAfrika" within local struggles, expanding diplomatic efforts, and organizing abroad made ambassadors Makeba and Amandla the producers of a unique cultural knowledge and authority that kept Black artists and exiles in close contact and camaraderie during the transition from a global focus on a U.S.-based Civil Rights Movement to the final decades of the apartheid regime in South Africa.

Antiphonies: Histories of Art and Activism

Turn-of-the-century South Africa was a nation on the verge of a century-long civil war. While there were numerous organizations and individuals of varying racial and ethnic identities working toward different, and often competing, projects of nationalism, community formation, and war making, the nation quickly moved toward a hard and fast binary: a nation in Black and white.[2] Although the country was originally administered from the top by the noninhabiting British, national policy development and its daily enforcement eventually were handed over to the Dutch, whose settlements in South Africa began in the seventeenth century. The deputized Dutch used their small, yet occupying, presence in South Africa to escalate Britain's race-specific system of governance. Late-nineteenth-century laws, including the Masters and Servants Acts enacted between 1856 and 1910, which regulated public and domestic spaces through prohibitions on the social and labor practices of unskilled workers, set the foundation for what would soon become the ideology and practice of "apartheid," an Afrikaner word, literally translated as "apart-hood." This radical segregationist policy codified and centralized racial difference through legislative maneuverings and violence. The seeds of the institution were already evident and became more draconian as the century progressed.

As indigenous communities across Africa struggled against colonial rule, they strategized and moved alongside other African-descended populations. Black Americans were crucial players in both the rhetorical and political maneuvers of Black South Africans. Historians Amanda Kemp and Robert Vinson argue that Black Americans were evoked by Black South Africans in two distinct ways: "[F]irst, black South Africans pointed to black American political, socioeconomic, and religious achievement as proof of African capacities to successfully traverse modern society. Second, black Americans, often coupled with black Caribbeans to form the generic category of 'American Negroes,' provided a political template for Africans seeking to improve their status in an increasingly segregationist-minded South Africa." Marcus Garvey and his Universal Negro Improvement Association (UNIA) became central figures in these formulations of solidarity. As chapter 1 argued, Garvey's Black nationalist designs of race-specific philosophies and institutions modeled the potential he saw elsewhere within diaspora. South African intellectual and activist James Thaele was a Garveyite who met with some success in his attempts to argue for African modernity through his work with the ANC and other leftist organizations, including the Industrial and Commercial Workers Union (ICU), which developed after the explosion of industry stemming from the late-nineteenth-century discovery of gold and diamonds. It was his education and experiences of travel that most radically shaped his worldview. After studying at South Africa's Lovedale Institute—a location described by Thaele as having failed "to teach the Blackman that culture of refinement and the Babylonian civilization of his forefathers"—Thaele went on to study at

Lincoln University, a historically Black college outside of Philadelphia that specialized in a liberal arts (versus industrial) education for Black men. After his departure from the ICU, Thaele focused his energies on building the previously moribund Western Cape branch of the nationalist ANC, "transforming it into the country's most militant organization by the late 1920s." He founded and edited the Cape's ANC organ, *African World*, from which he argued the "UNIA as the governmental authority over Africans similar to the League of Nations' jurisdiction over member European nations." His emphasis on Black self-government on a transnational scale ensured that Thaele would receive the wrath of watching officials. His activism revealed the ways in which Africans "relied on the modern concepts of race and nation to imagine a filial relationship with the American Negro as a means to disconnect modernity from whiteness," thereby advancing a protest agenda based in a deliberate diasporic frame.[3]

It was in the period of Thaele's return to South Africa that the ANC developed out of the South African Native National Congress (NNC), an organization that signaled what historian Francis Meli describes as the "creation of a loyalty of a new type—a non-tribal loyalty—which was inherently anti-colonial, and by implication, anti-missionary."[4] The early ANC constitution described the organization as a "Pan-African Association," a politico-ideological perspective later reinforced by a resolution among its membership, which urged the government to replace the word "native" with "African." This powerful suggestion on the part of the Black population explicitly demanded recognition of Black autonomy; their bodies had long been denied by the minority governments of the Dutch and British, and the act of self-naming suggested new, alternative subjectivities and ways of constructing and engaging in the body politic. This assertion implied "nationality and therefore modern citizenship rights" and linked the aspirations of the African majority to those African descendants who struggled in the minority abroad.[5] The moment of organizational transition and demands for recognition sparked the ANC adoption of the Xhosa hymn "Nkosi Sikelel' iAfrika." This is a pivotal moment in the history of the organization: it was not only reinventing itself within the public sphere and advancing a political agenda through its demands for a new national language on African subjectivity, but also launching its representational platform. Possibly taking another cue from Garvey—this time in the cultural realm—the song was institutionalized as the recessional hymn for ANC functions. It was used by the NNC as early as 1912, yet it was under the ANC that the song became an anthem.

By the time of adoption for "Nkosi Sikelel' iAfrika" by the ANC, the song had lived a life of local resistance. Nearly fifty years before the juridical adoption of apartheid Enoch Sontonga, a Xhosa clergyman, composed the anthem that, as sociologists Bennetta Jules-Rosette and David Coplan argue, "symbolize[d] more than any other piece of expressive culture the struggle for African unity and liberation in South Africa."[6] A musician and composer, Sontonga used his Christian belief system to order his piece; in composing the music and first verse, he relied on traditional Western hymn techniques, tonal formations, structuring, and message. "Nkosi Sikelel' iAfrika" is composed with four-part harmony in B-flat major. A repetitive melody—which is characteristic of both Western hymn composition and indigenous South African melodies— grounds the song.[7] The straightforward melody is offset by the rhythmic variations that Sontonga employs. Like "Lift Ev'ry Voice and Sing," the South African anthem opens with a series of eighth notes that hurriedly lead the singer to the longest note—a half note in measure 2, on the tonic (I). The rapidity of the line's movement is one of the most striking features of the song. While written in the formal hymn techniques of the eighteenth and nineteenth centuries—with major/minor tonal harmonies and abundant use of leading chord progressions (e.g., IV-I, the "A-men" coupling)—its quick pace betrays the slow, meditative performance traditions of this style. The flurry of eighth notes in the text move the song toward the redemption that the singers seek, as if the very speed of their singing will bring about the ends that they desire. It begins,

Nkosi, sikelel' iAfrika	Lord, bless Africa
Malupakam' upondo lwayo;	May her horn rise high up;
Yiva imitandazo yetu	Hear Thou our prayers
Usisikelele.	And bless us.

This prayer, delivered in various tempos, hinted at its eventual usage as a movement anthem and through its future visions signaled a protracted struggle.

The song's usefulness throughout the century was grounded by both the conditions of possibility presented to Black South Africans and the history of the nation's music. "Nkosi Sikelel' iAfrika" is a by-product of Sontonga's training in religious institutions as well as the cultural particularities of Black South African musics. Ethnomusicologist Charles Hamm described South African traditional musics as distinct from others in sub-Saharan Africa in that they "unfold over brief, constantly reiterated structures: in choral music these take the form of recurring vertical combinations of notes, or 'chords.'" In traditional music, these combinations are "built horizontally of different layers of sound, each contributing to the whole while maintaining some degree of individuality." The horizontal arrangement signals a rejection of hierarchies in sound and performance as musicians and audience members replicate the independence of the harmonic structure by taking liberties with the performance and distinguishing themselves throughout. Singers are particularly capable of creatively intervening in South African musics because "the dominant performance medium is the unaccompanied chorus, usually with one or more solo voices pitted against a larger group in call-and-response patterns."[8] The autonomy offered to the singer within the larger project of the chorus is in this music unique, and the regular use of antiphony (call-and-response) reinforces the soloist's role as a leader within the production.

The four-part harmonies of "Nkosi" imply a unified effort in its performance, but like "Lift Ev'ry Voice and Sing" the performance belies this easy association. Inclusivity is ruptured in measure 11, when the women, in unison, introduce the line "Yihla Moya" (Descend, O Spirit), with men following in unison afterward. This division offers melodic contrast but also demonstrates the importance of women within the musical and (later) political performance. The women's melodic line within the song is never broken; in contrast, the men have a four-count break while the women introduce the line in measure 11. The continuity of women's voices reflects their roles as leaders within the development and performance of culture as well as the religious elements that undergird the anthem. Their voices also serve as a bridge over those moments of silence that were part and parcel of both musical composition and political practice, as apartheid attempted to quiet the voices of a rebelling Black majority. As "Nkosi Sikelel' iAfrika" gained its reputation through usage in liberation movements across the continent, these moments of division and unity within it spoke to more than an artistic choice by Sontonga. The ever-present voice of women within the anthem suggests instead that they never rested in either the sound or function of the ANC and, by extension, the building of the nation.

Travel and geography were central to the anthem's reception throughout the region and continent. Sontonga's 1897 composition trekked across his native Eastern Cape through performances in churches and schools and two years later debuted at the ordination of a Shangan Methodist minister.[9] Poet S. E. K. Mqhayi continued in the efforts of the song and wrote the following seven verses in the early twentieth century. The issue of translation within and between diasporic peoples is evident in this piece, which early on spoke in Xhosa, Zulu, and Sethoso in order to demonstrate a broad appeal and address various linguistic and cultural communities within southern Africa. Sontonga employed a continental vision that requested blessings not just for South Africa, but for all of Africa. A Pan-Africanist aesthetic is demonstrated in Mqhayi's verses as well, which implore the creator to "Bless the ministers / Of all the churches of this land," and "Bless our efforts / Of union and self-uplift." This consciousness on the part of Sontonga and Mqhayi demonstrates an investment in cross-ethnic solidarities and futures, a constituent part of the Pan-Africanism and decolonization efforts spreading throughout the continent in the first few decades of the twentieth century.

The use of the anthem in ANC functions and protest events, as well as those of other Black organizations and nations later in the twentieth century, prompted the consolidating apartheid government to ban and replace it as a national icon. In 1938 Prime Minister J. B. M. Hertzog declared "Die Stem van Suid-Afrika" (The Call/Voice of South Africa) the national anthem of South Africa.[10] Officially adopted by Parliament in 1957, less than a decade after the election of the apartheid platform National Party, "Die Stem," written in Afrikaans, celebrates the pioneering spirit of the Dutch-descended Boer settlers. Their project of white unification, land accumulation, and political consolidation was everywhere present in the text, which extolled the virtues of a South Africa that they unequivocally claimed as their own. The first verse makes abundant use of the proprietary "our" when referencing the landscape;

"our blue heavens," "our deep seas," "our plains," and ultimately "our country" are the evidence of settler colonialism's logic of "territoriality," which historian Patrick Wolfe highlights as "its specific, irreducible element."[11] The mobilization of this logic through the performance of a selectively imagined, yet nonetheless national, symbol is grounded in both material acquisition of lands and resources and what cultural historian George Lipsitz argues is a "possessive investment" in the racial and social capital of whiteness.[12] This ownership claim is especially egregious and powerful within a geography where white people are the minority but have through coercion and force dominated the land and its inhabitants. Much like its formation in the United States, whiteness in South Africa functioned as a "status property," which critical race studies scholar Cheryl Harris argues is used to maintain and entrench the power of a few.[13] This minority in South Africa was unified under the apartheid umbrella, an infrastructure of violent exclusion based on race.

The installment and practice of apartheid in South Africa traverses a long history, one that defies finite dates and the logics of humanity. However, the formation of modern South Africa in the first decade of the twentieth century offers a moment from which to begin a brief dissection of a system that ruled the social, political, and economic existence of that country for nearly a century. Journalist Graham Leach argued that "since the 'South Africa Act' . . . [of] 1910 the shape of white politics in South Africa has almost entirely been determined by the Afrikaners." While the British, whose empire included South Africa until 1961, were also political forces, their role was secondary in the development and maintenance of a white supremacy grounded by Afrikaner nationalism. Efforts to consolidate white power across linguistic and cultural difference by political icons Jan Smuts, Louis Botha, and Hertzog led to a rebuttal in the form of a more staunch and virulent nationalism under D. F. Malan, whose National Party took government in the elections of 1948 on a straight apartheid ticket. With Malan, "a new breed of Afrikaner was at the helm, dedicated to an 'Afrikaner first' philosophy," which took effect immediately.[14] Under the banner of the National Party apartheid's most prominent architect entered politics.

Hendrik Verwoerd began his public political life as editor of the Afrikaner newspaper *Die Transvaler*, from which he supported the

National Party as well as the Germans during World War II. As a student (and later professor) of philosophy and psychology, Verwoerd understood the importance and effects of discourse, yet his writings demonstrate that he was also a social science methodologist, manipulating and expanding existing knowledges and practices through matrices of his own design.[15] This training and faculty no doubt facilitated his rapid political ascent into a position of incredible consequence; as minister of native affairs—the person responsible for the interface with and policy of or relating to that contested term "natives" or, as the ANC desired to be called, Africans—Verwoerd began the calculated erection of apartheid, itself a method, which he famously described as a "policy of good neighbourliness." His stunning achievement in promoting radical separation and white supremacy while minister of native affairs led to his 1958 election as prime minister of South Africa. From this position he brought "independence" to South Africa through the nation's withdrawal from the British Commonwealth and implemented the policies that maintained the radical partitions of apartheid. It was his arresting success in the formation of a racially exclusive governing system that made his reputation around the world. At the time of his assassination in 1966, Verwoerd was remembered as having "transformed South Africa's traditional but largely informal white baasskap (bossdom) into the rigid apartheid laws that classified and separated the races, in the process stripping the nonwhites of rights basic to all in most countries."[16]

Verwoerd worked diligently to make apartheid a present practice as well as a future vision, despite the fact that it was, both ideologically and practically, an impossible structure to maintain. Journalist H. Lindsay Smith argues that "to keep apartheid going over the years, an untenable position has had to made tenable; that oppression has had to be followed by more oppression; that repressive laws have had to be followed by more oppressive laws" while others were scrapped altogether.[17] The oppression indeed mounted and led to a flurry of laws in quick succession that demonstrated the haphazard and reactionary position of Parliament. At midcentury the Group Areas Act was introduced, which relegated Black bodies to the peripheries of the urban landscape in South Africa. Racial groups, which were similarly regulated through the Population Registration Act of 1950, were assigned to specific locations.

Black men and women were given limited access to the cities—primarily for the purposes of labor—and forced to reside in the outlying townships, with names such as Sharpeville, Alexandra, and Sophiatown. With the numbers of residents in townships increasing, Parliament followed the Group Areas Act with the Bantu Authorities Act, which provided for the establishment of "independent" homelands, or Bantustans, for Black South Africans. This policy displaced Black South Africans outside of the national frame and resulted in a frightening condition of statelessness: "It does not need much imagination to see that if, in the end, there are ten independent black states, as the white rules would have it, and six million workers recognized neither in their homelands nor in the white areas, there could be six million stateless persons—nearly a quarter of the population of South Africa in a stateless condition." As these "homelands" emerged and took advantage of their "independent" status, "efforts [were] made to force these workers to adopt the citizenship of their 'country' of origin,"[18] precipitating a potential offensive by the capitol in Pretoria to remove their South African citizenship. These radical policies sought to physically isolate and politically annihilate the already marginalized Black body and phantasmal Black citizen. The twists and turns of parliamentary rule under apartheid spun out of control as the century progressed, and ultimately the center could not hold. It was under Verwoerd that the violence of the apartheid regime exploded on an international scale and invited a radical repositioning in the strategies and procedures of the embattled ANC.

Dynamite and Dance: Youth Flight, MK, and Makeba

The first fifty years of the ANC's program for justice were characterized by nonviolence. Taking their cue from international icons like Mahatma Gandhi and the faith traditions of a growing Christian population, the leaders of the ANC used language in their manifestos such as "unity" and "harmony."[19] The message of "Nkosi Sikelel' iAfrika" replicates this peaceful imperative; its composition as a hymn draws on a tradition of delayed redemption, yet the pace of its performance was a new strategy that pushed for movement and recognition of the efforts of those singing it. This quickened pace was, by the middle of the twentieth century, being duplicated by the membership who performed the anthem. In 1944, after two years of announcing its arrival, the ANC introduced the Youth League, a group of students, activists, and workers who believed that, despite its significance and continued relevance, the ANC was sluggish and dated in its approach to liberation. These young people, many of whom came from the historically Black University of Fort Hare in the Eastern Cape, argued at the moment of apartheid's adoption that nationalism was the only method toward successful revolution: "It is known, that a dominant group does not voluntarily give up its privileged position. That is why the Congress Youth puts forward African Nationalism as the militant outlook of an oppressed people seeking a solid basis for waging a long, bitter, and unrelenting struggle for its national freedom." They saw themselves as aligned with "Africanism," a philosophy devised by the first president of the ANC Youth League, Anton Lembede. Africanism was a "nation-building faith" that Youth League leaders like Nelson Mandela and Oliver Tambo subscribed to instead of the "extreme and ultra-revolutionary" position of Marcus Garvey and his "Africa for the Africans," a battle cry employed by other freedom fighters in Africa.[20] While they understood Africanism to be a "moderate" model of liberation philosophy, the Youth League nonetheless pushed the agenda of the ANC left and became not only the voices but also the bodies of resistance in the coming decade.

The post-1948 moment of Black resistance in South Africa is marked by the defiance campaigns that heralded a new era in the South African liberation struggle. Strikes, protests, and public statements characterized much of the early response to the apartheid regime. These actions were grounded in two principles: first, that imprisonment was a step toward liberation. No legitimate leader of the people could escape this reality. The second principle was that oppressed people in South Africa would achieve their desired freedoms only through extraparliamentary processes.[21] The influence of U.S. civil rights discourse is present in these two positions, but each movement followed different paths. Historian George Frederickson outlined two shared points of debate between the Black liberation struggles in the United States and South Africa. One was the debate over relations with the white population; was it best to move toward a multiracial society, which Frederickson abbreviated as a "cosmopolitan" perspective, or was it more worthwhile to move toward independent nationhood or an "ethnocentric" agenda? Both movements were primarily organized around a cosmopolitan view, bolstered by the prominence of integrationist organizations and leaders like the NAACP and ANC, Martin Luther King, Jr. and Nelson Mandela. "The second dichotomy, which is not automatically resolved by adopting a cosmopolitan or an ethnocentric orientation," according to Frederickson, "concerns the nature of the struggle: will it be carried on by reformist or revolutionary methods?"[22] This second concern is where the two movements most radically diverged. While there were significant parallels between the two conditions of Black existence—parallels that were acknowledged on both sides of the Atlantic—the sociopolitical circumstances meeting Black South Africans convinced the ANC that their route to liberation would not survive under a strategy solely composed of civil disobedience; for the first time in fifty years, the ANC decided that violence would be met with violence.

This strategy was contested by a number of individuals within the organization, even as other members argued that the conditions facing Black South Africans left very little room for negotiation with a regime that so brutally abused the majority members of its nation. The bloody events of March 21, 1960, affirmed the shift in ANC strategy. The Sharpeville Massacre, as it is now known, began as a peaceful demonstration organized by the Pan-African Congress (PAC), another Black South African liberation organization, to protest the pass laws that governed the mobility of Black South Africans. The Defiance Campaign initiated by the ANC in the 1950s centered much of its effort on the issue of pass laws and continued to do so into the 1960s. The thousands of protestors who arrived at the event that day were mobilized by the PAC, the previous work of the ANC, and the new laws of 1952, which extended the pass laws to women. As the demonstrators approached the police station without their passbooks—the legal documentation required for all travel by Black South Africans—the police opened fire, killing 69 and injuring over 180 people. Most of those injured or killed by bullets were shot in the back as they turned to flee. A state of emergency followed that included the detention of thousands of men and women with no recourse to the international legal and humanitarian standard of habeas corpus, which guarantees a fair and timely trial, punishment commensurate with the crime, and uncompromised justice for the accused.

Many individuals were never charged, yet they were held in police custody for untold hours, days, weeks, or more.

The international domination of Black bodies through travel restrictions was a prominent tactic employed by colonial powers throughout the African world. The indigenous populations of these occupied nations daily encountered the reach of the colonial state, whose absolute paranoia led to the construction of legal structures that criminalized the most mundane of activities, including mobility. The Pass Laws of South Africa were "a mode of regulation somewhere conceptually between the polarities of brute coercion and ideological manipulation," which made them an integral element of the white supremacist-settler colonialist machinery under apartheid. Political scientist Philip Frankel argues that "the pass system profoundly aggravate[d] the [existing] social pathologies . . . by underwriting the most flagrant injustices of *apartheid,* disrupting the most elementary of human relationships, and exposing blacks to ruthless economic exploitation." What the architects and enforcers of apartheid in South Africa (and, similarly, those who devised and maintained Jim Crow in the United States) failed to realize was that their methods of domination were not fail-safe—they, in fact, often served to marshal the subjugated population: "[T]he tendency of the pass system to evenly spread humiliation, irrespective of status difference amongst blacks, contribute[d] to a sense of communal solidarity and integration which [was] a critical factor in their political mobilization."[23]

Women played a decisive role in the development of a program against the pass laws—all of this despite an uncertain role within the decision making of the ANC. Journalist and politician Frene Ginwala documents that membership for women within the ANC was constantly in flux. The draft constitution of the NNC named wives of members and "distinguished African ladies" as "auxiliary members," who paid no fees and hence had no vote. Without the franchise, this select group of women performed duties that were relegated primarily to the provision of "suitable shelter and entertainment for delegates to the Congress." The 1919 NNC constitution adjusted its language only slightly; auxiliary membership became a privilege extended to "all Women of the aboriginal races of Africa over the age of 18 years, who shall be members of the Bantu Women's National League of South Africa" and they were given the explicit rights to organize politically. It was in fact the success of the Bantu Women's League (founded in 1918) that provoked this adjustment in the NNC membership rules. The Bantu Women's League was formed in order to combat the extension of the pass laws to women through-out the Union more than forty years before Sharpeville.[24] Their ability to generate grassroots mobilizations—including demonstrations at government buildings and mass petitions—made these women a force to be reckoned with in the ANC and their communities. By the 1920s, there were numerous branches of the ANC Women's Section and activist Charlotte Maxeke was a recognized member of the ANC leadership body, "taking full part in proceedings and appearing on platforms at public meetings."[25]

The masculine imperative that undergirded the founding and maintenance of the early ANC was unexceptional. As gender studies scholar Cynthia Enloe argues, nationalisms have traditionally "sprung from masculinized memory, masculinized humiliation and masculinized hope."[26] According to historian Natasha Erlank, "Black nationalist activity [in South Africa] was not only premised on the exclusion of women, but also relied on the exclusion of women for its own legitimation."[27] Garvey's centrality to the discursive and strategic practice of Black Nationalism throughout diaspora—especially in Africa—helped to institutionalize the exclusive reliance on a powerful male figure in the design of the Black nation. This gendered imperative overdetermined the craft of nation formation. Yet the UNIA also demonstrated the limits of that endeavor; UNIA women, while undistinguished as political actors within their anthem "Ethiopia," nonetheless made their voices heard through creative interventions within the composition and their political actions within the organization. The same was true for the women of the ANC. It was their organizing strength that made them sought-after members of the organization, and pass laws were the issue that generated some of the earliest demonstrations of their might. Women were on the front lines in the fight against the pass laws because it intimately impacted their ability to manage both their financial and familial lives. While many men were seasonal laborers who temporarily relocated for their jobs, most South African women worked relatively close to the communities in which they raised children and/or had other familial relationships. Daily commuting from the townships to the urban areas where they worked primarily as domestics manifested their heightened exposure to the violences of the apartheid regime, especially in the form of pass requirements. In large part it was this reality that made Sharpeville so explosive.

The Sharpeville Massacre effectively ended the nonviolent phase that characterized the first fifty years of the ANC. The radical about-face in protest strategy was a public refusal to continually suffer at the hands of an increasingly militarized and aggressive apartheid police force in South Africa. No longer content to use tear gas and rubber bullets, this police force would under the new policy of the ANC be met with violence. Umkhonto We Sizwe (MK)—"Spear of the Nation"—was the answer. Formed in 1961, the MK, cells of men and women who trained in neighboring nations surrounding South Africa, mastered guerrilla techniques and the arts of sabotage. For the ANC Youth League, which was at the forefront of the charge to armed resistance, the message was clear; they fought because "white oppressors have stolen our land" and have the "fruits and riches," while Black people have "the backbreaking toil and the poverty." Black people "have to carry passes" and are "restricted and banished," while whites "move about freely." The MK made their reputation through interfering with, if not destroying, infrastructure in South Africa, including communication towers and military bases. Nelson Mandela helped to conceptualize and found the MK. His position on the move to violence was unequivocal:

Firstly, we believed that as a result of Government policy, violence by the African people had become inevitable, and that unless responsible leadership was given to canalize and control the feelings of our people, there would be outbreaks of terrorism which would produce an intensity of bitterness and hostility between the various races of this country which is not produced even by war. Secondly, we felt that without violence there would be no way open to the African people to succeed in their struggle against the principle of white supremacy. All lawful modes of expressing opposition to this principle had been closed by legislation, and we were placed in a position in which we had either to accept a permanent state of inferiority, or to defy the Government. We chose to defy the law. We first broke the law in a way which avoided any recourse to violence; when this form was legislated against, and then the Government resorted to a

show of force to crush opposition to its policies, only then did we decide
to answer violence with violence.

Mandela's strategy "made it known that we, the oppressed people of
South Africa, would fight for our rights. We made this known not only
with words. Dynamite blasts announced it."[28]

Explosive is an appropriate word to describe the South African
atmosphere in the post-Sharpeville moment. The turn to violence
as a strategy of ANC resistance was met with even harsher forms of
injury and harm by the apartheid government. Like Simone's realization of Black life's limited worth in 1963, indigenous South Africans too
understood that the most powerful members of the nation would not
prioritize their safety. The state of emergency implemented after Sharpeville included the detention of eighteen thousand people as the police
force swept the streets of the townships and cities. In addition to the
violences of passes, poverty, and surveillance, Prime Minister Verwoerd
moved to suspend the nation's responsibility for Black citizens. Alongside the construction and enforcement of Bantustans, he banned the
ANC and PAC and structurally imposed the unequal privilege of citizenship by revoking the passports of activists and artists who worked
against his machine. This moment signaled a new period within South
African resistance cultures. As jazz musician and Makeba collaborator Hugh Masekela argued, "[M]usic became an even more important
weapon in the struggle as any possibility of open legitimate protest had
come to an end after the Sharpeville massacre."[29] Verwoerd's attempts
to squelch Black resistance failed, however, as the voices of dissent were
pushed beyond the nation and forced to invent new networks, methods, and technologies of sound.

Perhaps the most iconic subject of South African banishment—and
its fallibility—was Miriam Makeba. Born Zenzile Miriam Makeba in
1932, Makeba gained her nickname, Mama Africa, through performances abroad in which she interpreted and combined the many linguistic traditions and contemporary political struggles of her nation
and continent. Singing variously in Xhosa, Zulu, and English, she
spoke to numerous South African communities while also making her
talent distinguishable and available to an international audience. In
the process, however, she encountered incredible scrutiny and finally

banishment from her native land in 1960. Makeba was, in this respect, not unlike the many men and women who fled South Africa post-1948, including jazz luminaries Masekela and Abdullah Ibrahim. Because of her condition as an outsider, she developed a reputation as "a singer who has made exile her profession and oppression her theme," marking her as an ideal troubadour for the myriad movements then under way among the African descended.[30]

Makeba was multiply capable of dissecting the conditions and governmentality of apartheid through her practice of a politicized commonsense, which directly impacted her musicianship. She decried Afrikaans as "the language of genocide" and argued "apartheid will only work if everything associated with blacks is worthless."[31] Her beliefs expose the death and destruction that constituted the apartheid regime; through structural and sociocultural reinforcements of Black devaluation, the minority government in South Africa sought to annihilate the Black populations physically and psychologically. Makeba counteracted this assault as a child by immersing herself in music. As a young vocal prodigy she joined in the alternative efforts of her community to be heard. She described, "We Africans have always been able to communicate with each other through singing. . . . Our songs mean more to us than the official media of the press and radio." Like the cultural practices described by anthropologist James Scott in southeast Asia, Black South African musics employed language difference and insider innuendo and code to construct subversive messages unrecognizable to government officials.[32] Once translated, their songs promptly were banned, yet the damage to minority governance was done and continued to erode as new songs developed to counter oppression. The communal response to shared conditions of domination was enforced by the act of singing and performance, thereby growing opposition multiply. It was largely through the practice of singing that Makeba understood her identity and future as intimately connected to her community; she believed, "My life, my career, every song I sing and every appearance I make, are bound up with the plight of my people."[33]

It was this nascent impulse that led Makeba to take risks early in her career. After participation in popular music ensembles, she struck out on her own and in 1959 released "Pata, Pata," which gained her national recognition and, ten years later, made her a star in the United States.

The pivotal moment of exposure for Makeba was her participation in the 1960 film *Come Back, Africa*, by U.S. filmmaker Lionel Rogosin. Filmed covertly (and under incredible threat of danger) in and around Johannesburg and the township of Sophiatown, *Come Back, Africa* told the story of Zacariah and his family who were unendingly displaced due to the violences of apartheid, namely the pass laws, and victimized by circumstances largely beyond their control. Poverty, criminality, race, and geography are intimately connected in the film, developing, to borrow from geographers Katherine McKittrick and Clyde Woods, "a clear picture of how the underside is, for some, not an underside at all, but is, rather, the everyday."[34] The examination and exposition of this quotidian Black South African experience on a world stage demanded retribution; not only was the film banned in South Africa, but Makeba was as well. She was denied entry into South Africa after touring with the film in Europe and the United States and was told that her passport had been invalidated. As evidenced by Paul Robeson in chapter 3, the passport was a technology of dissent for many African descended musicians and therefore became a weapon used against them by their nations. No longer a citizen of her country of birth, Makeba joined the exiled ranks of the South African stateless.

In this moment, music and its performance were her refuge and location of effective citizenship. She signed onto RCA records, the artistic home of mentor Harry Belafonte, and began to make a life for herself in the United States. The resonances of her home were everywhere present for her, however; on a trip to Atlanta, she was denied service at a hotel restaurant. There she experienced "a new country, but the same old racism. In South Africa, they call it apartheid. Here in the South, it is called Jim Crow."[35] This familiarity ultimately proved invaluable as she entered into the U.S. music scene. The conditions and practices of radical inequality that she faced in South Africa were present in myriad forms in her adoptive country and attuned her to the global condition of Black dispossession and abuse. She began in earnest to join in the efforts of other Black American and African diasporic musician-activists through participation in concerts benefitting civil and human rights causes. She also traveled as an ambassador to nongovernmental organizations abroad, including the United Nations (UN), to speak against the brutalities of South African apartheid. Seated before the UN in 1963, she asked, "Would you not resist if you were allowed no rights in your own country because the color of your skin is different to that of the rulers and if you were punished for even asking for equality?" Her experiences as a Black South African left her with a heightened foresight that led her to comment, "I appeal to you and through you to all the countries of the world, to do everything you can to stop the coming tragedy."[36]

Makeba attempted to manage the coming future by performing songs of South African protest, a performance practice encouraged by Belafonte, another musician-activist with deep networks in both communities. Like Robeson before him, Belafonte was a champion of "people's music" and consistently performed Black U.S. folksongs as well as songs from Jamaica and other Caribbean nations. He used his star power to further those traditions in other diasporic artists, including Makeba. In 1965 the duo joined forces for a full-length album titled *An Evening With Belafonte/Makeba*, which highlighted the cultural practices of diasporic communities, in particular the various linguistic and ethnic cultures of South Africa. The twelve tracks that compose the Grammy-winning album include Black work songs, lullabies, and traditional love songs. At the literal center of the album is track 6: "Ndodemnyama Verwoerd!" (Beware Verwoerd!). This song is different from a number of the other tracks offered on *An Evening*; it was by 1965 a long-standing protest song for Black South Africans. Written by famous ANC movement composer Vuyisile Mini in response to the 1948 election of the apartheid-platform National Party, "Ndodemnyama Verwoerd" announces, in Xhosa, the presence of a politicized and mobilized Black public:

Nantsi ndodemnyama	Here are the Black people,
Verwoerd pasopa	Beware, Verwoerd!

The song is composed in much the same way as other protest anthems; it is a moderately paced, common time (4/4), major key song that was sung and harmonized by groups who, from all appearances, had not a care in the world as they smiled and danced. Masekela commented, "It sounds like a fun song but it's really like, 'Watch out Verwoerd, here comes the black man. Your days are over with.'"[37] This performative subterfuge, along with the language barrier, allowed the song to remain in the movement repertoire for many decades undetected by the apartheid administration. Makeba's recording of the song buttressed her earlier declarations before the UN and brought to the United States and international audiences the sounds of a modern Black uprising.

Makeba's internationalism was not confined only to the West. She performed her convictions at independence and national holiday celebrations across continental Africa. By the high tide of African independence victories in the 1960s and early 1970s, Makeba was solidly a part of the "U.S. Third World Left" described by Cynthia Young.[38] She married Trinidadian-American militant and originator of the term "Black Power" Kwame Turé in 1969 after meeting him in Guinea, where both later lived and worked with president and African independence icon (Ahmed) Sékou Touré. Makeba's "terrain of exile [was] not wholly disadvantageous" for her political development and practice;[39] although she was unable to return home, there was a measurable freedom in the world at large that she would have never accessed as a subject under the South African apartheid regime. She used those freedoms of travel and expression to be present with and speak to African communities around the world that had achieved the rights for which her country still struggled. Her performances in numerous newly independent African nations signaled her repute as an icon for freedom on the continent, and her status as ambassador in exile meant that she carried to these locations the dreams and traditions of South Africa. "Nkosi Sikelel' iAfrika" was a central piece within this effort. As the adopted anthem of more than one African country—a practice demonstrating investment in collaborative movement building over exclusive nationalisms—the song symbolized both the specific conditions of her people in South Africa as well as the shared experiences of dispossession and eventual triumph that these independence festivities celebrated.

By the early 1970s, Makeba was labeled as "the greatest poet, historian, and storyteller" of her country.[40] Her recordings, international testimonies, and publications documented the conditions and cultures of her native land and continent for a global audience. Yet her role as griot was most pronounced on stage. Live performance was the greatest enactment of dissent for the subject of a country and continent under colonial siege. Indeed, as Masekela noted, "[t]he government despised our joy," and musical performance was a spectacular exhibition of the complex performances and pleasures of blackness.[41] To be sure, recordings had their place; they were valuable for international and otherwise distant audiences, fund-raising, and revenue for individual musician-activists. Recording was not, however, an always available vehicle for political speech. Although consistent, Makeba's work in the studio was mediated by her multiple exclusions as woman, South African, Black, and foreign, thereby limiting her access. Within the context of continental and global revolution, the studio also forestalled the immediacy and dynamism of camaraderie with a community from which the apartheid government of South Africa attempted to isolate her. As powerful and libratory as it was, the recording booth in the career of Makeba might also be read as an encumbrance to her political project because it undercut the spectacle and resiliency of the performing Black body. The fact that Makeba never produced a recorded version of "Nkosi Sikelel' iAfrika," a song that she was known to perform widely, is evidence of her efforts to build a shared rebellion against the constraints of intimidation and violence.[42] The voice and its expression are privileged within recordings, yet under apartheid, the moving, singing body was the stinging indictment and epic failure of the regime. Her desire to expose this collapse led her to travel the continent to sing an anthem that, through live performance, consolidated and further mobilized the liberated masses, ultimately garnering Makeba the title of Mama Africa.

Makeba's presence on stages in Zambia, Angola, and Tanganyika in the wake of each nation's independence was a strategic effort: it supported the successes of South Africa's neighbors and swelled the attention brought to the ongoing rebellion at home. In addition to its intimacy and dynamism, live musical performance was the method of delivery for this exchange because it offered "a way of circulating the intended texts of songs that had been altered due to censorship."[43] It also circumvented the censorship of the material musical object—cassette tapes, records, etc.—that caused "arrests and convictions . . . with distressing regularity."[44] In these live performance spaces Makeba and, through her voice, Black South Africans were free. Freedom from colonialism was marked sonically on numerous occasions. The celebration of independence in Tanganyika in 1961 was mediated by music as the indigenous populations celebrated their victory.[45] The *Tanganyika Standard* reported,

"TANGANYIKA is independent. She has experienced her greatest hour. A nation—and from today the latest member of the Commonwealth—has been born. At one minute to midnight last night, as the last notes of the British National Anthem hung on the air, 80,000 people looking down on the floodlit arena of Dar es Salaam National Stadium were plunged into darkness."[46] The sonic evacuation of the colonial anthem ("God Save the Queen")—with its "last notes . . . [hanging] on air"—was the event that captured the breaking of a new day in the ninth nation to gain independence from Britain. In its stead was placed the sound project of their compatriots to the south, "Nkosi Sikelel' iAfrika," which was renamed in Swahili "Mungu Ibariki Afrika."[47]

The practices of both diaspora and exile provided the mechanisms through which "Nkosi Sikelel' iAfrika" became the anthem for African nations beyond South Africa. The ANC was in large part responsible for this transmission through both its individual ambassadors, such as ANC President Oliver Tambo (1967–91), and its groups that trained and organized in the frontline nations. Indeed, "the hymn punctuated the ANC's victories and struggles as it traveled across borders into exile," thereby furthering the mission of the ANC and materializing the organization and its struggle through its iconic sound text.[48] Although "Nkosi Sikelel' iAfrika" was originally used as a liturgical tract, the song was, by midcentury, the defining sound text of an aggrieved majority under siege. Much like "Lift Ev'ry Voice and Sing," the hymn composition of "Nkosi" allowed for its adoption by organizations across the political spectrum; within the rise of African liberation movements, however, the song was primarily used as a mouthpiece for leftist liberation movements, a number of which had relationships to Marxist socialism. It is then unsurprising that "Nkosi Sikelel' iAfrika" was often performed at rallies and union events in South Africa, which had a large and increasingly powerful community of organized labor leading into midcentury. Since nearly all African national anthems date from the twentieth century,[49] there is embedded within them a radical engagement with questions of democracy, rebellion, and power that makes them applicable to other spheres of agitation and struggle both within and beyond the nation. This multipurpose and utility is their most important characteristic and allowed for a South African anthem that engaged the continent for more than a century.

Anthems like "Nkosi Sikelel' iAfrika" function as a setting or platform for more aggressive sociopolitical engagement; "Nkosi" is "a pre-
amble" that "serves as the basis for shaping a civil religion and civic culture across which dialogue can take place." As Jules-Rosette and Coplan
argue, the sacred nature of the song is particularly capable of bringing
these conversations into being because it "sacralizes unity by drawing
upon a powerful religious archetype that calls for justice beyond the
bounds of the state in the name of empowered and sacralized commu-
nitarian groups." This unity within "Nkosi" facilitated a transnational
vision, one that easily moved into diaspora, a "mutable field of political
discourse" that transcended ethnic and linguistic difference. Language
is therefore an important element within the history of the anthem. The
three original languages of composition were eventually expanded as
the song took hold around the Union and later, continent, to include
English and Swahili. Variations of the anthem were also composed in
indigenous dialects.[50] Translation here again displays its function as an
agentive production of dense historical reenactment and reinvention.
The anthem carries with it previous incarnations of struggle, combining them to form a layered production and shared set of ambitions. The
result is an impressive display of pan-African solidarity through sound.

A flurry of African independence celebrations between 1960 and 1975
solidified the recognition of "Nkosi Sikelel' iAfrika" as a continental
anthem. In "Introducing the Song of Africa," then president of the ANC
Oliver Tambo wrote, "From its very foundation, because it was a regional
organisation, the ANC perceived and defined its struggle in Pan African
terms. Hence the colours of its national flag, its slogans, and in particular,
the anthem—Nkosi Sikelel' I-Africa/Morena Boloka Sechaba [Sa Heso]—
which was adopted in the early years of its struggle and which addressed
all Africa. It was often referred to as the *Song of Africa*." The plurality of
voices—through language and condition—represented by the anthem
allowed it to be mapped across the continent: "As is well known, the music
of that song has, with various modifications, been adopted in the national
anthems of some countries of this region—Tanzania, Zambia, Zimbabwe
and SWAPO of Namibia, all in the spirit of African unity."[51] All of these
countries harbored, at one time or another, a significant South African
exile population and/or ANC headquarters and training camps. The use
of "Nkosi" in those locations was fed by both the universality of the song's

text and its usage by ANC members and performers in exile. The song, therefore, facilitated the coalescing of continental politics and liberation cultures in the last fifty years of African colonization.

Another level of transnational and pan-ethnic identification is present in early renditions of "Nkosi Sikelel' iAfrika." A 1934 commercial publication of the sheet music represented "Nkosi" as the "Bantu National Anthem." In the context of apartheid South Africa, "Bantu" was a category of classification that segregated the Black population, regardless of ethnic, tribal, or cultural affiliation. The Department of Bantu Education was one service designed to "support" this population, but as the later Soweto Uprising demonstrated, its practices were never intended to provide for the maintenance and development of distinct indigenous cultural practices and knowledges but instead to homogenize the diverse population under the universal rule of white supremacy. Bantu is an indicator of linguistic heritage that covers a broad spectrum of ethnic communities across southern Africa and was used in the anthem's subtitle to signal the song's service to populations across the continent. This identification with and performance of a shared Bantu cultural background through the anthem demonstrated its utility beyond the ANC and beyond South Africa—it, in combination with coordinated struggle, assisted in organizing a continental Black identity throughout the twentieth century. At an event celebrating the seventy-fifth anniversary of the ANC, the choir was described by Tambo as "consisting of Zambians and South Africans, [who] will present a special rendering of the Song of Africa, not as an anthem of any one country, but as a salutation by the peoples of this region to all Africa on the occasion of the 75th anniversary of the founding of the ANC."[52] While certainly privileged in this performance space, the ANC was not the only star within productions of "Nkosi Sikelel' iAfrika." Through the efforts of multiple performers and activists, it increasingly belonged to and reflected the power of an embattled continent.

Makeba's ambassadorship was one way in which the nationalist ANC was able to function in the absence of a nation. ANC contemporaries within Black struggle, including the UNIA, the National Association for the Advancement of Colored People (NAACP), and the Black Panther Party, did not face the conditions of estrangement and dislocation suffered by Black South Africans under the ANC and other banned organizations. The deportation of Marcus Garvey and temporary flight of Black Panther Eldridge Cleaver, which disrupted or reconstituted the centers for the UNIA and Black Panther Party, did not fundamentally dislocate the site of struggle. This was not the case with the ANC post-1960. Various waves of forced migration from the country meant that the ANC had to produce alternative ways of managing and organizing rebellion. Makeba significantly contributed to this project through her concerts and performances; she was a mobile and recognizable proxy for Black South Africans and the ANC in countries like Angola, Ethiopia, and Liberia. Her work as an individual artist, however, could not sustain the scale of work required for South African independence. Her work on behalf of the ANC required supplementation by other projects, which also grew from organized sound. With a popular presence in countries around Africa, North America, and Europe, the ANC expanded their communications networks in order to supply fighters and sympathizers with the day-to-day information that would make their organization and its realities legible.

The shift in organizational philosophy to consider direct action in all its forms brought with it changes to the organization's media platform. Employing violence as a strategy of defense within the struggle against apartheid required new educational efforts and responses to ANC critics. That outlet was Radio Freedom. Developed as a clandestine media assault in 1963, Radio Freedom was the major propaganda effort of the ANC Department of Information and Publicity (DIP). According to internal documents, it was intended to "project the ANC internally and internationally," "prepare the masses," "win political and material support," "counter enemy propaganda," and "build up morale."[53] As these expectations suggest, there was as much effort placed on considering how best to mobilize South Africans within South Africa as there was attention paid to audiences elsewhere. Moving bodies and resources in their occupied country was the preoccupation of this organization in exile. The ANC saw their "radios as directly responsible for the mass political mobilisation and direction of [the] revolution," and they used their broadcasts to update the South African public on ANC programs and victories abroad while also offering strategy for missions within the country. Language differences and state surveillance prohibited the mass distribution of written work by the ANC in South Africa,

but radio recouped the efforts of the organization to share information. Posts in Zambia, Ethiopia, Madagascar, and elsewhere were hubs
for Radio Freedom intelligence and worked diligently to assault the
apartheid Radio Bantu.[54] Limited technological infrastructure, jam-
ming techniques employed by the South African government, and the
necessity of constant movement by the embattled and surveilled ANC
forced Radio Freedom to periodically disappear from the airwaves. Yet
and still, the sounds of AK-47s that introduced their broadcasts were,
according to one listener, "sufficient to tell us that we must just carry on
with the struggle."[55] This ode to continued militancy was buttressed by
the call of nationalism through the playing of "Nkosi Sikelel' iAfrika"
and the announcer's call of "Amandla!" ("Power!"). This sonic advance
was marked by the signals that coalesced and mobilized the diaspora of
Black South African rebellion and solidarity across the continent.[56]

The anthem's travel to other nations by Makeba and through other
countries via Radio Freedom was expedited by the diaspora of artists and
activists who were expelled from South African society. This new wave
of exiles developed post-Sharpeville and was composed primarily of
young people. After ten years of engaging a strategy of violent resistance,
the ANC recognized that the military wing alone could not accomplish
their desired ends. In spite of its ability to galvanize membership, the
MK's effectiveness began to decline in the early 1970s. The Rivonia Trial
of 1963–64, in which ten ANC members were accused of treason and
sabotage, slowed the momentum of previous campaigns. The apartheid
government employed inflammatory language in its campaign against
the ANC; the label of "terrorist" was applied to the organization and its
leadership, including Mandela, who was imprisoned on a life sentence
after the Rivonia Trial. While the apartheid regime continued to spin
their narrative of ANC "terrorism," the extreme and irrational violence
enacted by South African police and military forces proceeded without interruption. Another vicious response to peaceful protest was witnessed globally in March of 1976 when students in Soweto organized
in response to the draconian demand from the Department of Bantu
Education that all students be instructed in Afrikaans. Arguing that it
was the language of the colonizer, students from across the area strategized and mounted a public response to this injunction. Petitions, community hall meetings, and strikes characterized the early program, but

by mid-month, a more public demonstration of defiance and solidarity materialized. The students, along with support from a number of family members and partnering labor organizations, took to the streets in a peaceful demonstration. Regimented formations and regulated dress characterized the protest of approximately fifteen hundred students and supporters who used songs to both pace and articulate the rationale behind their demonstration. According to participant Sibongile Mkhabela, "'Sizobadubula ngembhay mbhayi,' a song by Miriam Makeba was amongst the most popular freedom songs on that morning, but we also made up songs as we marched, converting religious hymns and choruses to freedom songs."[57] This musical impulse, which had for so long facilitated and moved social justice demonstrations throughout the Black world, would create in South Africa a new line of defense in the struggle.

Post-Soweto Blues: Mobilizing the Cultures of Exile

The performance troupe Amandla and the military MK organized diasporas of exile, both figuratively through the international composition of their membership and materially through the many travels and displacements that attended to their training and instruction. Between 1960 and 1994, there were forty-three exile missions established within continental Africa and abroad in countries such as India, Sweden, and Cuba.[58] Various languages, ethnic cultures, and ambitions circulated within these outposts, in the process composing dynamic groups that all served under the leadership of a similarly exiled ANC leadership. Although they did not constitute or represent themselves as a government, historian Raymond Suttner argues that "the ANC in exile exercised many of the functions of a state in relation to its members."[59] With so many young people under their care, the grand majority of whom were displaced and without an alternative home, the ANC took on the responsibility of education, shelter, and training for their recruits. They also instituted a series of formal procedures that maintained discipline and uniformity within their ranks. The symbols and subgroups employed by the ANC succeeded in developing three-dimensional allegiances that captured the multivocality of the organization and demonstrated music historian Shirli Gilbert's contention that "political and cultural work in exile necessarily had distinct priorities and aims."[60]

The Soweto Uprising necessitated a response unlike that to Sharpeville. The leaders of the ANC acknowledged as much in the paraphernalia that they sent out in order to mobilize support and resources from communities abroad. Under the heading "Hell Breaks Loose in South Africa," they described,

> Since the 16th June, when our students came out in Soweto onto the streets in their thousands, the struggle against the regime has escalated to a degree which has shaken the very roots of the regime, and the confidence of its imperialist backers. Our young people, unarmed, have marched . . . [while] the streets of our townships and even of its city centres became battlegrounds between unarmed people and armed police.

The flood of young people fleeing South Africa in the wake of violence in Soweto was channeled into the only established exile organization at the time: the MK. While the militarized response faced by the protestors may have warranted violence in kind, there was another logic at play that argued for alternative protest actions from these youth. The students themselves selected the course through their own methods of resistance; it was their uprising that encouraged "the voteless people" to "cry 'AMANDLA—POWER.'"[61] This cry articulated the stakes of their rebellion and signaled a future strategy with which to coordinate it.

Violence in the post-Soweto moment, while still organizing much of the ANC response to Pretoria, conceded space to culture as a method of tactical resistance. The relationship between the two strategies— violence and culture—is not coincidental or, necessarily, in conflict. Sharpeville unleashed a measured Black South African rage and led to violence as an organizing frame within the ANC program. It was physical, deliberate, and learned in that it was adopted from the actions of other resistance struggles across the continent and world while also signifying on the logics of violence that structured the apartheid regime. Martinican revolutionary intellectual Frantz Fanon theorized the turn to violence by the colonized as always entangled with culture. As he argued in 1961's *Wretched of the Earth*,

> The violence which has ruled over the ordering of the colonial world, which has ceaselessly drummed the rhythm for the destruction of native

social forms and broken up without reserve the systems of reference of the economy, the customs of dress and external life, that same violence will be claimed and taken over by the native at the moment when, deciding to embody history in his own person, he surges into the forbidden quarters. To wreck the colonial world is henceforward a mental picture of action which is very clear, very easy to understand and which may be assumed by each one of the individuals which constitute the colonized people.

Violence and culture ("customs" and "embod[ied] history") have no definite borders between them within the colonial project nor its response. Decolonization "brings a natural rhythm into existence, introduced by new men, and with it a new language and a new humanity. [It] is the veritable creation of new men."[62] The awakening and invention of new men and women are often recognized through the construction of art. While culture and its performance are often conceived of as organic and spontaneous, music—particularly the anthem as genre—exposes them as educated productions with anticipated ends.[63] The exodus of young people in response to Soweto instigated an intentional change in the organization. They brought with them a distinct cultural consciousness grown from the turn to violence and demonstrated that Black Power ideology and the musical and aesthetic cultures that stemmed from it in the late 1960s and 1970s were organizing elements within Black resistance movements globally. From the violence of their existence in South Africa and its strategic mobilization by the ANC, the Soweto youth found their intervention and their voice in the tandem projects of local solidarity and Black internationalism through the touring performance ensemble Amandla.

Made up of young men and women, many of whom participated in the Soweto protests and actions like it around the country, Amandla grew from a mass exodus from political and racial persecution. Initially members of the MK, these youth experienced both the pull of political solidarity and the push of forced exile; the protests that precipitated their formation generated a number of high-profile and excessive responses from the authorities, including the trial of the Soweto 11, in which eleven youths were charged with sedition. The events of the Soweto Uprising demonstrated the participants' knowledge of and reliance on civil disobedience as well as a continuation of the more aggressive student protests initiated at midcentury by the Congress Youth, yet the political consciousness of those who participated in the uprisings and later fled South Africa is debated. Historian Hilda Bernstein argues that the first wave of ANC figures who went into exile during the 1950s and '60s were "often middle-aged, and highly political, with a history of engaging in public political struggle," while the post-Soweto youth exiles were "overwhelmingly young, largely male; and though fired with political passion, they were often without real ideology or political pro-grammes." She goes so far as to describe these youths as "rebels . . . with no history in their heads."[64] While the impulses and knowledge bases of these two groups of exiles may be distinct, they were not as radically divergent as Bernstein's comments suggest, nor can the second cohort of exiles be refused the unique cultural knowledges and strategies that guided their exodus. Just as the rising decolonization efforts in Africa and the budding Civil Rights Movement in the United States influenced the early cohort, the second cohort was advised by successful national rebellions around the world as well as the changing discursive and cul-tural terrain of the United States.

Soweto youth were fed by contemporary cultural nationalisms, namely Black Power. Traveling by way of Stokely Carmichael's his-tory-making call for "Black Power!" in 1966 and the sensational(ized) rise of Black militancy through groups like the Black Panther Party, Black Power, as slogan and interpretive practice, organized transna-tional visions of Black self-determination, organization, and culture. It was a term, according to Young, "that suggested an ideological com-mitment—for example, to black control—even as the route to that goal remained contested."[65] This contestation came from within Black communities as well as from without. South Africa battled over Black Power's application and usefulness in public arenas of discourse and debate. The mobilizing philosophy of Black Consciousness, which was inspired by Black South African student organizing in the late 1960s and early 1970s, was the indigenous outgrowth of an aligned U.S.-based Black Power. Black Consciousness activists took advantage of the slo-gan in their literature and organizing and argued, following a surreal-ist tradition, that the liberation of Black South African minds was the first step toward total freedom. Steve Biko, one of the most prominent

Black Consciousness theorists, described it as "the realization by the black man of the need to rally together with his brothers around the case of their [oppression]—the blackness of their skin—and to operate as a group in order to rid themselves of the shackles that bind them to perpetual servitude. . . . It seeks to infuse the black community with a new-found pride in themselves, their efforts, their value systems, their culture, their religion and their outlook to life."[66] These two philosophies of Black solidarity offered prideful articulations of Black culture as an act of mobilization and harbinger of liberation.

The insistence by Black Power and Black Consciousness movements on cultural authority and political access was a means toward psychological freedom and constituted a future for native South Africans that caused alarm for the white minority rulers. By 1971, Japie Basson, a member of Parliament from the majority-white and increasingly liberal United Party, acknowledged that Black Power was a force to be reckoned with: "I have no hesitation in saying that Black Power in South Africa will grow and it will have to be accommodated. Nothing will stop it." This inflammatory statement did not go unchecked; Basson received a rebuttal from the president of the party, Sir De Villiers Graaff, who commented, "Black influence, Black inspiration, and Black Pressure, yes," but "I don't want it to be thought at any time that the United Party believes that a movement [for Black Power] exist[s] in South Africa now." Part of his rejection stemmed from the differences that he viewed between the discourse and practice of a revolutionary Black Power of the United States and that of South Africa. He lamented, "Black Power, with a capital B and a capital P, in the sense that it is used in the United States, ladies and gentlemen, please don't use that phrase."[67]

The distinction between South African and U.S. applications of Black Power was not lost on Black South Africans. However, they refused to allow those differences to obscure the visions shared between the two. Some Black South African leaders highlighted the similarities in order to internationalize and further legitimate their local freedom projects. The same article that quoted Graaff juxtaposed his comments with those of an unnamed Black South African who also commented on the terminology and its application. The author described the debate as "unnecessary confusion" and argued that "[Black Power] is essentially, and unmistakably, the same thing, and it is profitless to believe otherwise." While the

South African context is distinguished from that of the United States, "Black Power in South Africa and Black Power in the United States share an overriding characteristic: they represent a withdrawal into Blackness, an exclusion of Whites, and a closing of the ranks of Black people so that they may present their demands and wage their struggles as a united bloc." It is notable that the author described the move toward a shared blackness not as a retreat but as a "withdrawal," which represents a strategic and agentive choice, not simply a movement based on the demands of external forces. Black Power in South Africa was "present in a classic form" according to the author because it "reject[ed] the White liberal" and was fundamentally powered by those who most abhor apartheid's existence. Indeed, "apartheid, unwittingly, legitimates Black Power and gives it all the encouragement it needs" through providing opportunities—namely, segregated living and political spaces—where Black people's talent and power may be fostered and exercised.[68] It is exactly this process of radical racial isolation, and therefore solidarity, that made possible the conditions from which Amandla would erupt.

Amandla's formation, location, and relationship to the ANC followed a trajectory similar to that of the MK. The young musicians, actors, and dancers organized through Amandla were pulled from the ranks of the ANC military wing and trained in the frontline states, including Angola and Zambia, and used that distance to strategize structural and sustained responses to the apartheid regime. Although their targets were no longer physical objects, Amandla nevertheless enacted a cultural sabotage that was invested in attacking infrastructure. Their project was to dislocate and evaporate the savvy political maneuvering of the apartheid spin machine through performances that exposed truth to power and incited international attention and support for the antiapartheid struggle. Their training program demonstrates some of the seriousness with which Amandla was conceived. Their path as a group began in 1977 at the World Black Festival of Arts and Culture in Lagos, Nigeria. It was there that ANC members recognized the great potential of a touring cultural group in the struggle against apartheid. As Makeba's performances and other efforts demonstrate, culture was part and parcel of the ANC program for some time. A performance group named Mayibuye—named after the popular South African slogan (and, later, song), "Mayibuye iAfrika" (Let Africa Return)—developed in 1975 in London under the guidance of Barry Feinberg and Ronnie Kasrils and focused initially on poetry, with music added later. This group was successful in bringing attention to the struggle against apartheid and raising funds through limited, regional touring but was relatively short-lived due to membership turnover and the absence of long-term programming.

The ways in which Amandla made and narrated history were mediated by the power dynamics within the group. Like every other performance constellation discussed in these pages, Amandla attempted to manage and contain internal division with varying levels of success. An internal ANC memo from 1985 discussed the troubles facing the group, including "low morale, growth of individualism, poor artistic performance, in-group fighting and lack of discipline."[69] Undoubtedly, the long-standing struggle against the apartheid regime on the one hand and poor equipment with which to perform/fight on the other, led to questions of morale and "discipline," yet gender parity was a factor within the ensemble as well and may have contributed to the "in-group fighting." Of the eighteen members listed in an undated roster, ten were female. The "specialised field" for all ten women was "actress, dancer, vocalist," with the exception of two women whose descriptions read "actress, dancer, soloist." In comparison, the male members of the troupe were described as musicians with titles such as "violinist, pianist" and "trumpeter" in addition to receiving "specialised field[s]" including "vocalist, actor, poet" and "actor, dancer, poetry-reciter." Only one female member was described as an instrumentalist, holding the title of "pianist." Two men also held positions as "sound technician[s]" for the production.[70] This category of cultural labor was unavailable to the women, whose unilateral position as "actress, dancer, vocalist" signaled the possibility that they functioned as an homogenous chorus, versus agentive and distinguishable actors. Photographs of the ensemble encourage a reading of their roles as diverse, yet the limited language used to describe their participation in the group hints at the dissention that may have existed within the Amandla ranks.

Amandla was organized as a permanent fixture by the ANC in 1978, a formative year named by the UN General Assembly as "International Anti-Apartheid Year." The 1978 ANC Program of Action highlighted the "organisation of . . . solidarity fronts so as to widen the political base of the ANC internationally" as a strategic goal for the organization.[71]

Amandla fit this bill. Primary creative control was left in the hands of Jonas Gwangwa, a musician and activist, who became artistic director of the ensemble soon after its founding. As director he composed music and developed the show that Amandla performed around the world. The radical positionality of the group, both in relation to the regime in South Africa and within world politics, was demonstrated notably in the location of their first major performance. In 1978, Amandla debuted in Cuba at the Eleventh Festival of Youth and Students. The title of this showcase suggests its profound engagement with the particular value and talents of young people and included groups and organizations from around the world. The presence of Amandla on this occasion surely elicited the ire of the South African government. For many struggling under the yoke of oppression, Cuba symbolized the resolve and radical potential of a people's movement due to its admired 1959 revolution and continued resistance to domination by Western powers, most notably the United States. Yet for Pretoria its most immediate danger lay not in its communism but in its material support for armed revolutions in continental Africa. By 1976 Cuban military forces were planted in the frontline state of Angola, where they participated in the civil war between the established Marxist-Leninist government under Movimento Popular de Libertação (People's Movement for the Liberation of Angola) and the once-allied U.S.- and South Africa–backed União Nacional de la Independência Total de Angola (National Union for the Total Independence of Angola). Cuba was also allied with South West Africa People's Organization (SWAPO), who sought to liberate South West Africa (current day Namibia) from a colonizing South Africa. "Such operations," according to Leach, "plunged the South African forces into the cauldron of Angolan politics, setting the military against not only SWAPO but also the Cubans, the East Germans and the Soviets, and thrusting Pretoria into superpower politics."[72] This "thrust" manifest itself within a revitalized ANC as well; after the performance in Cuba "formal cultural activities under the banner of Amandla were enthusiastically developed in MK training camps in Angola."[73] This project represents the unique position of Amandla within the attempts by the ANC to communicate their solidarity with the frontline nation whose support meant solidified links to the arms-dealing Soviet Union and other socialist nations.

Amandla did not shy away from performances in countries without established links to the ANC, but they were discerning in their choices. The group never performed, for example, in Chile due to the dictatorship of Augusto Pinochet or Israel because they supplied arms to the apartheid military. After successful performances in Nigeria, Cuba, and Angola, Amandla developed a full-scale tour under Gwangwa's leadership that took them to Britain, Japan, Brazil, and elsewhere. They performed on nearly every continent for crowds with varying levels of engagement with their national struggle. Some audience members attended as card-carrying ANC members in exile, while others arrived with limited knowledge of the conditions of or responses to apartheid. Whatever their persuasion, audiences overwhelmingly praised Amandla.[74] Shows around the world sold out well past the decade anniversary of the group; ads read, "Tickets are selling like Paul Simon records, so get in quick!"[75] Paul Simon was a hugely popular musician during the time of this 1988 ad, yet his popularity did not insulate him from criticism for his 1986 *Graceland* album, which was recorded in South Africa despite the UNESCO (United Nations Educational, Scientific and Cultural Organization) cultural boycott of the nation. The ironic ad, used to encourage attendance for the Amandla performances, exposed an apartheid reality: white musicians and those Black South African artists who stayed on the right side of the regime continued to benefit from the riches of indigenous musical innovation in South Africa, while those who defied it struggled in the wilderness as stateless peoples. Although a harrowing project—often undertaken in countries with limited sympathies—Amandla's acts of culture provided evidence of escape as they organized a global audience and found protective cover in collective outrage.

Amandla demonstrated the ANC belief that "culture, more especially democratic culture in struggle, narrates the truth of a particular society."[76] The program developed by the group showcased the histories, arts, and talents that the apartheid regime actively obscured and submerged. Indeed, artist Bachana Mokwena argued,

This type of music is never played in South Africa. There are no schools of music or art in South Africa, not a single one, so people learn by ear. There are no facilities in the townships, where people could go to hear this music. It is considered respectable only among the oppressed, because it is their music. As for the white establishment, they couldn't care less for this music, because we are the downtrodden in their eyes. Barbaric. Our music, costumes, traditions and even our language are being crushed. They are killing our culture so we can never develop a spirit of oneness.[77]

Through their performances Amandla resolved the tension that existed within the ANC between the goal of international attention and solidarity on the one hand, and the work of nation building within South Africa on the other. The attention that they garnered internationally highlighted the plight of the oppressed racial majority and mobilized it through campaigns and donations, while their performances preserved and privileged elements of indigenous culture, a task, as Mokwena outlined, of tremendous significance for South Africa and its diaspora. Yet Amandla's efforts were not simply archival; they employed cultural excavation and exposure in service of contemporary sociopolitical circumstances and moved toward the disclosure of "truth" as a method of evidence against the apartheid regime. Gwangwa, in fact, described Amandla as "a documentary show," thereby highlighting their performative as non-fiction and a record of and response to ongoing, yet historically entrenched, events.[78]

Narrated as "the most successful attempt to create a truly representative culture," Amandla mobilized the dynamism of South African cultures by creating hybrid performances of newly composed and traditional musical texts.[79] Gumboot, a Zulu expressive form made famous by South African laborers, work, and resistance songs punctuated the various scenes in the show, which ran nearly three hours. Part 1 documented South Africa through the boom of worker and ANC activism in the 1930s and 1940s. Artistic highlights for this section included the "Flute Song," which was played on traditional penny whistles made of wood and copper, and the final gumboot dance. Part 2 began with a drum prelude "marking a turning point in the history of our national liberation—the introduction of armed struggle against the apartheid regime."[80] Drums are not indigenous to South African musical culture; they were introduced with European military and dance music during the seventeenth and eighteenth centuries.[81] In this way, the drum prelude of part 2 highlights both a sonic and sociopolitical departure as it introduces a new(er) vision of and method for Black existence in South Africa through sound. This type of intervention continued in "Piet Botha," named after the prime minister (1978–84) and later the first executive president of South Africa (1984–89). "Piet Botha" was "a song of warning to the South African President" for it prophesized that "the forces of liberation will crush his regime."[82] This type of militaristic posturing through the Amandla performances was a reflection of the performers' training in the MK as well as the aggressive art-politic articulated by Mayibuye years earlier. Amandla members were clear that their music was part and parcel of their decolonization efforts: "Our song calls on our people to rise up and fight for our country. We will destroy [Rhodesian prime minister Ian] Smith and [South African prime minister B. J.] Vorster with grenades and bazookas."[83] The relationship between cultural production and violence is here articulated as progressive: the songs mobilize the masses to use the "grenades and bazookas" that will eventually destroy the regime. Performance, as practiced by Mayibuye, Amandla, and others under apartheid, was a methodology that stressed the symbiotic nature of culture and violence; for results to be had, they recognized that the assault on apartheid needed to be cultural and physical, creative and material. Amandla serves as a microcosm for this symbiosis through its birth from the MK, the members' training alongside MK comrades, and their militaristic performances of Black South African culture from venues around the world.

The stage was set for the warnings of part 2 by "Nkosi Sikelel' iAfrika," which was used in the production to historically ground the sound for scene 2: "Formation of the African National Congress." By the time of Amandla's formation, "Nkosi," as the official song of the ANC, was the anthem of a government in exile. As the opening text for Amandla performances, "Nkosi" evidenced the historical seeds of organized, nontribal majority resistance in South Africa as well as the contemporary sounds of a stateless nationalism. In the absence of land, the ANC and other antiapartheid organizations organized for themselves an unrecognized citizenship that was sounded with an anthem. The special placement of "Nkosi Sikelel' iAfrika" within the program, therefore, compresses the political time-space continuum through a Janus-faced anthem that looks both backward and forward. Reviewers of the show

noticed the song's prominence within the performance and its importance to the national struggle. Margie Thomson wrote, "From the haunting opening rendition of *Nkosi Sikelel'I Africa* [*sic*]—the ANC's anthem
and the anthem of several African states—to the stomping, exuberant
melody of traditional dances with which the show ends, Amandla works
hard to tell us that black South African culture is alive and kicking."[84]
Both "Nkosi Sikelel' iAfrika" and Amandla were banned in South Africa
prior to 1990; the challenge to the apartheid government through Amandla's performance of "Nkosi" was therefore doubly impactful through the
sound and content of the show as well as the act of performance by these
men and women who disrupted, disarmed, and deconstructed their foe.

Through its performance by the MK and Amandla, "Nkosi Sikelel'
iAfrika" mediated the dual impulses of the ANC to broaden the reach
of their struggle to sympathetic parties and nations and to create an
inventive and incendiary culture in South Africa. The ANC necessarily was preoccupied with the practical and tactical education of its
groups in exile; as they traveled the world, these cultural producers
and military forces needed to be trained in the on-the-ground events
occurring within the nation of their birth. The DIP lamented this disconnect and argued that the propaganda wings of the ANC were "out
of touch with the internal situation they have the task to mobilise."[85]
The playing of "Nkosi Sikelel' iAfrika" on Radio Freedom and its shared
performance in South Africa and on Amandla stages in sites around
the world were the ties that bound the movement together in struggle. While site-specific instruction was crucial to ANC cohesion and
strategy as a nation in exile, the anthem was the mobilizing element
that transcended difference and instead became that which they shared.
That function made it invaluable. The anthem announced a nation in
the making, creatively reshaping itself and its future in dynamic performances that exposed their ethical higher ground. According to ANC
arts administrator Thele Moema, "People sometimes ask us how we
manage to laugh and dance in the midst of apartheid. And we say, yes,
the oppressor might think we are enjoying our oppression, but actually
we are gathering strength to confront him through dance, music and
theatre."[86] It was through cultural and emotional subversion and performance that Amandla struggled through the danger and pervasive fear
that surrounded them. This practice is not unlike those of other Black

performers, nor is Moema's acknowledgment of this practice unprecedented; he shares in it with W. E. B. Du Bois, who spoke of the spirituals as the language through which the slave "spoke to the world." "Such a message," according to Du Bois, "is naturally veiled and half articulate," insomuch as they are unwelcome and unpermitted utterances by those whose very existence was unordained.[87] The anthem provided structure and validation to a struggling majority and citizenship to the stateless of Amandla and other ANC ambassadors who performed in exile.

In the years following Amandla's launch, the antiapartheid program accelerated toward its final stage. The international attention and pressure organized by the ANC through Amandla and other campaigns weighed on the political and economic capabilities of the South African government under apartheid. The OAU, a continental unification and strategy group, had since the early 1970s called on participating African nations to end communications with the apartheid government, effectively isolating the political maneuvers of the regime within Africa.[88] Nonengagement was also requested of U.S. entertainers who were courted by the Pretoria government with large paychecks for their performances. Black artists in particular were targeted by South Africa because their performances were capable of bringing large crowds and the appearance of racial acceptance to the blighted land. The cultural realm again became contested terrain in the global struggle against apartheid and a focus for international protests of the regime. Antiapartheid leaders in the United States, some of whom gathered to form the Coalition to End Cultural Collaboration with South Africa, "realized that the failure to fully exploit the cultural arm had restricted access to potentially significant constituencies" and quickly set about a program in the 1980s to use Black artists to comment on the conditions of Black South Africans.[89] Like the fund-raising concerts of the U.S. Civil Rights Movement, antiapartheid concerts sprung up globally, lighting a fire in South Africa; those musicians who chose the paycheck over the movement, including Ray Charles and Aretha Franklin, faced their own boycott.[90]

The ANC request that no one visit or otherwise engage in economic exchange with South Africa was necessarily paired with their alternative ways of accessing the nation's communities and cultures. The answer was Amandla, which continued to tour until the ANC was unbanned.

The tours ensured that the struggle would always be accessible to a world that increasingly organized to protest South Africa's political system, practices, and products. By the late 1980s, sanctions and various other trade restrictions were imposed on South Africa by the United States (a longtime hold out on such action), the United Kingdom, and twenty-three other nations. The rise of divestment campaigns, particularly on college campuses in the United States, the end of the Cold War, and the 1989 turnover in the apartheid government made way for changes to the country's governance.[91] In 1990, newly appointed state president F. W. de Klerk announced the unbanning of the ANC, saying, "The prohibition of the African National Congress, the Pan Africanist Congress [PAC], and South African Communist Party and a number of subsidiary organisations is being rescinded. People serving prison sentences merely because they were members of one of these organisations will be identified and released."[92] By the end of 1991, South Africa, in consultation and negotiation with the UN, finalized an agreement that granted amnesty to an estimated forty thousand political exiles.[93] Within ten days of de Klerk's announcement, Nelson Mandela was released from prison after twenty-seven years behind bars. He immediately took up the mantle of the legal ANC and worked to develop and launch the first fully democratic elections witnessed by that country. In 1994, he was elected with the ANC nomination as the next state president of South Africa. As President de Klerk left his post, he concluded his speech in Xhosa, saying, "Nkosi sikelel' iAfrika."[94] The anthem was then played as Mandela assumed his position as head of state.[95] This was the transition that ushered Mandela into a presidential era premised on reconciliation; the outgoing apartheid-engineering National Party and the underground and exiled ANC collided on the dais through the anthem that had for nearly a century organized and marshaled Black South African populations against the violences of radical segregation. The anthem was, according to one author, "the beginning and the end of everything,"[96] and on that spring day in 1994 it heralded the beginnings of a new South African nation marked by universal suffrage and internationally renowned leadership. Makeba and Amandla carried and kept this future through their performance of the anthem that took Black South African voices where they needed to be in spite of exile and helped them to say what needed to be said in spite of censorship.

Conclusion

The Last Anthem: Resonance, Legacy, and
Loss at the Close of the Century

In 1989 Spike Lee released *Do the Right Thing*, a film that captures the lead-up to and effects of urban conflict in segregated Brooklyn. Infused within this visual catalogue was a soundtrack that punctuated the scenes of the film and carried its political power onto the radio and into the ears of millions across the country. Far and away, the most enduring single was track 1: Public Enemy's "Fight the Power." Beginning with an original speech by Chicago political activist Thomas Todd, the song launches into nearly five minutes of insistent demands (to "fight the power"), while taking advantage of numerous musical samples and resistance traditions. This song represents a particular moment in hip-hop, urban communities, and U.S. state formation. The applicability of the song to Brooklyn and numerous other locations, conditions, and political mobilizations marks "Fight the Power" as an anthem, perhaps the last Black anthem of the twentieth century. The song's growth from and response to collective Black struggle went beyond reporting to build discourse and debate; it was not simply narrative but was instructive, providing a pulsing cadence for Lee's fictive Brooklyn *and* the realities of Black neighborhoods in combustible Los Angeles. As a sound saturated by visuals (and vice versa), the anthem marks and is marked by the scenes in which it is deployed. According to Nicole Fleetwood, it is through this conjunction that "the visualization of black bodies was heard."[1] In the process, this song bridged East Coast and West, fiction and reality, and past and future through its critical dissection of the present.

"Fight the Power" spins through the methodologies and sounds of the past in order to create an alternative vision in the present. It lingers in dense and at times competing spaces of music, technology, politics, and mobilization, making use of them in combination in order to build a three dimensional movement of sound. As Mark Katz argues, "A look at Public Enemy's use of looping and performative quotation in 'Fight the Power' illuminates the mutual influences between musician and machine."[2] These sounds are not, however, trapped or contained by the machines that allow them to speak. The technological innovation wrought by deindustrialization makes hip-hop a type of wizardry all its own, yet the machine of Katz's description can be pushed further to represent a broad contraption inclusive of political systems. The music becomes the method of mobilization and models within it the synergies that the anthem accomplishes on the street. The captured voices in the introductory speech clip and the opening few bars of overlaced grunts, sighs, and snippets represent a cacophony of individual neighborhood subjects who collectively animate the project under way. Public Enemy makes ready use of iconography and period language, from the Universal Negro Improvement Association (UNIA) colors of red, black, and green to the Black Panther rebel yell "power to the people," thereby announcing an engagement with previous struggles even as they mount their own. The sampling further advances these connections; the cue to the exclamation "fight the power" at the end of each verse is a snippet of a Black man's voice, saying, "Lemme hear you say." This apparitional man is the second hype man in the production and backs up the always timely, clock-wearing Flavor Flav. His voice from the past is a push for Chuck D. and the rest of Public Enemy, who takes the cue and delivers it to their listeners in the contemporary moment.

The launch moment for both the film and the anthem is one of mainstream consumption of hip-hop, which became a vehicle for locally situated resistances in the late 1970s.[3] By the time of "Fight the Power," groups like Public Enemy were able to market themselves as a different brand of musician—while building on the reputation of hip-hop as a music "of the streets," they also catered to increasingly diverse audiences, many of whom would be unrecognizable as hip-hop fans ten years earlier. The music's wide reception in this moment was dually fed by both its format and usage. Multimedia exposure in films and commercials bolstered hip-hop and rap's exposure, while also adding to its everyday political applicability and adoption. The youth cultures that developed under hip-hop used the sounds of these artists as a core element of their political speech and mobilizations, in the process rapidly decentering the social justice organizations that defined the movements of their parents' generations. Beginning in the late 1960s, there was, according to political scientist Robert C. Smith, a "bewildering series of conventions, meetings, leadership summits, assemblies, congresses, institutes and so forth [that] replaced rallies, marches, and demonstrations and lawsuits as the principal routine activity of the black leadership establishment." These less conspicuous evidences of Black mobilization occurred without icons, like those that Smith laments in his book's title, *We Have No Leaders*.[4] In the absence of elected national representation or movement icons, Black men and women employed popular culture as their platform and method of democratic engagement. The rapid decline of the Black counterpublics described by political scientist Michael Dawson in the 1970s due to dramatic shifts in the nation's political economy led to the concentration of Black political speech within cultural production, an intensely situated and collective effort.[5] Following in that tradition, the visuals stemming from *Do the Right Thing* as well as the music video for "Fight the Power" mark two narratives of anthemic community mobilization in the post–Civil Rights moment that strategically move afield of their predecessors while negotiating ties to a powerful past. Through the anthem, *Do the Right Thing* models the still impactful ends to be gained from the decentralized organization that defines the political cultures of the post–Civil Rights period.

"Fight the Power" regularly "sample[s] a look back" by referencing historiographies of struggle among the African descended. Black movement slogans of the past, including "I'm black and I'm proud," signal a previous era that is collapsed in time and space through the reinvention of sonic materials and imagery. Like Smiley in *Do the Right Thing*, who hawks his Black nostalgia wares around the neighborhood, the video for "Fight the Power" similarly repeats the iconography of the most canonized period of Black politics by employing similar strategies of organization. Taking a cue from the Mississippi Freedom Democratic Party before them, the delegations that aligned to march on the Bedford-Stuyvesant neighborhood of Brooklyn made an explicit connection between political power and representation. Their protest, which was a mass mobilization and a performance, a political rally and a concert, emphasized the demand of Black communities that they be able to speak aloud their own truths. This is a scene of solidarity in the face of an unyielding and unrelenting majority public whose political systems—those that had officially incorporated Black demands twenty-five years earlier—eroded the social safety net and erected prisons to catch those who fell through its gaps. The participants within the "Fight the Power" video manifested the "crisis of victory" declared in the wake of 1960s civil rights legislation by labor leader A. Philip Randolph. Their moment called for new languages and alternative techniques of mobilization, both of which are present in the song that organized their coalition.

"Fight the Power" is an anthem, a term that I have outlined throughout this book as deliberate and situated. It was not representative of or used by an official organization, but was, like "Ol' Man River," adopted on varying scales by urban communities whose "spontaneous" uprisings were often anything but. The post–Civil Rights moment provides the framing for these politics that move through multiple media technologies and performances of collectivity and individuality, which are successful in part due to their significations on the past. It is the "post" in the title that marks its departure from the mobilizations that defined and contained the Black protest cultures of the late 1950s and 1960s. It also must be recognized, however, that they are contiguous—the "post" is literally attached to the movement(s) from which it is argued to have departed. Like the sound franchise genealogy represented throughout *Anthem*, there is a layered effect here, as the anthem in form and function builds on those movements and sounds that preceded it. "Fight the Power" exhibits a number of the compositional and performance aesthetics of Black music. Hip-hop is connected to the spirituals developed under slavery through rhythmic structures as well as the shared impulse to coordinate sound around stolen time, space, and resources. Just as enslaved Africans developed their music on time "liberated" from the

clock set by an overseer, coordinated communities despite the isola-
tionist practices of the plantation, and creatively redesigned materials
as instrumentation, the engineers of hip-hop similarly absconded with
time (from school and work), reappropriated urban public space, and
repurposed machinery. These traditions are carried over into "Fight the
Power," which announces its relationship to the Black anthems of the
past through its proximity to the long-held standard: James Weldon
and J. Rosamond Johnson's "Lift Ev'ry Voice and Sing," the organizational anthem of the National Association for the Advancement of Colored People (NAACP).

The two anthems are uneasily intertwined within the aural and visual
representations of Lee's *Do the Right Thing*, which pays homage to
urban youth culture, in particular rap music. The opening scenes of the
film emphasize the generational tensions within the Black community
through music, and "Lift Ev'ry Voice and Sing" is used as a pivot point
for two distinct Black political cultures. Film scholar Victoria Johnson
describes the procession: "Before the opening title sequence of *Do*, a
solo tenor saxophone plays a mournful variation upon 'Lift Every Voice
and Sing' over the symbol of Universal Pictures [the film's distributor].
The screen then goes black for a split second before a splash of hot red
colors reveals a woman dancing vigorously, in several different street
settings, to Public Enemy's 'Fight the Power.'"[6] The distinct difference in
tone and feel between these two musical interludes is magnified by their
proximity to each other in the sound scheme of the film. "Lift Ev'ry
Voice and Sing" is visually represented by a void—a dark screen with a
corporate logo—while "Fight the Power" is demonstrated in the literal
movement of the young dancer-actress Rosie Perez. Aurally, the somber
solo sax of "Lift" had no chance of besting the bass beats of "Fight." The
initial verbs that ground the titles of each song demonstrate the change
in context as a politics of respectability gives way to the demands of a
postindustrial urban insurgency.

These songs are represented in the film as the two sides of a bridge-
less gap in the political consciousness and mobilizations of the Black
United States. "Lift Ev'ry Voice and Sing" was carried by teachers,
preachers, and activists throughout the U.S. South for decades before its
adoption and formal usage by the NAACP. Its relationship to political
struggle is the link that connects it to this newest articulation of Black

mobilization, "Fight the Power," which disrupts the sound and the histories that "Lift" represents when it introduces Perez's free-form dancing. This image, which differently positions women within the contemporary youth cultures of rebellion, is a fitting representation of the sound motivating her movement; "Fight the Power" was the anthem for a generation whose later rebellion in 1992 Los Angeles appeared to most witnesses as anarchy. Congresswoman Maxine Waters argued instead that the "riot" exposed "the voice of the unheard."[7] When those voices were stilled in the streets, "Fight the Power" tapped and mobilized the still present anger in part through its continued (re)play through *Do the Right Thing.* The film was the representational mobilization of the rebellions that regularly occurred in communities like Bedford-Stuyvesant (Bed-Stuy); communities that, after years of political warfare, changed the scale of their interventions by launching filmic scenes of Black and brown streets into mainstream political debates.

It is not surprising that this anthem speaks to the rapid decline of urban communities on a national scale; the generation that the anthem marks felt the pressure of the crack cocaine epidemic and its response—the prison-industrial complex—which began in earnest one decade earlier but was by the end of the Ronald Reagan administration a multiparty issue that surveilled and caged Black men and women by the thousands. The Rosie Perez transition in the film is a visual disruption of the long-passed civil rights victories that the smooth jazz of "Lift Ev'ry Voice and Sing" was meant to represent, reminding us of the fight still left in this group one generation removed from the protests and violence of the 1960s. This difference rings in our ears and is emblazoned on our retinas as we are engulfed in the contrast of bright colors and silhouette. A new age through music is announced through this scene that disrupts (art) genre and (political) form. The political effects of "Lift Ev'ry Voice and Sing" were sonically mobilized by the harmonies of four-part choral singing, while the breaks, loops, and antiphonies of the spoken narrative within "Fight the Power" keep the receiver moving with head-nodding beats in anticipation of the next explosive comment from lyricist Chuck D. (neé Carlton Ridenhour). In this post–Civil Rights moment of crisis, "Fight the Power" does what "Lift Ev'ry Voice and Sing" cannot: it reviles an uplift mission in service of congealing and rallying an already powerful public of the disinherited.

The juxtaposition of the two songs within *Do the Right Thing* helps to ground "Fight the Power" as an anthemic text that takes the torch from a previous generation and announces the urban city as the frontier of contestation. As an anthem, "Fight the Power" is less the sound of a singular city than the sonic uprising of a multiply situated urban diaspora of the dispossessed. As Janice C. Simpson argued in *Time*, "The song not only whipped the movie to a fiery pitch but sold nearly 500,000 singles and became an anthem for millions of youths, many of them black and living in inner-city ghettoes."[8] The screams, breaks, and dreams of a pan-urban public are shared within this text that argues for freedom of speech and an end to representational violence—an argument also embedded within the film. While the visual scenes of the film are capable of countering false depictions through alternative representations, the diaspora of disenfranchisement that it highlights can best be organized by music, a form of political speech that is easily transferable and portable, as *Do the Right Thing* also portrays. Radio Raheem is the initial carrier for the anthem within the film. His master-blaster boom box is a big, black menace in his neighborhood that demands response. Carried atop the shoulder of the already formidable actor Bill Nunn, the boom box is the technology of rebellion that is literally attached to the Black male body, triply marking it as dangerous. Slowly the song takes on a life of its own; it detaches from Raheem's body singular and infiltrates the neighborhood as the sonic loop and context for Black bodies plural. This is its transition from song to anthem as it grows from its use by Raheem to its everywhereness as manifesto for a community under siege.

The song is used within the film to represent numerous moments of conflict, hysteria, and/or Black mobilization, including the escalation of the boycott at Sal's Pizzeria. The most explosive scene is the brutal beating and arrest of Radio Raheem in the wake of the confrontation at Sal's, a moment punctuated by the anthem. The smashing of Radio Raheem's boom box—from which streams a loop of "Fight the Power"— is the silencing of his voice and the spark for the violence that spills over from the pizzeria into the street. As the neighborhood watches, the police exercise unchecked violence on Raheem's body in order to secure white life and property. The film and the music video for the anthem document the police state and its use of surveillance and violence as methods of control. The numbers of police who turn out in response to the Brooklyn scuffle are also revealed in the streets of the "Fight the Power" video; by its end, the police have arrived and mingle among the marching mass. As Chuck D. attempts to man the bullhorn, a number of police officers cross his path. While the camera frame tightens, he casts the viewers at home a knowing look. This is a moment of recognition and reporting. He is acknowledging that the viewers have just witnessed the mobilization of a state that he has spent the last four minutes raging against. Like a reporter on the frontlines, Chuck D. is covering the events that will directly impact the viewing audience; as he famously argued, "Rap is CNN for black people," and his reporting from the stage of the conditions in the streets creates a dynamic "no spin" zone.[9] These are not canned engagements; they exist in real-time and are experienced as such, even when the reporting is on wax.

This reporting, in combination with Lee's film, is the documentary work that connects the anthem to places beyond its original location. In that way, the relationship between the Brooklyn and Los Angeles scenes is both visually and sonically materialized. Architecturally, the landscapes are distinct, but the film's introduction of the anthem through Perez invites a conversation between the two cities through the (Afro-) Hispanophone communities of each, namely the large Puerto Rican and Dominican populations in New York and the Mexican and Central American populations of L.A. The Latinos in the Bed-Stuy neighborhood of *Do the Right Thing* were present and fighting in the altercation with the police at Sal's. This scene recognizes Latinos, giving them the space that went largely unmarked in the rebellion three years later. The Korean shop owners in the film, who saved their store from vandalism by announcing their solidarity with the Black men and women at their doorstep, were also centrally configured within 1992 L.A. Numerous reports after the rebellion emphasized the divisions between the communities over economic standing, culture, and political beliefs; however, Lee exposed the multiplicity within urban neighborhoods and signaled the commonalities, in the process giving voice to the little-discussed interracial negotiations and efforts at community building that also occurred in L.A., both formally and informally. While differently configured within each city, the shared diversity of the cityscape is here acknowledged prior to the real-life events that would shake the West

Coast and the nation. Lee's film predicts the L.A. scenarios by staging them visually and announcing them sonically through "Fight the Power."

The street-level mobilization accomplished by "Fight the Power" is perfectly marked within its music video, also directed by Lee. The crowd who marched through Bed-Stuy moved as a delegation, holding signs to represent their crews in Miami, St. Louis, New Orleans, Philadelphia, Baltimore, Montgomery, and Selma. This was their coming out party, their national convention, and Public Enemy provided the anthem for their campaign, which expressed outrage at the violences of their present and approximated a vote of "no confidence" in outgoing President Reagan and his incoming proxy, George H. W. Bush. This practice resonated beyond the East Coast, taking root in Los Angeles in late April and early May 1992. "Fight the Power" joined in the lexicon of anthemic sound bites like "We Shall Overcome," becoming an oft-repeated way to signal the Black response to the acquittal of the four white LAPD officers who in 1991 brutally beat Black motorist Rodney King within a few inches of his life. The anthem played in the streets of the Palms neighborhood of west L.A. during the events, becoming a critical voice and strategy within the Black rebellion.[10] "Fight the Power" was the song that marked this last decade of the Black century—the violence of its turning and the innovation of its future. Through their Brooklyn performances, the members of Public Enemy were organizers whose sonic manifesto moved bodies and reconstituted the multiple centers of Black diasporic existence.

* * *

"Lift Ev'ry Voice and Sing" is not the only song represented in *Anthem* to have a presence within post–Civil Rights cultures. Whether it be through praise, critique, adoption, sound bite, or remix, all of the anthems continue to influence some dimension of contemporary Black political cultures. These anthems and their movements are resonant and compose a rich, multitextual legacy. Within African American and African diaspora histories and mobilizations, legacy is one of the stakes—we do today so that others can do tomorrow—and becomes an organizing framework, a dynamic structure of engagement that is not past but is part of a forward trajectory. These connections, both real and imagined, have offered insight into the community's formation over time and become the scaffolding for the future projects of their descendants. Music in the Black community offers testimony to formations of race and resistance through its ability to tell; it articulates and produces manifestos in order to expose the experiences of the African descended and their strategies for alternative ways of seeing and living in the world around them. The struggles that generated these songs produce a dynamic continuum out of which agents can create identity anew. As musicologist Tia DeNora argues,

> The telling [about the past] is a part of the work of producing one's self as a coherent being over time, part of producing a retrospection that is in turn a resource for projection into the future, a cueing in to how to proceed. In this sense, the past, musically conjured, is a resource for the reflexive movement from present to future, the moment-to-moment production of agency in real time. It serves also as a means of putting actors in touch with capacities, reminding them of their accomplished identities, which in turn fuels the ongoing projection of identity from past into future. Musically fostered memories thus produce past trajectories that contain momentum.[11]

Black music models this impulse while making plain the particular violences of difference. The politics of performance and performance of politics within Black musical traditions displays more than what we hear: it tells us how people live and love, work and play, survive and die over time. Black anthems are the evidence of Black music's vision, its relationship to previous sounds and struggles, and the organizing traditions that were built on, and then surpassed, previous political projects. An investigation of the anthemic event, therefore, demonstrates the complicated histories, exchanges, and compromises that hold the African diaspora in and through tension.

The previous chapters have exhibited the music of Black social movements as a principal and principled mode of engagement that bridges political thought and action in performance. The anthems that develop from these movements are often the artifacts that contemporary movement activists recover in order to build their own vision of change.[12] In this away, anthems are marked by their fantastic launch as well as by less ostentatious acts of resurrection and revival. The designation of anthem necessarily demands the continuance of the song in the popular, if not institutional-ized, memory of Black movements. It is important to this project then to briefly articulate the ways in which these songs resonate and how they are used beyond their original historical moment and circumstance to inform later periods of consciousness, mobilization, or nostalgia.

As the world changed, so too did the priorities and perspectives of its actors. Some of the anthems discussed here are now more diffuse and rare, even obscure, perhaps raising questions about their role as anthems. The demise of the organizations and/or movements that orig-inally supported and employed the anthem may have ended their polit-ical performance, yet the conditions that the organizations and songs spoke to largely remain intact. In investigating the resonance of these anthems I am concerned with the quality of their usage, not the quan-tity of their repetition; it is more important to take stock of how and where they reappear. Some of the anthems have taken new turns musi-cally or socially as they have been covered, remixed, or sampled by art-ists and activists. Whatever form they take, the nature of their contin-ued (non)usage is an important piece of their history. The six anthems within *Anthem* represent a rich variety of perspectives, positions, and traditions in African diasporic history and culture, and through each of them a connection or response between communities is witnessed in the post–Civil Rights generation. The ways in which the music contin-ues or fails to illicit comment and/or action in the Black United States and beyond is a commentary on the continuing legacies of Black politi-cal action and self-determination at the closing of the twentieth century and opening of the twenty-first.

The life cycles of the anthems presented in the previous pages are uneven. The UNIA, for example, is no longer a political contender in the Black public sphere, let alone broader progressive coalition politics in the twenty-first century. Marcus Garvey's deportation from the United States in 1927 led to the rapid decline of the UNIA, which in turn minimized the circulation and use of its anthem "Ethiopia (Thou Land of Our Fathers)." The obscurity of its performance has been duplicated within the litera-ture. Most scholars of Garvey and the UNIA have ignored it altogether, while those who do mention it offer only surface acknowledgment or dis-cuss it as a relic of the past. In his 1962 article on the varieties of Pan-Afri-canism and their relationship to expansion in Africa, historian George

Shepperson wrote that while "'Nkosi sikelel' i Afrika' [*sic*] is still a living force in many parts of Africa . . . the UNIA song ["Ethiopia"] is almost completely forgotten."[13] The pairing of these two texts signals the original reach of Garvey's UNIA throughout diaspora and the void that developed in its absence. While the UNIA ceased to function on a global scale by midcentury, "Ethiopia" made a direct connection with a movement that grew from Garvey's home country of Jamaica and has since taken root in communities around the world. Rastafarianism, so named for its icon Ras Tafari (better known as Haile Selassie), developed on the island in the 1930s as a response to a British colonialism characterized by "economic deprivation, political disfranchisement, and cultural alienation." While this distress fomented the organization of the Rastafarians, so too did the hope drawn from the crowning of Selassie as emperor of Ethiopia in 1930.[14] This combination of resistance to the white West and celebration of African achievement mirrored the program of the UNIA and serves today to support a global community of Rastafari.

While the Rastafari share in certain of Garvey's messianic visions and freedom dreams for the African world, the difference in their approaches to the liberation of Africa and its descendants is evident within the performance of the anthem. Although I have not found a recording of the original UNIA anthem to date, the importance of political aesthetics within reggae is clearly demonstrated by the continued performance and recording of "Ethiopia" by Jamaican artists. In Rastafarian ceremonies, the song is usually sung at the end of the event, but within a reggae performance, it can be incorporated into a song set. Popular reggae musician and Rasta ambassador Ras Michael recorded "Ethiopian Anthem" with his band The Sons of Negus. Their contemporary recording reveals alternative interpretations of Garveyism that better match their musical genre and geopolitical positioning. Sonically, the orchestration and rhythmic structure are altered to match the riddims of reggae. The song is accompanied by electric organ, which, after an introductory procession of harmonic chords, sets the backbeat by delivering a pulsating double-time beat beginning on the upbeat of 1. The prominent drumbeat is on the 2 and 4 in common time (4/4) versus the standard emphasis on the 1 and 3 in Western traditions. Rhythm guitar is used sporadically, while horns enter to fill in harmonic variation and introduce the singer's verse. Ras Michael's rendition of "Ethiopia" is a distinct departure from the version authored by Arnold Ford and Benjamin Burrell. The narrative style is consistent between the two songs, yet Ras Michael's message is significantly different and, in some ways, at odds with Garvey's agenda of modern Ethiopianism. Where the original UNIA sang, "as storm cloud at night suddenly gathers / our armies come rushing to thee," Ras Michael sings, "like bees to a hive swiftly gather / your children are gathered to thee." Ras Michael's articulation is decidedly less aggressive than the original; gone is the hallmark militarism of Garvey's UNIA, and in its place is a righteous tranquility of "truth and right," "love and light." The reggae version narrates the gathering of Jah's children in Ethiopia as an organic experience, in both the automatic outpouring of support to Jah/God and the relationship of Africa's children to the earth ("like bees to a hive"). The "red, black and green" of the Black nation's flag under the UNIA is replaced by the "red, gold, and green" of Jamaica's national flag. Jamaican nationalism in the 1930s was inspired by UNIA philosophies and grew "due in no small measure to the struggles of both the Rastafarians and the Garveyites."[15]

Garvey's legacy within Black liberation movements takes material form in Rastafarianism. Historian Leonard Barrett boldly asserts that "all Rastafarians revere Marcus Garvey as their inspirer; his picture is prominent in all homes and cult houses. His speeches are avidly read; songs and poems are written in his honor and, in the pantheon of the Rastafarians, Marcus Garvey is second only to Haile Selassie."[16] While his writings and imagery offer endorsement of his role within Rastafarian culture, the anthem of his organization on the lips of Rasta men and women is an important achievement because it connects the sociopolitical work of the early-twentieth-century UNIA with the continuing global impact of contemporary Rastafarianism. The performance of "Ethiopia" revives a powerful, global movement that was weakened by the prideful ambitions of a single man and destroyed by its surveillance and infiltration by U.S. and colonial administrations. The music refused silencing, however; its recital in Rastafarian services and its proliferation through the performances of popular reggae musicians make "Ethiopia (Thou Land of Our Fathers)" a hallmark of Black sonic materiality and a functional continuance of the once-powerful UNIA.

More than any other domestically produced song within *Anthem*, "Lift Ev'ry Voice and Sing" has retained the institutional title of anthem in the Black United States. The literary significance of James Weldon's poem and the song's southern performance roots and adoption by the NAACP ensure its contemporary placement within Black cultural rotations.[17] The anthem as musical text has received less attention than the poem in scholarship or public discourse, despite the claim by Julian Bond and Sondra Kathryn Wilson that "['Lift Ev'ry Voice and Sing'] is irrefutably one of the most stalwart and inspiring symbols in American civil rights history."[18] Unlike the poem, the music has retained a significant attachment to its location of origin. Initially composed for a choir of children, the song remains more identifiable within Black schools, particularly in the South. Political analyst and author Juan Williams recalled that his children learned the song in their all-Black elementary school in Washington, D.C. They sung it every morning along with Bob Marley's "Redemption Song," a provocative pairing that signals the diasporic impulse that is part and parcel of Black imaginaries. Blues scholar and author Albert Murray's attachment to the song also stemmed from its association with a school setting. He describes "Lift" as the "Brown American nation school bell anthem (the comb your hair brush your teeth shine your shoes crease your trousers tie your tie clean your nails rub a dub stand sit and look straight make folks proud anthem!)."[19] During the multiculturalism debates of the 1980s and early 1990s, education specialist Thomas J. Elward announced and discussed new methods for teaching *four* national anthems: "The Star-Spangled Banner," "America," "America the Beautiful," and "Lift Ev'ry Voice and Sing." Acknowledging the disjuncture between this last song and the previous three, Elward states, "Today's movement toward recognition of minority achievements and a multicultural outlook in schools increases the likelihood of using this song, especially in black urban schools."[20] Liberal platitudes aside, the inclusion of "Lift" within this cohort of texts materialized Johnson's intentions for the anthem on a national level. However, thirty years after Elward's article, the resonance of "Lift Ev'ry Voice and Sing" is limited as continuing generations of Black Americans lose touch with the song as anthem.

In spite of its firm grounding in Black Americana, the song appears less and less in the discourse on contemporary Black America, demonstrating an interruption in the potency and potential of the anthem. As I mentioned in the discussion of "Fight the Power," part of this break in the tradition has to do with a generational gap. The anthem continues to be used to inspire, but primarily by individuals who were adults or came to adulthood during the Civil Rights Movement—roughly, those born between 1930 and 1960.[21] Examples of these individuals' engagement with the song are ample.[22] The continued usage of "Colored" and "Negro" by organizations developed by the pre-hip-hop generations, such as the NAACP and National Council of Negro Women, contributes to the distance between their organizations and use of the anthem by post–Civil Rights generations.[23] Marking the generations by musical genre is an apt measure of political difference, as the sounds of these groups are intimately intertwined with their identities and agendas. As historian Leon Litwack notes, "Some forty years after the civil rights movement peaked, a new generation of Black Americans is less confident about its prospects, having experienced a serious erosion of the national commitment to civil rights. 'Lift Every Voice and Sing' would find little resonance (even recognition) among young blacks listening to Snoop Doggy Dogg, NWA (Niggaz With Attitude), Outkast, the Geto Boys, Urban Underground, Tupac Shakur, Lady of Rage, and ODB (Ol' Dirty Bastard)."[24] Indeed, the dominance of the prison and military industrial complexes in the lives of Black and brown youth and the global economic collapse begun in 2007 continue to mediate Black citizenship practices. Research conducted by sociologist K. Sue Jewell shows that one generation ago, only approximately two in three Black U.S. college-age students were familiar with "Lift Ev'ry Voice and Sing." As she notes, "With one-third of the students unable to recognize the song that symbolized unity and determination while serving as the basis for relentless motivation, it is reasonable to assume that [a] change has occurred" away from the civil rights agendas of midcentury.[25] Young people in this regard are finding it difficult to connect to their civil rights roots. The constellation of rap artists mentioned by Litwack offer a political range in music from a proclivity for political imagery and protest to political vapidity, yet they are all consumed at a rate that far outstrips the knowledge or performance of "Lift Ev'ry Voice and Sing."

For a song described by celebrated Black actor-activists Ruby Dee and Ossie Davis as a gauge of "the state of the race" in any given location, its absence in the practices and consciousness of contemporary

Black cultures speaks volumes about the way that the community imagines and articulates itself in the twenty-first century. While there are concerns associated with this disconnect—notably the histories obscured or lost by the anthem's nonperformance—attention must also be paid to the agency demonstrated through this silence. New anthems have developed in the absence of "Lift Ev'ry Voice and Sing."[26] The NAACP has not been displaced in the same way as its anthem, however. In addition to South Africa's "Nkosi Sikelel' iAfrika," "Lift Ev'ry Voice and Sing" is the only anthem in *Anthem* currently attached to a functional social justice organization.[27] The presence of the NAACP nationally mediates the absent knowledge of the song in performance, yet this silence surely reflects a change in its profile. For an organization once known by its anthem, the missing sounds of contest and victory mean something for the way that the organization fashions itself and its political work in the present.

The question of the present is important to the life cycles of all of these anthems, especially those offered to the world through solo singers, all of whom have since departed. In 2004, the American Film Institute (AFI) named "Ol' Man River" one of the "top movie songs of all time." Compiled and decided by a panel of industry judges based on the criteria of song (composition), cultural impact, and legacy, this list of one hundred songs was topped by the iconic "Somewhere Over the Rainbow," as sung by Judy Garland in the 1939 version of *The Wizard of Oz*.[28] The criteria employed by the AFI judges certainly laud legitimate characteristics of "Ol' Man River," but they fail to account for the song beyond its placement in the canon of film scores. As important as the "art" qualities of the film and its music are, the folk traditions, political consequence, and social reverberations of the song on a global scale are absented here in order to fit the anthem into a list that does not represent its peers. The significance of "Ol' Man River" is ultimately found in what it accomplished on the ground, not on the stage or screen, thereby exploding its original foundation in the art world.

Show Boat is read in the canon of musicals as an innovator in the integration of music and plot, making both dependent on each other in ways unknown previously. The music of the show is therefore as important to its success as the plot and is used to significantly grow and add nuance to the narrative. "Ol' Man River" is the standout of the musical and film version of *Show Boat* and is the only song from the film on the AFI list. It therefore serves to represent the film within the industry as well as within the popular imagination. Music critic Will Friedwald describes the song as a "Broadway anthem," one of "those gut-busting baritone ballads in which manly men assert their manliness." Other than the length of the chorus, everything about the song "is big, big, big. That description encompasses the scope of its philosophical content, the list of artists who have recorded it, the length of its verse . . . and, of course, the stories that are told about it."[29] The singers, musicians, and band leaders who have recorded versions of "Ol' Man River" include Bing Crosby, Frank Sinatra, Judy Garland, Duke Ellington, Bix Beiderbecke, and Screamin' Jay Hawkins. Part of the connection for jazz musicians, including Horace Henderson and his band, was the flexibility of the CM composition. Experimentation and improvisation through the simple melody offer tremendous opportunities for both rhythmic and melodic invention. Considering the numbers of Black male performers on this list, it is not a stretch to imagine that the history of struggle represented by and through Robeson was also a factor in their decision to cover the song.

The song's cultural impact is witnessed in the collective memory signaled by the AFI criteria, but the collective is not solely composed of moviegoers, nor is the song's impact relegated only to the art realm. The real potency of "Ol' Man River" is in its use by individuals and communities. This was accomplished only through the integrity and courage of Paul Robeson, who transformed the song as arranger and performer. His revision of the song "was closer to Woody Guthrie than Hammerstein," and it is the timeless political message of the song in concert with the extraordinary legacy of Robeson's activism that connects him to the Black political actors of the post–Civil Rights era.[30] Musician-actor-activist Yasiin Bey (then known as Mos Def—neé Dante Smith) invokes Robeson and his anthem in "New World Water" from his acclaimed 1999 release *Black on Both Sides*. The frustrations and anger of historical violence are announced when he says, "Fools done upset the Ol' Man River / Made him carry slave ships and fed him dead nigga."[31] The "upset" ol' man river of his text—who is burdened with the demand to degrade and cannibalize his own people—is balanced only by the real-life Robeson, whose indignation and refusal to be packaged and labeled by the mainstream reinvented sound as a weapon within twentieth-century political landscapes.

"Ol' Man River" continues to capture audiences, but its attachment to protest has vanished from the main stage. Acclaimed baritone William Warfield was a major contributor to the song's performance in the period following Robeson's last run of *Show Boat* in 1940. He began performing the role of Joe in 1951, starring in the Technicolor remake of Robeson's 1936 film. This performance launched his long relationship with "Ol' Man River," which he would go on to record for the second movie soundtrack as well as a Lincoln Center performance in 1966. His performance of the song paid homage to Hammerstein II, offering no deviation from the 1927 original. In his 1966 recording, the orchestra begins with an ornate introduction, leading Warfield into a methodical and slow vocal line. His tempo is unlike that employed by Robeson, who often sped up the vocal line in protest performances to distinguish its purpose from the concert stage. Robeson's radically paired-down accompaniment (piano) makes his performances a more casual and organic experience and highlights the text over the musical composition. Warfield's version uses the original Hammerstein text, effectively removing Robeson's political perspective and establishing "Ol' Man River" once again as simply an art composition designed to demonstrate defeat.[32]

Unfortunately, the song's labor in Black mobilizations, which is at the core of its role as an anthem, is no longer a significant part of its record. The song as protest was intimately associated with Robeson, who effectively was erased from American culture "as a result of a campaign of intimidation and harassment conducted by the [Federal Bureau of Investigation] and other agents of the [U.S.] government."[33] Historian Mark Naison describes Robeson as the "most complex and challenging African-American cultural figure of the twentieth century," yet "within a span of ten years, 1947–1957, [he] was virtually erased from historic memory."[34] The forced and deliberate removal of Robeson from U.S. culture and history effectively expunged "Ol' Man River" from the lexicon of Black protest musics. Although the AFI categories are useful and its recognition warranted, the lack of historical context for the anthem and its most famous singer does no justice to the work that it accomplished for a world far beyond stages and screens. The legacy of this great protest anthem has been relegated to an art canon that historically has had little regard for Black music or protest politics, the two spaces that Robeson combined to make his catalog of global resistance a crowning achievement of the Black Popular Front.

Unlike "Ol' Man River," "We Shall Overcome" has become a universal symbol. It invokes ideas of righteous struggle, suffering, and achievement. The movement that gave this icon to the world was not the Local 15 strike in Charleston (where it was born in protest) but the events that transpired ten years later, the traditionally located Civil Rights Movement dating from 1954 to 1965. Community protest in this period constellated around civil disobedience as the method of resistance, and the linked arms and swaying bodies of "We Shall Overcome" provided its defining anthemic event. While the nonviolent protest of Martin Luther King, Jr. and others was a premiere front in the struggle against U.S. racial oppression, there was a simmering and equally potent current of Black activism that utilized "any means necessary" to achieve freedom, and the anthem became a point of departure for these two positions. The Black Panthers, Deacons of Defense, and various branches of the Nation of Islam, to name just a few groups, achieved notoriety for their engagement with violence as a means of revolution, and their leaders drew both criticism and praise for this position. Malcolm X is the most revered and iconic of these leaders. He was consistently at odds with other figures over the project of civil rights and its means of achievement. For him, integration was not the end goal; ultimate justice for Black people (globally) was freedom from violence—physical, social, mental, and economic. The irony of course is that violence was a strategic option for Malcolm X, who famously argued that democratic freedoms for Black people would be achieved by either "the ballot or the bullet." Within his framework, the pining of interracial activists for the "someday" when we will overcome was seen as outdated and ill equipped to match Black reality.

Malcolm X's evaluation of the anthem drips with condescension and judgment in a number of his speeches after his break with the Nation of Islam in March 1964. In "The Ballot or the Bullet" he distinguishes between civil rights and human rights. He described, "Civil rights means you're asking Uncle Sam to treat you right. Human rights are your God-given rights." Like Robeson and numerous others before him,

he advocated taking the United States to the world court for their violation of human rights: "Uncle Sam's hands are dripping with blood, dripping with the blood of the black man in this country. He's the earth's
number-one hypocrite. He has the audacity—yes, he has—imagine him
posing as the leader of the free world. The free world!—and you over
here singing 'We Shall Overcome.' Expand the civil-rights struggle to
the level of human rights, take it to the United Nations."[35] After sharing a Harlem stage with Fannie Lou Hamer of the Mississippi Freedom
Democratic Party, Malcolm X was stirred to admonish the men of the
Civil Rights Movement for their inability to protect Black women saying, "[W]e [Black men] don't deserve to be recognized and respected
as men as long as our women can be brutalized in the manner that
[Hamer] described, and nothing being done about it, but we sit around
singing 'We Shall Overcome.'"[36] In this instance, Black men are emascu-
lated by Malcolm X's charge that they sing instead of act, thereby relin-
quishing their authority within traditions of Black resistance. His statement, however, obscures the active role that women took in making the
song a political tract and the ways in which their activism did not seek
out or require male approval or leadership.[37] Yet it is not only the singing but also *the song* that brings Malcolm X's condemnation. His vision
of Black revolution included a pointed attack on the anthem and its
singers as he challenged the Civil Rights establishment to consider the
reality of revolution: "Revolution is never based on begging someone
for an integrated cup of coffee. Revolutions are never fought by turning
the other cheek. Revolutions are never based upon love-your-enemy
and pray-for-those-who-spitefully-use-you. And revolutions are never
waged singing 'We Shall Overcome.'"[38]

For Malcolm X the song symbolized an obsolete guard of Black
activist who was more appeasing than demanding and more accommo-
dating than revolutionary. As the decade of the 1960s progressed, other
organizations and leaders began to feel similarly. Following closely in
the steps of Malcolm X, the Black Panthers arose as a powerful voice
among Black youth. They questioned the utility of "We Shall Overcome," and it slowly fell out of favor among Black movement actors,
particularly young activists who were turning their attention toward
armed revolt and the revolutions occurring in the project of the Third
World.[39] The anthem's absence in the U.S. context, however, has not

diminished its ability to bolster international camaraderie. Journalist Peter S. Scholtes writes that "today . . . [We Shall Overcome's] unfunky earnestness seems stranded in its era even as the lyrics are being taught in Arabic and Chinese. People everywhere else seem to believe this song still has something to tell them, even if Americans have heard it all."[40] What the Black hymn and labor ballad has to tell the world has covered the spectrum. It was used by Archbishop Desmond Tutu as sustenance in the fight against South African apartheid, at the Third Asia Pacific International Solidarity Conference in 2005 to highlight the courage of communist activists in India,[41] and, closer to home, it was used by the Harlem Boys Choir to heal the hearts of a grieving New York City post-9/11. The labor roots of "We Shall Overcome" were preserved by coal miners in Appalachia who went on strike in 1989 and used the song as a rallying call for their comrades. In that same year, workers were also a significant presence in the Tiananmen Square Uprising (Massacre) in Beijing, China, which sought to advance a more democratic government. Participants used the slogan "we shall overcome" as a visual representation of the movement on their T-shirts. The country's decades of communist leadership could not insulate the citizens from the thoroughly Western Civil Rights Movement and its anthem. According to journalist Rob Gifford, "Despite years of Communist indoctrination, the students turned out to be surprisingly media-savvy. They played to the Western news media, marching with banners emblazoned in English with some of the most sacred mantras of Western liberal democracy: 'Give me Liberty of Give me Death,' 'Government of the people, by the people, for the people,' and 'We Shall Overcome.'"[42] One American observer recalled that while they marched the students sang "We Shall Overcome" with a confidence and knowledge that surpassed his own. The protesters also sang "The Internationale," signaling the importance of labor and labor organization to the consciousness of the participants.[43] In its ability to condense struggle and (eventual) triumph into a sound bite, "We Shall Overcome" was for these students, and myriad other downtrodden populations globally, the mantra for a movement and future grounded by victory in collective struggle.

In spite of her dazzling political interventions, collectivity is something that largely eluded Nina Simone in her personal life. During her fifty-year career she achieved both brilliant flashes of international acclaim and prolonged absences and silence. Her tortured relationship with and withdrawal from the United States makes her disappearance from public discourse all the more inevitable. Her distance from U.S. popular consciousness was reflected in the obituaries that followed her death in 2003. According to historian Ruth Feldstein, "Many of these reports . . . depicted Simone as a historical relic from a bygone era."[44] This obscurity, however, has made her recovery that much more fantastic. None of the artists in this study command international acclaim in the same way as Simone. She is a cult figure whose recordings are collector's items often bought and sold through special dealers and distributors worldwide. This is both the frustration and euphoria of studying her in performance. Her prolificacy and the variation in her recordings make her work especially tantalizing for artists hoping to recover some element of her genius in their own work. Hip-hop has been a major forum for the reemergence of Simone's music. Artistic necessity, historical excavation, and community genealogies are the building blocks for the technology of sampling that launched Simone's voice for younger generations. Scholar Mark Anthony Neal argues that within the ravages of the post–Civil Rights order there developed a "postindustrial nostalgia" within Black popular culture, "loosely defined as a nostalgia that has its basis in the postindustrial transformations of black urban life during the 1970s." He notes, "The prevalence of nostalgia-based narratives in black popular culture would have particular effects on the maintenance of intra-diasporic relations, at once providing the aural and visual bridge to reaffirm diverse communal relations, particularly those across the generational divide."[45] These cultural acts contributed to the continuation of the aesthetic and oral traditions of the industrial urban Black centers that ceased to provide wages and goods for the post–Civil Rights generations.

Even as post–Civil Rights Black communities struggled with and rallied against the new conditions resultant of economic instability and mass incarceration, the tomes of the past spoke to them. Simone's art plays an important role in that production. Her political anthems were picked up on the other side of the Civil Rights Movement by musicians whose instruments were two turntables and a microphone. Many of the artists who have sampled Simone are commonly referred to as "conscious" or political rappers, including Black Star emcee and solo artist Talib Kweli (neé Talib Greene). For the introduction to his 2002 single, "Get By," Kweli uses a vocal moan from Simone's 1965 recording of "Sinnerman." Simone's ten-second cry is a fitting introduction to Kweli's story, which addresses the poverty, drug abuse, and rampant incarceration that depresses the Black community. His flow follows the twists and turns of Black life, mixing the events of the past with the realities of the present: "Mí abuela raised three daughters all by herself, with no help / I think about a struggle and I find the strength in myself / These words, melt in my mouth / They hot, like the jail cell in the South / Before my nigga CORE bailed me out."[46] His knowledge and mention of the Congress of Racial Equality (CORE) adds another layer to his return to Simone by including her activism. CORE's use of southern jails as a spectacle of injustice and antiracist strategy links their efforts to the activism grown from the contemporary prison-industrial complex, a central site of contestation for post–Civil Rights generations. Described by one reviewer as the "conscious hustler's anthem,"[47] "Get By" captures and struggles with the brutal realities of Black life in a way consistent with the Civil Rights storytelling and activism of Simone. This reinvention of her work has offered cultural cache to artists whose initial appeal is their proximity to "the streets."[48] In that way Simone's music is used as both an elevation of hip-hop's artistic and sonic quality and a reinscription of her relevance to Black struggle on the ground.

The sampling of Simone's music within hip-hop contains contradiction because she was not a fan or at all impressed by rap music. In a 1997 interview about her politics and music, she said, "I don't think that the new music, rap, is carrying on our ideals at all. . . . Rap is ruining music—it's just no good at all."[49] Her opinion of the music in this period is not surprising. Representations of the mid- to late 1990s rap scene were rife with violence after the murders of both Tupac Shakur and Christopher Wallace (aka The Notorious B.I.G.), yet the diversity of the form—both in that moment and since—offers a counterpoint to Simone's opinion of the music and its message. The presence of her art in hip-hop tells a story of continuity that bridges her past activism with the challenges of the present. Her anthem, "To Be Young, Gifted and Black," has carried over into the genre and is often referenced in popular recordings.[50] Underground emcee Gist, aka The Essence of Queens (neé Arthur Joseph, Jr.), has moved beyond the phrase, using the song and its message as the foundation for his 2007 single, "Young, Gifted & Black." The song begins with the faint but recognizable voice of Simone singing, "In the whole world you know / there's a million boys and girls who are . . ." This strain of the melody and lyric are carried throughout the song under emphasized horn breaks and bass beats. Gist and Simone have a conversation during the chorus of the song:

> SIMONE: . . . young, gifted and black.
> GIST: And I ain't never sold a ounce of crack / Never bust tre pound or mac
> SIMONE: and that's a fact.
> GIST: I'm just a youngin' that know how to rap / and I'm
> SIMONE: young, gifted and black.
> GIST: I might be the one to bring this back / 'cause I got the soul most dudes lack
> SIMONE: and that's a fact.
> GIST: I'm just a youngin' that know how to rap.

This back and forth between the two serves as one continuous thought as they begin and finish each other's phrases. His assertion that "I'm just a youngin' that know how to rap" is a tongue-in-cheek rebuttal to those who dismiss the hip-hop generation, both for their youth—associated with naïveté and a lack of knowledge—and their choice of music. He uses sarcasm to challenge those who believe that one person cannot make a difference and that music is not a vehicle for social change. He reclaims some of the momentum of the Civil Rights Movement and proves that his relationship to its legacy moves beyond his individual song and into the larger exposition of Black history when he describes that he has "[t]he fight of a old leader / Huey P. with the soul of Simone Nina."

For Gist, music is the mode through which the Black Radical Tradition takes shape. He makes explicit the idea of music as a political vehicle when he raps: "It feel good to make good black music / Ain't on the radio, still people is tuned in / Ain't quite crack but still people is usin' / Ain't there still but still people is movin' / Look at who's choosin' / *Young, gifted, black we're the movement.*"[51] His flow articulates a mobilization not reliant on the mainstream media and a faith in young Black people not as consumers but as actors. He revealed, "The inspiration that I got from [Simone] was to be proud of what you are. We're talented so there's no reason to not let the world know that we're talented. . . . Do what you know that you can do and be the best at it."[52] Acknowledging the role of young people in public culture and politics, Gist's call to "look who's choosin'" demands a closer interrogation of the potential of youth cultures. The biannual National Hip-Hop Political Conventions, which began in 2004, evidence the belief that hip-hop is a medium through which young people speak truth to power. Its narrative capabilities and growth from and relationship to Black communities and neighborhoods make the genre a prime location of information sharing. Sampling adds to the music's depth, power, and significance as the musicians absorb the histories, circumstances, and power of the original track, accumulating the political efficacy of its sound. Both Kweli and Gist made principled decisions to use Simone's work. In that way, their songs serve as complimentary exclamations built on the resonant musical and protest traditions of the past.

The past productively haunts all of these anthems, but since 1992 "Nkosi Sikelel' iAfrika" has had a possession all its own.[53] The institutionalization of the African National Congress (ANC) as South Africa's first party ensures that their anthem will have a utility and profile above and beyond what any of the previous anthems can achieve. This fact, however, does not mean that the anthem is unchallenged or uncontested. The ANC was empowered to govern South Africa by the nation's first universal suffrage election of 1992. In 1994, Nelson Mandela, the ANC activist and longtime political prisoner, was installed as president, in which capacity he would select the new symbols of postapartheid South Africa. Recognizing the power of his organization's anthem, he announced that the national anthem of South Africa would be "Nkosi Sikelel' iAfrika." As the leader of a government of reconciliation, however, Mandela did not stop there. He revealed that the anthem would, postapartheid, share the title with the apartheid anthem "Die Stem van Suid-Afrika." While melodically reconciled through composition in 1997, the hybrid anthem exposed a radical collision of ideologies that could not be resolved. A united nation under democracy could not hope to make peace with Afrikaner nationalism under apartheid. At the time of Mandela's election, "Die Stem" was the "official" anthem of South Africa, having been institutionalized by Parliament in 1957, while "Nkosi" was less than five years old by the standards of the apartheid government that unbanned it and its performance in 1990. The decision to fuse the anthems caused no uncertain amount of concern within the party and wider South African citizenry. The people's movement that made "Nkosi Sikelel' iAfrika" an anthem officially made its way to the national stage, but the performance that they might erect there was compromised from its first day by the still resonant and condoned sounds of apartheid.

Like all countries, South Africa deploys its national anthem in service of performing the unity of a sovereign and distinguishable nation. In the case of this relatively young nation, however, the anthem's performance also reads as an effort to reinforce the compatibility of two competing political systems through a coerced forgetfulness. The performance of the hybrid anthem at high-profile events is reliant on a national amnesia that forgives and, devastatingly, forgets the recent history of radical exclusion and violence that organized their twentieth century. The anthemic event enforces national dogma through ritual at national celebrations, notably sporting events, including the 2010 FIFA World Cup, where the anthem played in front of nearly 85,000 people at the Soccer City stadium en route from Johannesburg to Soweto. In spite of these very public evidences of the anthem in performative solidarity, there were a series of post-1994 mishaps with the anthem that signaled the failures of its composition and the lingering apartheid vestiges within the nation's representations. During a 2012 women's field hockey competition in Britain, "Die Stem" was played as the South African players' national anthem. What should have been a moment of pride for the players (who won the match) instead was described by South African hockey official Marissa Langeni as "a most embarrassing and uncomfortable experience." Stadium representatives in Britain apologized, blaming a contractor for the transgression: "Great Britain hockey and its contractor appreciate the sensitive nature of this unfortunate mistake and we apologise unreservedly for the offense caused."[54] Within the pantheon of national events, this scene is remarkable. It is unimaginable that athletes from Britain would experience a spectacle such as this. The entrenched nature of (Western) nationalism ensures that superpowers are welcomed with the proper sounds of their nation, which are imagined to be immemorial. The relatively recent politico-historical events of South Africa could be imagined as leading to the contractor's confusion, yet "Die Stem" was displaced as the national anthem of South Africa nearly twenty years prior to this match. In this scenario, it is clear that there is something more insidious happening in response to a national team representative of a distinct racial demography and present history of activism.

The fight over the nation's anthem is not simply performative or even ideological; it is also a material and economic consideration that has garnered increasing scrutiny postapartheid. South Africa is currently embroiled in heated debates over intellectual property and copyright concerns for "Nkosi Sikelel' iAfrika." More than sixty individuals, publishing houses, and corporations made copyright claims on the anthem in the late twentieth century. Whether through compositional or performance revision, the anthem has become a commodity that some argue should be profited from only by the government. According to legal scholar Owen Dean, however, the anthem copyright, with little exception, does not belong and cannot belong to any one person or group. The hybrid composition means that there are distinct copyright practices attached to all versions that combined to make the 1997 anthem. In addition to that, the music and lyrics are treated separately under law. Most all of the copyrights for the pieces of "Nkosi Sikelel' iAfrika" have expired due to the death of the composers. "Nkosi," therefore, "is not a national cash cow from which the South African government can or ought to derive wealth. Nor does it belong to anyone else. It may be part of our heritage but it is free for use for all."[55] The struggle over the anthem's profitability exposes the ways in which rebellion and revolution have been commodified in the postcolonial era. The movement that made the contemporary South African reality is, through its anthem, condensed and compressed into material objects that can be bought and sold in the marketplaces owned and managed by a powerful elite. The practice of "Nkosi Sikelel' iAfrika" as an anthem meant that it never belonged to any one person but rather to all who shared in its vision. The contemporary fight for ownership over the anthem highlights the postcolonial turn to nostalgic consumption and the erasure of a deadly recent past that has, discursively and sonically, become institutionalized within the fictive inclusivity of post-apartheid democracy.

* * *

From bombastic display to trace evidence, these anthems have retained a presence beyond their original designs. The quality of their engagements has, however, changed dramatically. The limitations of these anthems in the wake of their movement usage in the African diaspora derive from multiple conditions. Generational misrecognition within diasporic communities, the prohibition of materials of or related to race and culture in educational systems, and the structural breakdown of mass movement politics have contributed to varying levels of silence. There is also something within the anthemic formation that may be to blame—a lingering problematic that could impede future visions and mobilizations. Although often composed, and always performed, collectively, the imbedded singularity of *the* anthem may be its undoing. Like the messianic leadership that has proven troubled and inefficient time and time again, the isolation of a sonic text as the mouthpiece for a collective invites challenges that most anthems cannot withstand over time.[56] But instead of grieving for or fetishizing an idyllic past, it is important to recognize that "identity work is [also] achieved in and through the music to which [people] have *stopped* listening."[57] The fact that some of these songs have passed the time of their utility in movement cultures does not diminish their importance to the political histories and futures of the diaspora. Nor is their absence absolute. Bits and pieces of these songs, their musicians, their authors, and their movements linger in creative and political imaginations. The tangibility of that assertion is represented above. With every reference to these movements and musicians, with every performance, a conversation continues between the actors of the past and those of the present. The histories that these anthems have helped to build and the present efforts that they condone structure a radical movement timeline for members and actors within diaspora. Anthems, therefore, have a future, even if the nation does not. The project and practice of Black anthems represented here will, with any luck, mobilize another cohort with the talents to remake the world.

NOTES

NOTES TO THE INTRODUCTION

1. Erica Edwards dissects and troubles the "animating fiction" of charisma and charismatic leadership within twentieth-century African American literature, arguing that it is "a narrative and performative regime that works to discipline even as it enables social change." Erica R. Edwards, *Charisma and the Fictions of Black Leadership* (Minneapolis: University of Minnesota Press, 2012), x, 72. This project intends to similarly disrupt any easy association between singular leadership and progress by highlighting anthemic performance as a communally employed sound project of rebellion and political advancement among the African descended, while also acknowledging that these anthems expose conditions of conflict and, at times, collusion with structures of Western domination.

2. Jacques Attali, *Noise: The Political Economy of Music*, trans. Brian Massumi (1970; Minneapolis: University of Minnesota Press, 1985).

3. The 2010 kerfuffle over the status of "Lift Ev'ry Voice and Sing" as an anthem by literature scholar Timothy Askew, who argued the song was race neutral, is one example of a failed equation for anthemic production. Intention can be only minimally registered and is not a debate that I am interested in pursuing. The importance of these anthems is in their use, something that Askew does not consider. An investigation of performance produces evidence to support the fact that Johnson, for example, was not interested in an open exchange with the U.S. government through his anthem but instead wanted to dialogue with mobilizing communities of aligned difference. Timothy Askew, *Cultural Hegemony and African American Patriotism: An Analysis of the Song "Lift Every Voice and Sing"* (Deer Park, NY: Linus Publications, 2010). For a response to Askew, see Rudolph P. Byrd, "Song Reflects Racial Pride, Never Intended as Anthem," *CNN Opinion*, July 30, 2010, http://www.cnn.com/2010/OPINION/07/27/byrd.james.johnson/index.html (accessed August 1, 2010).

4. Simon Frith argues that music is a formative experience of identity formation that allows for the development of a self within a collective. Simon Frith, "Music and Identity," in eds. Stuart Hall and Paul du Gay, *Questions of Cultural Identity* (London: Sage, 1996), 110. My thinking on the political and theological response impulse within traditional anthems and its relationship to Black anthems was recognized through and indebted to conversation with Fred Moten.

5. Throughout the period of this study, those people who constituted family, friends, and neighbors were often those who lived under radical segregation, making their distance from the state and proximity to one another a shared condition from which to organize.

6. The class-focused socialist/communist/anarchist anthem "The Internationale" is another model of a sonic praxis of collectivity whose performance resists settling in any location or sphere of political influence. Its translation into dozens of languages emphasizes its ability to literally speak to various conditions, movements, peoples, and locations.

7. Here I pick up on historian Lisa Brock, who challenges scholars to develop a more diverse internationalism in the study of the African diaspora. See Lisa Brock, "Questioning the Diaspora: Hegemony, Black Intellectuals and Doing International History from Below," *Issue: A Journal of Opinion* 24, no. 2 (1996): 9–12.

8. Joseph E. Harris, "Introduction," in ed. Joseph E. Harris, *Global Dimensions of the African Diaspora* (Washington, DC: Howard University Press, 1982), 5; Hazel V. Carby and Tina Campt, "Dialogue between Hazel Carby and Tina Campt" (unpublished, 2006).

9. Stuart Hall, "Cultural Identity and Diaspora," in ed. Jonathan Rutherford, *Identity: Community, Culture, Difference* (London: Lawrence and Wishart, 1990), 222.

10. Olly Wilson, "Black Music as an Art Form," *Black Music Research Journal* 3 (1983): 2. In his work on Black music, Ronald Radano also champions the diversity of its formations, arguing, "Because of its intimate historical connection to ideologies of race . . . black music has inevitably assumed multiple manifestations. Its power and significance relate not simply to racial and semiotic indicators but also to a flexibility in articulating a broad range of meaning. Seen this way, black music's dynamism and heterogeneity become not limitations but sources of potency." Ronald Radano, *Lying Up a Nation: Race and Black Music* (Chicago: University of Chicago Press, 2003), xiii.

11. Fred Moten, *In the Break: The Aesthetics of the Black Radical Tradition* (Minneapolis: University of Minnesota Press, 2003), 14, 2.

12. Josh Kun, *Audiotopia: Music, Race and America* (Berkeley: University of California Press, 2005).

13. Robin D. G. Kelley, *Freedom Dreams: The Black Radical Imagination* (Boston: Beacon, 2002), 11.

14. Christopher Small defines "musicking" as a verb: "to music." Christopher Small, *Music of the Common Tongue: Survival and Celebration in African American Music* (London: John Calder, 1987), 50.

15. Contemporary resonances of this practice are recognized within the Occupy Wall Street movement, members of which assemble their voices to make audible the critiques, analyses, and comments of individual speakers.

16. John Dewey, *The Public and Its Problems* (New York: Holt, 1927).

17. Michael C. Dawson, "A Black Counterpublic? Economic Earthquakes, Racial Agenda(s) and Black Politics," *Public Culture* 7 (1994): 217.

18. My understanding of intracommunal difference and division is informed by Cathy Cohen's extensive reading of "marginality" within Black communities. See Cathy J. Cohen, *The Boundaries of Blackness: AIDS and the Breakdown of Black Politics* (Chicago: University of Chicago Press, 1999).

19. Kyra D. Gaunt, *The Games Black Girls Play: Learning the Ropes from Double-Dutch to Hip-Hop* (New York: New York University Press, 2006), 14.

20. Guthrie P. Ramsey, Jr., *Race Music: Black Cultures from BeBop to Hip-Hop* (Berkeley: University of California Press, 2003), xi.

21. Clyde Woods, *Development Arrested: Race, Power, and the Blues in the Mississippi Delta* (New York: Verso, 1998), 16.

22. Recent scholarship on the convergence of jazz with the Civil Rights Movement, for example, includes Robin D. G. Kelley, *Africa Speaks, America Answers: Modern Jazz in Revolutionary Times* (Cambridge, MA: Harvard University Press, 2012); Ingrid Monson, *Freedom Sounds: Civil Rights Call Out to Jazz and Africa* (New York: Oxford University Press, 2007); Scott Saul, *Freedom Is, Freedom Ain't: Jazz and the Making of the Sixties* (Cambridge, MA: Harvard University Press, 2003); Penny Von Eschen, *Satchmo Blows Up the World: Jazz Ambassadors Play the Cold War* (Cambridge, MA: Harvard University Press, 2004). For hip-hop scholarship and youth mobilization, see M. K. Asante, Jr., *It's Bigger Than Hip Hop: The Rise of the Post-Hip-Hop Generation* (New York: St. Martin's, 2009); Andreana Clay, *The Hip-Hop Generation Fights Back: Youth Activism and Post-Civil Rights Politics* (New York: New York University Press, 2012); Bakari Kitwana, *The Hip Hop Generation: Young Blacks and the Crisis in African American Culture* (New York: Basic Civitas, 2002); Imani Perry, *Prophets of the Hood: Politics and Poetics in Hip Hop* (Durham, NC: Duke University Press, 2004); Jeffrey O. G. Ogbar, *Hip Hop Revolution: The Culture and Politics of Rap* (Lawrence: University Press of Kansas, 2009); S. Craig Watkins, *Hip Hop Matters: Politics, Popular Culture, and the Struggle for the Soul of a Movement* (Boston: Beacon, 2005).

23. By "fantastic," I mean to signal scholar Richard Iton's use of James Baldwin, who masterfully destabilized the uses of Black popular culture. See Richard Iton, *In Search of the Black Fantastic: Politics and Popular Culture in the Post-Civil Rights Era* (New York: Oxford University Press, 2010).

24. Darlene Clark Hine, "Rape and the Inner Lives of Black Women in the Middle West: Preliminary Thoughts on the Culture of Dissemblance," *Signs* 14, no. 4 (1989): 912–20.

25. James C. Scott, *Domination and the Arts of Resistance: Hidden Transcripts* (New Haven: Yale University Press, 1990), 2, 4, 5.

26. David Krasner, *Resistance, Parody, and Double Consciousness in African American Theatre, 1895–1910* (New York: St. Martin's, 1997), 4, 146.

27. Historian Frank Guridy discusses the "translocal" through artists like poet-writer Langston Hughes, whose travel to Cuba invigorated discussions across the Caribbean and the United States. Frank Andre Guridy, *Forging Diaspora: Afro-Cubans*

and African Americans in a World of Empire and Jim Crow (Chapel Hill: University of North Carolina Press, 2010).

28. Cedric Robinson, *Black Marxism: The Making of the Black Radical Tradition* (1983; Chapel Hill: University of North Carolina Press, 2000).

29. Attali, *Noise*. These conditions are discussed in more detail in chapter 3.

30. Brent Hayes Edwards, *The Practice of Diaspora: Literature, Translation, and the Rise of Black Internationalism* (Cambridge, MA: Harvard University Press, 2003), 7; Paul Gilroy, *The Black Atlantic: Modernity and Double Consciousness* (Cambridge, MA: Harvard University Press, 1993), 102.

31. Gilroy, *Black Atlantic*, 19.

32. Benedict Anderson, *Imagined Communities: Reflections on the Origins and Spread of Nationalism* (1983; London: Verso, 2006).

33. Vijay Prashad, *The Darker Nations: A People's History of the Third World* (New York: New Press, 2007), 12.

34. Shana L. Redmond, "Citizens of Sound: Negotiations of Race and Diaspora in the Anthems of the UNIA and NAACP," *African and Black Diaspora: An International Journal* 4, no. 1 (2011): 19–39.

35. "A Tribute to Paul Robeson on the Occasion of His Forty-Sixth Birthday," April 16, 1944, Paul Robeson Collection, 1925–1956, 1943–1956, Schomburg Center for Research in Black Culture, New York Public Library, Astor, Lenox and Tilden Foundations, Microfilm: reel 1 (hereafter cited as Schomburg Center).

NOTES TO CHAPTER 1

1. Colin Grant, *Negro with a Hat: The Rise and Fall of Marcus Garvey* (London: Oxford University Press, 2008), 261.

2. Honor Ford-Smith, "Unruly Virtues of the Spectacular: Performing Engendered Nationalisms in the UNIA in Jamaica," *Interventions* 6, no. 1 (2004): 35.

3. In its original conception, the organization was known as the Universal Negro Improvement Association and African Communities League (UNIA-ACL). It retained the extended title but most often was referred to as the UNIA.

4. Booker T. Washington (1856–1915) was a dominant force in the economic and political discussions of, for, and by Black Americans post-Emancipation. Born into slavery, Washington later authored the classic *Up from Slavery* (1901) and went on to be founder and leader of the Tuskegee Institute in Alabama, where he taught industrial education to his Black student body. His deeply antagonistic relationship with another leading Black intellectual of the period, W. E. B. Du Bois, who was a proponent of liberal arts education for Black men and women, defined the poles of Black political engagement for the latter years of his life.

5. It is unlikely a coincidence that the Irish War of Independence, which was ongoing at the time of Liberty Hall's UNIA dedication in 1919, also had an impressive tradition of music making that, combined with armed mobilizations, composed a dynamic front against the colonialism of the British.

6. Grant, *Negro with a Hat*, 121.

7. Ibid., 106.

8. This text was drawn from the King James Version of the Bible.

9. David Cronon, *Black Moses: The Story of Marcus Garvey and the Universal Negro Improvement Association* (Madison: University of Wisconsin Press, 1955), 68.

10. "Opening of UNIA Convention," *Negro World*, August 3, 1920, in ed. Robert A. Hill, *The Marcus Garvey and Universal Negro Improvement Association Papers*, 3 vols. (Berkeley: University of California Press, 1983), 2:476 (hereafter cited as the *Garvey Papers*).

11. "Declaration of the Rights of the Negro Peoples of the World," in ed. Amy Jacques Garvey, *The Philosophy & Opinions of Marcus Garvey; or, Africa for the Africans,* vols. 1–2 (1925; Dover: Majority Press, 1986), 135.

12. Ibid., 140.

13. Universal Negro Improvement Association, Central Division Records, New York, NY, 1918–1959, Schomburg Center, reel 1.

14. J. Martin Daughtry, "Russia's New Anthem and the Negotiation of National Identity," *Ethnomusicology* 47, no. 1 (Winter 2003): 46.

15. See Edwards, *Charisma and the Fictions of Black Leadership*; Mary G. Rolinson, *Grassroots Garveyism: The Universal Negro Improvement Association in the Rural South, 1920–1927* (Chapel Hill: University of North Carolina Press, 2007); Martin Summers, *Manliness and Its Discontents: The Black Middle Class & the Transformation of Masculinity, 1900–1930* (Chapel Hill: University of North Carolina Press, 2004).

16. Universal Negro Improvement Association, reel 1.

17. Michelle Ann Stephens, *Black Empire: The Masculine Global Imaginary of Caribbean Intellectuals, 1914–1962* (Durham, NC: Duke University Press, 2005), 80.

18. Simone de Beauvoir, *The Second Sex*, trans. H. M. Parshley (1952; New York: Vintage, 1989), xxvii.

19. Ula Yvette Taylor, *The Veiled Garvey: The Life & Times of Amy Jacques Garvey* (Chapel Hill: University of North Carolina Press, 2002), 2.

20. William Isles, "The Negro and Music, Part II," *Negro World*, June 10, 1922, in "*The Negro World* (New York, NY)," Schomburg Center, reel 1 (hereafter cited as NW).

21. Williams Isles, "The Negro and Music, Part V," *Negro World*, August 5, 1922, NW: reel 1.

22. Marcus Garvey, "Propaganda," in ed. Amy Jacques Garvey, *Philosophy & Opinions of Marcus Garvey*, 8.

23. Marcus Garvey, "The Image of God," in ed. Amy Jacques Garvey, *Philosophy & Opinions of Marcus Garvey*, 44.

24. Roberta S. Gold, "The Black Jews of Harlem: Representation, Identity, and Race, 1920–1939," *American Quarterly* 55, no. 2 (June 2003): 209.

25. Jacob S. Dorman, "'I Saw You Disappear with My Own Eyes': Hidden Transcripts of New York Black Israelite Bricolage," *Nova Religio* 11, no. 1 (2007): 62.

26. Quoted in ibid., 69.

27. Ibid., 68, 69.

28. "Negro Jews Win in Rent Suit," *Amsterdam News*, December 23, 1925, 1.
29. By the time of this suit, UNIA members and leaders were amply aware of the significance of the courtroom. In 1923 Marcus Garvey offered a spectacular performance in a federal courtroom in his own defense against charges of mail fraud in connection with the collections for his Black Star Line shipping enterprise. He was convicted and in 1925 began serving a five-year sentence at the federal penitentiary in Atlanta, Georgia. President Calvin Coolidge later commuted Garvey's conviction, and upon his 1927 release he was deported to his native Jamaica.
30. Jeffrey R. Di Leo, ed., *On Anthologies: Politics and Pedagogy* (Lincoln: University of Nebraska Press, 2004), 1.
31. "First UNIA Court Reception," *Negro World*, September 3, 1921, in ed. Hill, *Garvey Papers*, 3:698.
32. Quoted in Lawrence W. Levine, "Marcus Garvey and the Politics of Revitalization," in eds. John Hope Franklin and August Meier, *Black Leaders of the Twentieth Century* (Urbana: University of Illinois Press, 1982), 121.
33. Ibid., 121.
34. "First UNIA Court Reception," 3:699.
35. Charles Mills, interview in documentary film *Marcus Garvey: Look for me in the Whirlwind* (DVD B00005TPCH; Public Broadcasting System, 2001).
36. Quoted in Tony Martin, *Race First: The Ideological and Organizational Struggles of Marcus Garvey and the Universal Negro Improvement Association* (Westport, CT: Greenwood, 1976), 237.
37. Wilson Jeremiah Moses, *The Golden Age of Black Nationalism, 1850–1925* (New York: Oxford University Press, 1978), 7.
38. Sterling Stuckey, *Slave Culture: Nationalist Theory and the Foundations of Black America* (New York: Oxford University Press, 1987), 156.
39. For example, in 1845 Garnet supported a resolution that maintained that people of color should have every right to defend the country through military service in order to maintain the government. These types of bids to inclusion within the nation—often made through an uncritical endorsement of national projects of war making, capital expansion, and the maintenance of other types of difference (gender, national, etc.)—condoned the violences of its formation.
40. Moses, *Golden Age of Black Nationalism*, 7.
41. Marcus Garvey, in ed. Amy Jacques Garvey, *Philosophy & Opinions of Marcus Garvey*, 9.
42. Levine, "Marcus Garvey and the Politics of Revitalization," 124.
43. Michael A. Gomez, *Exchanging Our Country Marks: The Transformation of African Identities in the Colonial and Antebellum South* (Chapel Hill: University of North Carolina Press, 1998).
44. Robinson, *Black Marxism*, xxxi.
45. Moses, *Golden Age of Black Nationalism*, 17.
46. This is not to say that morality was absent in the organization. As the significant representation of religious figures among the UNIA's leadership conveys,

questions of respectability and ethics were never far from the organization's message or purpose.

47. Robert A. Hill, "General Introduction," in ed. Hill, *Garvey Papers*, 1:xlv.

48. Randall K. Burkett, *Black Redemption: Churchmen Speak for the Garvey Movement* (Philadelphia: Temple University Press, 1978), 13.

49. Ibid., 6.

50. Levine, "Marcus Garvey and the Politics of Revitalization," 116.

51. Estelle James, interview in *Marcus Garvey* (PBS, 2001).

52. Arnold J. Ford, "The Password," in ed. Ford, *The Universal Ethiopian Hymnal* (New York: Beth B'nai Abraham Publishing, 1922), 13.

53. Burkett, *Black Redemption*, 5.

54. Ibid., 168, 171.

55. Rabbi Schlomo Ben Levy, "Biography of Rabbi Arnold Josiah Ford," *BlackJews. org*, http://blackjews.org/Bio%20of%20Black%20Rabbis/Biographies%20of%20 Black%20Rabbis%20in%20America.htm (accessed October 10, 2006).

56. Karen Sotiropoulos, *Staging Race: Black Performers in Turn of the Century America* (Cambridge, MA: Harvard University Press, 2006), 2, 7.

57. Reid Badger, *A Life In Ragtime: A Biography of James Reese Europe* (New York: Oxford University Press, 1995), 142.

58. *New York Age*, May 10, 1917, 6, reprinted in Badger, *Life in Ragtime*, 148.

59. Marcus Garvey, "The Conspiracy of the East St. Louis Riots," *Negro World*, July 8, 1917, in ed. Hill, *Garvey Papers*, 1:213.

60. Marcus Garvey, in ed. Amy Jacques Garvey, *Philosophy & Opinions of Marcus Garvey*, 4.

61. Quoted in Hill, "General Introduction," 1:lxxviii–lxxix.

62. Ibid., 1:xxxiii.

63. Edwards, *Charisma and the Fictions of Black Leadership*.

64. For histories of manhood (in the late nineteenth and early twentieth centuries), see Gail Bederman, *Manliness and Civilization: A Cultural History of Gender and Race in the United States, 1880–1917* (Chicago: University of Chicago Press, 1996) and Kristin L. Hoganson, *Fighting for American Manhood: How Gender Politics Provoked the Spanish-American and Philippine-American Wars* (New Haven: Yale University Press, 2000). For New Negro culture and politics, see Houston A. Baker, *Modernism and the Harlem Renaissance* (Chicago: University of Chicago Press, 1989); David Levering Lewis, *When Harlem Was in Vogue* (New York: Penguin Books, 1979); Alain Locke, ed., *The New Negro: Voices of the Harlem Renaissance* (1925; New York: Touchstone, 1997).

65. Angela Y. Davis, *Blues Women and Black Feminism: Gertrude "Ma" Rainey, Bessie Smith, and Billie Holiday* (New York: Vintage Books, 1998), xiii.

66. Quoted in Hill, "General Introduction," 1:lii.

67. Arnold J. Ford, "Legion's Marching Song," in ed. Tony Martin, *African Fundamentalism: A Literary and Cultural Anthology of Garvey's Harlem Renaissance* (Dover: Majority Press, 1983), 203–4.

68. Frank A. Guridy, "Feeling Diaspora in Harlem and Havana," *Social Text* 27, no. 1 (Spring 2009): 118.
69. For example, on the first day of the 1920 International Convention of the Negro Peoples of the World, the UNIA band played "The Star-Spangled Banner" in advance of Garvey's opening speech.
70. Carla Marano, "'Rising Strongly and Rapidly': The Universal Negro Improvement Association in Canada, 1919–1940," *Canadian Historical Review* 91, no. 2 (June 2010): 242.
71. In June 1919, a lieutenant with the U.S. Navy wrote that "Many signs point to the facts that all these negro [*sic*] associations [including the UNIA-ACL] are joining hands with Irish Sinn Feiners, Hindus, Egyptians, Japanese and Mexicans." Edward L. Tinker, "Radical Agitation Aimed at Negro Labor," June 14, 1919, quoted in ed. Hill, *Garvey Papers*, 1:433. It was true that Garvey communicated solidarity with many different nationalist movements, including those of Northern Ireland. For him, Black internationalism was not confined to what was already a broad notion of the Black nation or diaspora—it also drew from those with similar ideals and philosophies of liberation.
72. "Distribution of UNIA Branches Outside the United States, ca. 1926," in Martin, *Race First*, 16.
73. "UNIA Charter Unveiled in Puerto Padres," *Negro World*, February 19, 1921, NW: reel 1; "UNIA in Banes, Cuba Forging Ahead," *Negro World*, February 26, 1921, NW: reel 1.
74. B. G. Alfred, "Rousing Sunday Night in Havana," *Negro World*, February 19, 1921, NW: reel 1.
75. Printed (in Spanish) in *Sección en Español*, *Negro World*, March 19, 1921, NW: reel 1; translation: "Himno Bayamés," trans. J. Marin Varona (1899), University of Rochester Research, Eastman School of Music—Sibley Music Library, August 26, 2012, http://hdl.handle.net/1802/4195 (accessed May 5, 2013).
76. Maceo was incorporated into the UNIA's lexicon of diasporic heroes when in 1920 the organization unofficially named the third vessel in the Black Star Line enterprise the *Antonio Maceo*. Martin, *Race First*, 157.
77. Clifford L. Staten, *The History of Cuba* (Westport, CT: Greenwood, 2003), 53.
78. Guridy, "Feeling Diaspora in Harlem and Havana," 121.
79. Quoted in ibid., 135.
80. M.A. Figueroa, "Nuestra Raza," *Negro World*, December 3, 1921, NW: reel 1 (translation by the author).
81. Clarice G. Walters, "Gov. Colonel Alfredo Lora of Oriente, Cuba, Visits UNIA Meeting Amidst Tremendous Enthusiasm," *Negro World*, July 30, 1921, NW: reel 1.
82. Martin, *Race First*, 49.
83. Winston James, *Holding Aloft the Banner of Ethiopia: Caribbean Radicalism in Early Twentieth-Century America* (New York: Verso, 1998), 15.
84. Thomas C. Holt, *The Problem of Freedom: Race, Labor, and Politics in Jamaica and Britain, 1832–1938* (Baltimore: Johns Hopkins University Press, 1992), 356.

85. Ronald Harpelle, "Cross Currents in the Western Caribbean: Marcus Garvey and the UNIA in Central America," *Caribbean Studies* 31, no. 1 (January-June 2003): 39.

86. Ibid., 48, 49.

87. James, *Holding Aloft the Banner of Ethiopia*, 6, 78.

88. Alejo Carpentier, *Music in Cuba*, trans. Alan West-Duran (1946; Minneapolis: University of Minnesota Press, 2001), 259–60.

89. Jorge L. Giovannetti, "The Elusive Organization of 'Identity': Race, Religion, and Empire among Caribbean Migrants in Cuba," *Small Axe* 19 (February 2006): 8–11.

90. For a detailed accounting of this event and its consequences, see Frank A. Guridy, "'Enemies of the White Race': The Machadista State and the UNIA in Cuba," *Caribbean Studies* 31, no. 1 (January–June 2003): 107–37.

91. "Will White Cubans Support the Negro's Program for a Free Africa?," *Negro World*, March 26, 1921, NW: reel 1.

92. H. F. Campbell, "Cubans and 'Jamaiquanos' Idolize Morales for Fearless Utterances," *Negro World*, May 20, 1922, NW: reel 1.

93. Guridy, "'Enemies of the White Race,'" 110.

94. Tomás Fernández Robaina, "Marcus Garvey in Cuba: Urrutia, Cubans, and Black Nationalism," in eds. Lisa Brock and Digna Castañeda Fuertes, *Between Race and Empire: African-Americans and Cubans before the Cuban Revolution* (Philadelphia: Temple University Press, 1998), 124.

95. As with any organization, the locals were not without concerns. In 1923, James Cato of Division 194, Santiago de Cuba, wrote to *Negro World* to plead relief from "the assaults of many vicious and violent enemies within and without [the division]." James R. Cato, "Division 194 of Santiago de Cuba," *Negro World*, March 17, 1923, NW: reel 1.

96. Robaina, "Marcus Garvey in Cuba," 125.

97. Ethelbert Blackwood, "Eduardo V. Morales: An Appreciation," *Negro World*, June 17, 1922, NW: reel 1.

98. H. F. Campbell, "UNIA Not Organization of Africans, Haytians or 'Jamaiquanos,' Morales Tells Habana Hearers," *Negro World*, May 27, 1922, NW: reel: 1.

99. Rob. S. F. Blake, "Sunday School in Banes Oriente, Cuba, Renders a Cantata," *Negro World*, March 11, 1922, NW: reel 1 (emphasis added).

NOTES TO CHAPTER 2

1. H. C. McDowell to Frank Brewer, February 22, 1922, and H. C. McDowell, circular, February 7, 1930, quoted in Modupe Labode, "A Native Knows a Native: African American Missionaries' Writings about Angola, 1919–1940," *North Star: A Journal of African American Religious History* 4, no. 1 (Fall 2000): 5, 1.

2. James Weldon Johnson, "Race Prejudice and the Negro Artist" (1928), in ed. Sondra Kathryn Wilson, *The Selected Writings of James Weldon Johnson, vol. 2: Social, Political and Literary Essays* (New York: Oxford University Press, 1995), 397.

3. James Weldon Johnson, *Black Manhattan* (1930; New York: Da Capo, 1991), 135.

4. For histories of the NAACP, see in particular Gilbert Jonas, *Freedom's Sword: The NAACP and the Struggle Against Racism in America, 1909–1969* (New York: Routledge, 2004); Charles Flint Kellogg, *NAACP: A History of the National Association for the Advancement of Colored People* (Baltimore: Johns Hopkins University Press, 1967); B. Joyce Ross, *J.E. Spingarn and the Rise of the NAACP: 1911–1939* (New York: Scribner, 1972); Patricia Sullivan, *Lift Every Voice: The NAACP and the Making of the Civil Rights Movement* (New York: New Press, 2009).

5. Johnson, *Black Manhattan*, 143.

6. Kevin K. Gaines, *Uplifting the Race: Black Leadership, Politics, and Culture in the Twentieth Century* (Chapel Hill: University of North Carolina Press, 1996), 1–4.

7. Evelyn Brooks Higginbotham, *Righteous Discontent: The Women's Movement in the Black Baptist Church, 1880–1920* (Cambridge, MA: Harvard University Press, 1993).

8. James Weldon Johnson, *Along This Way: The Autobiography of James Weldon Johnson* (1933; New York: Da Capo Press, 2000), 309; Mary White Ovington, "How NAACP Began" (1914), reprinted on the official website of the NAACP, http://www.naacp.org/about/history/howbegan/ (accessed August 5, 2006).

9. W. C. Handy, *Father of the Blues: An Autobiography* (New York: Macmillan, 1941), 229.

10. Minutes of the Board Meeting of the NAACP, New York, NY, February 14, 1921, 4, National Association for the Advancement of Colored People (NAACP) Papers, Yale University, Microfilm: reel 1 (hereafter cited as NAACP Papers). Black Swan was the first Black-owned record label in the United States. Harry Pace founded the label in 1921 in New York City.

11. Mary White Ovington to "The Classmate," April 9, 1932, James Weldon Johnson Collection, Yale Collection of American Literature, Beinecke Rare Book and Manuscript Library, Yale University, series 1: box 8, folder 169 (hereafter cited as JWJ).

12. Rabbi Stephen S. Wise to James Weldon Johnson, March 2, 1928, JWJ, series 1: box 13, folder 311.

13. Johnson, *Along This Way*, 154–55.

14. Ibid., 156.

15. Richard A. Long, "A Weapon of My Song: The Poetry of James Weldon Johnson," *Phylon* 32, no. 4 (4th Qtr., 1971): 374.

16. James Weldon Johnson and J. Rosamond Johnson, eds., *The Books of American Negro Spirituals* (1925; New York: Viking Press, 1942).

17. Gilroy, *Black Atlantic*, 37–38.

18. Ibid., 31.

19. The three words on which the final I chord strikes are "(victory is) won," "(our bright star is) cast," and "(true to our native) land."

20. James Weldon Johnson, *Along This Way*, 152.

21. Ibid., 158.

22. Lucius R. Wyatt, "The Inclusion of Concert Music of African-American Composers in Music History Courses," *Black Music Research Journal* 16, no. 2 (Autumn 1996): 243.

23. Daphne Brooks, *Bodies in Dissent: Spectacular Performances of Race and Freedom, 1850–1910* (Durham, NC: Duke University Press, 2006), 224.

24. Sotiropoulos, *Staging Race*, 121.

25. Quoted in ibid., 42.

26. Krasner, *Resistance, Parody, and Double Consciousness*, 35.

27. Sondra Kathryn Wilson, "Introduction," in Johnson, *Along This Way*, xiv.

28. Milton C. Sernett, *Bound for the Promised Land: African American Religion and the Great Migration* (Durham, NC: Duke University Press, 1997), 37.

29. Johnson, *Along This Way*, 309.

30. Ibid.; Minutes of the Board Meeting of the NAACP, New York, NY, December 6, 1921, 3, NAACP Papers: reel 1.

31. Johnson, *Along This Way*, 314–15 (emphasis in original).

32. Ibid., 315.

33. Effie T. Battle to James Weldon Johnson, April 5, 1934, JWJ, series 1: box 3, folder 39.

34. Ron Eyerman and Andrew Jamison, *Music and Social Movements: Mobilizing Traditions in the Twentieth Century* (Cambridge: Cambridge University Press, 1998), 2.

35. Captolia T. Dent to James Weldon Johnson, February 24, 1932, and James Weldon Johnson to Captolia T. Dent, February 26, 1932, JWJ, series 1: box 6, folder 120.

36. Mabel Anderson to James Weldon Johnson, February 2, 1934, and James Weldon Johnson to Mabel Anderson, February 5, 1934, JWJ, series 1: box 2, folder 21.

37. Mrs. Lisbon C. Berry to James Weldon Johnson, May 21, 1933, and James Weldon Johnson to Mrs. Lisbon C. Berry, June 5, 1933, JWJ, series 1: box 3, folder 41.

38. Johnson, *Along This Way*, 155.

39. Mrs. L. H. Tyler to Edward B. Marks Company, February 14, 1934, JWJ, series 1: box 13, folder 311.

40. "The Star-Spangled Banner," *Wikipedia*, http://en.wikipedia.org/wiki/The_Star-Spangled_Banner (accessed August 26, 2006).

41. The official designation of "Lift Ev'ry Voice and Sing" as the Negro National Anthem lasted for decades and was noted on the official sheet music published by the Marks Company. Eventually the NAACP capitulated to concerns of patriotism and unity and requested a change to the song's unofficial title. In 1964 Marks Company President Herbert E. Marks wrote, "For many years it was known as the Negro National Anthem, but some time ago there was a protest from the N.A.A.C.P. pointing out that 'The Star Spangled Banner' is the National Anthem of American Negroes and asking us to change the description on our copies. From then on we have called it 'The Official Song of The N.A.A.C.P.,' having that distinguished organization's approval to do this." Herbert E. Marks to Rufus B. Easter, Jr., September 17, 1964, JWJ, series 1: box 12, folder 311. The contest between the two songs continued in various manifestations throughout the twentieth century and into the twenty-first as well.

42. Yasuichi Hikida to James Weldon Johnson, September 26, 1933, JWJ, series 1: box 9, folder 206.

43. Reginald Kearney, *African American Views of the Japanese: Solidarity or Sedition?* (Albany: State University of New York, 1998), xvii.

44. Historian Colin Grant notes that Garvey speculated within the pages of the *Negro World* that "the next war [following World War I] would be between the white and darker races, aided by the Japanese." Grant, *Negro with a Hat*, 125.

45. Kearney, *African American Views of the Japanese*, xxvi.

46. Ernest Allen, Jr., "Waiting for Tojo: The Pro-Japan Vigil of Black Missourians, 1932–1943," *Gateway Heritage* (Fall 1994): 39, 51.

47. Algernon Austin, "Rethinking Race and the Nation of Islam, 1930–1975," *Ethnic and Racial Studies* 26, no. 1 (2003): 56.

48. Ibid., 59, 58.

49. Nathaniel Deutsch, "'The Asiatic Black Man': An African American Orientalism?," *Journal of Asian American Studies* 4, no. 3 (October 2001): 198.

50. Yasuichi Hikida to James Weldon Johnson, September 26, 1933, JWJ, series 1: box 9, folder 206.

51. Edwards, *Practice of Diaspora*, 20, 5.

52. Yasuichi Hikida to James Weldon Johnson, September 26, 1933, JWJ, series 1: box 9, folder 206.

53. Ibid.

54. Reverend Koh Yuki to Masatane Mitani, June 4, 1933, JWJ, series 1: box 9, folder 206.

55. Yasuichi Hikida to James Weldon Johnson, September 26, 1933, JWJ, series 1: box 9, folder 206.

56. Paul Varley, *Japanese Culture*, 4th ed. (Honolulu: University of Hawai'i Press, 2000), 271.

57. Kenneth B. Pyle., *The Making of Modern Japan*, 2nd ed. (New York: Houghton Mifflin, 1996), 167, 184.

58. Varley, *Japanese Culture*, 296.

59. Kuei Chiu, "Asian Language Newspapers in the United States: History Revisited," *Chinese American Librarians Association E-Journal* 9 (November 15, 1996), http://cala-web.org/node/648 (accessed May 11, 2013).

60. Reginald Kearney, "The Pro-Japanese Utterances of W.E.B. Du Bois," *Contributions in Black Studies* 13, no. 1 (1995): 204.

61. Ibid., 201.

62. Quoted in ibid., 201.

63. Secretary of Japan Society (initials E. C. W.) to James Weldon Johnson, October 24, 1918, JWJ, series 1: box 11, folder 233.

64. "Institute of Pacific Relations," *Wikipedia*, http://en.wikipedia.org/wiki/Institute_of_Pacific_Relations (accessed October 26, 2010).

65. Johnson, *Along This Way*, 394.

66. Masao Kajimar to James Weldon Johnson, October 23, 1929, JWJ, series 1: box 12, folder 260.

67. Johnson's time as consul to Venezuela and Nicaragua as well as his extensive writings on Haiti after the 1915 U.S. occupation offer evidence of his global perspective on injustice, investment in bringing these conditions to light, and hopes for their eradication.

68. Johnson, *Along This Way*, 398 (emphasis in original).

69. W. E. B. Du Bois, "To the Nations of the World" in ed. David Levering Lewis, *W. E. B. Du Bois: A Reader* (New York: Henry Holt, 1995), 639.

70. Robin D. G. Kelley, *Hammer and Hoe: Alabama Communists during the Great Depression* (Chapel Hill: University of North Carolina Press, 1990), 116.

71. Yasuichi Hikida to James Weldon Johnson, September 26, 1933, JWJ, series 1: box 9, folder 206.

72. Ibid.

73. Ibid.

74. Ibid.

75. John Irwin to James Weldon Johnson, February 24, 1932, JWJ, series 1: box 7, folder 142.

76. James Weldon Johnson to John Irwin, February 26, 1932, JWJ, series 1: box 7, folder 142.

77. Johnson, *Along This Way*, 155.

78. James Weldon Johnson to Edward B. Marks Company, February 23, 1932, JWJ, series 1: box 13, folder 311.

79. Edward B. Marks to James Weldon Johnson, February 26, 1932, JWJ, series 1: box 12, folder 311.

80. James Weldon Johnson to Edward B. Marks Company, November 1, 1933, JWJ, series 1: box 13, folder 311.

81. James Weldon Johnson to Yasuichi Hikida, October 4, 1933, JWJ, series 1: box 9, folder 206.

82. James Weldon Johnson to Yasuichi Hikida, November 1, 1933, JWJ, series 1: box 9, folder 206.

83. James Weldon Johnson to Yasuichi Hikida, September 27, 1935, JWJ, series 1: box 9, folder 206.

84. Yasuichi Hikida to James Weldon Johnson, December 28, 1935, JWJ, series 1: box 9, folder 206.

85. Johnson did have a copy of the sheet music produced by Yuki with roman lettering in his possession but did not have a copy of the final publication.

86. Eric Lott, *Love and Theft: Blackface Minstrelsy and the American Working Class* (New York: Oxford University Press, 1995), 25.

87. Yonezo Hirayama (aka Yasuichi Hikida), "The World of Black People and the World of White People from the Perspective of Yellow People: Introduction of National Negro Anthem," *Ongaku Sekai* 8, no. 9 (September 1936): 92.

88. Ibid.

89. Ibid.

90. Ibid.

91. Japanese translation of "Lift Every Voice and Sing."
92. Kearney, *African American Views of the Japanese*, 84.
93. The Scottsboro case of 1931 involved nine young Black boys falsely accused of raping two white women aboard a train in Scottsboro, Alabama. The arrests and trials induced an international campaign for their freedom and racial justice, in large part due to the efforts of the Communist Party USA. Allen, "Waiting for Tojo," 47.
94. Kearney, *African American Views of the Japanese*, 83.
95. Sato Masaharu and Barak Kushner, "'Negro Propaganda Operations': Japan's Short-Wave Radio Broadcasts for World War II Black Americans," *Historical Journal of Film, Radio and Television* 19, no. 1 (1999): 15.
96. Kearney, *African American Views of the Japanese*, 152.
97. Joel V. Berreman, "Assumptions About America in Japanese War Propaganda to the United States," *American Journal of Sociology* 54, no. 2 (September 1948): 114.
98. Saul K. Padover, "Japanese Race Propaganda," *Public Opinion Quarterly* 7, no. 2 (Summer 1943): 19798. According to Padover, the Japanese broadcasted this information in Spanish to South America as well, thereby taking advantage of a broad of color alliance.
99. Quoted in Stanley Sandler, *Segregated Skies: All-Black Combat Squadrons of World War II* (Washington, DC: Smithsonian Institution Press, 1992), 63.
100. Gerald Horne, *Race War: White Supremacy and the Japanese Attack on the British Empire* (New York: New York University Press, 2004).
101. Ed Brooke, "Ed Brooke," in eds. Julian Bond and Sondra K. Wilson, *Lift Every Voice and Sing: A Celebration of the Negro National Anthem* (New York: Random House, 2000), 36.
102. "Unfortunately, since most broadcast records were lost or purposefully disposed of by the Japanese forces at the time of surrender [in 1945], there is no clear picture concerning the content of the actual short-wave broadcasts which had American Blacks as the target audience." Masaharu and Kushner, "'Negro Propaganda Operations,'" 17.
103. One of the most prominent examples of Afro-Asian political solidarity during the twentieth century was the Bandung Conference of Asian and African States that convened in Indonesia in 1955. This conference set a strong agenda for anticolonial revolutionaries and helped to inspire and mobilize a global political left. See chapter 3 and Cynthia A. Young, *Soul Power: Culture, Radicalism, and the Making of a Third-World Left* (Durham, NC: Duke University Press, 2006). For other examples of Afro-Asian connections, see Robeson Taj P. Frazier, *The East Is Black: Cold War China and the Black Radical Imagination* (Durham, NC: Duke University Press, forthcoming); Heike Raphael-Hernandez and Shannon Steen, eds., *Afro-Asian Encounters: Culture, History, Politics* (New York: New York University Press, 2006); Fred Ho and Bill Mullen, eds., *Afro Asia: Revolutionary Political and Cultural Connections Between African Americans and Asian Americans* (Durham, NC: Duke University

Press, 2008); Vijay Prashad, *Everybody Was Kung-Fu Fighting: Afro-Asian Connections and the Myth of Cultural Purity* (Boston: Beacon, 2001) and *Darker Nations.*

NOTES TO CHAPTER 3

1. Paul Robeson, "Paul Robeson's Message: Great Negro's View of the War," unidentified newspaper, n.d., Paul Robeson Collection, 1925–1956, 1943–1956, Schomburg Center, reel 2 (hereafter cited as PR).

2. "Labor Salutes the Armed Forces," program, New York State CIO, September 6, 1942, Lawrence Brown Papers, 1916–1972, Schomburg Center, reel 6 (hereafter cited as LB).

3. "Jo" in Ferber's novel became "Joe" in *Show Boat* the musical.

4. The original script—labeled #7430 by McMillin—outlined an Act 2 that reprised Robeson as an elderly Joe whose son, "a little pickaminny [*sic*]," would be advanced to adulthood in the form of Robeson playing himself and staging a concert recital of spirituals, flanked by a steady stream of chorus girls. In addition to being a psychoanalytic banquet, Robeson as Joe as father of Robeson is a dizzying portrayal of Black musical formations that disguises the tensions within the Kern/ Hammerstein composition of "Ol' Man River." Scott McMillin, "Paul Robeson, Will Vodery's 'Jubilee Singers,' and the Earliest Script of the Kern-Hammerstein *Show Boat,*" *Theatre Survey* 41, no. 2 (November 2000): 60.

5. Eslanda Goode Robeson to Lawrence Brown, March 20, 1928, LB: reel 3.

6. Paul Robeson to Lawrence Brown, April 19, 1928, reprinted in Paul Robeson, Jr., *The Undiscovered Paul Robeson: An Artist's Journey, 1898–1939* (New York: John Wiley, Inc., 2001), 150.

7. Geoffrey Block, "The Broadway Canon from *Show Boat* to *West Side Story* and the European Operatic Ideal," *Journal of Musicology* 11, no. 4 (Fall 1993): 527–28.

8. Thomas Dixon is most well known for his influence on the infamous 1915 D. W. Griffith film *Birth of a Nation*, which caused a national outcry from the Black community for its gross caricatures of Black people in the U.S. South. Boycotts of the film by the National Association for the Advancement of Colored People represent some of the earliest organizing by the U.S. Black community around negative stereotypes in American popular culture.

9. Hazel V. Carby, *Cultures in Babylon: Black Britain and African America* (New York: Verso, 1999), 147.

10. Edna Ferber, *Show Boat* (New York: Gossett & Dunlap, 1926), 31.

11. McMillin, "Paul Robeson, Will Vodery's 'Jubilee Singers,'" 62.

12. Ferber, *Show Boat*, 63.

13. Caribbean immigrant Bert Williams is perhaps the most iconic of these Black blackface performers. For a detailed account of his life and career, see Camille F. Forbes, *Introducing Bert Williams: Burnt Cork, Broadway, and the Story of America's First Black Star* (New York: Basic Civitas, 2008).

14. Ferber, *Show Boat*, 25.

15. Bethany Wood, "Ol' (Wo)man River? Broadway's Gendering of Edna Ferber's *Show Boat*," *Studies in Musical Theatre* 4, no. 3 (2010): 323.

16. Ferber, *Show Boat*, 120.

17. Jerome Kern and Oscar Hammerstein II, "Ol' Man River," performed by Paul Robeson and the Paul Whiteman Orchestra, 1928, CD JWJ 43-33, James Weldon Johnson Memorial Collection of Negro Arts and Letters, Irving S. Gilmore Music Library, Sterling Memorial Library, Yale University, New Haven.

18. Unknown author, *New York Evening Post*, January 26, 1926, LB: reel 8.

19. Jerome Kern and Oscar Hammerstein II, *Show Boat Song Book* (New York: Hal Leonard Corporation, 1927). All musical analysis is drawn from this version.

20. Eslanda Goode Robeson to Lawrence Brown, 1929, LB: reel 3.

21. Alexander Woollcott, "Ol' Man River—in Person: A Cosmopolitan Portrait," *Hearst's International—Cosmopolitan* (July 1933): 54, PR: reel 3.

22. Concert program, Theatre Royal, Drury Lane, London, England, 1929, LB: reel 4.

23. Concert program, Royal Albert Hall, London, England, December 1931, LB: reel 5.

24. Todd Decker, "'Do You Want to Hear a Mammy Song?': A Historiography of *Show Boat*," *Contemporary Theatre Review* 19, no. 1 (2009): 8.

25. Harry T. Burleigh, New York, NY, 1917, quoted in concert program, ca. 1941, LB: reel 7. This definition regularly appeared in Brown and Robeson programs during the 1920s and '30s.

26. Paul Robeson, *Here I Stand* (1958; Boston: Beacon, 1988), 49.

27. In 1936 a reporter wrote, "There were many old favourite songs, such as 'Swing Low, Sweet Chariot,' 'Didn't it Rain?' and 'Ol' Man River,' as well as others not so familiar, but they were all sung with real understanding of their character, and with that touch of almost childish simplicity, so typical of the negro [*sic*] race." Unknown author, "Trio of Artists: Celebrity Concert at Theatre Royal," *Irish Times*, February 3, 1936, LB: reel 8. This type of characterization— "childish" or childlike—was often applied to the spirituals to distinguish them from European "art" traditions. Robeson was similarly described as having an "incorruptible simplicity" early in his career. Woollcott, "Ol' Man River—in Person," 55.

28. Robeson, *Here I Stand*, 115.

29. Unknown author, "Paul Robeson Showed How Negro Songs Should Be Sung," *Montreal Daily Star*, October 14, 1935, LB: reel 7 (emphasis added).

30. Unknown author, "Art of Robeson: Establishing Mood in Song," *Belfast Telegraph*, March 28, 1929, LB: reel 7.

31. The song reappears on Robeson programs in 1941 in a musical theater set, not the spirituals set. Concert program, Portland, OR, November 15, 1941, LB: reel 5.

32. Unknown author, "Master Singer of Spirituals: Paul Robeson in Bradford," unidentified newspaper, 1939, LB: reel 7.

33. William R. Mitchell, "Paul Robeson Thrills Audience," *Pittsburgh Press*, December 4, 1929, LB: reel 8.

34. Concert program, New Brunswick, NJ, October 2, 1942, LB: reel 6.

35. In 1948, a columnist for the *Daily Worker* (New York) wrote to Hammerstein to encourage him to omit "all the Uncle Tom Business, the Negro as shiftless, lazy good-for-nothing—the Negro as the object of patronizing ridicule." Quoted in Decker, "'Do You Want to Hear a Mammy Song?,'" 10.

36. J. A. Rogers, *Amsterdam News*, October 3, 1928, quoted in Martin Baum Duberman, *Paul Robeson* (New York: Knopf, 1988), 114.

37. Unknown author, *Afro-American*, n.d., PR: reel 2. The word "darky" replaced "nigger" within the song lyrics. The constant amendment of this particular text ("nigger" to "darky" to "colored folk") signals the changing political identifications of Black Americans throughout the run of the show.

38. Decker, "'Do You Want to Hear a Mammy Song?'"

39. Duberman, *Paul Robeson*, 170–71.

40. Robeson, *Here I Stand*, 32.

41. Ibid., 32.

42. Ibid., 33. For more on Eslanda Goode Robeson's rich intellectual trajectory and radical politic, see Barbara Ransby, *Eslanda: The Large and Unconventional Life of Mrs. Paul Robeson* (New Haven: Yale University Press, 2013).

43. Gabriel O. Olusanya, *The West African Students' Union and the Politics of Decolonisation, 1925–1958* (Ibadan: Daystar Press, 1982), 6, 1.

44. Paul Robeson, "Negroes—Don't Ape the Whites," *Daily Herald*, January 5, 1935, PR: reel 2.

45. Paul Robeson, "How I Discovered Africa," in ed. Roberta Yancy Dent, *Paul Robeson, Tributes, Selected Writings* (New York: Paul Robeson Archives Inc., 1976), 68 (emphasis in original).

46. By 1930 the Labour Party had held two consecutive minorities within government, signaling their growing prominence within Parliament.

47. In 1935 and 1936 Robeson was identified as a patron of WASU on its official list of officers. Olusanya, *West African Students' Union*, 107.

48. Laura Tabili, *"We Ask for British Justice": Workers and Racial Difference in Late Imperial Britain* (Ithaca, NY: Cornell University Press, 1994), 42.

49. Duberman, *Paul Robeson*, 179.

50. Dianne Frost, *Work and Community among West African Migrant Workers* (Liverpool: Liverpool University Press, 1999), 77.

51. Robeson, *Here I Stand*, 32.

52. Colin J. Davis, *Waterfront Revolts: New York and London Dockworkers, 1946–61* (Urbana: University of Illinois Press, 2003), 14.

53. Paul Gilroy, *There Ain't No Black in the Union Jack: The Cultural Politics of Race and Nation* (Chicago: University of Chicago Press, 1991).

54. Gretchen Holbrook Gerzina, "Mobility in Chains: Freedom of Movement in the Early Black Atlantic," *South Atlantic Quarterly* 100, no. 1 (2002): 44.

55. Quoted in ibid., 48.

56. Paul Robeson, unpublished speech, ca. 1937, p. 2, PR: reel 1.

57. Duberman, *Paul Robeson*, 172–73.

58. Penny Von Eschen, *Race Against Empire: Black Americans and Anti-colonialism* (Ithaca, NY: Cornell University Press, 1997), 8.

59. Robeson would revive his role in *Show Boat* on Broadway in New York in 1932, in the film version in 1936, and in a run in Los Angeles in 1940.

60. Robin D. G. Kelley, "Introduction," in C. L. R. James, *A History of Pan-African Revolt* (Chicago: Charles H. Kerr, 1995), 4.

61. Von Eschen, *Race Against Empire*, 12.

62. Scott Reynolds Nelson, *Steel Drivin' Man: John Henry, the Untold Story of an American Legend* (New York: Oxford University Press, 2006).

63. The Black Codes (of 1865) were used to enforce a white supremacist social order in the U.S. South after Emancipation. These codes controlled Black social and physical mobility through curfew laws, work restrictions, and other personal and public limitations that ultimately translated into the de jure and de facto Jim Crow laws of the twentieth century.

64. Lawrence Brown, *Six Negro Folk Songs* (New York, 1943), LB: reel 4.

65. Mindy Thompson, *The National Negro Labor Council: A History* (New York: American Institute for Marxist Studies, 1978), 3 (emphasis added).

66. Ronald D. Scofield, "Rich Performance Given by Robeson to Big Gathering," *Sacramento Bee*, March 8, 1943, LB: reel 8.

67. Paul Robeson, "Statement by Paul Robeson," press release, May 3, 1954, PR: reel 2.

68. Robeson, "Negroes—Don't Ape the Whites."

69. Steven Fraser, *Labor Will Rule: Sidney Hillman and the Rise of American Labor* (New York: Free Press, 1991).

70. Henry W. Simon, "Robeson Returns to Carnegie Hall," *New York World Telegram*, October 7, 1940, LB: reel 8.

71. William L. Doudna, "Notes for You," *Wisconsin State Journal*, January 24, 1946, LB: reel 8.

72. Evans Clinchy, "Paul Robeson Sings 8 Scheduled Tunes, Plus 6 Encores," *Hartford Times*, November 17, 1952, PR: reel 4.

73. This text was not used in every performance.

74. C.H.T., "A Protest by Robeson," *Kansas City Times*, February 18, 1942, LB: reel 8.

75. Lee Goodman, "Music Review: Paul Robeson Knocks Throng for Loop in Concert at Wrigley Field," *Los Angeles, California News*, October 1, 1949, PR: reel 4.

76. Conrad Clark, "British Hail Robeson on His 70th Birthday," 1968, LB: reel 7.

77. Paul Robeson, *Paul Robeson Speaks to Youth* (pamphlet, New York, 1950), 12, PR: reel 2.

78. Event program, National Association for the Advancement of Colored People, Spingarn Ceremony, Hotel Biltmore, New York, NY, October 18, 1945, LB: reel 6.

79. The original Red Scare of 1917–20 was marked by an anticommunist panic that developed in response to the Bolshevik victory in Russia and other changes in U.S. society. The influx of large numbers of Eastern European immigrants, the development of the radical Industrial Workers of the World (IWW), and the public prominence of socialist intellectuals and activists, including Eugene

V. Debs—who ran for president of the United States on the Socialist Party of America ticket a total of five times between 1900 and 1920—contributed to the national panic.

80. W. Alphaeus Hunton, "A Note on the Council on African Affairs (Appendix D)," in Robeson, *Here I Stand*, 117.

81. Von Eschen, *Race Against Empire*, 20.

82. Paul Robeson, "Fight We Must," in ed. Dent, *Paul Robeson, Tributes*, 109.

83. Leslie Matthews, *New York Age*, September 4, 1949, quoted in the Westchester Committee for a Fair Inquiry into the Peekskill Violence, *Peekskill U.S.A.: A Documentary Report (Aug. 27; Sept. 4, 1949)* (Peekskill, October 1949), 19, PR: reel 3.

84. *New York Age*, September 10, 1949, quoted in the Westchester Committee for a Fair Inquiry into the Peekskill Violence, *Peekskill U.S.A.*, 3, PR: reel 3.

85. Alec Wilkinson, "The Protest Singer: Pete Seeger and American Folk Music," *New Yorker*, April 17, 2006, reprint, http://www.peteseeger.net/new_yorker041706.htm (accessed April 5, 2007).

86. The debate over Robeson and his politics was a heated one in the Black community. Major leaders discussed their positions publicly, often disagreeing with each other. In "Paul Robeson: Right or Wrong," (former) NAACP leaders W. E. B. Du Bois and Walter White argued their positions, with Du Bois offering support and White registering disapproval. "Paul Robeson: Right or Wrong," *Negro Digest* (March 1950): 8–18, PR: reel 3.

87. Paul Robeson, "My Father Was a Slave," in ed. Dent, *Paul Robeson, Tributes*, 89–90.

88. Tony Perucci, "'The Red Mask of Sanity: Paul Robeson, HUAC, and the Sound of Cold War Performance," *TDR: The Drama Review* 53, no. 4 (Winter 2009): 30.

89. Michael Denning, *The Cultural Front: The Laboring of American Culture* (New York: Verso, 1998).

90. Ibid., 35, 135.

91. Quoted in Westchester Committee, *Peekskill, U.S.A.*, PR: reel 3.

92. For studies in dialogue with the Black Popular Front, see Von Eschen, *Race Against Empire*; Martha Biondi, *To Stand and Fight: The Struggle for Civil Rights in Postwar New York* (Cambridge, MA: Harvard University Press, 2003); and Minkah Makalani, *In the Cause of Freedom: Radical Black Internationalism from Harlem to London, 1917–1939* (Chapel Hill: University of North Carolina Press, 2011).

93. Mark B. Salter, "Passports, Mobility, and Security: How Smart Can the Border Be?," *International Studies in Perspectives* 5 (2004): 72.

94. Edwards, *Practice of Diaspora*, 239 (emphasis added).

95. Paul Robeson, "Africa and the Commemoration of Negro History," *Spotlight on Africa* (January 1955): 18, PR: reel 7.

96. Radhika Viyas Mongia, "Race, Nationality, Mobility: A History of the Passport," *Public Culture* 11, no. 3 (1999): 528 (emphasis in original).

97. Ibid., 529.

98. Thompson, *National Negro Labor Council*, 9.

99. Ibid., 65.

100. Ewart Guinier, untitled speech, in "Get on Board the Freedom Train," NNLC Convention 1951, PR: reel 8.

101. Paul Robeson, "How Not to Build Canadian-American Friendship," in ed. Philip S. Foner, *Paul Robeson Speaks: Writings, Speeches, Interviews, 1918–1974* (New York: Brunner/Mazel, 1978), 312.

102. Ian Shaw, liner notes to *Paul Robeson: The Peace Arch Concerts*, 7 (compact disk, Folk Era Records, PRO1442D, 1998).

103. Lisa Gitelman describes "telepresence" as the "feeling that there's someone else out there on the other end of the line." In this scenario, it was someone who was forbidden from being physically present, adding intrigue and urgency to the person's voice and reception. Gitelman, *Always Already New: Media, History, and the Data of Culture* (Cambridge, MA: MIT Press, 2006), 4.

104. Afro-American Museum of Detroit, *Paul Robeson—In Conflict vs. the U.S. Immigration Service at the Peace Arch, Blaine, WA, 1952*, video documentary, 1977, quoted in Shaw, liner notes to *Paul Robeson*, 9, 10.

105. A. Hayes and E. Robinson, "Joe Hill," performed by Paul Robeson, 1952, *Paul Robeson: The Peace Arch Concerts* (compact disk, Folk Era Records, PRO1442D, 1998) (emphasis added).

106. Paul Robeson, "Intro. to 'No More Auction Block,'" performed by Paul Robeson, 1952, *Paul Robeson: The Peace Arch Concerts* (emphasis added).

107. Mark Katz, *Capturing Sound: How Technology Has Changed Music* (Berkeley: University of California Press, 2004), 40, 40–41.

108. Prashad, *Darker Nations*, 34.

109. Kweku Ampiah, *The Political and Moral Imperatives of the Bandung Conference of 1955: The Reactions of the US, UK and Japan* (Kent, UK: Global Oriental, 2007), 35.

110. Adam Clayton Powell, Jr., *Adam by Adam: The Autobiography of Adam Clayton Powell, Jr.* (New York: Dial Press, 1971), 116, 103, 118.

111. W. E. B. Du Bois, *Spotlight on Africa*, January 1955, PR: reel 7.

112. For a detailed accounting of the intimate relationship shared between the two men, see Murali Balaji, *The Professor and the Pupil: The Politics and Friendship of W.E.B. Du Bois and Paul Robeson* (New York: Nation Books, 2007).

113. Duberman, *Paul Robeson*, 431.

114. Paul Robeson, untitled speech at Bandung Conference, 1955, PR: reel 7.

115. In an undated, handwritten list of priorities most likely composed after his passport revocation, Robeson made special notice of his ambition "[i]n the cultural field—making records, concerts. . . . Will send special albums to the U.S.S.R. and People's Democracies + to other countries." Paul Robeson, "III," n.d., PR: reel 2.

116. Peter Manuel, *Cassette Culture: Popular Music and Technology in North India* (Chicago: University of Chicago Press, 1993), 2.

117. Pamela L. Caughie, "Audible Identities: Passing and Sound Technologies," *Humanities Research* 16, no. 1 (2010): 93.

118. Attali, *Noise*, 7.

119. Robeson, "Intro. to 'No More Auction Block.'"

120. L. van Beethoven and J. D. Bacon, "Hymn to Nations," performed by Paul Robeson, 1953, http://www.youtube.com/watch?v=bMA5A17IZSo (accessed May 6, 2013).

121. Robeson, untitled speech at Bandung Conference.

122. Prashad, *Darker Nations*, xv.

123. In his canonical text, *Black Skin, White Masks*, Martinican intellectual and revolutionary Frantz Fanon discusses his objectification as a Black colonial body: "[T]he Other fixes me with his gaze, his gestures and attitude, the same way you fix a preparation with a dye. I lose my temper. . . . Nothing doing. I explode. Here are the fragments put together by another me." Frantz Fanon, *Black Skin, White Masks*, trans. Richard Philcox (1952; New York: Grove Press, 2008), 89.

124. The movement employed the violence of police repression to bolster their moral higher ground, while the police state announced those same scenes as the consequences of continued rebellion. For a thorough study of the role of photography in African American justice movements, see Leigh Raiford, *Imprisoned in a Luminous Glare: Photography and the African American Freedom Struggle* (Chapel Hill: University of North Carolina Press, 2011).

125. Harry Belafonte, Chubb Fellow Lecture, Battell Chapel, Yale University, November 1, 2005.

126. Paul Robeson, "I Am the Same Paul," in ed. Dent, *Paul Robeson, Tributes*, 97 (emphasis in original).

NOTES TO CHAPTER 4

1. Concert program, Highlander Folk School, May 10, 1942, Lawrence Brown Papers, 1910–1972, Schomburg Center, reel 6.

2. Brandi Amanda Neal, "'We Shall Overcome': From Black Church Music to Freedom Song" (master's thesis, University of Pittsburgh, 2003), iv.

3. Bernice Johnson Reagon, "Let the Church Sing 'Freedom,'" *Black Music Research Journal* 7 (1987): 108 (emphasis added).

4. Lawrence W. Levine, *Black Culture and Black Consciousness: Afro-American Folk Thought from Slavery to Freedom* (New York: Oxford University Press, 1977), 6.

5. C. Vann Woodward, *The Strange Career of Jim Crow* (1962; New York: Oxford University Press, 2001), 11.

6. Robert Coles, *Farewell to the South* (Boston: Little, Brown, 1972), 83–84.

7. Ernest Lander, *A History of South Carolina, 1865–1960* (Chapel Hill: University of North Carolina Press, 1960), 167.

8. Gilroy, *Black Atlantic*, 89.

9. William E. B. Du Bois, *The Souls of Black Folk* (1903; Boston: Bedford Books, 1997), 185–86.

10. Ibid., 192–93.

11. Samuel A. Floyd, Jr., *The Power of Black Music: Interpreting Its History from Africa to the United States* (New York: Oxford University Press, 1995), 46 (emphasis in original).

12. Philip S. Foner, *Organized Labor and the Black Worker, 1619–1973* (New York: Praeger, 1974), 231.
13. Ibid., 231.
14. Brenda McCallum, "The Gospel of Black Unionism," in ed. Archie Green, *Songs about Work: Essays in Occupational Culture for Richard A Reuss* (Bloomington: Indiana University Press, 1993), 113.
15. Ibid., 117.
16. Quoted in Bernice Johnson Reagon, "Songs of the Civil Rights Movement, 1955–1965: A Study in Culture History" (Ph.D. diss., Howard University, 1975), 66.
17. Jon Michael Spencer, *Protest & Praise: Sacred Music of Black Religion* (Minneapolis: Augsburg Fortress Press, 1990), 85.
18. Horace Clarence Boyer, "Charles Albert Tindley: Progenitor of Black-American Gospel Music," *Black Perspective in Music* 11, no. 2 (Autumn 1983): 109.
19. Ibid., 113, 114.
20. Neal, "'We Shall Overcome,'" 6–9.
21. Gilroy, *Black Atlantic*, 89.
22. Reagon, "Songs of the Civil Rights Movement," 65.
23. Neal notes that the melody of "I'll Be Alright" is different from "We Shall Overcome" in the first two phrases but is otherwise consistent. Neal, "'We Shall Overcome,'" 10.
24. See, for example, James Fuld, *The Book of World Famous Music: Classical, Popular and Folk*, 5th ed. (New York: Crown, 2000).
25. Reagon, "Songs of the Civil Rights Movement," 25.
26. Wyatt Tee Walker, *"Somebody's Calling My Name": Black Sacred Music and Social Change* (Valley Forge, PA: Judson Press, 1979), 47.
27. Robbie Lieberman, *"My Song Is My Weapon": People's Songs, American Communism, and the Politics of Culture, 1930–50* (Urbana: University of Illinois Press, 1989), 72.
28. Reagon, "Songs of the Civil Rights Movement," 22.
29. "Over 70,000 Workers Idle in U.S. Strikes," *News and Courier* (Charleston, SC), June 22, 1945, 1.
30. "Most of Puerto Rican Sugar Workers Strike," *News and Courier*, February 13, 1945, 1.
31. "Soldiers Man Trucks during Chicago Strike," *News and Courier*, June 19, 1945, 1.
32. Eldred E. Prince, Jr. and Robert R. Simpson, *Long Green: The Rise and Fall of Tobacco in South Carolina* (Athens: University of Georgia Press, 2000), xv; Lander, *History of South Carolina*, 115.
33. Prince and Simpson, *Long Green*, xvi.
34. "The American Tobacco Company," http://www.smokershistory.com/ATC.htm (accessed October 12, 2007).
35. *The American Tobacco Company and Its Service to the Public: Some Interesting Facts About an American Business* (American Tobacco Company, July 1940), 7.
36. *Sold American! The First Fifty Years* (American Tobacco Company, 1954), 96.

37. The National Urban League, "'A Study of the Social and Economic Conditions of the Negro Population, Charleston, South Carolina' conducted for The Charleston Welfare Council by The National Urban League (for Social Service Among Negroes) *Community Relations Project*" (New York: 1946), 64, 1 (hereafter cited as National Urban League, "Charleston Study").

38. Ibid., 8, 9, 11.

39. Vicki L. Ruiz, *Cannery Women, Cannery Lives: Mexican Women, Unionization, and the California Food Processing Industry, 1930–1950* (Albuquerque: University of New Mexico Press, 1987), xvii.

40. Eleanor T. Royer, "Union Agreements in the Tobacco Industry," Bulletin No. 847 (Washington, DC: U.S. Department of Labor, Bureau of Labor Statistics, January 1945), 2.

41. Robert Rodgers Korstad, *Civil Rights Unionism: Tobacco Workers and the Struggle for Democracy in the Mid-Twentieth-Century South* (Chapel Hill: University of North Carolina Press, 2003), 3.

42. *The American Tobacco Company and Its Service to the Public*, 42.

43. Ibid., 45.

44. Quoted in Reagon, "Songs of the Civil Rights Movement," 72.

45. "White Cigar Makers Stick to Their Jobs," *News and Courier*, October 4, 1945, 1, 7.

46. Glenda E. Gilmore, *Gender and Jim Crow: Women and the Politics of White Supremacy in North Carolina, 1896–1920* (Chapel Hill: University of North Carolina Press, 1996), 3.

47. U.S. Department of Labor, Wage and Hour Division, "The Tobacco Industry: Cigarettes, Chewing Tobacco, Smoking Tobacco and Snuff" (Washington, DC, December 1941), 13.

48. Stuart Hall, "Reconstruction Work," *Ten.8* 16 (1984): 2.

49. Gender studies scholar Sarah Haley argues that the construction and maintenance of the punishment regime in the post-Emancipation South served to further obscure and queer the gender category of "woman" for the African descended, placing them outside of femininity and womanhood. These exclusions were central tenants of Jim Crow modernity. See Sarah Haley, "'Like I Was a Man': Chain Gangs, Gender, and the Domestic Carceral Sphere in Jim Crow Georgia," *Signs: Journal of Women in Culture and Society* 39, no. 1 (2013): 53–77.

50. "Tobacco Workers Seek Higher Pay, Ask Public Support," *News and Courier*, September 27, 1945, 14.

51. "Union May Pass Out Leaflets but Not Litter Street, City Rules," *News and Courier*, October 24, 1945, 1.

52. "Tobacco Union Opens Intensified Boycott Here," *News and Courier*, November 2, 1945, 6-B.

53. "American Tobacco Plants Strike for 25 Cent Raise," *FTA News*, November 1, 1945, 4.

54. "Tobacco Union Opens Intensified Boycott Here."

55. Ernest Obadele-Starks, *Black Unionism in the Industrial South* (College Station: Texas A&M University Press, 2000), 40.

56. Ibid., 53.

57. "1,200 Strikers to Picket Tobacco Plant Here Monday," *News and Courier*, November 3, 1945, 1.

58. "Tobacco Strike May Soon Be Ended CIO Leader Says," *News and Courier*, November 15, 1945, 8.

59. The criminalization of Black women was a tactic employed beyond the U.S. South; as historian Cheryl Hicks documents, these practices were present in New York City and followed a similar Jim Crow logic, which masqueraded itself as a necessary response to urban decline. The practices of surveillance and detention inflicted upon Black women, particularly Black women laborers, were therefore nationally reproduced structures of oppression. Cheryl D. Hicks, *Talk with You Like a Woman: African American Women, Justice, and Reform in New York, 1890–1935* (Chapel Hill: University of North Carolina Press, 2010). See also Sarah Haley, "Engendering Captivity: Black Women and Convict Labor in Georgia, 1865–1938" (Ph.D. diss., Yale University, 2009).

60. "Tobacco Strikers Pass Resolution," *News and Courier*, November 27, 1945, 11.

61. "Plant Manager Pleased at Cigar Output," *News and Courier*, January 15, 1946, 12; "Union Asks Public to Aid Strikers Here," *News and Courier*, January 18, 1946, 10.

62. "FEPC Bill Would Enable Hitler to Get a Job, Senate Hears," *News and Courier*, January 21, 1946, 1.

63. Gene Roberts and Hank Klibanoff, *The Race Beat: The Press, the Civil Rights Struggle, and the Awakening of a Nation* (New York: Knopf, 2006), 37.

64. Denning, *Cultural Front*, 353.

65. Quoted in Reagon, "Songs of the Civil Rights Movement," 74.

66. McCallum, "Gospel of Black Unionism," 115.

67. "McGinnis Says 300,000 Cigars Made Daily, Over 400 at Jobs," *News and Courier*, December 11, 1945, 1.

68. Biondi, *To Stand and Fight*, 8.

69. Unsigned, "Pickets Out of Character," *News and Courier*, March 16, 1946, letters to the editor, 4.

70. "NMU Gives Job Preference for Picket Duty at Cigar Plant," *News and Courier*, January 30, 1946, 12.

71. Ruiz, *Cannery Women, Cannery Lives*, xviii.

72. "Tobacco Strike Parade Today at White House," *News and Courier*, February 19, 1946, 1.

73. "The Strike Solid," *FTA News*, December 15, 1945, 5.

74. Ibid.

75. "Union Asks Public to Aid Strikers Here," *News and Courier*, January 18, 1946, 10.

76. Mary Notwen, "NMU on Picket Line," *News and Courier*, February 1, 1946, letters to the editor, 4.

77. A follow-up article on the Trenton workers was published the week following the Local 15 agreement. "Tobacco Workers Return to Jobs at Trenton Plant," *News and Courier*, April 4, 1946, 8.

78. National Urban League, "Charleston Study," 10.

79. Kelley, *Freedom Dreams*, ix.

80. *FTA News*, July 15, 1947, 8.

81. Aimee Isgrig Horton, *The Highlander Folk School: A History of Its Major Programs, 1932–1961* (New York: Carlson, 1989), 79, 93, 104.

82. Ibid., 117, 120.

83. Terese M. Volk, "Little Red Songbooks: Songs for the Labor Force of America," *Journal of Research in Music Education* 49, no. 1 (Spring 2001): 42.

84. Horton, *Highlander Folk School*, 148.

85. Peter S. Scholtes, "Something about That Songs Haunts You," *City Pages Blog* (Minneapolis/St. Paul), June 9, 2006, http://blogs.citypages.com/pscholtes/2006/06/something_about.php (accessed April 23, 2007).

86. Quoted in Reagon, "Songs of the Civil Rights Movement," 74.

87. John M. Glen, *Highlander: No Ordinary School* (Lexington: University of Kentucky Press, 1988), 102.

88. Local 15 member Isiah Bennett recalled, "The whites would never sing [on the picket line in Charleston]." Quoted in Reagon, "Songs of the Civil Rights Movement," 75.

89. Quoted in Reagon, "Songs of the Civil Rights Movement," 76.

90. Reagon, "Songs of the Civil Rights Movement," 65–66.

91. Hardeep Phull, *Story Behind the Protest Song: A Reference Guide to the 50 Songs That Changed the 20th Century* (Westport, CT: Greenwood, 2008), 2.

92. Horton, *Highlander Folk School*, 148. In his recollection of the song's formation, Pete Seeger admits that he is unsure who changed the line from "we *will* overcome" to "we *shall* overcome," saying, "It could have been me, but it might have been Septima Clarke, the director of education at Highlander. She always preferred 'shall,' since it opens up the voice and sings better." This admission serves again to only partially acknowledge the central role that Black women played in the development of the anthem that we know today. Pete Seeger, *Where Have All the Flowers Gone? A Singalong Memoir* (Bethlehem, PA: Sing Out Corporation, 2009), 33.

93. Guy Carawan, "Introduction," in eds. Candie Carawan and Guy Carawan, *We Shall Overcome! Songs of the Southern Freedom Movement* (New York: Oak Publications, 1963), 8.

94. Guy Carawan and Candie Carawan, eds., *Sing for Freedom: The Story of the Civil Rights Movement through Its Songs* (Bethlehem, PA: Sing Our Corporation, 1990), 12.

95. Seeger, *Where Have all the Flowers Gone?*, 33.

96. Phull, *Story Behind the Protest Song*, 4.

97. Literary scholar Bryan Wagner argues that instead of actually hearing Black folk music, collectors of Black culture in the early twentieth century heard "the residue from personification, the trace" of those performers and musicians. Bryan Wagner, *Disturbing the Peace: Black Culture and the Police Power after Slavery* (Cambridge, MA: Harvard University Press, 2009), 57.

98. Trad., "We Shall Overcome," performed in Hattiesburg, Mississippi, 1964, *Voices of the Civil Rights Movement: Black American Freedom Songs, 1960–1966*, side 6 (vinyl, Smithsonian Institution, R023A-F, 1980).

99. Spencer, *Praise & Protest*, 84.

NOTES TO CHAPTER 5

1. Ruth Feldstein, "'I Don't Trust You Anymore': Nina Simone, Culture, and Black Activism in the 1960s," *Journal of American History* 91, no. 4 (March 2005): 1353.

2. Quoted in Sylvia Hampton with David Nathan, *Nina Simone: Break Down and Let It All Out* (London: Sanctuary, 2004), 45 (emphasis in original).

3. Craig Werner, *A Change Is Gonna Come: Music, Race & the Soul of America* (New York: Penguin, 1998), 173.

4. Feldstein, "'I Don't Trust You Anymore,'" 1352.

5. Quoted in Hampton with Nathan, *Nina Simone*, 144.

6. Brian Ward, *Just My Soul Responding: Rhythm and Blues, Black Consciousness, and Race Relations* (Berkeley: University of California Press, 1998), 11.

7. Daphne A. Brooks, "Nina Simone's Triple Play," *Callaloo* 34, no. 1 (2011): 177–79.

8. Ibid., 178.

9. Then chairman of the Student Nonviolent Coordinating Committee (SNCC), Carmichael called for "black power" in a 1966 speech days after the attack of James Meredith, who marched in his attempts to integrate the University of Mississippi.

10. Nina Simone with Stephen Cleary, *I Put a Spell on You: The Autobiography of Nina Simone* (New York: Pantheon Books, 1991), 89.

11. Ibid., 90, 91.

12. N. Simone, "Mississippi Goddam," performed by Nina Simone, 1964, *Nina Simone: Anthology*, disc 1 (compact disk, RCA/BMG, B00009PJPJ, 2003). "Mississippi Goddam" is written in the style of the Broadway musical, a genre known for a "reflexive" quality that marks performances as particularly capable of delivering critique and instruction; "[t]he musical show offers a characteristically open, direct and ideologically unapologetic expression of the ideals, dreams, anxieties, feelings, fulfillments and frustrations of its audience." Paul Filmer, Val Rimmer, and Dave Walsh, "*Oklahoma!* Ideology and Politics in the Vernacular Tradition of the American Musical," *Popular Music* 18, no. 3 (1999): 381–82.

13. Simone speeds up the civil rights clock, arguing, "This whole country is full of lies / You all gonna die and die like flies / I don't trust you anymore / You keep on sayin' 'go slow.'" She insists that the demand to slow down is exactly the problem: Simone: "Desegregation." / *Chorus*: "Too slow!" / Simone: "Mass participation." / *Chorus*: "Too slow!" / Simone: "Unification." / *Chorus*: "Too slow!" She disrupts the incremental steps proposed and maintained by the political infrastructure of the white South and instead demands movement paced by her clock.

14. Simone with Cleary, *I Put a Spell on You*, 90.

15. N. Simone, "Four Women," performed by Nina Simone, 1965, *Nina Simone: Anthology*, disc 1 (compact disk, RCA/BMG, B00009PJPJ, 2003).

16. Hortense J. Spillers, "Mama's Baby, Papa's Maybe: An American Grammar Book," *Diacritics* 17, no. 2 (Summer 1987): 65.

17. Simone with Cleary, *I Put a Spell on You*, 117.

18. Tammy L. Kernodle, "'I Wish I Know How It Would Feel to Be Free': Nina Simone and the Redefining of the Freedom Song of the 1960s," *Journal of the Society for American Music* 2, no. 3 (2008): 312.

19. Combahee River Collective, "A Black Feminist Statement," in ed. Beverly Guy-Sheftall, *Words of Fire: An Anthology of African-American Feminist Thought* (New York: New Press, 1995), 233.

20. Historians Dayo Gore and Erik McDuffie separately document the long history of Black women's radical and leftist activity within the Communist Party USA, Congress of Industrial Organizations, and other anti-imperialist and activist organizations. The demands made by many of these women to overthrow (hetero)patriarchy, capitalism, and racism throughout the period of decolonialism and the Cold War carried over into the next generation as the elder women continued to mentor, write, and advise generations throughout the twentieth century. Dayo F. Gore, *Radicalism at the Crossroads: African American Women Activists in the Cold War* (New York: New York University Press, 2011) and Erik S. McDuffie, *Sojourning for Freedom: Black Women, American Communism, and the Making of Black Left Feminism* (Durham, NC: Duke University Press, 2011).

21. Kimberly Springer, *Living for the Revolution: Black Feminist Organizations, 1968–1980* (Durham, NC: Duke University Press, 2005), 4, 5.

22. Public radio stations on the East Coast of the United States were met with a flurry of responses when "Four Women" was released. While the song continued to play in New York City, a jazz station in Philadelphia was concerned by critical calls from listeners. Station manager Dolly Banks pulled the song from rotation "after reading an article in a local paper which said that the song was insulting to Negroes." Not surprisingly, the vignette that induced the most vitriol was that of Peaches. Earl Calwell, "Nina Simone's Lyrics Stir Storm of Protest," *New York Post*, September 2, 1966, Simone Clippings, 1925–1974, Schomburg Center (hereafter cited as Clippings). Simone's explicit mention of slavery and defiant, violent reaction to it offered too close a proximity to the history that the country struggled to dismiss, and too militant a posture in the context of the Civil Rights Movement as it progressed in 1966. As Spillers documents, "[T]he familiarity of [the slavery] narrative does nothing to appease the hunger of recorded memory, nor does the persistence of the repeated rob these well-known, oft-told events of their power, even now, to startle. In a very real sense, every writing as revision makes the 'discovery' all over again." Spillers, "Mama's Baby, Papa's Maybe," 68–69.

23. Simone with Cleary, *I Put a Spell on You*, 96.

24. August Meier and Elliot Rudwick, *CORE: A Study in Civil Rights Movement, 1942–1968* (1973; Urbana: University of Illinois Press, 1975), 405.

25. August Meier, "New Currents in the Civil Rights Movement," 1963, pamphlet, Congress of Racial Equality Records, Wisconsin Historical Society, series 1: box 6, folder 10 (hereafter cited as CORE).

26. Muste's mark on FOR specifically and the Civil Rights Movement in general is most thoroughly realized in his brainchild, the sit-in. During the 1940s, Muste suggested that FOR combine Mahatma Gandhi's nonviolent *satyagraha* with the sit-*down* protest technique of the Detroit automobile workers under the United Auto Workers union (UAW-CIO), thereby developing the sit-*in*.

27. James Farmer, *Lay Bare the Heart: An Autobiography of the Civil Rights Movement* (New York: Arbor House, 1985), 80.

28. Ibid., 104.

29. Ibid., 185.

30. Ibid., 187, James Farmer to Guy Carawan, January 12, 1962, CORE, series 1: box 5, folder 5.

31. Robert Brookins Gore, "Liner Notes for SIT IN SONGS: SONGS OF THE FREEDOM RIDERS," CORE, series 5: box 35, folder 8.

32. Ibid.

33. Ingrid Monson, "Monk Meets SNCC," *Black Music Research Journal* 19, no. 2, New Perspectives on Thelonious Monk (Autumn 1999): 190.

34. Meier, "New Currents in the Civil Rights Movement," 7.

35. Kobena Mercer, "Black Hair/Style Politics," in eds. Ken Gelder and Sarah Thornton, *The Subcultures Reader* (London: Routledge, 1997), 420, 421, 423 (emphasis in original).

36. See, for example, Kelley, *Freedom Dreams*; Nikhil Pal Singh, *Black Is a Country: Race and the Unfinished Struggle for Democracy* (Cambridge, MA: Harvard University Press, 2005); Young, *Soul Power*.

37. Hampton with Nathan, *Nina Simone*, 47, 43, 39, 56–57.

38. Simone with Cleary, *I Put a Spell on You*, 98.

39. Meier and Rudwick, *CORE*.

40. By 1966, Farmer had resigned as national director of CORE. According to the new leadership, racially exclusive schools would allow Black children the opportunity to learn in schools of comparable quality to those of white children. Whitney M. Young, "3 Meetings Show Black Diversity," *Chicago Daily Defender*, September 26, 1970, 8; "Conn. NAACP Blasts Black 'Separatism,'" *New York Amsterdam News*, March 28, 1970, 48.

41. Simone with Cleary, *I Put a Spell on You*, 100.

42. Bryant Rollins and Les Matthews, "Candidates Warned: Must Deal with Both Black Nationalists and Integrationists or Get No Support," *New York Amsterdam News*, October 16, 1971, A-1.

43. Simone with Cleary, *I Put a Spell on You*, 108–9.

44. Saul, *Freedom Is, Freedom Ain't*, 6.

45. Get well card, n.d., Lorraine Hansberry Papers, Schomburg Center (hereafter cited as LH).

46. Merrill Singer, "The Social Context of Conversion to a Black Religious Sect," *Review of Religious Research* 30, no. 2 (December 1988): 178.

47. Simone with Cleary, *I Put a Spell on You*, 86.

48. Fanon Che Wilkins, "Beyond Bandung: The Critical Nationalism of Lorraine Hansberry, 1950–1965," *Radical History Review* 95 (Spring 2006): 191–92, 199.

49. Simone, *I Put a Spell on You*, 87.

50. These salons, occurring in cities such as New York and Washington, DC, fostered collaborative efforts in the arts and letters by intellectuals, poets, musicians, and visual artists, and played a role in the formation and maintenance of a diasporic Black public. See Edwards, *Practice of Diaspora*.

51. Simone with Cleary, *I Put a Spell on You*, 87.

52. Documentation of the relationship shared between Simone and Hansberry is scant beyond Simone's autobiography and limited photographic materials. I argue that the greatest evidence of the women's engagement with each other is heard, rather than read. The conversion of Hansberry's *To Be Young, Gifted and Black* and its performance by Simone is the most powerful evidence of their personal and political intimacy.

53. Simone with Cleary, *I Put a Spell on You*, 26.

54. Ruth Wilson Gilmore, *Golden Gulag: Prisons, Surplus, Crisis, and Opposition in Globalizing California* (Berkeley: University of California Press, 2007), 261.

55. Robert Nemiroff, "Foreword," in Lorraine Hansberry, *To Be Young, Gifted and Black: Lorraine Hansberry in Her Own Words*, adapted by Robert Nemiroff (1969; New York: Vintage Books, 1995), xxvi.

56. Hansberry, *To Be Young, Gifted and Black*, 126, 131.

57. Ibid., 256 (emphasis in original).

58. Cheryl Higashida, "To Be(come) Young, Gay and Black: Lorraine Hansberry's Existentialist Routes to Anticolonialism," *American Quarterly* 60, no. 4 (December 2008): 904.

59. Hansberry, *To Be Young, Gifted and Black*, 17, 11.

60. J. Rado, G. Ragni, and G. MacDermot, "Ain't Got No/I Got Life," performed by Nina Simone, 1968, *Nuff Said* (compact disk, Sony/BMG, B0001ZXMBS, 2004).

61. Hansberry, *To Be Young, Gifted and Black*, 206, 209.

62. Ibid., 209.

63. Ibid., 53, 51 (emphasis in original).

64. Stephen Holden, "A Rare Gig for Nina Simone," *New York Times*, June 3, 1983.

65. Hansberry, *To Be Young, Gifted and Black*, 257 (emphasis in original).

66. Ibid., 228 (emphasis in original).

67. Historian Robin D. G. Kelley uses this phrase to illuminate the radical visions of life and liberation developed by Black artists and activists in the twentieth century. Kelley, *Freedom Dreams*; Hansberry, *To Be Young, Gifted and Black*, 257.

68. Hansberry, *To Be Young, Gifted and Black*, 201.

69. Kodwo Eshun, "Further Considerations of Afro-Futurism," *CR: The New Centennial Review* 3, no. 2 (Summer 2003): 293.

70. Hansberry, *To Be Young, Gifted and Black*, 213–14.

71. It was in this year that SNCC expelled its white members, whose services, it was argued, would be best used to organize their own communities.

72. William Worthy, "They USED to Be Colored . . . ," *Realist* (May 1964): 23, 24, 25, CORE, series 5: box 16, folder 5.

73. Hansberry, *To Be Young, Gifted and Black*, 21 (emphasis in original).

74. Worthy, "They USED to Be Colored . . . ," 24.

75. Avery F. Gordon, *Ghostly Matters: Haunting and the Sociological Imagination* (1997; Minneapolis: University of Minnesota Press, 2008), 190.

76. Lee Dembart, "Nina Simone: Soul on Voice," *New York Post*, March 15, 1969, 29, Clippings.

77. Gordon, *Ghostly Matters*, xvi.

78. Hansberry, *To Be Young, Gifted and Black*, 261.

79. James Baldwin, "Sweet Lorraine," in Hansberry, *To Be Young, Gifted and Black*, xix.

80. Simone with Cleary, *I Put a Spell on You*, 50, 51.

81. National Public Radio, "Jazz Profiles: Abbey Lincoln," produced by Sandy Placksin, 2007, http://www.npr.org/programs/jazzprofiles/archive/lincoln.html (accessed November 19, 2007).

82. See Sara Evans, *Personal Politics: The Roots of Women's Liberation in the Civil Rights Movement and the New Left* (New York: Knopf, 1979).

83. Monson, "Monk Meets SNCC," 197.

84. Feldstein, "'I Don't Trust You Anymore,'" 1365.

85. Cynthia Kee, "Singing for Her Life: Nina Simone Voices Her Personal Pain and Frustrated Passion," *Saturday Review* (May/June 1985): 58, Clippings.

86. Quoted in Ward, *Just My Soul Responding*, 302.

87. Dorothy Randall Tsuruta, "I Ain't About to Be Non-Violent, Honey," *Black Scholar* 29, no. 2/3 (1999): 55; Nadine Cohodas, *Princess Noire: The Tumultuous Reign of Nina Simone* (New York: Pantheon Books, 2010), 129. In working with other scholars, I have also received questions around her gender (performance). This listener concern—indeed, discomfort—with the sound of her voice has followed her legacy into the twenty-first century.

88. Brooks, "Nina Simone's Triple Play," 179.

89. Tsuruta, "I Ain't About to Be Non-Violent, Honey," 54.

90. Crossroads Theatre program, n.d., LH.

91. Hansberry, *To Be Young, Gifted and Black*, 228 (emphasis in original).

92. Camille Sands, *New York Times*, April 18, 1971, LH.

93. Baldwin, "Sweet Lorraine," xviii.

94. Nat Hentoff, *New York Times*, May 29, 1969, LH.

95. N. Simone and W. Irvine, Jr., "To Be Young, Gifted and Black," performed by Nina Simone, 1969, *Black Gold* (vinyl, RCA, 82876596242, 1970).

96. N. Simone and W. Irvine, Jr., "To Be Young, Gifted and Black (Live)," performed by Nina Simone, 1969, *Nina Simone Forever Young, Gifted & Black: Songs of Freedom and Spirit* (compact disk, RCA, B000CNE15A, 2006).

97. Feldstein, "'I Don't Trust You Anymore,'" 1359.

98. Lott, *Love and Theft*, 4.

99. "Cherokee Charlie Says," *Chicago Daily Defender*, December 29, 1969, 15.

100. "Top 10," *New York Amsterdam News*, January 3, 1970, 12; "Top 10," *New York Amsterdam News*, January 31, 1970, 16.

101. Ward, *Just My Soul Responding*, 302.

102. We understand now that AMSAC's investment in the selection of primarily politically moderate and/or early-career artists and intellectuals did not stem simply from their own liberal anticommunist and Black middle-class perspectives—it was also representative of the mandates of the organization's major benefactor, the Central Intelligence Agency (CIA), whose ties to the organization were not exposed in the U.S. press until 1967. Historian Hugh Wilford documents that AMSAC was "the CIA's principle front organization in the African American community." See Hugh Wilford, *The Mighty Wurlitzer: How the CIA Played America* (Cambridge, MA: Harvard University Press, 2008), 198.

103. Langston Hughes, untitled welcome remarks, AMSAC program, Lagos, Nigeria, December 18 and 19, 1961, JWJ, MSS 26: box 371, folder 6038 (emphasis in original).

104. Simone with Cleary, *I Put a Spell on You*, 80–81 (emphasis in original).

105. Conrad Clark, "Pan-African Cultural Festival Draws Blacks," *New York Amsterdam News*, July 26, 1969. The Algerian War for Independence lasted from 1954 to 1962. Guerrilla tactics marked much of the battle by the National Liberation Front (Front de Libération de Nationale, FLN), and "counterterrorist" acts were employed by the French military. In July 1962, Algerians voted overwhelmingly for independence instead of a continued relationship with France. The war of liberation was the subject of the famous film *The Battle of Algiers* (1966), and diasporic icon and Martinican intellectual-revolutionary Frantz Fanon assisted in the war effort on the side of the Algerians prior to his death in 1961.

106. In 2002 the Organization of African Unity (OAU) became the African Union (AU).

107. "Organization of African Unity (OAU) Charter," 1963, http://www.au.int/en/sites/default/files/OAU_Charter_1963_0.pdf (accessed May 11, 2013).

108. Ward, *Just My Soul Responding*, 211.

109. Brown described, "Right up until the time I left for 'Nam I continued to receive stern warnings from certain Black leaders that by going over there I was, in effect, supporting an extremely unpopular war, and because of it, I was hurting not just myself but my people." James Brown, *I Feel Good: A Memoir of a Life in Soul* (New York: New American Library, 2005), 154.

110. Quoted in Patricia Smith, "Singer Nina Simone Puts Forth a Brash Image," *Chicago Sun-Times*, June 27, 1985. In the 1970s, while incarcerated at Attica Prison in New York, H. Rap Brown converted to Islam and changed his name to Jamil Abdullah Al-Amin.

111. N. Simone, "To Be Young Gifted and Black (Interview)," performed by Nina Simone, 1969, *Protest Anthology* (compact disk, Artwork Media/Andy Stroud, B0015HK2I2, 2008).

112. N. Simone and W. Irvine, Jr., "To Be Young, Gifted and Black," performed by Donny Hathaway, 1970, *Everything Is Everything* (vinyl, Atlantic, B0045WZXS8, 1970).

113. Franklin's title dismisses the "To Be" of the original and is simply "Young, Gifted and Black."

114. N. Simone and W. Irvine, Jr., "Young, Gifted and Black," performed by Aretha Franklin, 1972, *Young, Gifted and Black* (vinyl, Atlantic/Wea, B0000335M, 1972).

115. Daniel P. W. Ellis, "Identifying 'Cover Songs' with Beat-Synchronous Chroma Features," *Music Information Retrieval Evaluation eXchange, University of Victoria* (2006): 1; Mark Butler, "Taking It Seriously: Intertextuality and Authenticity in Two Covers by the Pet Shop Boys," *Popular Music* 22, no. 1 (January 2003): 1.

116. Ellis, "Identifying 'Cover Songs,'" 1.

117. Simone first took residence in Barbados, then in Liberia, and later in various European countries, finally settling in France, where she passed away in 2003.

118. Hansberry, *To Be Young, Gifted and Black*, 257 (emphasis in original).

NOTES TO CHAPTER 6

1. Cohodas, *Princess Noire*, 112.

2. The categories of "Coloured" and "Indian" marked racial difference as well. The Coloureds were designated as those of mixed-race ancestry, while the Indian populations were largely immigrant, arriving in South Africa from colonial India as laborers beginning in the late nineteenth century. Throughout the twentieth century, these two populations negotiated their relationships to whiteness and blackness, often arguing proximity to whiteness within juridical spaces and solidarity and communion with Black South Africans in the streets as the anti-apartheid struggle gained momentum. Within this framework, then, white and Black continued to be the poles of opposition with both Coloureds and Indians falling legally and socially somewhere in between.

3. Amanda D. Kemp and Robert T. Vinson, "'Poking Holes in the Sky': Professor James Thaele, American Negroes, and Modernity in 1920s Segregationist South Africa," *African Studies Review* 43, no. 1 (April 2000): 143, 145, 148–50.

4. Francis Meli, *A History of the ANC: South Africa Belongs to Us* (Bloomington: Indiana University Press, 1988), 40.

5. Kemp and Vinson, "'Poking Holes in the Sky,'" 150.

6. Bennetta Jules-Rosette and David B. Coplan, "'Nkosi Sikelel' iAfrika': From Independent Spirit to Political Mobilization," *Cahiers d'Études Africaines* 44 (1–2): 344.

7. Kay Kaufman Shelemay, *Soundscapes: Exploring Music in a Changing World*, 2nd ed. (New York: Norton, 2006), 384.

8. Charles Hamm, *Afro-American Music, South Africa, and Apartheid* (Brooklyn: Institute for Studies in American Music, Conservatory of Music, Brooklyn College of the City University of New York, 1988), 6, 5.

9. D. D. T. Jabavu, "The Origin of 'Nkosi Sikelel' I Afrika,'" in *Lovedale Sol-fa Leaflets, No. 17: "Nkosi Sikelel' I Afrika"* (Alice, South Africa: Lovedale Press, 1934), 4.

10. Graham Leach, *South Africa: No Easy Path to Peace* (Bergvlei, South Africa: Century Hutchinson, 1986), 19.

11. Patrick Wolfe, "Settler Colonialism and the Elimination of the Native," *Journal of Genocide Research* 8, no. 4 (2006): 388.

12. George Lipsitz, *The Possessive Investment in Whiteness: How White People Profit from Identity Politics* (Philadelphia: Temple University Press, 1998).

13. Cheryl I. Harris, "Whiteness as Property," *Harvard Law Review* 106, no. 8 (June 1993): 1709.

14. Leach, *South Africa*, 93, 94.

15. Verwoerd's published scholarship includes a journal article on how to control and manipulate emotion. Hendrik V. Verwoerd, "A Method for Experimental Production of Emotions," *Journal of American Psychology* 37, no. 3 (July 1926): 357–71.

16. "South Africa: Death to the Architect," *Time*, September 16, 1966, http://www.time.com/time/magazine/article/0,9171,836363-2,00.html#ixzz1DUoT7GG6 (accessed February 1, 2011).

17. H. Lindsay Smith, *Anatomy of Apartheid* (Germiston, South Africa: Khanya, 1979), 7.

18. Ibid., 8, 23.

19. ANC Youth League Manifesto—1944, African National Congress website, http://www.anc.org.za/show.php?id=4439 (accessed May 30, 2011).

20. Meli, *History of the ANC*, 114, 109, 116.

21. Ibid., 121.

22. George Frederickson, *The Comparative Imagination: On the History of Racism, Nationalism, and Social Movements* (Berkeley: University of California Press, 2000), 136.

23. Philip Frankel, "The Politics of Passes: Control and Change in South Africa," *Journal of Modern African Studies* 17, no. 2 (1979): 200, 205, 206.

24. Frene Ginwala, "Women and the African National Congress, 1912–1943," *Agenda*, no. 8 (1990): 80, 84, 85. By "Union," I am referring to the Union of South Africa, which was the nation's official title prior to its departure from the British Commonwealth in 1961, after which time it became the Republic of South Africa.

25. Ginwala, "Women and the African National Congress," 86.

26. Quoted in Igor Cusack, "African National Anthems: 'Beat the Drums, the Red Lion Has Roared,'" *Journal of African Cultural Studies* 17, no. 2 (December 2005): 236.

27. Natasha Erlank, "Gender and Masculinity in South African Nationalist Discourse, 1912–1950," *Feminist Studies* 29, no. 3 (Autumn 2003): 668.

28. Nelson Mandela, untitled, n.d., Oliver Tambo Papers, National Heritage and Cultural Studies Centre, University of Fort Hare-Alice, file B2.8.3, box 33 (hereafter cited as Tambo Papers).

29. Quoted in Anne Schumann, "The Beat That Beat Apartheid: The Role of Music in the Resistance Against Apartheid in South Africa," *Stichproben* 14, no. 8 (2008): 25.

30. John Cunningham, "Wednesday Women," *Guardian*, January 27, 1988.

31. Miriam Makeba with James Hall, *Makeba: My Story* (Johannesburg, South Africa: Skotaville, 1988), 5, 33.

32. James Scott, *Weapons of the Weak: Everyday Forms of Peasant Resistance* (New Haven: Yale University Press, 1987).

33. Makeba with Hall, *Makeba*, 22, 1.

34. Katherine McKittrick and Clyde Woods, "No One Knows the Mysteries at the Bottom of the Ocean," in eds. Katherine McKittrick and Clyde Woods, *Black Geographies and the Politics of Place* (Boston: South End, 2007), 3.

35. Makeba with Hall, *Makeba*, 100.

36. Miriam Makeba, "Miriam Makeba, UN, 1963," YouTube, http://www.youtube.com/watch?v=uWP5mBJ4HWs (accessed June 13, 2011).

37. Hugh Masekela, interview in documentary *Amandla! A Revolution in Four-Part Harmony* (HBO/Kwela Productions, 2002), scene 3.

38. Young, *Soul Power*.

39. Tom Lodge, "State of Exile: The African National Congress of South Africa, 1976–86," *Third World Quarterly* 9, no. 1, The Politics of Exile (January 1987): 2.

40. Solomon Mbabi-Katana, "Introduction," in eds. Miriam Makeba and Jonas Gwangwa, *The World of African Song* (Chicago: Quadrangle Books, 1972), 21.

41. Hugh Masekela and D. Michael Cheers, *Still Grazing: The Musical Journey of Hugh Masekela* (New York: Three Rivers Press, 2004), 70.

42. According to Graeme Gilfillan, the executor of the ZM Makeba Trust, Makeba never recorded "Nkosi Sikelel' iAfrika." Interview by the author, December 20, 2010, Johannesburg, South Africa.

43. Schumann, "Beat That Beat Apartheid," 27.

44. Extreme cases of arrests for censored musical material include these: "Jacob Mashigo received five years imprisonment in August 1983 for possessing a cassette with *one song* by Miriam Makeba and Harry Belafonte. Thabo Moloi received two years imprisonment for possessing a cassette with a speech by ANC President Oliver Tambo, interspersed with Freedom songs. Derek Tsietsi Makomoreng received five years imprisonment in January this year for possessing a 60 minute cassette with the music of the ANC Cultural Ensemble Amandla on it." "Music and Censorship in South Africa," *Rixaka: Cultural Journal of the African National Congress* 2/86 (n.d.): 29 (emphasis in original).

45. Tanganyika merged with the newly independent island of Zanzibar in 1964, forming the nation of Tanzania.

46. Quoted in Martin Sturmer, *The Media History of Tanzania* (Tanzania: Ndanda Mission Press, 1998), 104 (emphasis in original).

47. Kelly Askew argues that within Tanzania, "the key symbolic markers of national identity encompassed a national language (Kiswahili), national anthem ('Mungu Ibariki Africa'), national holidays, national monuments, a national *ngoma*

[traditional dance] troupe, and national arts and language competitions. . . .
The national anthem, however, hailed from South Africa, the national *ngoma*
troupe performed acrobatics learned in China, and the national arts competitions
included a *kwaya* competition—*kwaya* being the musical consequence of interaction with Western Christianity. Thus despite considerable rhetoric to the contrary,
it was not the perceived 'indigenousness' of something that rendered it acceptable
to official post-independent nationalism, but how well it fit with reigning political
paradigms and objectives." This fact evidences the deliberate politico-ideological
impulse behind the adoption of "Nkosi Sikilel' iAfrika" by postindependence
African states. Kelly M. Askew, *Performing the Nation: Swahili Music and Cultural
Politics in Tanzania* (Chicago: University of Chicago Press, 2002), 277.

48. Jules-Rosette and Coplan, "'Nkosi Sikelel' iAfrika,'" 345.

49. Cusack, "African National Anthems," 238.

50. "Mwari Komborera Africa" is described by Jules-Rosette and Coplan as "an inspired
version of 'Nkosi Sikelel' iAfrika.'" Written and performed in various languages,
including the Shona dialect Manyike, and locations, including the Congo and Zimbabwe, the song extends the reach and potential of "Nkosi" through its affiliation and
shared vision for an Africa "bless[ed]," "help[ed]," "save[d]," and "remember[ed]" by
God. Jules-Rosette and Coplan, "'Nkosi Sikelel' iAfrika,'" 361, 362, 356.

51. Oliver Tambo, handwritten note, January 8, 1987, file A5, Tambo Papers.

52. Ibid.

53. "ANC and Information Policy," internal document, n.d., p. 8, ANC Department of
Information and Publicity, DIP General Papers, file B7.1.5.6., box 35, Tambo Papers.

54. Radio Bantu, started by the minority government in the 1960s, fed the radio market, boosting the number of transistors from 103,000 sets in 1962 to 771,000 in
1966 and to over 2 million in 1968. They delivered news and music from Pretoria
in various languages in order to divide and conquer the Black population. See
Charles Hamm, *Afro-American Music*, 24–25.

55. Quoted in Sekibakiba Peter Lekgoathi, "The African National Congress's Radio
Freedom and Its Audiences in Apartheid South Africa, 1963–1991," *Journal of
African Media Studies* 2, no. 2 (2010): 143.

56. "Transcription of ANC Freedom Broadcasts Heard in Johannesburg, Cape Town,
Durban, Port Elizabeth and East London (S.A.) Recently," n.d., DIP Internal Propaganda, Radio Unit, Radio Commentary/Scripts, file B.7.1.6.2.2.1, box 36, Tambo
Papers.

57. Sibongile Mkhabela, quoted at Hector Pieterson Museum, Soweto, South Africa
(visited December 26, 2010).

58. Roger Pfister, "Gateway to International Victory: The Diplomacy of the African
National Congress in Africa, 1960–1994," *Journal of Modern African Studies* 41, no.
1 (2003): 52.

59. Raymond Suttner, "Culture(s) of the African National Congress in South Africa:
Imprint of Exile Experiences," *Journal of Contemporary African Studies* 21, no. 2
(2003): 190.

60. Shirli Gilbert, "Singing Against Apartheid: ANC Cultural Groups and the International Anti-Apartheid Struggle," in ed. Grant Olwage, *Composing Apartheid: Music For and Against Apartheid* (Johannesburg, South Africa: Wits University Press, 2008), 177.

61. African National Congress, *A Message to Western Europe*, pamphlet, p. 1, African National Congress Papers, National Heritage and Cultural Studies Centre, University of Fort Hare-Alice (hereafter cited as ANC Papers).

62. Frantz Fanon, *Wretched of the Earth*, trans. Constance Farrington (1961; New York: Grove Weidenfeld, 1963), 39–40, 35.

63. For a detailed discussion of the educated nature of Black musics, see Jones, *Blues People*.

64. Quoted in Suttner, "Culture(s) of the ANC," 187.

65. Young, *Soul Power*, 44.

66. Steve Biko, *I Write What I Like: Selected Writings* (1978; Chicago: University of Chicago Press, 2002), 49.

67. *Sunday Times*, September 26, 1971, 48, ANC Papers.

68. Ibid.

69. Barbara Masekela to ANC Secretary General, February 26, 1985, file B8.2-B8.2.1.1, box 38, Tambo Papers.

70. "Female Members of Amandla" and "Male Members of Amandla," n.d., Department of Arts and Culture, file B.8.2.2.5-6, box 39, Tambo Papers.

71. "African National Congress (S.A.) Programme of Action for 1978," n.d., "ANC-General Reports, 1967–1983," file B2.3-B2.3.1, box 29, Tambo Papers.

72. Leach, *South Africa*, 209.

73. Gilbert, "Singing Against Apartheid," 167.

74. There are notable exceptions to Amandla's positive reception. Protests were reported outside of Amandla performances in England and Australia, for example. Small groups, composed primarily of peace activists, challenged the ANC on the use of violent tactics, including "necklacing," in which used tires were placed around the necks of the accused and set on fire.

75. "Foot-Stomping Cries for Freedom," *New Zealand*, April 1988, ANC Papers.

76. "Political Education and Culture," n.d., p. 3, ANC Papers.

77. Steve McLeod, "Dance and Song Ring Out Protest," *West Australian*, May 7, 1988, xi, ANC Papers.

78. "Amandla: The Show" (1989), 2, ANC Papers.

79. Zimbabwe Tour Program, 2, ANC Papers.

80. Ibid., 4.

81. Hamm, *Afro-American Music*, 5–6.

82. Zimbabwe Tour Program, 4, ANC Papers.

83. Gilbert, "Singing Against Apartheid," 162.

84. Margie Thomson, "Black South African Culture Alive and Kicking," *New Zealand Herald*, n.d., ANC Papers.

85. Sizakele Sigxashe to R.C. Secretariat, April 14, 1980, Department of Information and Propaganda, file B7.13, box 35, Tambo Papers.

86. Quoted in Margie Thomson, "Politics as Art," *New Zealand Herald*, February 24, 1988, 1, ANC Papers.

87. W. E. B. Du Bois, *The Souls of Black Folk*, in James Weldon Johnson, Booker T. Washington, and William E. B. Du Bois, *Three Negro Classics* (1970; New York: Avon Books, 1999), 382.

88. The Organisation of African Unity (OAU), formed in 1963, was disbanded in 2002 by then chairman of the OAU and president of South Africa Thabo Mbeki and replaced by the African Union (AU).

89. Donald R. Culverson, *Contesting Apartheid: U.S. Activism, 1960–1987* (Boulder, CO: Westview Press, 1999), 114.

90. "Entertainers Boycotted in 1982 for Performing in South Africa," in ibid., 115.

91. State president P. W. Botha suffered a stroke in 1989, after which he resigned. His unwavering support for apartheid and staunch anticommunism marked him as a dying breed within South African society.

92. F. W. De Klerk, "Unbanning Speech," track 5, *The Winds of Change: A Journey Through the Key Music and Moments That Gave Birth to a Free, Democratic South Africa*, disc 2 (compact disk, African Cream Music, ACM-CD023/3, 2004).

93. "S. Africa OKs Amnesty for Political Exiles," *Los Angeles Times*, August 17, 1991, http://articles.latimes.com/1991-08-17/news/mn-461_1_south-africa (accessed August 14, 2012).

94. Ingrid Bianca Byerly, "Mirror, Mediator, and Prophet: The Music Indaba of Late-Apartheid South Africa," *Ethnomusicology* 42, no. 1 (Winter 1998): 35.

95. "In Praise of . . . Nkosi Sikelel' iAfrika," *Guardian*, November 2, 2007, http://www.guardian.co.uk/commentisfree/2007/nov/03/southafrica.comment#start-of-comments (accessed August 14, 2012).

96. Andre Abrahamse, *Winds of Change*, liner notes, p. 14.

NOTES TO THE CONCLUSION

1. Nicole R. Fleetwood, *Troubling Vision: Performance, Visuality, and Blackness* (Chicago: University of Chicago Press, 2011), 3.

2. Katz, *Capturing Sound*, 161.

3. This moment was not without its contests, however. The protracted debates over the First Amendment right to free speech were at fever pitch in the mid-1980s as future second lady Mary "Tipper" Gore and her organization, Parents Music Resource Center, launched an offensive against the use of profanity and sexual language in popular musics, namely heavy metal, punk, and rap.

4. Robert C. Smith, *We Have No Leaders: African Americans in the Post-Civil Rights Era* (Albany: State University of New York Press, 1996), 24.

5. Dawson, "A Black Counterpublic?," 195–223.

6. Victoria E. Johnson, "Polyphony and Cultural Expression: Interpreting Musical Traditions in *Do the Right Thing*," *Film Quarterly* 47, no. 2 (1993): 20.

7. Quoted in Anna Deveare Smith, *Twilight Los Angeles, 1992* (New York: Anchor Books, 1994), 162.

8. Janice C. Simpson, "Music: Yo! Rap Gets on the Map," *Time*, no. 135 (February 5, 1990): 60.

9. Jeff Chang, "Rapping the Vote: The Former Public Enemy Front Man on the Political Power of Hip-Hop," *Mother Jones*, September/October 2004, http://www.motherjones.com/media/2004/09/chuck-d (accessed January 13, 2013).

10. According to an eyewitness accounting of the L.A. rebellion, "Fight the Power" was playing in the streets as the city burned. Comment by Daphne Brooks, Sounds of the City, Experience Music Project Conference, New York University, March 24, 2012.

11. Tia DeNora, "Music and Self-Identity," in eds. Andy Bennett, Barry Shank, and Jason Toynbee, *The Popular Music Studies Reader* (New York: Routledge, 2006), 143.

12. Eyerman and Jamison, *Music and Social Movements*.

13. George Shepperson, "Pan-Africanism and 'Pan-Africanism': Some Historical Notes," *Phylon* 23, no. 4 (1962): 351.

14. Ennis Barrington Edmonds, *Rastafari: From Outcasts to Culture Bearers* (New York: Oxford University Press, 2002), 29.

15. Rupert Lewis, "Marcus Garvey and the Early Rastafarians: Continuity and Discontinuity," in eds. Nathaniel Samuel Murrell, William D. Spencer, and Adrian Anthony McFarlane, *Chanting Down Babylon: The Rastafari Reader* (Philadelphia: Temple University Press, 1998), 148. Jamaica gained independence from Britain in 1962.

16. Leonard E. Barrett, *The Rastafarians*, 20th anniversary ed. (1977; Boston: Beacon, 1997), 67.

17. The circulation of the phrase "lift every voice" in scholarship on, about, or by African Americans signals its enduring resonance within the lexicon of Black advancement narratives. Studies in education, theology, and history have often used the phrase, including, for example, Rosella B. Camper and Natalie Tyler, *Lift Every Voice . . . Echoes from the Black Community of Maryland's Eastern Shore* (Wye Mills, MD: Chesapeake College Press, 1999); Philip S. Foner and Robert James Branham, eds., *Lift Every Voice: African American Oratory, 1787–1900* (Birmingham: University of Alabama Press, 1998); Dorothy Sterling, Benjamin Quarles, and Ernest Crichlow, *Lift Every Voice and Sing: The Lives of Booker T. Washington, W. E. B. Du Bois, Mary Church Terrell, and James Weldon Johnson* (New York: Doubleday, 1965); Mary Potter Engel and Susan B. Thistlewaite, eds., *Lift Every Voice: Constructing Christian Theologies from the Underside* (Maryknoll, NY: Orbis Books, 1990). Numerous local and national histories of civil rights activism employ this prose as a title. Authors, activists, and public intellectuals have built on this history and used the phrase to announce their own histories, including famed Harvard law professor Lani Guinier, whose memoir, *Lift Every Voice*, details the 1993 scandal surrounding the withdrawal of her nomination to head the Civil Rights Division of the U.S. Justice Department. That phrase helped her to recognize that "when we struggle with others we gain a sense of our own power to resist injustice and to make things better for more than only ourselves."

Guinier's comment reflects the continued necessity of reading James Weldon Johnson's text literally as an act of resistance against the silencing of Black voices and as a call to collectivity. Lani Guinier, *Lift Every Voice: Turning a Civil Rights Setback into a New Vision of Social Justice* (New York: Simon & Schuster, 1998), 112.

18. Julian Bond and Sondra Kathryn Wilson, "Introduction," in eds. Bond and Wilson, *Lift Every Voice*, xvii.

19. Juan Williams, "Juan Williams," and Albert Murray, "Albert Murray," in eds., Bond and Wilson, *Lift Every Voice*, 252, 185.

20. Thomas J. Elward, "Oh Say, Can You Sing Our National Songs?," *Music Educators Journal* (February 1982): 53.

21. There was a prominent national display of the poem/anthem delivered as a prayer by civil rights icon Reverend Joseph Lowery at Present Barack Obama's 2009 inauguration.

22. Myrlie Evers-Williams, widow of slain civil rights activist Medgar Evers, praised the song, highlighting its role in the 1996 NAACP Convention that signaled the organization's "rebirth." Former presidential candidate and activist Reverend Jesse Jackson notes the song's function in the events of his organization, the Rainbow/PUSH Coalition: "Traditionally, to begin our Saturday morning forum, we honor our culture through the Negro National Anthem, 'Lift Every Voice and Sing,' because it exemplifies the human spirit and the pride of millions of African Americans." Dorothy I. Height, president emeritus of the National Council of Negro Women (NCNW), described numerous instances of "Lift" at work and argued that "it [is] a trusted leadership tool [that] stimulates unity. It motivates." In performance the anthem "never failed." Myrlie Evers-Williams, "Myrlie Evers-Williams," Jesse Jackson, "Rev. Jesse Jackson," and Dorothy I. Height, "Dorothy I. Height," in eds. Bond and Wilson, *Lift Every Voice*, 85, 130, 117.

23. As of the mid-1980s, sociologist K. Sue Jewell documented that nearly 75 percent of Black college-age youth in her study identified as "Black" whereas only 8 percent of the youth identified as either "Negro" or "Colored." K. Sue Jewell, "Will the Real Black, Afro-American, Mixed, Colored, Negro Please Stand Up? Impact of the Black Social Movement, Twenty Years Later," *Journal of Black Studies* 16, no. 1 (September 1985): 63. Scholar Todd Boyd has also noted the ironies of the NAACP's continued usage of the word "Colored." See Dahleen Glanton and Kayce T. Ataiyero, "NAACP Buries the Hated N-Word," *Chicago Tribune*, July 9, 2007. This critique, however, does not mean that the organization's disconnect from contemporary political cultures is complete. The NAACP has active youth divisions, the NCNW is affiliated with numerous organizations including many Black sororities, and Jesse Jackson's involvement in recent racial justice campaigns including efforts following Hurricane Katrina (2005) and the Jena Six incident in Louisiana (2007) has inserted Rainbow/PUSH into the public political discourse. Under the leadership of president and CEO Benjamin Jealous, the NAACP has also taken a more public role in racial justice issues, including the 2012 Trayvon

Martin case, as well as progressive positions in other national political concerns, including same-sex marriage.

24. Leon Litwack, "Leon Litwack," in eds. Bond and Wilson, *Lift Every Voice*, 173.

25. Jewell, "Will the Real Black, Afro-American, Mixed, Colored, Negro Please Stand Up?," 70.

26. Most often, the term "anthem" has been employed by rap and hip-hop emcees as a way to measure popularity, not political intent. However, the twenty-first century has produced its own anthems within Black youth cultures, namely 2001's "Hip-Hop" by Brooklyn-based duo Dead Prez, in which they ask, "Would you rather have a Lexus or justice? / A dream or some substance? / A beamer, a necklace or freedom?" C. Gavin, L. Alford, V. Williams, and A. Mair, "Hip-Hop," performed by Dead Prez, *Let's Get Free* (compact disk, Relativity Records, B00004DRZS, 2000). This song was attached to mobilizations that occurred during the 2004 U.S. presidential election by the National Hip-Hop Political Convention, which worked to oust then president George W. Bush.

27. Due to the nonadoptive role of the anthems of chapters 3 and 4, I am not considering the (inter)national labor movement and the Highlander Folk School in this statement. All unions discussed in these chapters exist in some formation, although a number of them, including the Food, Tobacco and Agricultural Workers, have merged with other (inter)national unions. The Highlander Folk School is also in existence, although it is now known as the Highlander Research and Education Center, which suggests a move away from direct organizing.

28. American Film Institute, "AFI's 100 Years . . . 100 Songs," June 22, 2004, http://www.afi.com/100years/songs.aspx (accessed May 14, 2013).

29. Will Friedwald, *Stardust Melodies: The Biography of Twelve of America's Most Popular Songs* (New York: Pantheon Books, 2002), 114, 106.

30. Ibid., 122–23.

31. D. Smith and L. Fernandez, "New World Water," performed by Mos Def, *Black on Both Sides* (compact disk, Priority Records, B00001XDNV, 1999).

32. Oscar Hammerstein II and Jerome Kern, "Ol' Man River," performed by William Warfield, 1966, *Greatest Hits: Broadway* (compact disk, Sony, B0000029PM, 1996).

33. Henry Foner, "Foreword," in eds. Joseph Dorinson and William Pencak, *Paul Robeson: Essays on His Life and Legacy* (New York: McFarland, 2002), 3. With the exception of a postage stamp released in 2004 and a few landmarks in his native Princeton, New Jersey, Robeson is unrepresented in U.S. culture on any scale.

34. Mark D. Naison, "'Americans Through Their Labor': Paul Robeson's Vision of Cultural and Economic Democracy," in eds. Dorinson and Pencak, *Paul Robeson*, 187.

35. Malcolm X, "The Ballot or the Bullet (April 3, 1964)," in ed. George Breitman, *Malcolm X Speaks: Selected Speeches and Statements* (New York: Grove Press, 1965), 35.

36. Malcolm X, "With Mrs. Fannie Lou Hamer (December 20, 1964)," in ed. Breitman, *Malcolm X Speaks*, 107.

37. Histories of Black women's activism document their unique strategies and leadership styles during the long Civil Rights Movement. See, for example, Gore, *Radicalism at the Crossroads*; Danielle McGuire, *At the Dark End of the Street: Black Women, Rape, and Resistance—A New History of the Civil Rights Movement from Rosa Parks to the Rise of Black Power* (New York: Knopf, 2010); Barbara Ransby, *Ella Baker and the Black Freedom Movement: A Radical Democratic Vision* (Chapel Hill: University of North Carolina Press, 2005).

38. Malcolm X, "The Black Revolution (April 8, 1964)," in ed. Breitman, *Malcolm X Speaks*, 50.

39. Prashad, *Darker Nations*.

40. Scholtes, "Something about That Songs Haunts You."

41. Neal, "'We Shall Overcome,'" 1.

42. Rob Gifford, "How the West Was Lost," *BBC News*, June 2, 1999, http://news.bbc.co.uk/2/hi/special_report/1999/06/99/tiananmen_square/359000.stm (accessed January 4, 2008).

43. Ish, "China Stories Pt. 22: To the Square," *The Original Pawns of Comedy Blogspot*, April 1989, http://theoriginalpawnsofcomedy.blogspot.com/2006/08/china-stories-pt-22-to-square.html (accessed January 4, 2008).

44. Ruth Feldstein, "Nina Simone's Border Crossings: Black Cultural Nationalism and Gender on a Global Stage," in eds. James T. Campbell, Matthew Pratt Guteral, and Robert G. Lee, *Race, Nation, and Empire in American History* (Chapel Hill: University of North Carolina Press, 2007), 296.

45. Mark Anthony Neal, *What the Music Said: Black Popular Music and Black Public Culture* (New York: Routledge, 1998), 126.

46. T. Greene and K. West, "Get By," performed by Talib Kweli, *Quality* (compact disk, Rawkus/UMVD, B0000719UL, 2002).

47. Amazon.com review of Talib Kweli, *Quality*, http://www.amazon.com/Quality-Talib-Kweli/dp/B0000719UL (accessed January 4, 2008).

48. Emcee Common (formerly known as Common Sense) has sampled Simone on more than one occasion, including "Misunderstood" from *Finding Forever* (compact disk, Universal Music Group, B000RN86BK, 2007). Kweli used Simone's "Four Women" to construct his critique of patriarchy and celebration of women in a track of the same name. T. Greene, T. Cottrell, and N. Simone, "Four Women," performed by Reflection Eternal [Talib Kweli and Hi-Tek], *Train of Thought* (compact disk, Rawkus/UMVD, B000067CLQ, 2000).

49. Michael Bracewell, "Dangerous Diva," *Guardian Weekend*, December 6, 1997, 30, Clippings File, 1975–1988, Schomburg Center.

50. In 1989 Big Daddy Kane released "Young, Gifted and Black" on his album *It's a Big Daddy Thing* (compact disk, Warner Brothers/Wea, B000002LI2, 1989). While the song is not a political commentary, its title nonetheless connotes a connection to the pride that originally attended the Simone version.

51. A. Joseph, Jr., N. Simone, and W. Irvine, Jr., "Young, Gifted & Black," performed by Gist aka The Essence of Queens, *Young, Gifted & Black* (mp3, http://www.gistmusic.com/YGBsite2.htm, Transcendent, 2007) (emphasis added).

52. Interview with Gist aka The Essence of Queens (neé Arthur Joseph, Jr.) by the author, telephone, January 13, 2008.

53. By "productive" I mean both celebratory and critical histories, exultation and derision. All perspectives lend evidence to the three-dimensionality and significance of these texts.

54. Sportsmail Reporter, "National Anthem Mix-Up Leaves South Africa Squirming through Apartheid-era Song," *Daily Mail* (UK), June 6, 2012, http://www.dailymail.co.uk/sport/othersports/article-2155283/National-anthem-mix-leaves-South-Africa-squirming-apartheid-era-song.html (accessed August 15, 2012).

55. Owen Dean, "An Anthem to Ignorance: South Africa's Case of 'Nkosi Sikelel' iAfrika,'" *Intellectual Property Watch*, June 20, 2012, http://www.ip-watch.org/2012/06/20/an-anthem-to-ignorance-south-africas-case-of-nkosi-sikelel-iafrika/ (accessed August 15, 2012).

56. For a detailed analysis and critique of representations of the messianic Black male figure, see Edwards, *Charisma and the Fictions of Black Leadership*.

57. DeNora, "Music and Self-Identity," 146 (emphasis in original).

ABOUT THE AUTHOR

Shana L. Redmond is Assistant Professor of American Studies and Ethnicity at the University of Southern California. She is a former musician and labor organizer, and a Midwest native.

9 780814 770412